THE COMPLETE GUIDE TO WRITING PARANORMAL NOVELS

Volume 1

D1593730

Edited by Kim Richards

With Contributing authors:
Rae Lori
Danielle Ackley-McPhail
Barbara Baldwin
Shannah Biondine
Elizabeth Burton
Karina L. Fabian
Jerri Garretson
Kelly A. Harmon
Lee Killough
Linda Madl
Ripley Patton
Lee Masterson
Sheri L. McGathy
Kathryn Meyer Griffith
Rosemary Laurey
Bob Nailor
Ryan Peverly
Kim Richards
Jane Toombs

THE COMPLETE GUIDE TO WRITING PARANORMAL NOVELS

Volume 1

The Complete Guide to Writing Paranormal Novels: Volume 1

ISBN 978-1-897492-41-3

Dragon Moon Press
www.dragonmoonpress.com

Printed and bound in the United States of America

DEDICATION

To Tina Morgan,
Our inspiration and to whom we
owe a debt of gratitude.

TABLE OF CONTENTS

TABLE OF CONTENTS

INTRODUCTION

By Kathryn Meyer Griffith

Oh, how we love our paranormal literature…angels, ghosts, vampires, sprites and fairies, or any of the supernatural entities that go bump in the night. Scare us. Amaze us. Take us to another world where such creatures exist and where they love us, hate us, help us or war against us. We love the wonders of time traveling to strange places or times to right a wrong or stop one; to delve into the mysteries of the mind and the psychic powers it can control. Distract us from our sometimes tedious mundane lives with tales of shift changers, fairies and demons.

We love the supernatural and all things mystical. What doesn't—what could never—exist except in our imaginations. It's part of being human, this inner spiritual search for the intrinsic answers of the universe.

Because most of us are terrified of dying and death, of losing all we know so well in this mortal plane, we want to know: is there life after death? Do ghosts walk the earth? Vengeful or benevolent spirits? Immortals such as vampires and werewolves? Does good always win against evil? As human beings we'd love the answers to these questions and if we can't find them, prove them, well, then we'll invent, create, worlds where we can.

That's where the paranormal fiction writer comes in.

Now I must say right off that I can't be considered a true skeptic when it comes to the supernatural because at the tender age of sixteen I *saw* a *ghost*, or what I believed was a ghost. My great Aunt Mary had died two days before. Not unexpectedly. She was old, had been in a nursing home for months, and we knew it was coming. Before the nursing home, though, she'd lived ten years with my maternal grandmother, whose name was also Mary, and had been happy there. The night before the funeral I'd been sleeping in my bed and something—to this day I don't know what it was—woke me and I wandered down the dim hallway to use the bathroom.

And there was my dead Great Aunt Mary standing at the end of the hall in an eerie pulsating ball of light. She looked so *real*, as if I could reach out and touch her and my fingers would feel flesh. She was gesturing excitedly to me and rattling off a string of words that had to be German because I couldn't understand a word of it. The old woman had been an immigrant who'd never learned our language, which is one of the reasons she'd been so content living with my grandmother; they'd both spoken German. The only word I could understand was *Mary* as she kept repeating the word over and over. I assumed my aunt was calling for my grandmother, as if my aunt were lost, and looking for her favorite niece. It's the only explanation I have for the visitation.

Why she appeared to me, I'll never know, but she did. I remember thinking: *It's Aunt Mary. Oh my God! But she's dead. Dead.* When it finally hit me, I was so frightened I turned and scurried back to my bedroom and dived beneath my bed covers. To this day, my mind swears I didn't see what I thought I saw…Aunt Mary's spirit…but my heart and my senses chide me and say, *yes, you did. You saw a ghost. A real ghost.* So there.

Since that day I've never been able to laugh at the possibility of the paranormal existing. The thing is, because I consider myself a down-to-earth realistic person, if someone asks me if I believe in ghosts and such I often as not hesitate before I admit that I *might* have seen one. Might. No one wants to be thought of as unbalanced. Seeing spirits is only one step above seeing little green men or pink elephants.

I wanted to be taken seriously. I mean, I was a writer, not a nutcase.

All toll I've been a writer of paranormal fiction for forty years and proud of it. I've written about spirits, benevolent and malevolent; ghosts;

angels; demons and all manner of vampires and unexplained creatures; and even, once, a possessed gun, and a woods haunted by an entity that was an eternal killer. Can't get more paranormal than those, can you?

Ah, I'm ahead of myself. Let's go back a little in the old time machine. My love of the supernatural began long before I saw my Aunt Mary's ghost and innocently enough when I was a child of about ten years old. The year was nineteen-sixty.

In those long ago days our school would get what they called the Weekly Reader which was chock full of stories and adventures for children our age. Puzzles. Riddles. Fables. Little tidbits of interesting fluff and fillers. It also encouraged us to order books once a year. That's how it begun for me. As part of a class order, I picked out a hardcover fictional anthology of short stories on ghosts, mesmerized by the intriguingly spooky cover. I can still remember the excitement when the cardboard box arrived at school and our teacher opened the box and handed out everyone's copies. When I held the book in my hands I breathed in its luscious paper, glue and fresh ink scent, ran my small hands lovingly over its beautiful smooth cover. It felt like Christmas.

Years later, I can't recall if the stories were good or not, but I loved them and I wanted to read more like them. And in the years to come I did. I gobbled up everything paranormal. Books and short stories about ghosts, spirits, angels, demons, and any other paranormal creatures such as vampires, werewolves or mythical monsters. I devoured movies about vampires and werewolves and little alien green men. Oh, I know aliens are more science fiction than paranormal, but, as a kid, I lumped everything scary or unexplained into one big genre.

When I became older, a teenager, I was a devoted fan of Stephen King, Anne Rice, Peter Straub and Dean Koontz from early on. I loved the way they wove simple humanity, with all its frailties and peccadillos, into their stories and made you *care* about the characters.

That's what differentiates a great story from a good one, in my opinion. The characterizations. If a writer gets you to care about a character or characters then you'll care what happens to them. You'll root for them or condemn and boo them. Either way, the writer will engage the reader and hopefully compel them to finish the book and find out what happens to them. After that, or so the plan goes, the reader will then want to seek out our other books and stories and read them. Voilà, a lifelong fan and someone who'll plunk down coins for our next book.

Remembering how much I'd adored Peter Straub's *Ghost Story* when I read it many years ago, I recently sat down to write some short stories with ghosts in them myself. I wanted a twist, though, something different than a lot of spirit stories I'd read, so in *In This House* there are two old people narrating the story, reminiscing over their long happy lives together and how worried they are that their only daughter hasn't found the love of her life yet. Yet at the end the reader discovers that the two old ones are really ghosts themselves haunting their long gone home. They stick around just long enough to arrange a special meeting between their live daughter and the man, a young friend of theirs, they believe is her true love. Of course, the two hit it off and all ends happily ever after. Except for the ghosts, they're still dead. Oh, well. You can't have everything.

In *Don't Look Back, Agnes*, my two-thousand and eight ghostly novella, I use a ghost as a way to wreak revenge on a spectral killer who twenty years before murdered him and two of his teenage friends out in the woods…and is now threatening his childhood sweetheart who's returned to care for her ailing mother. The ghost passes as a real person for most of the story, though there are hints for the reader most of the way that he isn't at all what he appears to be, until the end when the woman protagonist recognizes that he is her long dead boyfriend. The ghost then protects her from the killer by summoning a real life cop to her aid.

Two different types of ghosts for two very different stories but yet the main theme behind both of them is love. The finding and, once found, the protecting of that love.

Truth is, I've used ghosts many times in my paranormal novels. I even use the ghost of a witch as my main antagonist in my nineteen-ninety-three novel *Witches*. Rachel was an accused witch in the seventeenth century in Canaan, Connecticut, who was drowned by a murderous mob of her townspeople. She dies in Black Pond but returns to exchange places in the twenty-first century with a white witch named Amanda. I throw in a bit of time traveling when the story follows Amanda into the past where she not only changes the townspeople's bad opinion of her doppelganger Rachel but she meets and falls in love with an earlier reincarnation of her dead husband from the present. Her future. His past.

In my nineteen-ninety-four novel *The Calling* I use a ghost as a lifelong beacon to call my female protagonist to present day Egypt so she can discover how the ghost's royal family was brutally murdered three thousand years before. The ghost haunts and bullies her until she gets what she wants. Justice. And for the world to know what truly happened to her and her doomed family. There's no actual time traveling but I allow the main character glimpses through the ghost's eyes and senses, her memories, of what her life had been like in eighteenth dynasty Egypt. The ghost had been a pharaoh's daughter, a pharaoh's queen and widow but after her family was deposed and nefariously slain, she ended her days hiding in a necropolis, a city of the dead, among the tomb slaves, tending to the mummies and their final resting places. The ghost had a lot to demand justice for.

Well, enough of ghosts.

In many paranormal books faith and the use of religion is a fertile basic foundation. I'd been raised a Catholic mainly by my Grandmother Mary Fehrt's devotion and influence. The same Mary who my aunt was searching for that night so long ago in my murky hallway. My grandmother was extremely devout and attended Mass every Sunday morning. She was one of those rare people who truly believed in God, heaven and hell, and made me believe, as well.

Later, in a book where I used a strong secondary theme of religion I called on her memory to fashion a sweet-natured character that believed the end days were coming. My grandmother was a special person. One of those rare women who was always there for everyone else, as my father was; a true giver. I've learned over the years there aren't a lot of people in the world like that.

My mother, her only daughter, had seven children, three boys and four girls, a ragtag of a brood of which I was the second oldest. My Grandmother would bribe us three oldest ones with pastries (I loved the whipped cream puffs and the fluffy cheesecake I've never found an equal to to this day) afterward at a local bakery if we'd go to mass with her. Clever woman.

I long ago realized the influence my religion has had on my fiction. Being a Catholic, with all the pomp and rituals, the saints and martyrs, I'm sure, opened me up to the possibility of miracles, and thus, eventually, all that was supernatural. It gave me a genuine sense of the divine and, then, on the other side of the door, what was evil. If miracles happened, and God existed, then there had to be angels… and then, thus, on the flip side, Satan ruled hell and there might be demons. This belief enabled me to write a book many years later called Before the End: *A Time of Demons*, an apocalyptic quest saga about two everyday people, a loving brother and sister singing duo, who in the end days must battle world-wide attacking demons and fight beside grimly authoritative angels to save those left behind after the Rapture.

I have no doubt that my religious childhood, formed when I was an impressionable young girl, and spiced up with the supernatural stories of my youth, influenced me. Looking back at my work, I can see that the religious angel-against-demon, good versus evil, universal theme repeated in quite a few of my novels and short stories.

Evil Stalks the Night is one such. It pits an eternal evil in a haunted wood against the beliefs and inner strength of a good woman who's also dealing with a devastating divorce and a hideous nemesis from her childhood that lures her back to finally face and defeat it.

Blood Forge is another book with that good versus evil theme. A demon possessed gun is conquered and destroyed after centuries of carnage it creates by a caring married couple who believe in themselves, a greater being (an angel in a priest's robes in this case) and the timeless power of love.

Another ingredient in the recipe that would entice me to write paranormal fiction were the spooky stories my grandmother would weave for us. My immigrant grandmother had come to America on a boat when she was only six years old, fleeing from Austria and the tyranny of Hitler's Germany. Among all the other things she was, she was a born story teller. Probably that's where I get it from.

When I was a child, my older sister, Carol, my younger brother, Jim, and I would often spend the night before church with her and she'd delight and frighten us with her own brand of Austria ghost stories and weird tales. We'd sit in the semi-dark in her remodeled basement (my stoic German grandfather was a self-taught carpenter and their house was full of his beautiful handiwork) and listen raptly to her stories. I can recall many an evening, as the rain howled outside on a chilly autumn night, or the snow fell, how we'd sit in that darkened basement and be scared out of our wits by my grandmother's macabre yarns; jumping at any strange or unexpected sound outside while the trees scratched the glass windowpanes with skeletal fingers. We loved it.

Or we'd stay up late with her and watch Spook Spectacular or Chiller Theater where my growing hunger for all that was spooky was indulged and fed until I was as fat as a tick. Other days Grandma Fehrt would drop me and my two siblings off at Saturday or Sunday matinees at a local theater. It was one of those elaborate theater palaces with all the polished wood and shiny mirrors, plush balconies, and heavy scarlet velvet curtains across an endless screen. Later I'd recreate that theater or one like it, making it almost a character in itself with its eerie but haunted ambience, in a novel I called *Vampire Blood*.

It's no wonder I grew up to write horror and paranormal fiction.

There was one spooky story my grandmother told that I'll never forget. It was about this rich young girl in the early nineteenth century who came down with a mysterious wasting away illness. According to my grandmother, as she told it, the beautiful girl eventually died and her family, with much weeping and wailing because she was well loved, buried her in a wooden coffin in the icy winter's ground in their private family cemetery.

In those days, as was the custom, they didn't embalm the body but cleaned and dressed it in fine clothes with their favorite jewelry and just buried them. It so happened that this girl had a diamond and gold ring she always wore and it was interred with her on her cold white hand. The times were hard, though, for poor families. The rich were very rich while the poor...lived in rags, starved and watched the wealthy with haunted, envious eyes.

One of the gravediggers, dressed in his tattered clothes, helped to cover the girl's coffin with earth, but not before he'd seen and noticed the sparkling ring on the corpse's finger before they'd closed the lid. Now, the man was desperate. He had a sick small child at home, as well, and many other hungry mouths to feed. It'd been a long, bitter winter and there'd not been much game to hunt. Not much work anywhere, though he'd looked for months. He had no money. That ring, he thought, would buy enough food and warm clothes—and medicine for his little sick one —to solve all his problems. Something I, as a child with six brothers and sisters, understood all too well. Hunger. Need. Want. Many times my siblings and I had gone hungry, had need of things we couldn't afford. Mine was a hardscrabble childhood, too, but one always filled with love...of family. I understood that kind of desperation. Anyway, the man thought: what use did that poor dead child in her coffin need with fancy trinkets? She was a corpse and beyond caring if that bauble was with her or not.

So in the middle of that first night after he'd helped bury the girl, in the snow and freezing cold, he snuck back into the cemetery and dug her up. Cut off her finger and took the ring. Yikes.

Wait…there's a happy ending. It seems the girl wasn't actually dead at all. She'd had what they called in those days the sleeping sickness. Where a person looked dead, passed for dead, but *wasn't really dead.* Cutting off her finger started the blood flowing and the dead girl woke up! She climbed out of her coffin and stumbled home to her shocked, but eternally grateful parents as the gravedigger threw the finger with the ring at her and ran off as if the hounds of hell were after him. He'd seen the dead rise. *Ta da.*

Wow, my siblings and I loved that story, even though it scared the bejesus out of us. Imagine being buried alive? Clawing at the wooden coffin lid with broken, bloody finger stumps. Knowing your air was going. No one was going to help you because no one knew you were there. Still alive. Buried. Ugh.

Again, years later I wrote a romantic paranormal novel called *The Last Vampire* and used that scene in the climax of my book. My main character, who was an unwilling and basically good vampire, was buried alive in an isolated cemetery as punishment by the other wicked vampires she'd crossed. She tries to dig her way out, but can't, and the hero ends up rescuing her by locating the coffin (there was an earthquake that dropped it further into the shifting earth) and pulling her out at the last minute before she would have been buried deep in the ground forever.

That early story of my grandmother's in some ways also influenced my newest vampire novel *The Woman in Crimson;* which is about a ghostly vampire that haunts an ancient family cemetery during the middle of a snowy, harsh winter. The winter, the icy ivory snow and the graves covered in white is the backdrop to a beautiful civil war era evil vampire who wanders around it and the tombs below in a tattered crimson gown. Crimson against white. Crimson blood. White snow. Now that's an eerie atmosphere. A haunted ambience that is so prevalent in a lot of paranormal novels.

I even toss in a benevolent and wise spirit as further contrast. It's the dead father of the main character, Caroline, who is summoned by a vampire psychic to help them find a way to get rid of the voracious vampire. I had no intention of writing a novel with a supernatural trifecta of vampire, ghost and psychic…it just happened. The characters demanded more help and I gave it to them.

Well, enough of vampires and ghosts. There's much more to paranormal fiction than those two entities, though I believe ghosts and vampires seem to be among the most popular these days.

At this point I'm going to make a confession. Part of this book deals with good and bad fairies. It alludes to them as perhaps being gods, or fallen angels, tall elf-like creatures endowed with magical abilities, or beautiful beings born in the realms of mist, or winged creatures no bigger than one's thumb or even spectral shades of the dead that are no longer a part of our world—or the sum of what some people might believe are any other number of supernatural beings. Perhaps vampires, ghosts, werewolves, the whole pantheon of paranormal creatures are really just fairies in their various disguises. Could be. Who knows?

But, as I said, I don't know much about fairies. Oh, I watch the yearly Saint Patrick's Day moldy oldie movies on television about magical elves, winged sprites and leprechauns that invariably are on twenty-four seven for the holiday. I adored The Lord of the Rings trilogy, with those hunky seven-foot tall enigmatic elves, and enjoy any films about Ireland's little people. Tinker Bell is one of my granddaughter Caitlyn's favorite little buddies. Her room (until just last year when she announced she was too big, too grownup to like the tiny creature any longer and then, at nine, became obsessed with all things vampire and Twilight—yep, she's my blood all right) had been plastered with Bell posters and figurines. Yet I don't know much else about them but that. Let's just say I equate fairies more with swords and dragons, mythical realms full of Hobbits, earth elementals, water nymphs, Fauns and Satyrs, and...fantasy. Hey, if anyone's seen one of these little buggers... let me know. Other than that, I'm a virgin in the land of fairies and elves. Lucky for you, though, we have an expert on all things fairy in this book. I'm sure she'll illuminate the subject for you with her extensive knowledge.

I mentioned psychics earlier. Now ESP, telepathy, clairvoyance, precognition and psychics I know. In fact, my first published novel, written on a typewriter with sticking keys and a case of White-Out, in the dark ages before The Internet was about a woman psychic. Let's see, that was about, uh, nineteen-eighty-four or so. The book was titled *Evil Stalks the Night* and was about a reluctant psychic whose family, was she was a little girl, was butchered in the forest behind her childhood home and, many years later, after a devastating divorce, is forced to return to the scene of the crime, so to speak, to claim a much needed inheritance. Her spooky (was or was she not a witch?) grandmother's rambling old house. In the book I describe how she feels about being psychic. Here our protagonist, Sarah, as a child, talking to her also psychic grandmother, first suspects she has psychic powers:

"Yes." She stared at me and I could see how she fought with herself over what she should tell me and what she shouldn't. "Have you ever heard the word psychic or medium before?"

"Yes. In books."

"Ah, then you know about them?"

"A little." My eyes were guarded by then, my heart raced. I'd read about people who could see the future or talk to spirits and I also knew that sometimes they were considered freaks. I didn't want to see the things they claimed they saw. It must have shown in my face because my grandmother kissed me and soothed me with hugs. She understood.

"Your great-great-grandmother had it, though we don't talk about her much." My grandmother stared out the window again. "She was the girl with the ring."

"What happened to her . . . later?"

She sighed and kept her face away from me. "They burned her for a witch when she was thirty. So young. Those were terrible times." She looked back at me and smiled encouragingly at my look of shock. "It's better these days."

Or later, when she's a grown woman, and knows full well she's psychic, and what a toll it's taken on her life already. Scared off her first husband. Made her a pariah in her community. Knowing things other people don't has made her enemies. Knowing things she—and they— would rather not know because they were usually bad things had jaded her. She hates her powers:

It was bad enough that the dreams scared me.

The cranks and the letters, the telephone calls in the middle of the night, were harder to hide, though. Jonathan and I had lived in Benchley, a middle-sized town located just outside St. Louis, where Jonathan worked on the police force. By leaving the place where my psychic reputation had become common knowledge, I had also left behind my fame. I liked the idea. Blessed anonymity.

I was sick of the accusing letters and the quacks that called day and night. I had realized just recently that I always felt safe, though, because I lived with a cop and felt protected; now my son and I were alone and vulnerable.

Something inside warned me to remain anonymous and save us both a lot of unnecessary grief. I had decided for many reasons that I would be more careful revealing my psychic powers. If I were smart I would ignore them and try to lead a normal life. I was going to try to forget what I had been. I had to, for my son's sake.

You must remember that I first began this novel around nineteen- eighty or so, though it took four years longer to come to print and the bookshelves. One of the main themes in the book is that Sarah *doesn't want* to be psychic. Abhors it. It's done nothing but make a mess of her life. That truth plays a huge part in what happens later in the novel.

I mean, think about it? Would you really want to know when a crime was going to happen or, worse yet, *live* it or *see* it? Would you want to be plagued by nightmares of good and bad events…and carry the guilt if you can't/won't try to change things for the better? Couldn't it take over your whole life in ways you could never imagine?

I used this concept, too, in my two-thousand-and-ten horror novel Before the End: *A Time of Demons*, where my main character,

Cassandra, is first getting her precognition and demon-seeing powers. She can look at a person and see if they're about to die. The first of her so-called gifts from God. Yow, who'd want to be able to see that? Then you'd have to do something about it, right? Wrong? What happens if you know you can't change their coming death, you've tried, and must be fated forever to just have that awful knowledge…and have to live with it? I wouldn't want it, would you?

Now we come to another important ingredient for most paranormal novels. Romance. Sex. I'll tell you that in all my novels and short stories there is a huge dose of romance; sometimes sex. In good taste, of course. For me, romance and love (not necessarily sex except in the erotic stories) are the glue that holds a paranormal or a horror novel together. Not just romantic woman-and-man love, either, but the love of family, of a mother or father, or between sisters and brothers or between friends. Love is the single strongest weapon, besides religion at times, to combat evil or fend off the nasty spirits, vampires or what not. I use it a lot. In the apocalyptic novel above it is familial love between the brother and sister and the affection between them and their aunt and uncle; between them and their friends, and in the end, between them and the humans of the world that give them their strength.

In my *Witches* it's the love between three sisters and even the love between Cassandra and her feisty mischievous familiar cat Amadeus that gives them the edge.

In my *The Last Vampire*, it's the love, pure and carnal, between the two main characters Emma and Matthew, as the world is falling apart around them, humanity is dying, and Emma is transforming into a blood–thirsty vampire, which sustains them. Emma fights to keep from feeding on Matthew and Matthew fights to protect the woman he loves. Love binds them together when there's nothing else left. The earth is shaking itself apart. Humanity has been decimated and turned the survivors into pathetic savages. Emma's love for Matthew pits her against her greatest enemies, a band of vicious vampires who either want her to join them or they'll kill her. Matthew's love for Emma drives him, in the end, to track her through a dangerous terrain under horrible conditions with vampires hounding him and trying to kill him. Love enables Emma and Matthew to persevere over all the odds and end up together…until the world finally turns dark. Until the end they have each other.

Because for love, a human will fight to the death, defend another in times of trouble, remain loyal or believe something they'd never normally accept. For love most people will sacrifice *everything*. That's a powerful motivation and I've always maintained that, in a fictional story, it's essential that every character, good or bad, must have a solid motivation for what they believe and what they do. A convincing motivation. Motivation is as important as character or plot. In my opinion, of course.

I've noticed in the last few years, especially as e-books and e-short stories have grown in popularity that sex, eroticism, have also grown in leaps and bounds. Years ago I fought writing these erotic stories. I always was a prude. But recently, even I've seen how, if handled tastefully, eroticism can add a new exciting dimension to a story. In my *The Nameless One* erotic short story I weave the sex into the plot by making it about a married couple who are on an archeological dig in Egypt. They love each other. The sex scenes are between them. Finding the tomb of a cursed ancient pharaoh's lesser wife, who is also an iniquitous sorceress, a lust spell entrances them. That's part of it. In the tomb itself I also create animated characters on the golden walls that seem to come alive and make lusty love for any human eyes watching. This is a sacrilege, because for me, eroticism without real love as a base or an end product makes it more animalistic and much less fulfilling.

Another section of this guide deals with time travel and in many paranormal romances time travel is used as a way to set a love story in an exotic or strange time, which also complicates the love affair in different ways. We've all loved books that take us away, literally, to another time and place. We suspend believability and experience the strangeness of the different time and see the people and the place through our own eyes. I've written two time travel novels; quite different, and one novel, *The Heart of the Rose* I actually set in fifteenth century England. All three took immense amounts of research. Which is why I haven't written a new one in quite a while and don't intend to in the near future. It takes too much work. My hat's off to all the historical writers and all the research they must have to do. It isn't easy.

One of the time travel books, *Egyptian Heart*, a true romantic paranormal in that the romance and the time traveling are the strongest focal points of the novel. I send my main character back to ancient Egypt, around the time of Nefertiti and Akhenaton. Like my time travel stories, and my one historical romance, I tried to make the times historically accurate but wove a *fictional* heroine, in this case Maggie Owen, into that history. Maggie, an Egyptologist, in the present, hasn't found her true love and senses that she never will. She longs for him. Aches for him. Perhaps, she thinks, the love of her life doesn't even live in her time.

Then an ancient magical amulet necklace she finds in a tomb sends her back to the days of Nefertiti and she finds him. Ramose Nakh-Min. She's mistaken as a slave, his slave, and confusion ensues. He's immediately intrigued with her pale coloring, green eyes (eyes like a jinn, which is superstitiously looked upon by ancient Egyptians and sometimes feared) and blonde hair; unbeknownst to her, there's a prophecy he's aware of that says his true love will have that coloring and be a stranger to his land.

Of course, after some trials and tribulations, they fall madly in love. But how can she love him, she broods, when the scarab amulet she wears around her neck could send her back to her time without warning…and she has no idea when or even if that will happen. It would break her heart, and his if she gives him too much of her heart, to lose her true love now. In the meantime, she adapts to his time and finds a place, the love and respect of others, for herself there. The romance and the magic make this book what it is.

My other time travel is the before mentioned *Witches*. Amanda, the white witch from present Canaan, is dragged back to seventeenth century Canaan, where she must fit in. In a time where witches are imprisoned and hung just on the word or accusation of another. She, too, finds her true love there. But unlike Maggie in *Egyptian Heart*, she'd already found him in this life, but lost him to death. She finds him again in the past as a reincarnation of her dead husband.

Amanda also has the added problem that the black witch she's been forced to exchange places with had been poised to be arrested for witchcraft and executed. So Amanda not only finds herself alone in a strange hostile time, but in great personal danger, and must also try to find a way to change the townspeople's unsavory opinion of the woman she's replaced. And when she finally gets to go home to the present, it isn't alone. No, she doesn't get the reincarnated husband, but I give her a baby (she's pregnant) to take home. A baby she and her dead husband had always wanted to have, but couldn't.

Anything, if explained plausibly, can happen in paranormal fiction and isn't that exactly why we love it?

So, hurray to romance and magic! The supernatural. To angels, ghosts, beings of the night, elves and fire elementals. Fairies and vampires. To all the paranormal cast of characters we love to love. If you keep reading them, we'll keep writing them.

The rest of this Guide will give you useful tips on not only writing exciting dialogue but how to self-edit your grammar and punctuation, how to create realistic dialogue, how to find an agent or publisher for it and, lastly, the importance of heeding each agents' or publisher's rules of submission and why it's so important to follow them to the letter.

Now go ahead, turn the page, and read everything you'll need to know about writing, plotting, editing, polishing and submitting paranormal fiction. Then…start writing.

Written this day of February 19th, 2011
by Kathryn Meyer Griffith

Part One

SPIRITS, SPRITES AND SPOOKS

ANGELS & BENEVOLENT SPIRITS

By Shannah Biondine

Here's an interesting fact that may surprise you and possibly persuade you to consider the use of good spirits or angels as paranormal characters in your fiction: *The majority of Americans believe in angels.*

According to various surveys and polls taken within the past decade, nearly sixty percent of adults in the United States believe in the existence of angels. A large percentage of people worldwide profess to a similar belief. The conviction that such spirits exist appears to span religious, regional and educational lines. Even among survey respondents who described themselves as having "no religion, " two-thirds of a sample indicated they believe in God and approximately half confirmed acceptance of angels or unseen but positive spiritual beings.

One study at Baylor University found that a majority of respondents not only accept as fact the existence of such beings, but claimed to recall specific incidents when they believe they witnessed a guardian angel protect them or another person from harm.

In an age of GPS systems, cell phones, laptops, video clips, and a global network of data, economics, and breaking news stories, a large segment of us believe in angels. Not just a handful of throwback hippies in a commune somewhere growing their own tofu or third-world farmers. A significant portion of the world's population, many of these people quite educated. Even secular types claiming no religious affiliations believe in the existence of invisible and benevolent spirits.

Interesting and maybe all the more remarkable when one considers the state of the world economy, recent natural disasters, wars, and so on. But is this fact significant for you as a fiction writer?

Definitely, because it means a large number of readers will be predisposed to accept a story premise featuring spiritual beings. *(Note: within the context used in this chapter, all references are to helpful spirits.)* A reader who believes in the existence of angelic spirits is unlikely to balk at a story with such a character in its plot. Whether main or secondary characters, whether they're central to and propel the story action, or merely appear briefly in one pivotal scene, readers are likely to be engaged and keep reading because they don't need to "suspend their disbelief." Thus your tale may be poised from the outset to touch readers on a deep, psychological level.

I recently participated in a panel discussion about writing fiction. Inevitably, various opinions were offered as to why writers are drawn to crafting fiction, and why readers seek and appreciate it. My personal philosophy is that fiction—while primarily understood to be a form of entertainment or escapism—performs a vital underlying, and frequently overlooked, secondary role.

Fiction fills a human psychological need for order and structure. For all that it is "pretend," fiction stands as a safe haven against the disorder and chaos of real life. Fiction lets its readers explore remarkable events, cause and effect, dramatic outcomes, and the workings of the other minds. Within a created stage and story, readers can take desperate chances, fall in love, or fight a war. A good novel is the literary equivalent of riding on an amusement park ride.

Everyone knows that in life, bad things happen every day to good people. Humans behave in ways both reprehensible and admirable. The core difference between a good work of fiction and everyday life is that in fiction the reader is provided a comprehensible *reason* for madness or mayhem. Events aren't random, and you as the writer understand this.

As authors we agree to a basic tenet, guaranteeing readers that by our tale's resolution whatever was amiss will have been corrected. Our protagonist will be richer somehow for having survived the plot events, better for having striven against some powerful obstacle or long odds. The protagonist's striving and effort will have won an emotional payoff. Since readers are along for the ride while the protagonist experiences various plot events which lead up to the final chapter, they will be touched in some emotional way by the storyline.

Thus you're not only setting out to entertain readers, but move them. The best and most enduring stories last because they strike a universal chord. They reach deep within the human psyche to frighten, amuse, stir affections, reassure, or strengthen reader self esteem. They make readers believe in themselves, in justice, in the milk of human kindness, in things "larger than life."

Few issues qualify better than religious beliefs. Religion sparks wars and divides people just as capably as it unites them. Every person has opinions about the purpose of life and the potential existence of an "afterlife." Readers *care* about spiritual matters, no matter what label they put on themselves…even if they don't label themselves at all.

So using invisible beings, sympathetic to mortal plights, understanding of mortal weaknesses and causes, seems a natural fit for writers of the paranormal. We have already chosen to walk the fine line between light and shadow, between what is and what might be, making the ordinary more extraordinary. Readers of paranormal genres have a taste for all that is murky and arcane, seemingly a greater willingness to stretch the bounds of belief into what cannot be seen with the eye but may be perceived by the soul.

Angels and spirits can be a very special weapon in our fiction's arsenal, but there are things to consider when crafting such work. Here are some observations to bear in mind:

ANGELS & BENEVOLENT SPIRITS AS STORY CHARACTERS

Enduring fictional characters generally must possess some quality that makes them unique, or at least striking and unusual enough to be memorable. Obviously divine beings qualify by their very definitions, but you must not overplay the obvious or rely on that fact alone. Make sure there is something human about the character, as well. Humans must relate to this being, so a minor weakness or mortal tendency is generally a smart idea.

Spiritual essences are often assumed to be invisible to the mortal eye, but don't ignore the old saying that "Angels are among us all the time" without our being aware of it. Whether the spirit in your tale is visible or not to other characters or the reader is your choice. The particular entity in your tale may appear as a person, an animal, tree or plant. Spirits can be bodies of water, gusts of wind, mountains, or other inanimate objects. There's no reason why a positive spirit must be a natural object, either. A benevolent angel could appear in a tale as a human creation—even something like a knife or gun. *Will* it be a killing weapon in your hero's hand? Only you know the answer, but it's an intriguing question.

Readers often accept the notion that children or pets are more "sensitive" to spiritual essences. This can work for or against what you're trying to accomplish. You don't have to adhere to any hard and fast rule about this, but you should be aware of this basic reader expectation. Consider *The Sixth Sense* and whether the story would have been as powerful if the mother saw dead people and her son struggled to believe her. Maybe not.

Timing of a "spiritual appearance" can be critical. While you're free to write a spiritual being into any scene, note that certain timeframes may work to your advantage. Holidays and happy gatherings for humans—reunions, weddings, big family dinners—are particularly ripe for "special visitors." A divine being might turn up at an ill parent's bedside on Mother's or Father's Day, arrive as an uninvited guest when families gather for Thanksgiving, Easter, Passover, or Kwanzaa.

Faith moves to the forefront of most people's minds during such celebratory moments. Of course stories featuring Christmas angels have been done many times, however, that doesn't mean you can't still write one with a different slant. Some people would hold that Santa himself is the quintessential "Christmas angel," and many choose to believe in the spirit of generosity he embodies.

The flip side of timing is equally appropriate: angels are frequent visitors to crash sites, battlefields, hospitals, graveyards, and courtrooms. Traumatic events or major life crises offer ideal backdrops for spiritual appearances. Dark and troubling times make readers expect, and even request divine intervention. A critical plot point may even be the point where a reluctant character finally accepts the truth of the spiritual realm or concedes that he/she cannot "go it alone" any longer and have readers cheering events to their ultimate resolution.

Don't forget to put limitations on the magic. Appropriate timing, visual appearance, and a quirk or two are not enough. If your benevolent spirit is all powerful, you destroy your own tale. If an archangel shows up and readers sense this being can simply wave his hand and fix everything that's gone wrong, from your human's broken-down car to his slipping career or unraveling marriage, what's the point in turning another hundred pages?

The trick is to think of your angel much like a high-wire artist. This artist has no fear of heights, or at least appears not to fear them. He can confidently balance on a bicycle or chair leg perched on a taut segment of thin wire high above the ground. Danger surrounds and death lurks below, yet the tightrope walker makes it to the other side.

Give your good spirits one or two particularly strong talents like tightrope walking. Let them be sensitive, aware, wise, patient...but don't let them be impervious to all harm or capable of too many amazing feats. Perhaps the laws of physics or mortal courtrooms don't apply, but spirits must still be subject to God's laws or the laws of the Universe. There has to be something your spirit is incapable of, some weakness, some manner in which the humans in your tale must still take up the sword and fight their own battles or readers won't care enough to hang in for the showdown.

PLOT FUNCTIONS & AVOIDING STEREOTYPES

While I basically favor indulging reader expectations rather than playing against them, the one area where I recommend being a trailblazer is in the use of stereotyped characters. Angels are themselves archetypes, symbols of all that is good and righteous. This doesn't mean your spirits have to or should be utilized in the way readers might anticipate.

Here's what I mean. It's fine to have an angel appear in a hospital setting, but I wouldn't make that heavenly helper a nurse or ER doctor. That's already been done too many times. The same goes for firefighters, police officers, soldiers, and other stock characters. These roles are by definition "guardians" of human society, so where's the novelty or freshness in having such a person be guardian angel? There's no mileage for you as a storyteller with that.

Wouldn't it be more interesting for readers to discover the angel's some homeless guy nobody even noticed in the prior scene? Or the annoyingly slow elderly woman who counts out every last penny at the grocery store while your hero's impatiently agitated in line behind her, desperate to get out of there so he can save the day? Not the handsome young doctor but the ordinary, middle-aged pharmacist.

Keep in mind how invaluable a spiritual helper character can be to *you*, as author. Need a message delivered in a particular scene, but all your humans are scattered and busy with other things? Need to mend fences between feuding neighbors or get your hero that vital but highly unlikely social invitation? Use your angel. Need a touch of humor to lighten or darken the mood? Angels might be the answer, if that will naturally flow with your story action. Avoid excessive or unwarranted angelic intrusions. Actions of your spirits need to be plausible, not simple plot devices that feel arbitrary or "faked."

The trick is not limiting your angels to primary roles. They can make great secondary or minor characters, too. A good spirit can serve as your protagonist's best friend or a child's mentor. An angel can be the black sheep, whose main purpose might be as an example for others of how *not* to behave. While it's true readers won't expect guardian angels to lie, cheat, steal, or get drunk, what if the angel is exhibits such frailties in order to help someone else? Then it would be acceptable. Even negative behavior on the part of a very positive character may be forgiven if you set up the proper character motivation.

Last but not certainly not least, think of angels when you consider death. An angel can take the bullet meant for someone else or even *be* the bullet.

Sometimes we writers need to kill off a character to serve the larger plot, and having an angel hovering in the background can make this a truly powerful scene for readers. Going back to what I said about making sense and order in our fictional worlds, don't forget that death is the ultimate taboo, the largest subject most people cannot truly wrap their minds around. Your benevolent spirit can help other characters understand the transition, accept the finality, and ultimately find strength to go on in the face of death.

The ways you as author harness the abilities of special beings are nearly limitless. There are dozens of intriguing possibilities, so begin by asking that ultimate writer's question, "What if....?" If you want to write paranormal fiction, you've chosen to think outside the box, to create from a place without mental boxes. Leaps of faith are the norm; you shouldn't be afraid to take one.

CAN I USE A SPIRITUAL BEING AS MY PROTAGONIST?

The answer would be yes, but this could be tricky. Remember what I said about flaws, and consider that protagonists need a character arc. You'll need to be especially careful in crafting this growth and change for a divine being; justifying early why this specific angel isn't already perfect. You'll also need to be really vigilant about character motivation throughout the unfolding plot. Readers may accept angels, but they'll also automatically demand that such evolved spiritual beings consistently live up to higher standards of ethics than ordinary mortals.

You can give a hero wings, but you can't grant him a free pass.

This also may affect your story resolution. It won't be enough to simply "tie up all the loose ends." In saving himself from damnation, your hero-angel must also somehow save the planet or all of mankind. The stakes are naturally higher, so your payoff must be as well. You may also find, as several authors noted during the panel discussion, that you encounter a problem with finishing your novel and realize it's because you've demanded certain characters do something you—and probably your readers also—know deep down is essentially wrong, something that particular character would be unwilling to *ever* do. For a character to have changed this much, great impetus would have had to affect him/her. Did you create that?

For example, is your angel going to save one life at the cost of a hundred others? If so, you have to ask tough questions: Would a heavenly angel truly be able to wreak such havoc? Or would he sooner sacrifice his own soul before keeping such a terrible bargain?

Will the plot work as you outlined it, or do you need to rethink the motives and scenes propelling the characters and story action to the climax? This is where many writers get blocked, and just one example of how a reading partner or critique group can be of tremendous help. You need someone you trust to brainstorm with you while you verbalize key points may clarify problems and get your writing flowing again.

I utilized guardian angels as secondary characters, where they meddled in human lives and helped mortal men and women find true love. This was a deliberate choice from the outset, as I knew I planned installments in a series. So far there are only two volumes, but I can use both the same two angels again, or give either a different partner in a future installment. There are no limits to the humans I can have them guide or interact with. Nor do they have to remain in the same Old West town.

Some writers and critics say a series is successful because the setting is so dynamic, readers long to return to that place and time. This may be the case for tales set in a particular era or fantasy realm, but it's also true that characters bring readers back eager for more. This holds for many works of genre fiction. There's no reason it can't be true for books that feature special angels or divine beings.

VARIETIES OF POSITIVE SPIRITUAL BEINGS

Here's a palette from which to choose in crafting spiritual beings. Keep in mind that you can bend some of these descriptions to suit your needs, or even pick and choose attributes to create your own unique characters.

DEVAS. Derived from Sanskrit and referring to "a being of bright light," the term Deva is used to indicate a spiritual essence lacking the corporal body of humans. Also known as Elementals, these entities go back to Pagan beliefs predating Christianity.

Devas are believed to invest their energy and knowledge in a particular area. There are devas associated with growing acorns into oak trees, devas of lakes or fields, etc. Some people believe that all plants and animals, even planet Earth itself, has its own deva. Devas or Elementals who choose to aid human beings do so for mutual benefit. (Got a Tree-hugger character in mind? What could be better than a Deva to help out?)

GNOMES are considered Earth Elementals, living in rocks, under tree roots, below the ground or in soil itself. They may or may not be helpful to humans.

SYLPHS are air spirits and often found on mountaintops. Sylphs are believed to aid humans in receiving creative inspiration and are associated with the arts. They are generally sympathetic toward humans.

UNDINES are water spirits. They may resemble humans in appearance and size but inhabit streams or ponds and lakes rather than land. They are graceful, emotional, sensitive beings often found behind the veils of waterfalls or under lily pads.

SALAMANDERS are the spirit of fire. Believers say you cannot light a match without a salamander present near you.

They are considered the most powerful of all the elementals and are particularly inclined to help mortals who "keep their heart fires burning."

In Scottish folklore, BROWNIES are invisible sprites believed to perform helpful tasks at night while the human household is sleeping. Germans call a similar invisible helper a KOBOLD. (Other sprites, elves and fairies are covered more extensively in a separate chapter of this guide).

If your work is associated with a particular region or culture, I encourage you to research its folklore and history for other spiritual beings. The list of possibilities throughout history and various regions of the world is virtually bottomless, particularly as you have no time restrictions. An ancient being who comes to the aid of modern mortals might make your tale even richer by lending additional depth or atmosphere.

CHRISTIAN ANGELS & THEIR CHOIR

These benevolent beings are generally considered both messengers or helpers sent by God. They communicate with and defend mankind. This is what most everyone agrees upon. However, there is disagreement amongst the major religions as to the specific hierarchy, powers, and number of angels. I have provided details as to the Nine Choirs of Angels (also known as The Hierarchy) according to standard Christian theology, and recommend that if your work is directed for a specific religious market, you will need to conduct further research.

In the Old Testament, only two orders of angels are cited—the Seraphim and the Cherubim. Saint Paul added seven other orders in the New Testament, thus bringing the total to nine. These are listed in descending order (of power, or "closeness to God Himself").

THE FIRST TRIAD is highest, and made up of the Seraphim, Cherubim, and Thrones.

SERAPHIM are described as angels of love, light, and even fire. They are involved in humanitarian and planetary causes. They are alternately depicted as having six wings and four heads, being "fire serpents," or having no embodiment at all, merely appearing as light essences.

CHERUBIM are the angels of harmony and wisdom. They guard the light and the stars, keep negative energy from getting through to Divinity, and shine so brilliantly that humans are thought to be unable to see them.

THRONES are angels of justice and will. They are also called the "many eyed ones." They create, collect and send energy to oversee relationships and planetary issues.

THE SECOND OR MIDDLE TRIAD is comprised of the Dominions, Virtues, and Powers.

DOMINIONS are angels of intuition and wisdom. They combine the spiritual and material aspects of life, oversee cause and effect, and are useful in mediating/arbitrating when adjustments need to be made with churches, politicians, leaders, and human laws.

THE VIRTUES are angels of movement and choice. These are often known as the "Miracle Angels." They are said to aid those who strive to go above and beyond, to accomplish what others call impossible. They offer healing through the elemental energies of earth, air, fire, and water.

THE POWERS are angels of space and form. They keep track of human history, have organized the world's religions, dispense justice or chaos, and mainly serve in roles of defenders over home/family/friends.

THE THIRD OR LOWEST TRIAD is composed of The Principalities, Archangels, and lower basic angels of every stripe.

PRINCIPALITIES are beings that guard continents, countries, large cities or groups. They work towards global reform and channel positive energy. They may be involved in issues such as the extinction of animal species, leadership problems, human rights issues or discrimination amongst humans.

ARCHANGELS are ruling angels, also called Angels of Fire. These are the angels probably most often portrayed in films or fiction, because they enjoy human contact and are able to belong to several levels in the angel hierarchy at once. They also have different individual attributes. Familiar names here would be Gabriel, Michael, Raphael, and Uriel.

Lowest of all the ranks are beings simply called **"ANGELS."** These are the various messenger angels, nature angels, and those typically assigned to humans. When acting as Guardian angels, they provide guidance specifically during transformation, birth, and death, as well as protection during the course of mortal life.

A guardian angel can come from any level within the choir and can communicate with other angels at various levels. They may need to be asked and do not always interfere unless the mortal seeks assistance.

FRAMING YOUR STORY

By now you've probably imagined a range of plot possibilities. Whether your tale involves corporate greed, global warming, a murderer on the loose, or two misguided lovers, I'm sure you noted some spiritual being or angel who'd be perfect for helping when your plot thickens.

Here's an exercise that may be helpful even before you begin plotting your tale. Think of a book or film you love. Take that same basic storyline and inject an angel or deva into it.

Why, you wonder? Well, it's an important test because paranormal works shouldn't work just because they're paranormal.

A story about a werewolf or ghost or angel needs to be first and foremost a good story, with all the essential other ingredients in place. A strong protagonist, solid conflict. Take a great story near and dear to your heart, and plunk a good spirit in there somewhere. Doesn't matter where. Add a secondary character or change the protagonist. What do you get?

A whole different story, yet still an excellent, satisfying tale. Or did the plot change? Did the entire parameter of the tale collapse in on itself, or morph into something wholly different than what you started with? Would this story stand on its own as a single title, or have you evolved it into something you could easily imagine as part of a longer series? Is it no longer a cohesive epic, or just a piece of a larger puzzle?

These are some of the tough questions you face. If you're attempting your first paranormal work, the task may seem daunting. Remember what intrigued you about writing a paranormal to begin with, and recall all the myriad possibilities. Your characters can be different and fresh, make unusual choices most mortals do not face, have options closed to many characters in stock novels.

There's a broad array of facets and elements to work with. Plus you can always ask for help from your "writer's" angel.

We writers all have one, and has been touched or guided by an invisible spirit no one else can fully appreciate. We just prefer to call it our "muse." It will guide you. Just open your inner ears and listen.

Yes, Virginia, There are Ghosts

By Linda Madl

Years ago at a book signing a reader taught me the best lesson I can share about writing ghost stories. In my historical romance, *Bayou Rose,* I had written in a grandfather ghost subplot though I'm a skeptic. I had spent little time considering how to handle the ghost. I just went with my instincts and my reading of ghost stories—fiction and non-fiction. So, I was unprepared for a wary reader's question.

She hovered over my table as she perused the back cover copy. The story was set on a Louisiana antebellum plantation and had turned out very well. The eye-catching cover was rich and sensual without being too revealing, and the promotional copy mentioned the ghost. I was proud of the book, which received good reviews and eventually went into a second printing.

The reader frowned over the blurb describing the ghostly subplot. Without looking up, she demanded in a voice loud enough to make everyone in the store turn my direction, "Is it a real ghost?" Before I could respond, she squinted at me over her reading glasses, leaned closer, and added in a not-to-be-contradicted tone, "I hate it when they aren't real ghosts."

On the spot, I managed to smile at her oxymoron. Real ghosts? I had never thought about it exactly that way. Still I recognized what she meant. Thank heavens, I could say there was a "real" ghost in the book. He was introduced in the beginning and revealed himself at the end. But there was more to the haunting of the old plantation than the spirit of the grandfather. The plot included a hoax ghost. I had written in both real and false specters, yielding to my own desire to leave a bit of mystery around the grandfather spirit. Just like Virginia longing to believe in Santa and this reader's desire for "real" ghosts, I too found it more satisfying to write as if ghosts actually linger among us.

Superstitious, illogical, and unscientific though it may be, many of us want to believe in ghosts. We grow impatient with a TV ghost hunter that always finds a practical explanation for a haunting. We scorn a ghost story that turns out to be about phony phenomenon. We long for the mystery and the wonder of beings beyond our ken, real ghosts.

In other words, if the ghost you're writing about isn't a bona fide spirit from the other side, your readers will be disenchanted.

When you decide to write a story with a ghost, your job as a writer—your contract with the reader—is to create a believable, chilling, and heart-stopping specter.

Ghosts have been part of storytelling for millenniums. Readers understand their role as focus of the story or as a device. From the Egyptians, Greeks, Chinese, and Will Shakespeare, Charles Dickens, M.R. James, Henry James, O. Henry, Edith Wharton to Ruth Rendell, Stephen King and the X-files. Remember the Christmas episode with Lily Tomlin and Ed Asner playing the ghosts in the old mansion? One of my favorites. The point is, ghosts stories are more than scary tales told at slumber parties or around campfires. They are an ancient and honored story form. Many of the great authors have indulged in writing ghost stories. Readers, like the woman at my book signing, have expectations.

During the Nineteenth Century the fireside reading of ghost stories was a household ritual, not just at Halloween but also throughout the Christmas holiday and the winter. Magazines of the time published ghost stories for family reading. The reading public snapped them up to be enjoyed after supper by young and old. Many of the favorites are reprinted often and are still found in bookstores and libraries.

Many of today's readers have watched a ghost hunter on TV, gone on a Halloween ghost tour, or read any one of numerous books of "true" ghost experiences. Many have read ghost stories extensively during their teenage years. Readers come to the genre with a basic knowledge about ghosts and seeking certain experiences.

Ghosts are classic. A well-written ghost story is gripping and cathartic for all ages.

They are also fun to write. Maybe that is one of the reasons so many of the great authors have turned their hand at ghost stories.

GHOSTLY ESSENTIALS

Before you start writing, let's discuss some basics:

First, What is a ghost? It is the spirit, image, or presence of a departed person (sometimes of an animal) who is able to enter the physical world of the living instead of passing on to the afterlife. A ghost is not an immortal like a vampire, a shapeshifter such as a werewolf, or a soulless entity like a fairy or a demon. A ghost is a manifestation of a deceased human being or an animal that remains in this world or is caught between the worlds of the living and the dead. Thus a ghost seems unnatural to the living and most people are afraid them.

Aspects of this definition vary from culture to culture. Ancient Greeks believed the departed crossed the River Styx into the underworld. Egyptians thought they sailed to the west beyond the setting sun. Christian cultures believe the departed ascend to heaven. The Victorian spiritualists supposed spirits of the deceased crossed to another plane, the Beyond or Summerland. Whatever the departed's destination, a great many people, ghost story readers aside, feel safest living by the axiom that 'there is no such thing as ghosts.'

Ghosts of inanimate objects have also been reported and make good material for a story. These reports include ships, riverboats, coaches especially old-fashioned hearses, houses or buildings, villages, and trains. In *Haunted Heartland* by Beth Scott and Michael Norman witnesses tell of hearing or seeing Abraham Lincoln's funeral train as it chugs along the tracks from Washington D.C. to Springfield, Illinois on the anniversary of its sad trip in 1865. However, for the purposes of our discussion, these appearances fall into the category of place memory or slips in time. If you are working on a story that falls in this category, you might want to also read about time travel.

GHOSTLY MOTIVATIONS

What traps a ghost in the world of the living? Here are the generally accepted reasons for ghosts to remain caught between the world of the living and their final destination:

- Revenge or justice for a wrongful death (such as the ghost of Hamlet's father who's revelation about his death sets Hamlet in action).

- Closure of unfinished business such as carrying out a promise, waiting for a loved one to return, or finding something important the ghost lost.

- Communication of information vital to the living but known only by the ghost (as in the movie *Ghost Town*.

- Gratitude to the living for good deeds.

- Reenactment of the ghosts' death or traumatic events in their life (i.e. usually an imprint in haunted houses or on battlefields).

- Forewarning of events (as Marley does in *A Christmas Carol*) or of an imminent death.

- Protection of a treasure, a significant secret, or a loved one (as Sam does in the movie *Ghost*).

- Desire to remain in the home or location where they were the happiest.

- Unaware that they are dead and should move on.

Every one of these motivations presents the stuff of story conflict. Develop your own motivations for your ghost. Just about any desire that would compel a living person to make a long journey could serve as the motivation for a ghost to remain in our world and interact with the living.

GHOSTLY MANIFESTATIONS

For the most part, a ghost appears as a living person at the age it died and is clothed in the fashion of the period in which it lived. However, a story may portray the ghost as a young man or woman even though the departed died of old age. The ghosts of children remain children. They do not grow up over the years. The ghost will behave with the personality of the deceased individual it represents. A sweet gentle soul will remain gentle. A bully will still be a bully.

Some respected paranormal investigators and ghost story writers take issue with ghostly wardrobes. Why do ghosts appear clothed at all? Garments don't have spirits. Logically, wouldn't a ghost—as the spiritual projection of a deceased person—appear naked? I'll leave you to theorize about ghost clothes. An amusing story or two have been written based on the premise.

The ghost may appear wispy and shapeless, partially formed, full form but transparent, in black and white or full color, or even as solid as a living person. Often the living are convinced they see a real person until they note the image is floating above the ground or it vanishes into a stone wall. If death was violent, the ghost might appear with bloody wounds, a disconcerting sight for the living witness.

Ghosts may be seen during the day, at twilight, at night, in dreams, or in other borderline states of consciousness. They are seen everywhere: indoors, outdoors, in cars, on planes, aboard ships, or on horseback. Sometimes a servant, child, or a pet accompanies them.

They may also manifest as sounds or smells instead of a visible image. Disembodied footsteps or rappings in walls are common. The scent of cooking might fill an empty kitchen. A lady's fragrance may linger in a vacant parlor. Laughter might echo in a long-deserted barroom. These events often take place on anniversary dates of a death or a murder. They might occur before a death as a warning. They may be repeated throughout decades, even centuries, or they may fade after a time. Disturbance of a grave or the remodeling of a house might trigger the appearance of a ghost.

Other evidence of ghostly manifestations includes disappearance of items only to be found days later in an unexpected place. A whole room of furniture may be rearranged within an impossibly short time. Lights flicker. Television channels change without human command. Food or liquor disappears; however, I personally attribute vanishing victuals to living agents. As a rule ghosts don't eat. Sometimes an unexpected image appears in a photograph though no one saw the ghost at the time the shot was snapped. Ghost images may also reflect in a mirror, but remain invisible when viewed directly, the reverse of a vampire.

WHO SEES GHOSTS?

Commonly, persons with psychic ability more readily perceive ghosts than average folks. As in the TV series *The Ghost Whisperer,* Melinda sees the spirits, but her friends and husband do not. Remember in the movie *Ghost* how psychic Oda Mae Brown is the only one who sees and hears Sam in a room full of her friends and clients.

A ghost may appear to a group or to one individual. It may remain invisible to everyone in a room while a psychic or a child or a pet sees the ghost plainly. The accepted explanation for this phenomenon is that psychics, children, and animals retain their capacity to perceive the unseen while we ordinary adults outgrow the sensitivity. Others who might be especially attune to seeing a ghost would be someone emotionally close to the departed such as a spouse, sibling, dear friend, colleague, or beloved servant.

However, that does not mean that the average individual like you or me is immune to seeing ghosts. Lots of people will testify to that.

GHOSTLY POWERS AND LIMITATIONS

Call them superstitions, traditions, or conventions, there are beliefs in every culture about what ghosts can do and cannot do. Some of those conventions in western culture are:

Touching a ghost or having a ghost pass through you is unpleasant or possibly dangerous. At the very least you will experience a tingling chill or perhaps other symptoms such as sneezing like in *Ghost Town*.

· Ghosts cannot cross water (some say running water).

- Ghosts only appear at night or at the witching hour (which is not so).

- Ghosts can pass through walls or doors.

- Ghosts may be able to speak like a living person or may communicate through telepathy, gestures, or dreams.

- Appearance of a ghost is preceded by a bone-chilling sense of cold.

- Ghosts may interact with humans or may seem unaware of people.

- Ghosts appear to float rather than walk; they may or may not leave footprints.

- Ghosts must be invited to enter a dwelling where they did not die (not necessarily so).

- Ghosts are not confined to a locale, but may attach themselves to a living person.

- Ghosts of drowning victims are said to be especially powerful.

These traditions can be useful in ghost storytelling, or you can defy any of the above and create your own set of ghost laws. Just inform the reader of your rules and be consistent.

GHOSTLY FORMS OR TYPES OF HAUNTINGS

Over the years paranormal investigators have developed categories for ghost phenomenon and most readers are familiar with them.

The most common ghosts are *trapped souls* who are unaware that they are dead, are unable to make a full transition to the afterlife, or are unwilling to go. They may be trapped by their own private motivations discussed earlier. They may or may not attempt to communicate with human witnesses. Sam in the movie *Ghost* is a trapped ghost. He wants justice, and he wants to protect his wife, but he finds himself unable to communicate with her.

Another common ghost is the *psychic imprint* or *recording*, the product of an emotionally charged event such as the ghost's death or the death of a loved one. These ghosts are frequently connected to violent events: battlefields, a tragic duel, murder scenes, or site of a fatal accident. However, in some cases the imprint is of an individual or a group happy with their life in that place and time. On many occasions astonished witnesses have seen and heard the monks of Whalley Abbey in Great Britain chant in Latin with their heads bowed as they walk in a procession which vanishes into the fog as described in *Ghosts and Spirits* by Rosemary Ellen Guiley. The psychic imprint of ghostly monks appears, goes through the motions of an event without acknowledging human witnesses, and then vanishes.

A third type of haunting is frequently labeled a *thought form*. This entity, though not a form of a deceased human, is energized by human emotions and may behave and take on the form of a ghost. Or the entity may remain an undefined presence that conveys pain and suffering to those who encounter it. It is usually connected with a negatively charged site: a battlefield, a dungeon used for torture, or an insane asylum.

Poltergeist activity is frequently connected with ghosts. However, a poltergeist, which is German for noisy ghost, is an invisible mischievous spirit or energy. Some investigators theorize that poltergeist activity is projected by the psyche of a living individual, frequently an angry adolescent in the family. Others believe that the naughty spirit is an entity, which feeds on negative human energy such as that of a rebellious teenager. Poltergeists manifest as bad smells or flying objects or objects disappearing to reappear at a later time. The activity may be as benign as water splashing out of nowhere on the ceiling, pebbles showering onto the roof, or as dangerous as knives flying across the room. The phenomenon usually begins and ends suddenly. It may last for a few days or go on for years. It may or may not follow the family if they relocate. In some cases there is communication between the poltergeist and the person who is the focus of the activity. The activity may occur inside or outside the house and is quite unnerving for those who live with it.

The Bell Witch story of Tennessee is a famous, unsettling 'true' poltergeist story. This particular poltergeist even learned to speak and may have committed murder. It is a chilling, well-documented story.

Check your local library or Internet sources to learn more about this weird tale.

A fifth type of ghost (this doesn't fit within our definition of a ghost as a deceased person, but I think it worthy of mention) is a *fetch* or a *doppelganger,* one's ghostly double or an apparition of a living person. The phenomenon is sometimes called *bilocation.* In British and Irish folklore seeing a fetch is an omen. Seeing one's double in the morning foretells long life. Seen at night, the fetch foretells one's imminent death. There is a famous story about the poet, Percy Bysshe Shelley seeing himself weeks before his drowning death in Italy. What's even stranger is a friend saw him also when it was known he had gone for a visit in a neighboring town. It is a spooky phenomenon and material ripe for paranormal stories.

How to Banish Ghosts

So ghosts trouble your story characters. It is generally accepted that ghosts cannot physically harm a person. However living with the fear or a negative atmosphere can be nerve wracking enough to make cleansing a room or house necessary. Call *Ghostbusters?* The movie certainly offers some imaginative ways to deal with nasty ghosts. Here are some more conventional options:

1. Your story characters might hold a séance to communicate with the ghost. Once they learn its motivation for lingering, they can find a way to resolve its conflict. In the television series, *The Ghost Whisperer,* Melinda communicates with the trapped spirit and discovers how to help it crossover. Some well-trained mediums can cleanse a room or a house of negativity without needing to know the reason for the ghost's lingering presence, but this doesn't make for a very satisfying ghost story.

2. Your characters could have a house blessing. Clergy are not required for this ritual, though it's a nice touch if they participate. During a house blessing a number of actions may be performed: prayers are recited in each room, a

white candle is lit, holy water is sprinkled into the air, or sage is burned to cleanse the dwelling of spirits. Often rock salt is spread in a circle around the house for protection against the spirits' return. Sometimes such rituals work, but frequently the ghosts lie low to return later and resume or even increase their frightening activities.

3. Exorcism may be resorted to if all other efforts fail. The various religious denominations have different beliefs about exorcism. Clergy frequently resist performing an exorcism because of personal skepticism or fear. It is generally believed the ghost will respond only to the faith it practiced in life. This may or may not be known, depending on how much history your story characters have about the haunted site.

From a storytelling point of view, resolution of the ghost's conflict, which is linked to the living, sets up the most satisfying story outcome. Know your characters and your ghost and use your creativity.

WHAT MAKES A GOOD GHOST STORY?

The Oxford Book of English Ghost Stories used the follow criteria to determine a good ghost story and I think their point is right on.

> Each story should reveal to the reader a spectacle of the returning dead... and their actions; there must be dramatic interaction between the living and the dead ... with the intention of frightening the reader...

In other words, a good ghost story is about the living relating to the dead, and it is a scary experience. Not gross, mind you. Gore belongs in the horror genre.

A good ghost story scares the bejeebers out of your reader. He expects it. She wants it. Your goal is to make the reader cast an uneasy peek over his shoulder while reading. Or jump when the cat meows unexpectedly. Or be compelled to get up and turn on all the lights before settling back to read more.

Readers want to be scared. They want to be creeped out. They want the catharsis of spine-tingling fear that morphs into a safe, satisfactory ending. It is a cozy feeling to be frightened until you're covered in goose bumps then find all turns out well. You close the book still secure in your favorite chair.

Even Charles Dickens's *A Christmas Carol* is scary. Forget all the bad movie versions and read the original tale.

Ghosts are inherently frightening because they are manifestations of the dead. We do not understand death. Ghosts have powers to move about in ways we do not understand, like walking through a wall. They make disembodied sounds or appear in icy preternatural silence. They can invade our dreams or alter our mood. All are unfathomable actions to us living. It's not hard to make them scary.

Having said all this, I would like to point out that it isn't necessarily the ghosts who provide the fright. In Neil Gaiman's work *The Graveyard Book* the ghosts are friendly, some even endearing. It is the living and the serpent-like creature deep inside the hill that are truly terrifying and dangerous.

ARE GHOSTS EVIL?

Writers and investigators of the supernatural of earlier centuries often lumped ghostly activity with witchcraft and evil. In their religious system, witchcraft was an instrument of the devil. The odd bump in the night, the vase flying across the room, or the sudden appearance of a long-dead neighbor on his favorite woodland path could only be the work of the Devil.

Don't confuse ghosts with demons. You want to be clear about who and what your ghost is, its motivation, and its action. Just as there are evil people, there are evil ghosts. Just as there are misunderstood or misguided people, so are there misunderstood or misguided ghosts. While ghosts can influence people through dreams and thoughts, they do not posses them. Possession is a demon's power. Demons are soulless, evil entities. They are altogether different from ghosts.

MAKING GHOSTS REAL
FOR YOUR READERS

Here are some pointers for creating your ghost story:

CHARACTERIZATION

Given that ghosts are spirits of the living, they have attitudes, flaws, virtues, and mannerisms just like humans. Characterize them just as you characterize your living characters. Use their looks, their dress, their speech, their likes and dislikes, their life history, and their occupations or preoccupations. All the aspects of a person will hold true in death as in life. Ghosts can be jealous, loving, vengeful, forgiving, stingy, generous, sloppy, meticulous, vain or self-effacing. They will express these traits in gestures, facial expressions, tone of voice, syntax and even vocabulary— in every way that they relate to the living. The attributes often will be described by the living who encounter the spirit, unless the story is told from the ghost's point of view. (see POV below). Whatever a person was in life, his or her ghost will reflect as a spirit. Of course, the depth of the characterization reflects the ghost's importance to the plot.

PLOT

A slice of life narrative does not make a satisfying ghostly tale. Ghost stories need a plot. The reader expects a beginning with conflict, middle with deepening conflict, and an end that entails resolution. As stated in the above quote from *The Oxford Book of Victorian Ghost Stories,* the conflict involves the living interacting with the ghosts. More must be going on than the main character encounters a ghost in a house one night, is scared witless, and never returns to the place. There must be interaction between the living and the spirit. This interaction may be physical or psychological. In *The Turn of the Screw,* a classic example of a psychological ghost story by Henry James, the children are haunted by a pair of ghosts, and they play head games with the governess. The plot of *Emily's Ghost* by Annette Stockenberg reveals a physical or external plot in which Emily encounters a ghost, takes him home with her, and agrees to help him solve a historic crime for which he was hanged. Psychological or external plot is your choice.

Atmosphere

The tone, setting, and the emotional mood of the story creates the atmosphere. The most effective way to create a realistic and unsettling mood is to make use of the five senses: smell, sight, hearing, touch, and taste. From the Ghostly Basics I outlined above you can see how ghosts lend themselves to mood setting. The use of well-selected sensual details manipulate the mood, give immediacy to the narrative, and carry the action forward with subtle story questions. Use as many of the five senses as you can in a scene without telling everything. You want just enough detail to creep the reader out. Here's an example from my story "One Night at Whistling Woman Creek," a story of a frontier woman, in the anthology *Trespassing Time: Ghost Stories from the Prairie*. Can you find the three senses I used?

> Martie rose from the table, lit a lantern, found the shotgun behind the door, and carried the light and the firearm out onto the porch.
>
> The wind grabbed her skirt, but she ignored it. There was no moon, no stars, only the soft darkness of a cloud-covered night. The dogs barked on. She could just see their stiff tails on the edge of the lantern light. They faced the southwest, barking for all they were worth.
>
> Bossy the cow gave a nervous low. Martie glanced toward the barn to see the horses circling in the corral, the wind lifting dust from their hooves—like smoke coming off their feet.
>
> She was immediately aware that her stocking feet itched something awful. She rubbed one foot on top of the other for relief. All of a sudden the sense of being watched overwhelmed her.
>
> "Anybody out there?" she called. A drifter might make the dogs bark like that. "Make yourself known, sir. I'll call off the dogs."
>
> Nothing. The dogs persisted with their barking.

A number of visual references are used in the excerpt above, including light and darkness, stars and moon, and the dust from the animal's hooves. Touch or feel is also used: the tug of wind on her skirt and the itch of her feet. All through the scene is sound: the lowing of the cow and the barking of the dogs. When you put your mind to it, there are lots of ways to make the five senses work for your ghost story.

POINT OF VIEW (POV)

In the traditional Victorian ghost story—the golden age of ghost stories some believe—the tale is usually told from the main character's POV and often in the first person. The narrator's voice gives the story immediacy. Almost never did the ghost tell the story. However, more recent ghost novels and stories are recounted from the ghost's POV and quite effectively. The novel *The Lovely Bones* by Alice Sebold and *The Mercy of Thin Air* by Ronlyn Domingue use the ghost or spirit's perspective.

The different 'camera' angle literally gives an additional aspect to the conflict and to the important characters in the action. The spirit may be observing the scene from an opened dresser drawer or the upper corner of the room where no human could possibly be. Keep in mind this added dimension as you establish your ghost character's narrative and relationship with the living. Obviously in these ghost POV tales the frightening aspect readers so relish comes not from the POV ghost but from the living.

I couldn't resist a ghost POV story for *Trespassing Time*. It's entitled "Halloween at the Gates of Hell." See what I mean by expanded perspective?

> The ghost awoke slowly, disturbed not so much by the call of Halloween or the loud music that three young men had brought to the cemetery as by their dark, swirling vortex. He fumbled his way to consciousness, responding to their self-absorption and vanity, their arrogance and pettiness, like a sleeper to the smell of fresh brewed coffee, like a lover to his name on his beloved's lips.

> He stretched cold, vaporous limbs into the far corners of the graveyard and yawned with a gaping, vacuous mouth. Welcoming their darkness, he turned to the three young men. But the light of their fire assaulted him. Momentarily stunned, he shrank back into the shadows.

> A bonfire was a rare thing in a cemetery, especially the Lutsville Cemetery. Among the century-and-a-half old headstones was no place for mortals to linger after dark, let alone build a fire and commune around it.

> ...The ghost pulled himself together and swirled upward to gaze down on the youths and to better appraise the ... opportunity they presented to him.

As you can see, a ghost's POV will go well beyond that of the living's.

Another interesting aspect of telling the story from the ghost's POV is how the ghost deals with existence in the physical world of the living. In the movie *Ghost*, Sam must learn how to get from one place to another and how to move physical objects. Remember his encounter with the other ghost in the subway?

Author Lee Killough also deals with this challenge in *Killer Karma*. Cole Dunavan, a police detective, tries to solve his own murder, but must learn how to get from one place to the next and how to communicate with the living. How your ghost meets these challenges provides another way to show what kind of a person they were.

The Ghostly Ending

The only requirement for a ghost story ending, or for any story, is a satisfying conclusion. It might be happy. It might be sad. It might be unexpected or even uncertain—though foreshadowed throughout the story. It might be scary. Scary is really good as long as the conflict is resolved to the reader's satisfaction.

I personally like endings where the main character reaches a point where he or she must make a choice between two options that address the conflict. The choice between the options must be difficult. Keep the reader on tenterhooks to the very last.

Conclusion

To wrap it up: Make good use of characterization; ghosts are like people. Engage the reader with effective use of the five senses. Build a plot that delivers surprises, goosebumps, and a satisfying beginning, middle, and end. Use your creativity and have fun. If you're into it, your reader will get into it too.

Ghost story readers want to believe in ghosts just as Virginia wanted to believe in Santa Claus. In 1897 newsman Francis Pharcellus Church of New York's *Sun* wrote in his response to the eight-year old girl, "Did you ever see fairies dancing on the lawn? Of course not, but that's no proof that they are not there. Nobody can conceive or imagine all the wonders there are unseen and unseeable in the world."

That includes ghosts in my book. Don't disappoint your reader with a faux specter regardless of how technically sophisticated the ghost perpetrators might be. Leave that glitzy visual stuff to Hollywood. If you're not writing about a real ghost, you're not writing a ghost story. Remember, it's about the departed interacting with the living for important stakes. It's about giving your reader a satisfying boo-licious scare.

READING LIST

In the resources section at the end of this book is a list of ghost story reading. It is hardly an inclusive list, but features some good reading and a wide sampling of the genre.

Fae, Fey, Faery, Fairy—A Quick Glance into the Abyss

By Sheri L. McGathy

Good fairies, bad fairies, wee ones or tall. No matter how we think of them, or what name we choose to call them, the notion of fairies and their lore has been with us for thousands of years, perhaps longer. Fairies have captured our imaginations since the first tale, told by the first storyteller, came into being. Tales of fairies are ever changing and constantly evolving, often reflecting the era they were born within, as well as the joys and fears of that time.

Mention fairies and you'll get a variety of opinions as to who or what they are. Most will agree that fairies are mysterious creatures, but not all agree on exactly what they are or where they came from or even what they can do. Some will insist fairies are tiny people that live in deep pockets of nature—magical, wild areas untainted by the human hand. Some think fairies are free from the constraints of time and space. Others say they are whimsical creatures that spend their time flitting from flower to flower or from stream to field to grove.

Many fairies were believed to be gods, or if not gods every bit as powerful and just as unpredictable. Fairies have been labeled soul stealers and baby thieves even while being praised for their concern and caring ways toward mortals. There is even the belief that fairies are the true source of alien beings and sightings of little green men as well as the culprits behind human abduction stories. Back in the 1990s, there was an interesting cartoon based on this controversial theory called *Roswell Conspiracies: Aliens, Myths and Legends*. The premise of the cartoon series was that aliens were the true source of all Earth's myths, folklore, and legends concerning fairies, werewolves, vampires, and other creatures from the paranormal realm. The show was one of many examples of how writers can take existing myth and reshape it to create their own unique spin. The opinions concerning fairies vary as widely, and are as contradictory, as the tales of how they came to be amongst us. This variety can provide very fertile ground for writers.

So, just who or what are fairies? Are they tall, elf-like creatures endowed with magical abilities? Painfully beautiful beings born in the realms of mist? Are they little green men or small, winged creatures no bigger than one's thumb? The answer is elusive. Could they be the souls of the Pagan dead, spectral shades that are no longer a part of our world, but still seek its light?

Do fairies wish to do harm or to do good or perhaps a little of both? Are they supernatural beings, once powerful gods and goddesses now diminished in both stature and memory? Forgotten to time? Perhaps, or perhaps they really do exist in their many forms on another plane. Perhaps only when the energies are right, are we able to see them and they us. It is said only those born with the gift of second sight or the very young who still believe without question can see the fairies. But I wonder at the truth of this since so many tales abound. Given the mischievous natures of fairies, I suspect they appear and disappear when it suits them and show themselves to us only if they please, whether we possess the second sight or not.

In the Scandinavian region of northern Europe, we find stories that tell of fairies being the forgotten children of Adam and Eve, hidden from the eyes of Man as punishment for Eve's attempt to hide them from God. In another version of this story, we hear of a mother who had only managed to wash half of her many, many children when God came to her cottage. Ashamed of those children still dirty, she hid them from him. God was so angered by her actions he decreed that those she had hidden from him would be forever hidden from all mankind. These children became known as the "Hidden People" or the fairies.

Other tales handed down from the Nordic countries and Scotland, as well as in some areas of Ireland, speak of fairies as fallen angels and tell how they fell from Heaven when the gates were flung open to expel the hosts of Satan. These fallen angels were neither bad nor good, but amoral in nature and were not fated to follow Satan. So, when the gates were finally closed, the angels stopped their fall wherever they were and took on the essence of their surroundings.

Some took on the mantle of air and wind. Some made their homes on frozen mountaintops and became as cold and bitter as the northern gales. Others landed in the dense forests, or within the open fields and meadows to become one with the rich earth. Many splashed into the waters of the world, be they brook or stream, lake, river, or ocean. Some gathered the essence of light and fire about them while others chose the cloak of darkness and cool shadow.

In more recent years, scholarly debate has suggested there was once a race of Man, small of stature, nature-loving, peaceful folk who were forced into hiding for their survival. These people chose mounds deep within the earth or caves far beneath a mountain, or managed to track deep into ancient forests where few would follow. And there they stayed, keeping to their ways, the memory of them lingering in the minds of those who came after, yet the truth of their race, who they had been, fading into myth and lore. Eventually, they became known as the beings we now call fairy.

Perhaps there's a hint of truth hidden within all the many and varied lore, a moment or point in time that transforms an event from ordinary to extraordinary. The story is told, and retold, and retold again and again to eventually take on the air of myth. Somewhere buried in all the tales of fairies, there hides a truth as to who and what they really are, it's just waiting for us to find it.

A few years back, I found myself absorbed in a fascinating discussion with another author on the subject of fairies. He wondered why the fairy folk appeared in the lore of so many cultures throughout the world. Why so many stories were devoted to them and so many people believed these beings existed and exist still.

I pondered this. "The Little People," as he fondly called them, did indeed appear in countless lore. The Irish leprechauns were the first to come to mind, but not the only references to little people. Leprechauns are said to shun humans, preferring instead their own company and their crock of gold for comfort. Described as little old men standing no taller than a human knee, leprechauns are said to dress all in green and wear big-buckled black shoes and a large three-pointed floppy hat. They are crafty tricksters, especially when caught by humans who wish to take their crock of gold. If you manage to capture one but take your eye off them, even for a blink, your hold on them will be broken and they will disappear taking their gold with them. If you do manage to keep your eye trained to them, don't be fooled by a leprechaun's offer of silver or charms in exchange for his freedom. The treasures he so eagerly offers will turn to leaves or some other worthless thing before the day is done.

Both written and verbal stories of little people or fairies, tricky or otherwise, persist in most cultures throughout history. Some Native American tribes have tales of little people who assist the tribe by watching over young children or finding lost or misplaced items.

In Scotland, Wales, and England, similar beings known as Brownies exist. Other names: Broonie, Bwbachod (*boobachod*) or Bwca (*booka*), and for the more ominous ones, the Nis or Goblin, just to name a few. Brownies are for the most part helpful creatures or spirits of Fairy with brownish skin and just as brown, if not browner clothing, sometimes wearing a hooded cloak over a shaggy body, sometimes not, depending on where the tales are told. They are said to help with household chores or tend the fields and livestock, doing mostly unfinished tasks that humans failed to complete before the sun set to end the day. Humans repay this kindness by leaving out saucers of milk and grain as a way to show how grateful they are for the fairy's aid.

Folly to those who forget the fairy "gifts," for it's well known that fairy folk anger quite easily and can take offense at the slightest thing. Forgetting to please a fairy could cause the forgetful person to be stung by a fairy dart or suffer a fairy stroke! At the very least, they may find that they now have to do their chores without the nightly helper.

The realm of Fairy and its lore tell of dwarves and pixies, elves and sprites, white and green ladies, black ones, red ones, and even those said to be blue and gray. There are even Green Men and the Green Man.

Fairy lore regales us with tales of beautiful, solitary female guardians who live in the trees or dwell within the water even as they keep us ever watchful for a procession of trooping fairies crossing a field under the ghostly light of a full moon.

Creatures not unlike great serpents lurk beneath dark waters or water horses wait to take you below the waves. Seals that shed their skins to become enchanting maidens and beings that are part man or woman, part animal or fish abound in fairy lore.

Stories exist of the fairies of light, whose spirits are kind and their guiding hand a comfort while other tales warn of fairies who lurk within the shadows, their natures as dark as the world they inhabit, ever waiting to do the unwary human harm.

There are fairies who live deep within the ancient forests or make their homes beneath mounds of rich earth. Some live high upon the mountaintops, while others choose to inhabit the lands of ice and snow. There are fairies in the air floating gracefully upon the breeze and fairies that thrive upon the havoc of storms, their every move designed to create the booming threat of thunder. Let us not forget the fairies who tend the crops, care for the animals, and ward the fires through the long nights.

Fairies can offer blessings or dole out curses on a whim. There doesn't seem to be many places that a fairy doesn't dwell or a blessing or curse they can't summon. Many a human affliction has been blamed on fairies.

Guardian spirits are prevalent in the world of Fairy, existing as a myriad blend of ancient mythology and fairy lore. These spirits, called Elementals, are spirits of the air (mind), of the earth (body), of fire (spirit), and water (soul). Elementals are said to hold the ability to act as portals to the fairy realm.

I believe Elementals are the core, the very heart of all things Fairy. They represent the spirit of a place, its very essence. Elementals give voice to a silent world, and are the governing influence for all who dwell within their realm. They are the manifested guardians of and the embodiment of nature in all its beauty and rage. They are nature's spiritual custodians.

Elementals offer balance. Even the Christian belief that fairies were fallen angels carries the essence of air, earth, fire, and water, the elements of life. These elements also represent the four realms of Fairy. Fairies of all shapes and sizes fit somewhere within one of these four realms.

AIR ELEMENTALS

Sylphs are the Elemental spirits of the air and wind, taller than humans and stronger, and like the wind they are unpredictable and prone to sudden changes of mood and mind.

EARTH ELEMENTALS

As an Earth Elemental, the Gnomes are said to be quite small, yet at times can grow as large as giants. They are of the earth, concerned with the rich minerals within and the process of transformations. It is said that Gnomes are able to "swim" through the earth as if it was water.

FIRE ELEMENTALS

Salamanders represent the ever-changing fires. They are the raw expression of passion and fearless, free will. They are the spirits of fire and can be just as consuming and temperamental.

WATER ELEMENTALS

UNDINES, water elementals, resemble humans but can change their form to that of a fish or serpent, sometimes becoming half human and half fish. They are as free and fluid as the water they inhabit.

Undines are often referred to as water nymphs. Though born of water, these nature spirits of Fairy known as nymphs are found throughout the world. Nymphs are said to be quite beautiful maidens who live amongst great beauty.

NAIADS are nymphs that live within the freshwater streams, springs, and creeks. Oceanids live in the oceans, and the Nereids make their home in the waters of the Mediterranean Sea.

DRYADS are guardian nymphs of the woods and of the trees. Forests and woods teem with wildlife and plant life. Things fairies are drawn toward. Oreads are nymphs of the mountain forests.

FAUNS AND SATYRS are male nature spirits of the Fairy Realms, man-like creatures, small of stature, with horns on their heads and legs that look like those of a goat. They are the guardians of the animals that inhabit the woods and fields. They are sort of the bad boys of Fairyland, with their fondness for drink and their constant pursuit of amorous pleasure.

Many nature spirits such as the Flower Fairies are thought to be quite small. These plant fairies have lacey, delicate wings with clothing and skin tones that match the flowers they tend. Other fairies of nature can be as tall, if not taller than Man. Their concerns are primarily with the plants, the earth, the sky, and all the animals that inhabit the land and water. They are the protectors of nature and do not take Man's interference lightly.

Fairy lore is laced with omens and warnings and describes fairy beings whose sole purpose is to give truth to these omens and warnings. There are fairies that warn of death, either by an eerie wail (the Irish death spirit known as the banshee/bean si/bean sídhe—fairy woman who wails for the ancient families of Ireland) or by washing the bloody shroud or the grave clothes of the soon-to-be departed in a stream at night (Scotland's bean-nighe).

The bean-nighe is also believed to be the ghosts of women who died in childbirth, their clothing left unwashed after their death. Thus, each bean-nighe is doomed to wash them until the year arrives at what would be their natural death.

People will sit wide-eyed and fearful, huddled in the dark after the banshee wails listening for the rumble of the death coach even as they pray that the sound they hear is nothing more than the wind rattling their locked doors. They sing of golden-haired enchantress' and of wild hunts even as they warn others to beware. Many a person has crossed the road to avoid an old crone they encountered late at night or carried charms to ward against any fairy wishing to do them harm. Iron or Cold Iron, as it is sometimes called, was said to offer a strong protection against those of Fairy as the fairy folk have a natural aversion to the metal. Iron was also considered a special ward against witches, ghosts, and other supernatural beings.

We tell our children of the tooth fairy who takes their newly lost milk teeth and leaves a silver coin in trade. We read them bedtime tales about the fairy godmother whose kindly interference could mean the difference between a prince and a toad even as we warn of fairies that will suck the life from them or steal them away to Fairyland. Interesting to note, originally the fairy godmother bestowed charms to a child at birth, giving them grace, beauty, good fortune among other gifts or even cursing the child to be forever bereft of these same charms.

Fairies enchant and entrance, beguile and bewilder and none more so than the fairy nobility. These tall, god-like beings desire the light and warmth of the mortal soul as much as mortals desire the fairy's beauty and youth. Many a fair maiden or a comely young lad was rumored to have succumbed to the beguiling looks of a fairy noble. Though most of these tales take oral form and change from teller to teller, there are written accounts or fanciful tales of humans who sought out or took fairy brides though rarely do such unions end well.

Dunvegan Castle, on the Scottish Isle of Skye, is the ancestral home of The Clan MacLeod. On display in this castle is a tattered fragile piece of cloth claimed to be a fairy flag given to a Clan Chief by his fairy bride. The flag is believed to date back to the 7th Century. There are two sets of thoughts on how the flag came into the possession of the MacLeods. One speculates it came into the MacLeod possession through the Crusades, the other that the flag was given to the Chief of the MacLeod Clan by his fairy bride. I prefer the fairy version, and while there are several versions of the tale, I like the one told by the Clan MacLeod the best.

It seems that a fairy princess fell in love with the then Chief of Clan MacLeod, a very handsome young man, he was, and she wished to marry him at first sight. Her father, the fairy king, refused to allow the union, but eventually allowed his daughter to wed the young MacLeod, but under one condition: she could only be his wife for a year and a day.

The daughter agreed and their happy union produced a son. Too soon though, the year and a day came to an end, and she knew she had to return to Fairy. Before leaving, she begged her husband never leave their son alone and that he should never be allowed to cry, for she knew her heart could not bear the sound of his sadness. Her husband promised, and kept his word. That is until the night of a big celebration and the maid watching the young son, left him alone to watch the dancing. No sooner had the son started to cry than his fairy mother came to him, held him close, dried his tears, and wrapped him in her fairy shawl.

After he fell asleep, she whispered magic words in his ear, kissed his forehead, and vanished. Years later, when the son was older, he remembered his mother's visit and her whispered words: the shawl was in truth a magic talisman, it was to be kept in a safe place, and none but those of Clan MacLeod might touch it or it would vanish in a puff of smoke. If ever a MacLeod faced mortal danger, the shawl/fairy flag, was to be waved three times and the hosts/knights of Fairy would ride to the Clan's aid. There were to be three such blessing, or three times the flag could be used. To this day, the flag has been waved twice, the last blessing still remains.

THE SELKIES/ROANES (seal folk) from the Shetland and Orkney Islands in Scotland's West Highlands are often mentioned in the stories of mortal and fairy unions. The women of the seal folk are enchanting and beautiful. The men, while just as enchanting and handsome, are said to be quite amorous, often shedding their sealskins to court mortal women. If a mortal woman wished to call a male selkie to her bed, she need only sit upon a rock at high tide and shed seven tears into the sea. The male selkie would come to her at night. But if the mortal hoped to keep the selkie by her side, she would soon be disappointed. The selkie male would always return to the sea, leaving both the woman and any offspring the union produced.

Mortal men often coveted a selkie bride for their beauty and kindness, and so would wait in the shadows at night when the selkie would leave the sea to shed her sealskin and dance in the moonlight in her human form. While she danced, the mortal would steal her sealskin, promising only to return it if she would agree to be his bride. The selkie would have little choice but to agree, as she could not return to the sea without her sealskin. Rarely did the human keep his promise to return her skin, as he wished to keep his enchanting wife at his side until the day he died.

As she promised, a selkie would be the model wife, bear children, care for the home, cook, clean, sew, become everything a man could desire, but she would never stop wishing to return to the sea. In these tales, it was usually one of her children that would discover where the father hid the sealskin and return it to the mother. The selkie would then return to the sea, sometimes taking her children with her, most times leaving them behind.

There are still families in Scotland who claim selkie blood ties. The children from these unions were often regarded with both respect and sympathy. They were usually very attractive with an almost supernatural air about them. Some possessed the second sight or the healing touch. They also held a keen understanding of the sea.

It is interesting to note that some of the same theories which surround fairy origins are quite similar to selkie origins. Many ancient tales claimed them fallen angels condemned to live as animals until Judgment Day, or that they were once human and had done something so awful that they were now doomed to live as a seal the rest of their days. Similar to the belief that fairies were the dead, the old storytellers told tales that the selkie folk were actually the souls of the drowned, allowed to leave the sea to take human form one night only each year.

Selkie lore can also be found in Ireland as well as along the western and northern coasts of Scotland though they are often referred to as selchies or silkies. A wonderful movie, *The Secret of Roan Inish (1994)*, based on the book *The Secret of Ron Mor Skerry* by Rosalie K. Fry, explores the legends of the selkie folk based on Irish and Orkney folklores.

The child in me imagines the seal folk have white coral fairy courts far beneath the foaming waves of the sea, the envy of the fairy world. The author in me suspects that fairy courts are as varied and as imaginative as the lore about Fairy, each as enchanting and awe-inspiring as the next.

For me, one of the more interesting as well as well-known fairy courts is the underground court of the **DAOINE SÍDHE** (*theena shee*), the fairies of Irish folklore. The **SIDHE, SÍDHE,** or Aes Sidhe (*ess shee*)—the People of the Mounds or People of the Hill—are the aristocrats of Fairy, the nobles, "The Gentry." They are considered trooping or heroic fairies. They live in groups and travel in long regal processions known as Fairy Rades, mounted on magnificent unearthly steeds of great beauty and grace, with a swiftness that rivals the wind.

Also referred to as the "Good Neighbors," those of the Daoine Sídhe are believed descended from the legendary **TUATHA DE DANANN** (People of the Goddess Dana), one of the earliest conquerors of Ireland.

The Tuatha de Danann or Tuatha de Danaan were purported to possess magical abilities as well as the skill to become invisible at will. Unusually beautiful people of great intelligence, the Tuatha de Danann (*Tootha day danan*) were thought to be immortal gods.

In time, the Tuatha de Danann became the conquered and were driven underground into the earthy, grassy mounds known as sidh. There, it is believed, they as the Sídhe exist still, in an otherworldly place where time and space do not mirror our own, still possessed of great magical powers, beauty, intelligence, and immortality.

In Scotland, you'll find the Seelie (beneficent) and Unseelie (malign) Courts. Like the Daoine Sídhe in Ireland, the Seelie or Blessed Court consists of aristocratic elves and fairies living in underground palaces of both crystal and gold. Their regal processions are often spied at twilight.

Like the Daoine Sídhe Court, those of the Seelie Court are touted in lore as beautiful, noble creatures, enjoying the general merry-making of a gathering to feast and dance, as well as taking great joy in the hunt. Generally, those of the Seelie Court are considered no threat to humans if the proper measures and acts of respect are offered: food and water, milk, tobacco, and even whiskey.

In contrast, the Unseelie Court is comprised of darker creatures of Fairy, described as ugly, hideous beings in looks or nature or both with a passion for harm. They are also referred to as The Sluagh or The Host. Those of the Unseelie Court are thought to be the unblessed dead, malignant spirits who wish to do their greatest harm to humans and are considered to be quite evil. They are usually solitary in nature, living in the wilds or places where there was once great bloodshed. Yet, it is said they flock in groups, flying out of the west to pass in the night sky like a great dark cloud of doom. The night belongs to the Unseelie.

Despite all the warnings that exist, we fall in love with Fairy nobility, even though not all are noble or the love they offer particularly healthy for humans. If one takes a fancy toward a mere mortal, it could mean great harm to that human.

One such being is the Snow Queen—a fairy queen whose mesmerizing beauty causes even the delicate loveliness of the snowflake to pale in her presence. She is the queen of the ice realm, a cold, ancient spirit who travels within the blizzard's frigid breath to entice mortal men to follow her, to love her. Yet to do so, meant one's death.

Like the Snow Queen, there are many fairies with reputations for doing harm from the very dangerous and quite evil female vampire/succubus of the Scottish Highlands known as Baobhan Sìth *(baá-van)* to the fairy mistress Leanan-Sídhe *(lan-awn shee)*/Lhiannan-Shee *(lannan-shee)* of the Isle of Man whose beauty so enchants and drains that her human lover's muse burns bright yet short in her arms. Fairy lore contains many a tale of monstrous creatures and shadowy beings of the night that ride the winds and prey upon the unwary traveler.

It is interesting to note that many village folk tales speak of fairies traveling within the winds. A dust devil or tiny twister seen near dusk is believed to be a group of fairies returning to Fairyland. It was thought that if you saw these wind funnels, you must throw your shoe into the spinning mass and force the fairy or fairies within to release whatever they had "borrowed" from our world. Fairies are great "borrowers." Often "things" they acquired included humans.

In fact, humans have blamed fairies for many of their woes, from crop failure to personal misfortune, streaks of bad luck, and even deaths. People hung charms over cradles to ward against the fairy folk taking their babies and leaving a changeling, offspring of the fairy, in the baby's place. And many a maiden has claimed enchantment by a fairy prince to explain away a night's passion with a local boy.

Yet fairies were also credited with many of the good things in life, granting blessings as easily as curses. They could heal the ill and aid in finding lost objects, bring the rains, or deliver a cooling breeze on a hot day. Fairies could gift one with good luck instead of bad, help bring about a bountiful harvest, find water, or guide a weary traveler safely home. They might find lost animals, locate misplaced items, or even help a shy young man gain the favor of a fair maiden. The lists of blessings as well as curses could be quite lengthy, depending on who you were and where you lived and who was creating the list.

The variety of beings of Fairy seems as vast and rich as the many tales of where the fairy folk dwell: Fairyland, Elfhame, Tir-na-nÓg/Tir nan Og/Tir Na N-og *[(teer na nogue)(Land of the Ever-young or*

Eternal young)] Avalon and other lands of myth. Places such as fairy forts and mounds of earth, lakes, and forests, or certain trees (oak, ash, hawthorn), even the tall and silent standing stones, serve as homes for fairies or provide portals to their mysterious realms.

Many people believe the standing stones are set on or form points over ley lines, and thus the stones are imbued with earth energy. Others believe the stones serve as a conduit for this energy to be passed on as a constant cycle of renewal. Some claim the energy in ley lines is generated from passed souls or from the fairies themselves. As to whether that power comes from remnants of past lives, or the earth, or fairies, I don't know, but it certainly is something to ponder.

There are those who believe these ley lines are actually the old fairy paths (trails that fairies traveled) of folklore only now are less powerful than they were a hundred years ago.

Why is that? Could it be because so few of Fairy now travel these ancient lines or that fairy energy has grown weak? Perhaps. Either could make for an interesting plot or subplot for your story. Once you attempt to answer why fairies would turn away from treasured energy sources or what happened to cause fairy energy to wane, the ideas begin to take shape and the story builds.

Some theorize that the fairies protective powers are decreasing, that as the world's wild places shrink and Man's belief in the good folk fades, so, too, will the fairies. In time, fairies will diminish to a point they will disappear from our world forever.

There are still pockets of nature, places where the ancient magic is strong and the essence of the Elementals fills the place. Here fairy rings, and Fairy Forts or Ráths, and the ancient paths or ley lines, still carry the ability to attract fairies or point the way to their world.

HOW TO FIND THEM, WHERE DOES ONE LOOK?

As noted earlier, untouched pockets of nature still attract fairies, as do ancient sites such as ringforts and stone circles. Ringforts, also called Fairy Forts or Ráths, are the remains of early medieval circular structures/

settlements with earthen (ráths) or stone (caiseal—northwestern Ireland/cathair—southwestern Ireland) banks or mounds. A ringfort called a dún was thought to be the site of a ruler. In some of the more ancient sites, a circular impression in the ground is all that remains to mark that a ringfort once stood there.

Ringforts are considered to be magical places for the fairies, places where the old energy still lingers and remains strong. Fairy Forts are also considered portals to the realm of Fairy. True believers will not touch or alter these mounds and steer clear whenever possible.

The mounds are not the only way to enter Fairyland. The Fair Folk themselves may lead you in, or "borrow" you and take you to their realm. In Ireland, Scotland, Wales, and England, many believed that the fairies were the souls of the dead or even the guardians of the dead keeping them safe underground in the Fairy realm. In some more whimsical tales from the region, it was thought the dead were taken to Fairyland through these mounds or other portals so they could laugh and sing for a year and a day.

Stepping into a Fairy Ring is another way to enter the Realm of Fairy. It is a common belief that Fairy Rings are created when fairies dance in circles starting on Midsummer Eve. Toadstools or mushrooms usually appear to outline the rings in autumn, providing much needed seating for the tired fairies dancing since midsummer.

It is important to remember the grass within the Fairy Rings should be avoided. As noted earlier, one does not want to anger the fairies, or risk being magicked. An old wife's tale speaks of using the dew from the grass just outside of a ring as a cream for a girl's complexion, or even for a love potion. But warns that one should never touch the grass within the ring, as it might make your complexion worse!

Another theory for the appearance of Fairy Rings was the belief that the circular patterns were formed in the grass by sleeping dragons. The newly formed rings were said to mark the spot where the dragon hid his treasure before he flew away. Note here, you can't find the dragon's treasure without the aid of fairies.

It is important to remember that one should never enter a Fairy Ring, for if you do, you are a captive of Fairy, doomed to live the rest of your days as either a slave or servant to fairies. Of course, there is always a clause, a sort of safety net that can save you if you were unfortunate enough to step within a ring or find yourself compelled to dance with the Fair Folk. If another human, or a chain of humans can pull you free, then you will be rescued from your fate.

In one of my stories, *Thief of Dreams*, I played upon the lore of a Fairy Ring to both send someone to Fairy and to rescue them. The ring served as a portal to the realm of Fairy and only true love could see him free. By merging the old with new, you can weave imaginative, compelling tales of your own.

Other portals include the wild, untouched pockets of nature, places where the energy of the ley lines is strong such as woods, forests, lakes and other bodies of water, and the many standing stones throughout the world. Even ancient caves long forgotten by Man still harbor the possibility of providing passage to Fairyland.

Of course, one might try to remember that should they find themselves in Fairyland, whether by enchantment or love, never eat or drink anything there. It is also wise to recall that time moves differently in Fairy. What may appear as merely a moment can be a lifetime in the real world. Since fairies hold a natural aversion to iron, charms and wards made from the cold metal might ensure that the fairy folk pass you by.

Christianity and the Victorian era of cute and small winged creatures that flitted from flower to flower, and more recently books and movies depicting fairies as helpful little sprites, have played havoc with our perceptions of fairies. I credit authors such as J.R.R. Tolkien *(The Hobbit,* and his trilogy *The Lord of the Rings)* and Marion Cockrell *(Shadow Castle)* for introducing me to fairy creatures, mainly elves, that were tall and elegant and a far cry from the tiny pixie Tinkerbell of Disney's animated version of *Peter Pan* of my youth.

As stated earlier, fairies weren't always so sweet or so small. They were once thought of as tall, elegant beings, taller than man, painfully beautiful, extremely mysterious, and often dangerous. Fairies were steeped in myth and ancient lore, idolized even as they were feared. A far cry from the cute little winged beings of the Victorian era.

If one wishes to write of fairies that are more than the small sweet variety, one must set aside these modern day notions, seek the mysteries beyond the great veil of mists, step back to an era where the belief in magic was an everyday occurrence and omens were given great respect and heed. Back to a time when fairies were powerful, and at times, evil beings. Beautiful, alluring, and dangerous creatures, able to appear and disappear at will with the power to change their shapes, wield magic, and create illusions to lead an unwary human astray.

There's a wealth of fairy lore out there for the taking, enough to allow anyone to create believable, enchanting stories. While readers expect certain elements of the known traditional fairy lore in your creations, you don't have to simply rehash the old. Be inventive, add a dash of this lore, a sprinkle of legend, a healthy dose of imagination, and before you know it, you've created your own fairy lore.

That's what I like to do. I enjoy coming across some scrap of lore, and reworking it, making it my own. I try to retain the essence of that lore, yet I want it to be more than just the same old story retold to fit my story idea.

While this chapter barely touches the surface of fairies and their lore, I've tried to give you an overview of some of the areas that I find fascinating. For further research, there is a reading list in the resource section at the end of this book.

A Map to the Charted "Unknown"

An Author's Look at ESP

By Danielle Ackley-McPhail

Let's face it; everyone wants to be special. Everyone wants to be able to do something no one else can. To know what no one else can know. In theory, anyway… At the same time, no one wants to be singled out as "different". Kind of screwed up, isn't it? What can I say? It's human nature.

One of the ways mankind has always grasped at to aspire to this dichotomous existence is ESP, or extrasensory perception; whatever the skills or the theories behind their origins. Throughout known history there have been those who claimed special abilities beyond the five traditional senses, because of this, it is not surprising ESP would become a staple of the paranormal author's tools of the trade.

Why? Well because in more ways than one, characters need something to set them apart, to give them an edge, and authors need characters who are cursed…blessed…something more. Sometimes it is events, destiny, station, or physical nature that marks a character or (God of your choice help them) all of these above. In paranormal writing, however, it is often,

ESP that is the distinguishing factor. Is this a good thing, or a bad thing? Depends on the skill of the author. Often it is both, simply because it is difficult to find an approach to ESP that hasn't been done before, making the characteristic itself cliché, or a crutch. Some might even say: the easy-out. This doesn't have to be the case if you are willing to put some effort into it. Yes, there are plenty of bad examples. I am sure you can call a few to mind yourself without even thinking about it, so instead I will attempt to direct you toward examples of how it has been done well. First, let's take a look at what ESP is.

According to The Merriam-Webster Dictionary:

> extrasensory perception (noun, circa. 1934): perception (as in telepathy, clairvoyance, and precognition) that involves awareness of information about events external to the self not gained through the senses and not deducible from previous experience —called also ESP

Yeah…kind of dry, but it gives us a basis to work from. Now… where does it come from?

TOUCHED BY GOD... OR SOMETHING

Gods. Demons. Evolution. Science. ESP is attributed to many different sources. Each lends a unique spin on a character and can have an influence on their development and the advancement of the plot. This is because it is not their own perception alone which must be addressed, but that of any character they encounter, making it an excellent source of tension, plot complication, and character motivation on many levels.

THE GOD INFLUENCE

One of the most common sources to receive the credit (or blame) for otherworldly powers is divine bestowment. Whether this is a good thing or a bad thing depends on the universe it's happening in. When seen in a good light such skills have generally been referred to as The

Gift, The Touch of God, The Sight, The Holy Flame or other such glorified names. When in bad, it is The Curse or the Devil's Work. Such gifts may or may not be attributed to an organized-religion-based deity. In the *Valdemar* series by Mercedes Lackey there are many different cultures touched upon; all of them possessing paranormal mental abilities of one sort or another. The Heralds have a natural skill affiliated with magic and the elements. They are recruited by a force for good in the form of the Companions, but it is never clearly defined in relation to a belief system, just a Greater Good. Their Karsite counterparts have the same skills and similar, if in lesser quantity, corollaries to the Companions in their Suncats, and the source they attribute the gifts to is firmly religious. Other examples of this can be found in *God Stalk* by PC Hodgell, where ironically the skills of the gods are attributed to those that believe in them even as the extra skills of those people are linked to a relationship with certain gods.

EVIL'S INFLUENCE

Whether by magic or possession, evil forces are known likewise to bestow such powers on an individual, either willingly or unwillingly. There is more torment in this approach if not for the character in question, then for those the character interacts with. It's up to you to decide how to take this. Is your character a good guy trapped by an evil spell, or is he a villain calling up things better left alone? While the source of the power might be evil, that doesn't automatically dictate that the character is. This could be the crucible in which his nature is tested, or tempted. In my *Eternal Cycle* series I have a character, Tony, who had dormant mental/magical abilities. In *Yesterday's Dreams* he is snared by the evil force and enlisted as a minion. He isn't completely comfortable with the situation, but goes along with things because he doesn't know how to extract himself. By the end of the book it is too late and he has been possessed by an evil god who triggers his latent skills. In book two, *Tomorrow's Memories*, that god, Olcas, commits all manner of heinous acts through the use of Tony as a vessel and his inherent ability of mindreading and magic as the means. Tony is trapped but for brief moments when the god's hold loosens. Is the evil

Tony's, or Olcas's? We won't know until book three if Tony can manage to both free and redeem himself.

BIOLOGICAL ADAPTATION

Some theorize ESP is just another stage in our evolution as a species. That we all, in effect, have the latent potential somewhere in our make-up, and at some point those extra senses are temporarily or permanently unlocked. Whether the skill is a natural outcome of genetics, or a biological response to severe trauma, it can lead to interesting developments in a story.

Take my mother for example (okay, odd example and not literary at all, but it works). She was in a car accident a few years back. The car was struck by another car on the side where she was sitting. By her account she found herself standing outside the car trying to see if the kids in the other car were okay, but when she looked at her own car, there was no way she'd opened her door to get out. To my knowledge she had never before and has not since shown evidence of this ability. Creepy, huh? I can't tell you if this is or isn't true, but is an excellent example of trauma-induced teleportation.

From fiction you can look at the novel *Tigra* by R.H. Leahy. In it there is a race of tiger-like creatures. At one point they were a highly developed civilization even more advanced than mankind in terms of scientific development and culture. Until five thousand years in their past a planet-wide catastrophe gave them the gift of a racial mind link… of course, it destroyed their sense of self-awareness and eventually reduced them back to animal instinct, but it shows how paranormal skills can take away as much or more than they give and presents quite the conflict to be resolved in story-time.

ARTIFICIALLY INDUCED

The lines between fantasy and science fiction have blurred when it comes to the paranormal, particularly ESP. If you believe we all have the potential for ESP (or are just using it as a plot point), then it stands to reason that such potential can be triggered or unlocked. Whether induced chemically, through hypnosis, surgically, or by subjecting a character to extreme trauma: the means don't matter, only the end result.

An excellent example of this is the work of Anne McCaffrey. Predominantly it is seen in her *Pern* series, but also in her Talents series, starting with *To Ride Pegasus*. In this series, "Talents", or those with ESP, are unifying to gain protected status and to learn, measure, and refine their skills. Some are born with the special abilities; others are not. Like Peter, a young boy completely paralyzed when a wall falls on top of him. He discovers he can initiate an electrical gestalt that powers great feats of telekinesis, allowing him restored mobility and much more. This series and those spawned by it, go into the science of expanded senses.

In the *Alliance Archives* series by Mike McPhail, scheduled for release in 2010, telepathic skills have been developed in select military subjects by means of a protein-coated, self-assembling nano-antenna, basically a synaptic interface overlaid on the brain. This becomes an inherited trait when the protein enzymes pass from mother to child and continue through the genetic line through children of both sexes. Finally, though it is a media reference, in the movie *Serenity*/series *Firefly* the character River Tam has been manipulated and engineered into a super-soldier, complete with clairvoyance/precognition. How much of her ability is from natural skill and how much from alterations made by the scientists working on her we are not privy to, but without doubt she has been altered. This is both a source of internal conflict and plot advantage for the character as often only her preternatural knowledge has allowed her and her fellow characters to survive a variety of encounters.

As you can see, there are plenty of theories as to how and why super-senses may be possible. How then do you figure out which one to use? All, or none; world-shaking or subtle? There are so many aspects to consider. It all depends on the character and the story you want to tell.

THE ESP UMBRELLA

Now that we have touched on where ESP comes from, let's look at what "skills" fall under the scope of ESP. There are a few basic ones that just about everyone can name, and then there are adaptations found throughout fiction that refine those basics. As the author, you can do whatever you want, as long as you can explain—or justify it—enough for it to make sense to the reader. (For simplicity's sake, all the following definitions are from *The Merriam-Webster Dictionary* and include pronunciation, part of speech, and the year it first appeared, where known). The possible handicaps listed are qualities that can prevent your characters from becoming "too" powerful.

CLAIR·VOY·ANCE (\kler-vòi-ən(t)s\, noun, 1838): the power or faculty of discerning objects not present to the senses 2 : ability to perceive matters beyond the range of ordinary perception.

VARIANTS: Clairsentience, Clairaudience, The Sight, Precognition

POSSIBLE HANDICAPS: "blind" to events pertaining to self or those close to them; only receives visions of "x" type of event, such as murders; only receive partial visions where key details are not known

LITERARY EXAMPLES: Richard Peck's Ghosts I Have Been and The Ghost Belonged to Me; Anne McCaffrey's To Ride Pegasus

EM·PA·THY (\'em-pə-thē\, noun, 1850): the action of understanding, being aware of, being sensitive to, and vicariously experiencing the feelings, thoughts, and experience of another of either the past or present without having the feelings, thoughts, and experience fully communicated in an objectively explicit manner.

VARIANTS: Telempathy

POSSIBLE HANDICAPS: adversely affected by high emotion; only sense a particular type of emotion; can be blocked by falsely projected emotions; can be attacked by an overload of generated emotion; traumatized by sensing negative emotion; absorbs or reflects outside emotion

LITERARY EXAMPLES: Alan Dean Foster's Flinx and Pip series, Mercedes Lackey's Heralds of Valdemar series

PSY·CHO·KI·NE·SIS (\ˌsī-kō-kə-'nē-səs,—kī-\, noun, 1914): movement of physical objects by the mind without use of physical means (teleportation, 1931).

VARIANTS: telekinesis, levitation, pyrokinesis

POSSIBLE HANDICAPS: limited in weight that can be lifted; physical stress caused in proportion to paranormal activity; exponentially increased use of energy out of proportion to same action performed physically; line-of-sight required

LITERARY EXAMPLES: Stephen King's Carrie

PSY·CHOM·E·TRY (\sī-ˈkä-mə-trē\, noun, circa 1842): divination of facts concerning an object or its owner through contact with or proximity to the object.

VARIANTS: dowsing

POSSIBLE HANDICAPS: false impressions left on items by another; adverse emotional responses to visions experienced; confused images caused by various subjects handling the item; lack of control over visions triggered by handling everyday objects or chance touches by others

LITERARY EXAMPLES: Laurie Faria Stolarz's Deadly Little Secrets, James Patterson's Maximum Ride series, L. J. Smith's Dark Visions Trilogy, Susan Cooper's The Dark Is Rising series

TE·LEP·A·THY (\tə-ˈle-pə-thē\, noun, 1882): communication from one mind to another by extrasensory means.

VARIANTS: mind-speaking, mind-hearing, mind-reading, animal mind-speaking

POSSIBLE HANDICAPS: inability to use by conscious effort; inability to block the thoughts of others; inability to connect with a particular person; unaware of the ability and thought mad; only able to hear a particular kind of thought (ie; thoughts of violence; erotic thoughts, etc.)

LITERARY EXAMPLES: Robert A. Heinlein's, Time for the Stars, Tony Vigorito's Just a Couple of Days, Joan D. Vinge's Psion, Brenda W. Clough's How Like a God

This is just a basic list; the stuff most of us know anyway just because our society has always had a fascination with this discipline. This list is by no means complete, but I have listed some resources at the end of this chapter where you can learn more about what is and isn't considered a psychic ability, at least according to various Psychical Research Associations.

SOCIAL RAMIFICATIONS

The bearer of such unusual abilities is revered or feared, depending upon the claimed source of those abilities, the level of faith and piety of the characters encountered, and how much those characters have to hide. The treatment received also depends on the benevolence, or lack thereof, seen in the character possessing the skill. Once their talents are known, the gifted character rarely seems to be treated as the person they are; the gift seems to overshadow their humanity in the view of support characters. How will your character deal with this? In what ways will it complicate their lives? Is there danger inherent in the situation from those that are afraid or misunderstand? All aspects you must determine as the author. Whatever you choose, always represent a variety of social responses to round things out for your characters. You will never have one pure response throughout a community. Fear, awe, envy, hatred… there are so many possible responses. Fascination, even… Consider what will be most beneficial to the plotline and expand from there. Here is a checklist of questions you can ask yourself when developing a storyline involving paranormal abilities:

- How does the character with the ability feel about it?
- Is it something the character has always been aware of, or something that developed with age/by accident/ or intent?
- How would this skill advance the plot?
- What drawbacks are there to this ability?
- Is the skill general knowledge or secret?
- Does the character have a handicap (social, physical, mental) from which this added skill stems from, or that is a counterbalance to the skill?
- Is there a way to short-circuit or cancel out the ability, either permanently or temporarily?
- Is the special ability key to the plot or just a secondary point used to distinguish the character and feed them information they would not otherwise know?
- What danger is inherent in the use of this skill (internal or external)?
- How do those close to the character (friends and family) respond to the ability?
- How does the general populous respond?

- How will any religious groups view this ability?
- Who would be the most adversely affected by your character's abilities?
- Who is most likely to want to exploit your character?
- Who in the story is there to defend/help your character?

You are not limited to these questions, but answering them or coming up with similar questions of your own will help to clarify the structure of your society, who your character is and how they would act, and what challenges the character faces independent of the major plot line of the story. Even if you do not include the specific answers in the text itself, knowing the answers gives you a better understanding of what has gone in to making your characters who they are.

WHAT IS YOUR KRYPTONITE?

Okay, not yours, but your character's. After all, unstoppable powers can be a drag. To the story, I mean. I've touched on this a little bit in the definitions above, but I'll expand here. You need to temper any special abilities your character possesses with a governor. Sometimes it is something as basic as energy out requires energy in (or even twice energy in), only it's not always easy to replenish. It can be something natural such as an allergen, which inhibits the ability to See. Anything, really, as long as it brings the character down a peg, which in the eyes of the reader makes them more human, more "approachable". Of course, in the case of your bad guy, it gives the hero something to discover that can allow good to triumph over evil. Such handicaps can be artificially caused, temporary, or regional. They can even be unpredictable or of unknown causes with known effects; anything to maintain a sense of challenge to balance the extra abilities. After all, haven't you noticed how annoying it is when a character is "all-powerful" removing all sense of urgency, or in the case of the bad guy, hope for your hero? That's just setting you up for having to whip out a dues ex machina or other contrived method of defeat if you haven't built one in already. No one is ever happy with such fixes so best avoid them from the very start.

On writing PSI

Most of what I have touched on here has dealt with the concerns of character development, however, there is one mechanical consideration to be addressed. When you have a character that speaks or hears speech with their mind, reads thoughts, or receives visions, how do you depict it? There are several literary conventions that have been employed in the past to visually distinguish telepathic communication or visions from dialogue or narrative. The most common is to have the psi episode in italics. Personally, in regards to telepathy, I have employed bracketing asterisks in place of quotation marks. For visions or flashbacks I use italics. As an author, one thing you can do to determine how to write psi events is to check out other books that employ them, particularly any produced by publishing houses you are considering submitting too. If they have a style for such things then use that formatting. If not, as long as you are consistent and clear in how you distinguish psi from normal occurrences, it doesn't really matter how you do it.

Summing up

The theories on ESP and other paranormal skills are diverse and in many cases speculative. When using this in your writing the primary thing to keep in mind is that you must think things through and understand the how's and why's and what-for's in relation to your plot and your characters (those with the skills and those who interact with them). Where there is research and "common" knowledge, utilize it; where there isn't, be sure to take a logical approach so your reader isn't left confused or frustrated by unclear concepts. Have fun with, but don't forget to follow your own rules once you establish those how's and why's and what-for's. There is nothing worse in fiction than a story that violates its own continuity. Decide how things work and stick with it and you will have the reader in your grips until the end!

LOVE, ROMANCE, SEX AND...

Writing the Naughty Bits

By Rosemary Laurey

(also writing as Georgia Evans and Madeleine Oh)

Looking for a way to ratchet up the tension and conflict between your characters? Need to give your story a boost when it slows down or drags? Why not let sex rear its throughly fascinating head.

Any time you have two adults thrown together, sexual interest flutters—even if the response is "Oh, my god, no! I'd rather join a nunnery/monastery or travel steerage on the Titanic." And if the response is, "Wow!" or "Yes, please!" The connection has been made, the tension set up, you have another layer to your story and a wonderful opportunity to torture your characters as they save the world, solve the problem or find the murderer.

Sex scenes, love scenes, sensuality, sexual tension, romance— all varying shades of the same human emotion, are an integral part of genre fiction, a marvelous vehicle for raising tension, showing character, moving the action along and creating plot twists. But, it is vitally important to bear in mind that adding sex (in whatever degree) to your story must serve a purpose within the story or character arcs. Sex just dumped into the plot at editorial fiat or in the belief that 'hot' stuff sells better risks ending up superfluous, and quite possibly downright boring or even verging on the ridiculous. Witness some of the quite astounding passages that end up as finalists for the annual Bad Sex Award.

Keep in mind the differences between paranormal, science fiction or futuristic romance, where the relationship between the two protagonists makes up more that fifty percent of the story and science fiction, fantasy or paranormal fiction with a strong romance thread, but where the main plot and action are not the relationship. Your targeted genre affects how you balance the plot and the relationship. Then there is erotica in which the sexual relationship or encounter is the plot and frequently much of the action. So, how best to go about adding sexual heat and/or sensuality etc. to your fiction?

Bear in mind the distinction between sensual and sexual. The latter refers to the evocation of sensual experience, the awakening of the five senses. It can certainly be sexual, in fact a sex scene devoid of sensuality is worse than dull, but by no means does sensuality always imply a sexual theme. Think of walking along the beach barefoot as the tide comes in, holding a tiny baby, eating a ripe, juicy peach right off the tree and warm from the sun, or sitting by a crackling log fire. All are examples of sensual experiences without a sexual theme. Although they could be used (with the exception of the baby!) as sensual elements in a sex scene.

So, on to incorporating sexual elements, love scenes, hot bits (call them what you will) into your fiction. To make them an integral part of the plot there are two good reasons (and only two) for adding explicit sex: to show character or to move the plot along.

If this sounds awfully arbitrary think about it, how a character behaves before, during and after sex says a great deal about them, and adding the element of consummated (or even interrupted) sex into the situation almost invariably ratchets up the tension and adds a nice complication to the plot.

Not that an explicit love scene is the only way to accomplish this, far from it. The love thread is just one tool at the writer's disposal but one that's quite a lot of fun for all concerned.

Would your story benefit from a little light (or heavy) sex? Maybe. Before you start in this direction, look inward, ask yourself if you enjoy reading the sexy parts? Or are you a reader who skips them to get back to the main plot? If you're the latter—then honestly you'll be much happier stopping right now and skipping ahead to the next chapter. Forget adding sexy bits, you won't enjoy the writing thereof, and ten to one your lack of enthusiasm will come through to your readers. As I said earlier no one gets any sort of thrill from boring or dull sex. If writing and reading explicit sex isn't your cup of tea, stay with flirtation, or insinuation. After all, in an earlier time, when most fictional sex scenes featured a couple watching the embers fading, or the sun dipping over the horizon followed by a row of asterisks, everyone knew exactly what was going on. Readers added their own detail as needed. Having said adding sex or love scenes isn't necessary, let's move on to the writing thereof, for those who do enjoy reading the naughty bits.

Leaving aside erotica, which is a whole different genre, let's focus on popular fiction, and the how, when and where to add some spice to your plot.

How? Like any good writing, it takes practice. The best way to start is by reading some of the spicier fiction, deciding your own comfort level and sticking with it. I can't repeat this often enough, begin were you feel confident, whether it's just s sensual kiss and romantic stroll hand in hand along a beach in the moonlight or a wild, all clothes off, go at it, explicit action, find your comfort zone and settle there. At least for now. You may find after several books that you are ready to go further.

As for when, to my mind it is absolutely vital to know your characters, not just well, but intimately (in every sense). Immerse yourself in their emotions, thoughts, ethics, hopes and fears. The sexual encounters must be in character—or if they're not you'd better let the reader know why the inconsistency. If your characters are vampires, shape shifting dragons, inhabitants of a fantasy universe, or a future world, that adds another important layer to the character and the encounter. Have fun with it.

And now where? By this I mean where in the story. You hear all sorts of nonsensical 'rules' about how often you should add your love scenes, that publisher A expects one thing, publisher B another and editor C at publisher D doesn't want sex in the first chapter. My advice to flow with your story and write in the spicy scenes as the plot and the characters indicate. Of course this works nicely for me since I'm not a 'plotting in advance' writer. My characters drive my books and I've learned to listen to them. If you are a writer who prefers to plot closely and stick to your outline, I'd suggest finding the peaks of emotional connection between your characters: the points when a few pages or paragraphs of intimacy fit in naturally and tucking the love scenes there. Another good spot is a moment of peace and connection when lurking disaster is about to shatter that period of calm. Interrupting the tender interlude and leaving the characters stressed and frustrated is a good way to up the tension—but beware over doing this. You can definitely have too much of a bad thing here.

Having slipped inside your characters' skins, felt their attraction and desire, and chosen the perfect spot in the narrative for them to get intimate, let me drop in a word or two about vocabulary. Please, please, unless you are writing a spoof, eschew all and every trace of purple prose. We've all encountered it—particularly in some of the older books from the 60s and early 70s. Ban it from your book. Phrases and descriptions such as 'dew laden petals of love' or 'throbbing monolith' (I swear I did not make those up! I have seen them in print) not only yank the reader out of the story while they struggle to regain their composure. They also reduce your carefully developed characters into strange creatures. Even if they are strange or alien creatures, they don't deserve to be made ridiculous.

When I encountered the throbbing monolith, I had this image of a granite jackhammer and frankly I can think of few things more likely to jolt your average reader out of the mood. Same thing for those darn petals of love, dew laden or otherwise, makes me wonder if there are thorns lurking.

Forgive that little aside, but I really, really want to reinforce avoiding ludicrous euphemisms and stick to everyday vocabulary your reader will not only understand but glide over as they read. Choice of vocabulary may be dictated to some degree by your editor and the house style, but most of all it needs to be in character with your protagonists and their world. Earthy, blunt sorts might be comfortable with four letter Anglo-Saxon terms. Not everyone is, pick your words to suit your characters. In an alternative or future world story, it's possible to invent your own vocabulary, but be darn certain it is one hundred percent comprehendible to your readers. You don't want them lurching out of the story to ask. He did what? Where did she touch him? And, this is one of my cardinal rules, for each body part, action, etc, choose one word (in each viewpoint if necessary) and use it consistently. Makes for a much smoother read. Avoid having a cock in one paragraph, a dick in the next, and a penis in the next sentence (unless you're character is a multi-endowed alien and it's necessary for the scene to distinguish between his many parts) and please forget the turgid manhoods. (Honest, didn't make that one up either.) So pick your words, be sure they fit your characters, and stay with them, this is one place where repetition works best. You want your readers focused on the interaction between your characters, not wondering what body part you're going to spring on them next.

A WORD ABOUT POINT OF VIEW AND PRONOUNS

The most practical approach is to stay in the pov you're using for the rest of your story. However I really feel that omniscient pov doesn't work for love scenes (and judging by most published work, seems editors agree here). Omniscient pov pretty turns your reader into a voyeur. Fair enough if that's your aim, but keeping your reader involved works best. Since most popular fiction is written in first or third person the odds are you'll be using one or the other. If it's first person, the pronouns are easy enough: you have your viewpoint character and the other one.

In third person, and assuming you have a heterosexual couple, keep close in the viewpoint character's head,(now is not a time to head hop, trust me) focus on emotions, feelings and reactions, and all should go smoothly. You know who's she and who's he and you can take everything along to finish the scene. Things get trickier in third person pov if you have a gay male or lesbian couple. Writing 'He stroked his cock' could leave the reader wondering who's doing what to whom or if it was self-service. Same for 'She kissed her breast'. See my point? Here you have to write skillfully and go over it a gazzillion times to make sure everything is clear to the reader. Use names by all means, but that can get wordy after a while. Other tricks to use are focusing on physical characteristics, hair or eye color, skin tone, a tanned hand stroking fair hair is distinctive enough—a certain tone of voice or accent identifies a speaker, as do individual physical characteristics: a beard rubbed against skin, a scar or tattoo. If one character is a vampire, werewolf, alien or what have you, focus on the white skin, cool to the touch, strength, hairiness, a voice like a growl, pointed ears, unusual skin tone or height etc. All help ease the pronoun confusion, of course if one character is an alien hermaphrodite; you need to get really creative over the pronouns.

Don't forget the pre and post coital scenes. The seduction or invitation can be as much fun as the lovemaking itself and the aftermath is a fantastic chance to open up your characters. Within the framework of your story, something has to change after the love scene: how your characters feel about each other and themselves, where they go on from here, either together or apart, and how this changes their relationship and the dynamics of the story.

Don't skip on rewriting. Go over your love scenes time and time again. Refining and polishing until they are as perfect as you can make them. Ask yourself do you find them interesting? Intriguing? Arousing? Yes, arousing. If you don't feel at least a flutter of sexual interest, you can be pretty certain neither will your reader. A well written love scene should stir a reaction in both author and reader. Work at your writing until that happens.

So, enjoy taking your character's clothes off, it makes a fun diversion from the tension and action, gets your reader close to your protagonists, helps move on the story, and above all, it's fun!

'TIS A MYSTERY

By Lee Killough

Paranormal mysteries. Great fun to write. A challenge to write well.

If you are not already a mystery reader, it is a good idea to familiarize yourself with the conventions of ordinary mysteries by sampling those on the shelves at the library or local bookstore.

Putting together a mystery itself is challenge enough, though it seems simple. Stripped to its essence, to bare bones if you will, a mystery is a puzzle story. A crime is committed—most often a murder but not necessarily so—and a sleuth must find who dunnit, why dunnit, and in some cases, how dunnit. A crime and a sleuth seeking answers. But oh, how many ways to flesh out the skeleton.

Start with the format. My personal favorite gives the reader a chance to solve the crime along with the sleuth, and maybe beat him to the answer, by showing all the clues. Whatever the sleuth sees and hears, so does the reader. The trick there is making it a worthy contest ... hitting neither sleuth nor reader over the head with the clues. Obfuscation is the name of the game. Burying relevant facts among red herrings. Place a crucial item in the middle of a long list or description of a room, where it may be glimpsed in passing so as to seem unimportant. A critical name is tossed in off-hand. The author plays against expectations, perhaps making the bad guy *so* obvious he is dismissed, or hiding a steel trap mind or vicious streak behind a woman's ditzy facade. I heard a mystery author, whose name I wish I remembered, say he wants twenty per cent of his readers to beat the sleuth...and the rest giving themselves a head slap at the end: "Of course! Why didn't I see that!"

Other mysteries try to keep the reader in suspense until the Big Reveal at the end. They show what the sleuth does, but not all the sleuth sees or hears. *She leaned close and whispered a name in my ear.* What that name is, isn't disclosed. Alternatively, this kind of mystery can hold back information by having a naive narrator who misinterprets what he sees, misleading himself and the reader...or an *unreliable* narrator who deliberately lies to the reader. Agatha Christie used the unreliable narrator several times, mostly famously in *The Murder of Roger Ackroyd*, where the end twist revealed the killer as the narrator himself. This is frustrating if the reader wants to play detective, but with engaging characters or a unique situation, readers may just go along and enjoy the ride.

A third approach shows the reader who, why, and how from the beginning. Then while the reader wonders if/how the sleuth will win out, the story follows the hunt from both sides as the sleuth tracks the villain and the villain tries to evade detection and capture. Frederick Forsyth's *Day of the Jackal* being an outstanding example. The book's plot involves a plan to assassination France's then President Charles de Gaulle and though we know from history that de Gaulle was not assassinated, it still holds the reader to the end. And as a mark of the Forsyth's writing skill, the reader wavers between rooting for the Jackal and Inspector Claude Lebel.

The sleuth is not always the hero in these novels. They are often caper stories, with personable criminals and clever crimes leading the reader to cheer for them instead of the police.

What about sleuths? They cover the spectrum...pros, semi-pros, and amateurs. Pros include all branches of law enforcement: local and state police, sheriffs, marshals, district attorneys, and investigators for all branches of government and private organizations such as insurance companies and the Jockey Club in England. There are private Investigators of all types, including Thomas Sniegoski's fallen angel Remy Chandler. These sleuths require research to make sure the characters ring true and the department structural and procedural aspects are correct.

Semi-pros are not trained for police work but work in professions that may bring them in contact with some crime they feel compelled to investigate: ex-cops (included here because being "ex" cuts them off from authorized use of crime labs and the official authority to question witnesses and suspects), bounty hunters, anthropologists, lawyers, psychiatrists, reporters, crime scene cleaners—to name just a few. Of course the author should be sure to research these professions, too.

The largest sleuth group, though, are amateurs. Of every shape, size, age, and sex, involved in every possible hobby and non-law enforcement profession, from Academics and artists through athletes, white and blue collar workers, hobbyists, and shop owners to zoo keepers.

Whatever the format, whoever the sleuth, the mystery should be engrossing, and maybe teach readers something new and interesting. What I love about writing paranormal mysteries is exploring the nuts and bolts of what it is to be a vampire, werewolf, or ghost. Don't we all enjoy hearing inside info? Paranormal mysteries let you take readers inside the world of paranormal beings and psychic talents.

Don't forget that just as the protagonist is the character most affected by the outcome in any other novel, the sleuth in a mystery should have a personal stake in solving the crime. Amateurs become involved to protect a family or friend who is suspected of the crime, or clear his own name or protect his business. Above doing his job, the professional may be driven by a personal reaction to the crime: outrage at the crime itself, memories of a similar case he could not solve, a personal connection to the victim and/or victim's family. A new kid on the block, maybe a woman in a formerly all-male unit, may want to prove herself. Or a sleuth in professional trouble needs to repair his reputation.

Because a mystery is a puzzle, your pieces must fit together: the clever or compelling crime, characters the reader can care about, a number of suspects, plenty of clues that include red herrings along with the ones pointing to the perpetrator. Everything leads to a resolution that serves justice and leaves the reader satisfied.

Every author has his own way to write, from outlining extensively to plunging in without knowing there the story will end. All correct methods if they work ... though mysteries need at least *some* planning. In the paranormal you might start with a cool sleuth, or an interesting paranormal way to do someone in. In the former case you need to come up with a crime for him to investigate and in the latter, find a sleuth. Then decide what evidence will lead to the uncovering the perpetrator, and work out how to plant that evidence so your sleuth can find it. Make it difficult for him and lead him into some blind alleys along the way. Sometimes it helps to write mysteries backward, from solution to investigation. Don't be afraid to over-write. The excess can always be edited out later. Cutting is much easier than adding. When I sold my first mystery, the editor asked me to add two chapters of red herrings. *Two chapters!* Talk about writing agony.

I like laying out a time line on a calendar page or note cards— story-boarding the plot—and using that to decide where the various events will happen and what will be learned with each. It gives me an overview I can't have on my computer screen and see where I may need to reshuffle events.

While constructing a mystery is a challenge, the beauty of mystery is that, being a plot form, it plays well with other genres. Almost any of the above formats and sleuths can be combined with science fiction, fantasy, young adult, westerns, historical and military fiction, and certainly with the paranormal.

That's where the fun comes in. Mixing genres gives the writer wonderful freedom to broaden the possibilities of who, why, and how. Even as it creates challenges beyond just those of constructing a good mystery.

One of the biggest challenges is making the paranormal elements essential to the mystery. That is critical. The mere presence of the paranormal is not enough.

For example, in Denise Dietz's *Eye of Newt* the protagonist Sydney Saint Charles is descended from a line of reputed witches and runs an apothecary shop selling potions and charms. While charms are described in the book, and the possibility that Sydney is a witch makes her an interesting character, magic has nothing to do with the mystery. Not even when Sydney fears a charm she sold is responsible for the death of a rock star. It turns out not to be so and her actual investigation of the death—interviewing, finding clues, being led astray, and putting herself in danger—involves nothing paranormal. So entertaining as the book is, I don't consider it a paranormal mystery.

Nor are Dean James's humorous Simon Kirby-Jones mysteries. Yes, Simon is a vampire, but special pharmaceuticals let him go out in daylight and indulge in regular food and drink. Being a vampire does not affect the plot except for making it easier to move around at night and enter places for snooping—activities that could both be handled without vampiric abilities.

There is nothing wrong with adding color to a mystery via paranormal trappings as in the books above. If your intent is a true paranormal mystery, you need the paranormal shaping and driving it.

Consider Shirley Damsgaard's Ophelia and Abby series. In *Charmed To Death*, the plot could not work the way it does without magic. It both helps witch protagonist, Ophelia Jensen and makes her a target. At one point, the killer uses witchcraft to try to kill her.

The paranormal is even more critical to Charlaine Harris's Grave series. Harper Connelly has the psychic ability to sense dead bodies. Take that away and the story completely disappears. In Kat Richardson's Greywalker series, vampires and a necromantic object are central to the plot of *Greywalker*, a vicious laboratory-created spirit to that of *Poltergeist*, and a monster from local Indian legend to *Underground*.

Equally challenging is playing fair with the reader, when you have paranormal characters or possibilities beyond our familiar reality for who, why, and especially *how* dunnit. Because to give readers a chance at out-guessing the sleuth, you have to let them know what those new possibilities are. You want them to finish the last page triumphant, or thinking: "Oh, *right!*" not "Huh?"

The mystery, the paranormal elements, and characters are always most important, but every story happens somewhere and that somewhere— big city, small town, resort town, agricultural community—is going to help shape the activities and personalities of story characters, and maybe add interesting atmosphere. You need to know your setting and keep it in mind as you write.

The story settings of paranormal mystery vary. Many use our here and now real world, or a period setting like the early 1900's in Barbara Hambly's vampire mystery *Those Who Hunt the Night*. Others sidle away from the real world until they become alternative or fantasy worlds.

Real world settings are good for single or limited paranormal elements. Apart from giving you less to explain to readers, a real world background provides contrast to the story events. A murder disrupts normal life anyway but that disruption becomes all the more dramatic when the paranormal also shakes up characters' worldview.

If your sleuth is has a paranormal talent, using it openly make life difficult. Despite years of success psychically finding bodies, Harper Connolly is always regarded with suspicion by police agencies who hire her. They have trouble believing she isn't a charlatan, or at best, an opportunist preying on victims' families.

Victoria Laurie's Psychic Eye, Abbie Cooper, also advertises her clairvoyance to make a living, but doesn't go to the police with details she senses about a crime, for fear they will think she is involved. Other characters with paranormal gifts such as witch Ophelia Jensen also hide their ability in order to keep below law enforcement radar. Paranormal cops such as my vampire, Garreth Mikaelian, and werewolf, Allison Goodnight, hide what they are. If your character doesn't try to hide his talent, perhaps it is because he doesn't believe in it himself. Warren Ritter of David Skibbins' *Eight of Swords* give his Tarot readings on a street corner and shrugs off his ability, considering himself a con man.

In a real world setting, *crime* of paranormal origin becomes not just dramatic but a challenge for the sleuth—because real world detectives don't believe in vampires, werewolves, demons, and ghosts. They have to be convinced of paranormals' existence. In my book *Blood Hunt*, Inspector Garreth Mikaelian was a workaday detective investigating a murder that turned out to be committed by a vampire. A possibility that unfortunately never occurred to him until the vampire turned him into one, too.

When you use the real world, you need to let the reader know early that this mystery involves the paranormal.

Charlaine Harris, following science fiction author Ted Sturgeon's advice to writers to "Shoot the sheriff in the first paragraph" shows what is coming in the first line of *Dead Until Dark:*

> I'd been waiting for the vampire for years when he walked into the bar.

Casey Daniels also goes for immediate notification in *Don of the Dead*, and sets the light-hearted tone of the book:

> I have to admit, the first time Gus Scarpetti spoke to me, I didn't pay a whole lot of attention. After all the guy had been dead for thirty years. How much could he possibly have to say?

Shirley Damsgaard starts *Charmed to Death* with a magic ceremony in the woods.

The opening line of my book *Killer Karma* is:

> He found himself standing in a parking garage with no memory except of his murder.

Not all stories introduce the paranormal that fast. Kat Richardson's *Greywalker* needs several chapters before protagonist Harper Blaine discovers she is dealing with the supernatural. Which is fine as long as the opening has a hook that will keep the reader turning pages. Shoot the sheriff in the first paragraph, remember? *Greywalker* has Harper savagely attacked—an attack which Harper and readers discover has turned her into a Greywalker.

In a mystery, discovery of the story's crime is another good hook. L. L. Thrasher starts *Charlie's Bones* with a skeleton unearthed in the course of putting in a swimming pool. Tanya Huff's *Blood Price* immediately snags the attention with a bloody murder, and while protagonist Vicki Nelson, who almost witnesses it, is unaware of paranormals at this point, she feels the presence of something dangerous and evil. That keeps readers hanging on until, along with Vicki, they are introduced to vampires and demons.

Some series with a real world setting involve a number of paranormal beings: Vicki's world, Charlaine Harris's Sookie Stackhouse, and Kat Richardson's Harper Blaine. In each case the real world can become overshadowed and pushed into the background. If this is true of your stories, you need to remember the world is still there and will affect the interactions and reactions of your characters. Keep in mind the average Joe reacts differently depending on whether he is unaware of paranormals, knows they are around and wishes they were not, or accepts their presence.

The approach Carole Nelson Douglas and Kim Harrison use for playing with multiple paranormals is to invent a reality-changing event that brought all paranormals into the open. Carole Nelson Douglas has the Millennium Revelation in her Delilah Street series while the Angel virus is responsible in Kim Harrison's Rachel Morgan series. A new world order naturally requires explaining it to the reader but you want to avoid the deadly info dump.

Carole Nelson Douglas named her event to tell the reader a great deal by itself: Millennium Revelation. Further explanation comes briefly. As a single sentence, for example, in *Brimstone Kiss*, the second book of the series:

> Vegas was wicked, of course, long before the turn of the twenty-first century brought all the bogeymen and women of myth and legends out of the closet and into human lives and society. More details about the world appear gradually as the story progresses and Delilah becomes involved with various supernaturals in their clubs and activities.

Harrison's Angel virus needs more explanation. In the first novel of her series, *Dead Witch Walking*, she gives it in one lump. But not right away. The book starts with no explanations, just action ... as if the reader already understands this world. Only on page 37, with the story well under way, does she explain the virus and then it is as a train of thought Rachel follows while packing up to leave her job. Mixing information with character action helps keep the story moving forward.

While not a mystery series per se, a couple of the Bordertown stories—in short story collections edited by Terri Windling and the novel *Finder* by Emma Bull—*are* mysteries, and the Bordertown setting is another one shaped by a world-changing event. In this case, the reappearance of Faerie. Bordertown, as the name suggests, sits where the World and Elfland meet, a city reshaped by its geographical location and the mixture of machines and magic that both work erratically. The first page and a half of the short story "Danceland" sets the stage. The viewpoint character lolls in the sidecar of a motorcycle powered by a spell box, watching his mechanically-minded elf partner head into a store with machine parts and magical objects in the window, and watching the mixture of elf gangs, halfies, and human kids eyeing each other warily outside a club. After that, the reader clued in, the world can unfold with the story, and only bits of explanations here and there as necessary.

Yet another approach is a paranormal world within but separate from the real world, such as Limbo in Chris Freeburn's *Dying For Redemption*, and Simon R. Green's Nightside stories.

Freeburn's Limbo is just that, the afterlife stop on the way to Heaven or Hell. Her protagonist, Calamar Callous, is a soul who was a private eye in life and has chosen to stay in Limbo, knowing his destination if he moved on, so he continues as a PI, helping the recently murdered learn who did them in so *they* can move on. Her Limbo needs little explanation, other than showing the "rules" of Limbo and those of the ghost Callous becomes when in the real world, because her Limbo is a copy of the real world.

Not so Green's Nightside, which protagonist John Taylor describes as "the wicked heart of London." In the first book, *Something From the Nightside*, Green gives the reader a taste things to come during the Underground ride to Nightside where a fellow passenger is reading a newspaper dated next week and the car has no windows. Because you don't want to see what is out there, particularly whatever is pounding on the top and sides of the car fiercely enough to partially cave in the car. A car that heals itself once the menace has been left behind. By creating a setting apart from the real world, Green was free to pull out all the stops and dazzle the reader with a host of quirky characters, aliens, houses and cars that eat people, time slips, gods, and artifacts from all of time and space.

Using a setting like this offers you the chance to let your imagination loose, too. But you must build from a solid base. Know how the landscape looks, how people in it look and act, and mundane as it sounds, know how the infrastructure works. The Nightside stories, despite the appearance of hurling everything including the kitchen sink into each new book, maintain an underlying consistency. That is always key in building a believable world: laying out the rules—as fantastic as you want them—and sticking to them. *Something From the Nightside* establishes the nature of Nightside and John Taylor's bag of psychic tricks, and no matter the twists in subsequent stories, they grow from the foundation of the first book.

Finally, you can divorce your setting from the real world altogether. True, this requires the most world-building, but lets you play with situations and characters no other setting can. For example, a reality where magic is commonplace, taking the place of our science. Randall Garrett's Lord Darcy stories investigate crime scenes using spells that serve the same function as our CSI techniques, and magic plays a part as well in the commission of some crimes Darcy investigates.

An alternative world can let you explore the paranormal of another culture. Which Liz Williams does with her Inspector Chen novels, using Chinese culture. In her Singapore Three, Heaven and Hell lie close to the "real" world and Chen, whose job in his police department is investigating crimes involving the supernatural—such as, in *Snake Agent*, determining why the soul of a dead girl failed to arrive in Heaven as it should have—visits both Heaven and Hell in the course of his cases, he is partnered with a demon.

An alternative world can also let you go over the top or down and dark. As in John Meaney's duology *Bone Song* and *Black Blood*, where his city Tristopolis has streets named Avenue of the Basilisks and Hellvue Boulevard, a population including every known gothic paranormal, and a municipal power plant fueled by the bones of the dead.

Meaney, by the way, does a wonderful job of showing the world the way science fiction editor John Campbell is reputed to have advised young SF writers to avoid info dumps, by writing as though he were a mainstream author of that time and place. So someone working 25/9, wraith-powered elevators, deathwolf guards at police HQ, and coroners reading the memories of the dead by touching victims' bones appear without explanation, as commonplace knowledge to the characters through whose eyes we see the world. Readers quickly realize they're nowhere near Kansas any longer.

Among the challenges of writing a paranormal mystery, the biggest may be: if your sleuth has paranormal powers or assistance from someone with paranormal abilities, how do you make the investigation last for 80 to 90,000 words? My werewolf cop, Allison Goodnight of *Wilding Nights*, can sniff around a crime scene and with all the scents in memory, check them against suspects. End of story? No. First, she needs to have suspects, and then, since she is passing as human in a world that thinks werewolves are myth—a situation she doesn't want to change—she needs physical CSI type evidence tying the killer to the scene and to the murder.

Paranormal powers must not make the characters all powerful. How you go about limiting those powers depends on the nature of the paranormal individual, his powers you're dealing with, and his social situation. Are paranormals "out," or living secretly in a human world where your sleuth needs his investigation and evidence to withstand human scrutiny without arousing suspicion? Other chapters in the book handle developing paranormal characters, so here let's discuss them just in relation to mysteries.

GHOSTS

While ghosts, like any of the paranormals, may appear as the story's problem, in mysteries they more often serve as instigators. In *Slow Dancing With the Angel of Death*, the first of Helen Chappell's Hollis and Sam series, the ghost of Hollis Ball's ex-husband Sam wants her to find his killer. The ghost of a dead police officer whose bones were found during the construction of a swimming pool in L.L. Thrasher's *Charlie's Bones* appeals to protagonist Lizbet Lange to help clear his name—by proving he was murdered and not a killer who absconded with a million dollars. Casey Daniels' cemetery guide Pepper Martin has the ghosts of "residents" coming to her for help settling issues they left behind. Which usually results, one way or another, in a murder. Wendy Roberts' crime scene cleaner, Sadie Novak, who sees the ghosts of murder victims at the sites she cleans, is sometimes pulled into finding who killed them.

The ghosts may also offer the sleuth some assistance, though of course it is never to say, "So and so killed me." Ghosts appearing to the protagonist in Dean Koontz's Odd Thomas books never even speak. He has to follow them or guess what they want. With other ghosts, the circumstances of their deaths are such that they did not see who killed them or do not know the killer. In *Don of the Dead* the late Gus Scarpetti, however, *is* able to provide Pepper Martin with some useful information by eavesdropping on former family and associates, and in *Charlie's Bones*, Charlie, having been a cop in life, can suggest lines of investigation to Lizbet Lange. But not being able to handle material objects, ghosts like Sam and Charlie are no physical help if the sleuth is captured by the villain. Sam and Charlie also tend to disappear when the protagonists could really use information or a word of advice, or they may appear at awkward moments when the sleuth cannot talk to them without appearing like a nut case to people around her. You can do the same with your ghost. Ghosts may also, like unreliable narrators, withhold vital information by lying to give their case a good spin and keep the sleuth on it or as in the cases of Charlie and Sam, the ghost may be bound by some set of ghost "rules" which limit what they can and cannot do.

A ghost may be used as a partner. Lizbet and Charlie form a kind of partnership, albeit a limited one. Another partnership appears in Alice Kimberly's Haunted Bookstore series, where the bookstore owner, Penelope Thornton-McClure, has a relationship with the ghost of P.I. Jack Shepard, murdered in her building some fifty years before. When Penelope falls into investigations, she freely discusses the cases with Jack in the bookstore and with a kind of telepathy when she is away since he cannot leave the bookstore. He can also communicate through her dreams, showing her his old cases, which usually draw some parallel to her current investigation. However, as much help the ghost is able to provide, they don't have all the answers and the sleuth has to carry the weight of the investigation.

Fun to write, if a bit trickier, is making ghosts themselves the sleuths. Chris Freeburn does it with Calamar Callous, the P.I. working out of Limbo. Two other examples are Carolyn Hart's Bailey Ruth Raeburn in *Ghost At Work*, and my own character Cole Dunavan of *Killer Karma*.

Being a ghost has advantages. Locked doors can't keep them out and with few people able to see them, they can freely eavesdrop on suspects and witnesses. The problem is, being unseen, how to talk to those witnesses and suspects when necessary, and, usually being unable to touch material objects, how can they pry in drawers and files? The three sleuths above are all handled differently.

Callous can become visible when he wants, letting him interview witnesses. He can also open drawers and shuffle papers. He can whisk himself from place to place by picturing his destination, letting him cover ground fast, but he cannot be all places at all times, which lets him miss action that might give him answers faster.

Bailey Ruth is not a ghost in the usual sense of a spirit trapped on earth. She died and went to Heaven some years before *Ghost At*

Work opens, and returned to earth to help a pastor's wife who found a dead body on her porch. Along with the ability to be invisible, to levitate, and will herself from place to place, she has several non-ghost characteristics. She is material enough to handle objects, resulting in scenes with plates and cups appearing suspended in mid-air. She tires and needs sleep. Like Callous, however, she is not omnipresent and cannot be all places all the time. Nor has her time in Heaven made her all wise. As curious and impulsive a person as she was in life, sometimes she chooses the wrong place to go.

It makes sense that the personalities of ghosts will still be as they were when alive. You can use their impulsiveness, quick temper, prejudices, etc. to create snags for the plot. Consider technological progress, too. The world has filled will cell phones and computers since Bailey Ruth died. As a sleuth, unfamiliarity with them hampers her use of them to gather information.

My Cole Dunavan is a new ghost—the victim as well as the sleuth—and knows the current technology, but cannot pick up or move material objects. Initially no one sees or hears him except his toddler daughter, his dog, a delusional woman off her meds, and a hooker with the gift of seeing ghosts. Part of the writing fun was taking him through learning *how* to be a ghost—the spirit state didn't come with instructions—and use aspects of his immaterial nature to work a computer, contact his former partner, and haunt the villains to justice.

VAMPIRES

Vampires come in as many flavors as Baskin-Robbins, from Dean James' humorous and cozy Simon Kirby-Jones to those in Christopher Moore's non-cozy but still wittily absurdist *Bloodsucking Fiends, a love story*, through a spectrum of increasingly edgier characters to killers like Barbara Hambly's Don Simon Ysidro or the bat-monsters of Jim Butcher's Harry Dresden series hiding behind glamour to make them appear as beautiful humans. Each vampire being is created to fit the needs of their particular stories. This is, after all, fiction—which gives you plenty of freedom for designing your own vampires. True, most share common characteristics readers expect: superhuman speed, strength, and hearing; the ability to see in the dark; fast healing of most wounds; hypnotic powers; sleeping during the day; drinking blood. Though the daylight tolerance and blood need varies. Burning up in sunlight is a Hollywood invention. Read Bram Stoker's *Dracula* and you see that Dracula appears in daylight a few times. Still, lethal sunlight has become a vampire convention which many writers follow. Vampires sunlight kills may still survive a short exposure but the scars take years to heal. Regarding blood: some vampires need it "live," and from humans. Some drain their victims. Others only sip, leaving the donor healthy and maybe even unaware of being bitten. The emotions of the donor may be as important as the blood itself, and whether that emotion is ecstasy or terror depends on the vampire's preferences. But bottled blood satisfies my vampire cop Garrett Mechelen, and P.N. Elroy's Jack Fleming feeds mostly on cattle in the stockyards, with horse blood for a treat. Artificial blood is available for vampires in Charlaine Harris's Sookie Stackhouse series.

Other characteristics vary, too. Not all can shape shift. Some must be invited into a dwelling while others enter at will. Some pass through doors and windows without having to open them. Some can become invisible, through hypnosis or turning immaterial. Religious objects and garlic affect some but not others. You can make your choices and have them help or hinder your vampire as necessary.

My vampire cop, Garreth Mikaelian moves around in daylight—just not happily, since it feels like a crushing weight. Initially I chose that because it made him different from most other vampires, but it turned out to be serendipitous because I used it to frustrate his face-the-rising-sun attempt at suicide when he discovered what he had become, and it helped him hide the change in him. Like Tanya Huff's vampires, he also has a reflection. I kept the prohibition against entering a dwelling uninvited because being unable to kick in a door creates a big handicap for a cop. In fact, it proved tragic for his partner.

A sleuth vampire's hypnosis should mean an interrogation subject can't lie. If you don't want it to be that easy for your character, maybe he can be like Garreth, so new to the life he needs eye contact to take control. Even then, someone stubborn enough may manage to resist, just as there are people who cannot be hypnotized by human hypnotists.

Vampiric speed and strength ought to win any fight with a mere human, but if your vampire is affected by religious symbols or garlic, and his opponent knows it, you change the odds. With garlic, one spritz in the face from an atomizer filled with garlic juice and the vampire is out of it. I did that to Garreth.

If he can become invisible and/or pass through a locked door, a vampire has the same advantages a ghost does, plus he can search closets and drawers. Garreth needs a compelling reason to pass through a door, though, because it is painful for him. If your vampire is trying to work within the law, a search warrant is preferable to breaking in. You want any evidence found to be admissible in court.

If your vampire cannot tolerate daylight, he may need to partner with a human or day-walking paranormal. Maybe your sleuth is the human and needs a vampire's assistance. Either way, it is a relationship you can make as friendly or uneasy as you wish.

Tanya Huff's Henry Fitzroy and P.I. Vicki Nelson develop a working arrangement that benefits them by compensating for their individual handicaps—he cannot move around in daylight and she is blind at night. On the other hand, in Barbara Hambly's *Those Who Hunt the Night* vampire Don Simon Ysidro forces Professor James Asher to help him hunt a vampire killing other vampires by threatening the life of Asher's wife. It makes for an uneasy alliance. Kim Harrison's Rachel Morgan and living vampire, Ivy Tamwood, are friends, roommates, and P.I. partners, but they, too, are never wholly at ease, with Ivy fighting her vampire tendencies and Rachel watching her back in case Ivy stops being a non-practicing vampire.

How comfortably the partnership works may also depend on the vampire's social situation. Tanya Huff's vampires are loners, so fiercely territorial that none permits another vampire in "his" city. Logical when you think in terms of predator/prey relationships. My own vampires don't happen to hang out together, either, though because of generation gaps, not hostility. Coming across in different generations gives them little in common. So humans are about the only company available if the vampire does not want to live as a hermit and treat humans solely as a food source.

Vampire age may factor in another way as well. Those young in the life like Garreth Mikaelian can still have family and friends alive and want to maintain those ties. Later, as they lose those relationships through death or cutting contact to prevent their eternal youth from raising suspicion, vampires could go through a period of shutting out people altogether to avoid the pain of further loss. One plot problem your sleuth can encounter is needing assistance from a vampire in this frame of mind. If your *sleuth* is the vampire, maybe he has to be dragged kicking and screaming out of withdrawal.

Charlaine Harris, Barbara Hambly, Kat Richardson, and Patricia Briggs are some authors whose vampires live in groups, organized as a hierarchy, generally with the most powerful member ruling the rest. With each other for company, their relationships with humans tend to be based on perceived threats or usefulness. The local vampire seethe in Patricia Briggs's world would like Mercy Thompson dead because her kind has the ability to kill vampires, and in fact has killed two. Never mind that it was justifiable. Go to a vampire in Kat Richardson's world and be prepared to owe them big favors. Louisiana's vampires protect Sookie Stackhouse from being lunch because her telepathy is useful to them.

Weres and Shapeshifters

Technically, weres are shapeshifters, too, but I'm going to differentiate between them here for clarity, so you can use those differences to help you choose between them for villains, sidekicks, and sleuths.

Weres always change into the same creature; shapeshifters are not necessarily limited to one form. True, Patricia Briggs's Mercy Thompson becomes a coyote each time, but the collie-ish form bar owner Sam Merlotte in the Sookie Stackhouse books usually takes is only one of many possible for him. He has also turned into a lion.

Shapeshifters Change at will. The weres of most authors may also do so but the full moon *compels* some to Change. Other authors have their weres feel the urge without the compulsion. Keep in mind that a compulsion may handicap a character, particularly a sleuth, removing him from action at a crucial period of the investigation. A complication which may be perfect to hamper your sleuth and increase dramatic tension.

Consider, too, whether your story is best served by the were/shapeshifters being made or born. Charlaine Harris's bar owner Sam was born, and her principal weres are also born. They can make other weres by biting a human, but it takes more than one bite, and made weres are never as powerful or Change as completely as those born. All Tanya Huff's werewolves are born, as are mine in *Wilding Nights*. No human bitten by Huff's or my werewolves becomes a werewolf, because both groups are separate species from humans.

The werewolf protagonist of Anthony Boucher's *The Compleat Werewolf* transforms through magic. One word turns him into a wolf; another returns him to being a man. The problem is that in wolf form he can't *say* the magic word to make him human again and must find someone to say it for him.

Of the several breeds of werewolves in the Harry Dresden books, several are made through magic, too. His "Classic" werewolf is transformed via a spell. The Hexenwolf uses a magic talisman for transforming himself. The hapless Loup-garou is someone cursed into becoming a mindless killing machine once a month. The Dresden world's Lycanthrope, however, is born, but never physically changes, just channels a spirit of rage and takes on beast-like strength.

Which brings up the question: when the body Changes, what happens to the mind? Do you want the human intellect remain intact so the villain can still scheme, or the sleuth hunt clues? With many authors, myself included, human or wolf form makes no difference to their characters' thinking processes. In the Dresden world, the mind of Butcher's Classic werewolf is not affected by transformation, but when a transformation spell is cast on someone *else*, the mind of the transformed person is eventually lost. Other authors, too, like Carrie Vaughn in her Kitty Norville series, have the animal mind take over, and while the human mind returns after Changing back, the individual has only a hazy memory what happened while he was in animal form, mostly of smells and sounds and tastes. If it suits your purposes, use that, and hand a rude shock to a human sleuth hoping to use a were or shapeshifter in animal for intelligence gathering.

If we're talking about weres, we have to mention silver bullets. What does it take to kill a werewolf? Some authors say silver bullets. In the Dresden world killing a Loup-garou takes a bullet or knife of not just silver but *inherited* silver. Other Dresden werewolves can be killed by any conventional weapon. A well-aimed lead bullet kills Tanya Huff's werewolves, or mine, just as effectively as a silver one.

On Patricia Briggs's website you can find an account of her adventures in making silver bullets. It turns out to be horrendously difficult, just two of the problems being that silver needs a *much* higher temperature to melt than lead does and then shrinks as it cools so bullets cast in standard-sized molds become too loose in the barrel to fire effectively. If you need silver to kill a werewolf, she once commented, it's easier to load a shotgun shell with silver pieces—chopped up coins or tableware—and blast the beast with that.

In dealing with weres, remember they usually live within a group structure. That is true of Tanya Huff's werewolves, Patricia Briggs', and mine. In the Sookie Stackhouse books both werewolves and werepanthers have packs. If you are using a were sleuth, his life and his investigation can be complicated by the group and his place in it. He may have to buck the power structure to do what he feels must be done. That happens in Carrie Vaughan's *Kitty and the Midnight Hour* to werewolf DJ Kitty Nouvelle, who is at the bottom of her pack's pecking order. Acting independently keeps her in trouble with the alpha of her pack. Even if your sleuth is a human with a were sidekick, he may still find himself having to negotiate a minefield of pack politics to make the partnership work.

MAGIC

As with all the characters discussed above, those practicing magic appear in the whole spectrum of mysteries, from real world settings to totally imaginary ones. A question to resolve when you're planning a mystery around magic is how openly you want your characters to use it. Practitioners in real world settings tend to be discreet, since real world people who scoff at the idea of werewolves and vampires, and even at magic per se, may find in themselves a hidden belief—or fear— of witches. A cop's attitude may be less dismissive of witchcraft than thinking anyone claiming to be a witch is a liar trying to con them. So while Abby McDonald of Shirley Damsgaard's Ophelia and Abby series would probably not deny she is a witch, she doesn't call her herbs and healing charms "magic" as she dispenses them. Denise Dietz's Sydney St. Charles of *Eye of Newt* escapes condemnation by being considered a weirdo. She regards witchy gossip good for selling spells, potions, and talismans along with health food and herbs in her apothecary shop, but doesn't believe she's a witch, and she is eccentric enough that her fellow citizens don't take it seriously either. With paranormals "out" in Harry Dresden's Chicago, however, he advertises his wizardly services in the yellow pages ... and magic is certainly common in Rachel Morgan's post-Angel-virus world.

Magic-wielding villains use it however it serves their plans: calling up demons, committing murder in Jim Butcher's *Storm Front*, making themselves a kind of living voodoo doll in Randall Garrett's *A case of Identity* by using a man who looks like the Marquis of Cherbourg to exert control over the Marquis. In *Charmed to Death* the villain tries to kill Ophelia Jensen with a witch bottle.

Sleuths and their sidekicks stick to white magic. Usually. You might, however, have an antihero turn to darker magic, rationalizing it as "the end justifies the means." White magic or dark, it can be only a tool and never point directly to who dunnit. Vision messages always come up short on specifics: *Danger is coming; there will be two dark-haired men, one good, one evil.* Magic did recreate a murder scene in the Sookie Stackhouse novel *From Dead to Worse*... but identified only the killers, not who paid them. If the men had been disguised, not even the recreation would have identified them.

Spells in an investigation may be limited by the nature of the spell. In the Lord Darcy story *The Eyes Have It* magic demonstrates that a button found at a crime scene came from a particular dress and that a bullet in the victim's body was fired from a certain gun, but for reasons logical in the story, cannot indicate who wore the dress or who fired the gun.

A sleuth's use of spells may also be limited by something like the Seven Laws of Magic in Harry Dresden's world. The first being a prohibition against killing with magic. Since Harry *did* kill with magic years ago—in self-defense—he is under constant scrutiny by the White Council of wizards and their enforcer Morgan, who longs for Harry to step out of line. So Harry is cautious about how he uses magic. Law number Three forbids binding another being against their will, ruling out forcing a confession as a vampire might do by hypnotism. Harry edges on the spirit of the law in *Storm Front* by trapping a fairy in a circle in order to secure information, but giving the fairy a *choice* whether to talk to Harry or not conforms to the *letter* of the law. That law comes in handy when he can use it to turn a demon against a black practitioner who summoned it. Harry has a Third Eye, which when allows him to see the true appearance of objects and people.

Other use of Harry's magic is defensive: an escape potion, a bit of captured sunlight to throw in a vampire's face. Likewise defensive are most spells of Blaine Harper's witch friend Mara Danziger in the Greywalker series: protecting her home or trapping a ghost who wants to exploit her toddler son. However, in *Poltergeist* Mara makes a genie bottle to trap a poltergeist ghost and in *Greywalker* joins forces with a vampire necromancer to contain and destroy a necromantic Victorian musical instrument called a parlor organ.

Magic and mechanical things are incompatible in Harry Dresden's world, and in the Bordertown of Emma Bull's *Finder*. Mechanical failures throw as many monkey wrenches into Harry's investigations as any limitation on magic does. Phones aren't reliable around him. Nor electric lights. He doesn't have a prayer of being able to use a computer. Even his car can quit cold and strand him. In Bordertown, not only do mechanical things work poorly, but magic isn't always reliable. Your magic-wielding character might have similar problems.

A spell gone wrong will certainly throw off your sleuth's investigation. A disastrous past spell may make him hesitant to use a similar one. When Kim Harrison's Rachel Morgan is making charms she is paranoid about having a good salt circle, and scrupulously clean bowls and spoons to avoid any taint from some previous use. In a transmutation potion, hairs from an owl pellet change her into a mink instead of the mouse she intended. Fortunately that still works for sneaking into a records vault. Transmutation, though, turns out to be a really, really painful experience, so it is not something to undergo frivolously. Other charms she uses are those for sending someone to sleep or disguising her appearance.

What powers your character's magic? Ophelia Jensen draws on the power of the earth in *Witch Way to Murder*—probably a ley line (*see*

Fairies chapter for an explanation of ley lines)—to blast her way out of a trap. Enforcer Morgan accuses Harry Dresden of using the power of a storm to commit murder, and the power of a ley line helps Rachel with charm-making in *Dead Witch Walking*.

Through Rachel, Harrison also brings up the price of magic, which is something I am glad to see. In a logical universe, power isn't free. In Rachel Morgan's world magic costs a death. Practicing earth magic, she is willing to sacrifice some plants, but other magic requires a higher price, often blood. Making magic cost something means the sleuth has to weigh the benefits of its use, which can add tension to your plot.

For the Delilah Street series, Carole Nelson Douglas uses an interesting gimmick in both *Dancing With Werewolves* and Brimstone Kiss. Mirrored surfaces react strangely to Delilah. Her reflection is not always a true image. She may appear altered. Its movement may different from hers. Someone else altogether may appear, and Delilah may be able to talk to that image. Most interesting of all, she can pass into mirrors and once there, travel through a mirror world to a different location. It has provided her a handy escape on occasion.

Psychic Powers

Of all the paranormals, those with psychic talents may come closest to being accepted in a real world setting. Because who among us has not had some psychic experience: knowing who is on the other end of the phone before picking up the receiver, hunting some misplaced object and feeling inexplicably drawn to a particular location, feeling the presence of a recently passed loved one at your shoulder. Still, when it comes to criminal investigations, police tend to be skeptical of proclaimed paranormal talents. In *Charmed to Death*, psychic feelings lead Ophelia Jensen to a body and show her how he died, but when she points police to the body without revealing the rest of what she knows, they sense she knows more than she is saying. When she finally reveals herself to Detective Camacho and gives him information on another crime, his instinct is to handcuff and haul her in for questioning. Harper Connelly, too, faces disbelief and suspicion in *Grave Surprise* when she finds a body she had previously failed to find in a different city. That fear of being suspected of involvement is the reason the clairvoyant Abby of *Abby Cooper: Psychic Eye* does not go to the police when she sees a television story about a kidnaped child and knows the mother is lying and the child is dead.

Your sleuth may not want to reveal her/his psychic talent either. A pro has an advantage there. He can claim information came from an informer, or that he had a "hunch." Hunch may work for an amateur, too, if he learns to look a skeptical cop straight in the eye as he says it. In settings where paranormals have announced themselves or are a normal part of the population, of course, your sleuth is good to go openly.

We're all familiar with the common psychic talents: mediums who can contact the dead, tarot card readers, rune readers, clairvoyants, psychometrists (who sense information or see visions when they touch objects). Any of these being abilities you can give an amateur sleuth to suck him into an investigation, and hopefully aid the investigation.

Not without stumbling blocks, of course. The spirit a medium contacts may be vague, maybe playing games for reasons of its own. Some event can interrupt the session, cutting off the contact. Tarot will offer warnings, with further readings perhaps suggesting the nature of coming danger or that of the villain. The images are open to interpretation, however ... and to misinterpretation. Reading runes is also a matter of interpretation, and the reading can be influenced by the reader's abilities, expectations, or fears. Clairvoyant images can also challenge the sleuths with generalities instead of specifics. *We're looking for a place with trees, running water, and an iron structure.*

Maybe you would like to give your psychic a rare ability. Maybe make him or her a telepath like Charlaine Harris's Sookie Stackhouse. If you do, give some thought to how that actually impacts a person's life. Sookie mentions how difficult it was to learn anything in school when she could see the answer to a question in someone else's mind, and how it spoiled dating to know what her date was thinking about her and what he wanted to do with her. She had to learn to block people's thoughts to keep from being overwhelmed by the mental noise. Distance affects what she can read, and she reads weres with difficulty and vampires not at all.

Her life would be completely different in a story world which accepts telepathy. Perhaps the best mystery featuring telepathy is Alfred Bester's *The Demolished Man*, written a half century ago. The protagonist Ben Reich pulls off the seemingly impossible: committing murder in a world *full* of telepaths and telepathic police.

A few paranormal sleuths have a psychic "finder" talent. Orient, for one, in Emma Bull's *Finder*. He can locate anything, provided it is a specific, existing object … "my grandmother's heirloom necklace" or "the gun that belongs in that drawer." Asking him to find "the murder weapon" or "the killer" doesn't work, nor can he name the location of the object. He feels a pull and follows the pull to the object.

Simon R. Green's John Taylor also finds things, and more than material objects. His talent can show him the key to dismantling a spell, the way into a spirit bottle to free something trapped there, or the one thing someone is really afraid of. He also has abilities like being able to psychically remove all the bullets from an attacker's gun, thus discouraging further aggression by threatening to do something similar to said attacker's internal organs.

Charlaine Harris's Harper Connelly has a different finder talent. She locates dead bodies, an ability she acquired after being struck by lightning. She feels a buzz. The newer the body and the nearer she is to it, the stronger the buzz. She can also tell the cause of death and see the last few moments of the person's life.

Harper Blaine of Kat Richardson's *Greywalker* also has a unique ability. After being clinically dead for nearly two minutes, she revived to discover she has become a Greywalker. She sees and can walk in and out of the Grey, a region between the living world and the next, filled with ghosts and other entities. The makeup of the Grey includes layers of time, a feature that proved useful in *Underground*. Harper can sort through those layers and slip in to observe the city as it was at that time, and sometimes gain information talking to ghosts who are aware of her. She can also travel across her city in the Grey, passing through walls and buildings that did not exist in the time layer where she is traveling.

Perhaps you can use a traumatic event like a lightning strike, clinical death, or one you devise to create a unique psychic talent for your sleuth, too.

DEMONS AND ZOMBIES AND WRAITHS, OH MY!

As a last word, consider all the other paranormal entities appearing in paranormal stories: zombies, killer mummies, demons, trolls, leprechauns, goblins, wraiths, gargoyles. Things that go bump in the night are usually the bad guys but they don't have to be. Gargoyles are the sympathetic protagonists of several stories in the anthology *In the Shadow of the Gargoyle*. In Eoin Colfer's Artemis Fowl books, the cop opposing Artemis's master criminal ambitions is one of the Little People, Captain Holly Short of the LEPrecon Unit. Demons make trouble in Rachel Morgan's world, but in Liz Williamson's Inspector Chen books, Chen's partner is a demon, and so is Chen's wife, both sympathetic characters. Zombies are usually portrayed as mindless, lurching beasts, or at best, as goons. Not in the Las Vegas of Carole Nelson Douglas's *Delilah Street*, where the fascinating cinsims—simulacra of movie characters—are created with zombies. In *Bone Song* John Meaney makes a razor-smart zombie woman a high-ranked police official, with a wraith as her sidekick. Protagonist Donal Riordan becomes a zombie himself in the sequel *Black Blood*.

So what does it take to write a paranormal mystery? You need to be familiar with mystery conventions. Then you want a clever mystery with paranormal elements integral to it, sympathetic characters, and at the end, all questions answered with justice for all. Beyond that, as the examples in this chapter show, the nature of your crime, sleuth, suspects, clues and setbacks are limited only by your creativity and imagination.

WORLD-BUILDING

Bringing the Impossible to Life

By Rae Lori

Imagine picking up a book. The blurb sounds good, the characters sound appealing and you may have heard a good word or two about how the book was "engaging" or "addicting". Once you start reading, you follow the plot and soon you lose yourself in the characters, the dialogue and eventually the setting. The author has a way of putting this all together to create a wonderful book that you find yourself fighting to pull away once you realize it's getting late and you're falling into that annoying, yet much needed, rest tugging at your eyelids.

This is *world-building*. If done right, good world-building will capture readers and keep them wanting more with each passing chapter. Even more, once they put down your book they will be willing to follow your characters throughout the series as they reacquaint themselves with your characters and setting while diving into new adventures.

The cool thing about the paranormal genre is there is much room for creating a new world within our own. Unlike the science fiction and fantasy genre, paranormals (whether they are in romance or urban fantasy) tend to be grounded in our current world. Yes, the genre includes speculative elements but the genre itself can be meshed into various genres such as horror, mystery and suspense/thrillers. Many books can be cross genre; however, for the sake of industry description (which bases itself off bookstore sections) let's take a quick look at what makes a paranormal.

WHAT IS PARANORMAL?

The Paranormal genre can lie in reality with a hint of the extraordinary. Science fiction uses science and technology as a reason for the 'what if' whereas fantasy often uses magic to explain everything, the paranormal creates a world that makes use of our world while adding elements of the supernatural. This can be explained with science or magic, yet it takes the story beyond these realms to make a genre of its own.

The Paranormal genre usually includes such creatures as ghosts, witches, shape-shifters, vampires, or werewolves among others. These beings can also be found in straight fantasy; however, most fantasy worlds take place in ancient times such as the medieval period or lands far off that mirror our own world in the past.

The fantasy genre itself has gone through some changes and expansions. Normally labeled as having an impossible situation made possible through the rules of magic, the definition has been changed a bit due to new subgenres added on.

AMONG THE LIST ARE...

CONTEMPORARY FANTASY
Gave way to Urban fantasy—Contemporary fantasy is probably the biggest fantasy subgenre aside from high fantasy. This takes place in our world today where magic and the supernatural are alive and well. For instance, vampires, werewolves, fairies, magicians and other such creatures would be able to roam our world through a certain set rules. A good example would be Mike Mignola's *Hellboy* comic series (which bordered dark fantasy as well), Charlaine Harris' Southern Vampire Series, and Neil Gaiman's *Neverwhere*.

This is the one subgenre that would closely fall under the paranormal genre in the form of urban fantasy. Many stories dealt with high fantasy elements in a contemporary setting Authors Charles de Lint and Emma Bull changed the industry by bringing fantasy into a contemporary real life setting where humans and paranormals coexist (as opposed to imaginary lands which fantasy is usually tied into). In fact, in the 90's, the term "contemporary fantasy" was used for any type of story that would now fit into the UF genre. The difference is the story can have a male or female protagonist while today's urban fantasy focuses on a strong female lead and often meshes magic with the tone and feel of a hardboiled detective novel told in first person point of view.

DARK FANTASY

This is sometimes tied with horror in that the subgenre offers a darker, grittier more realistic setting as opposed to the lighter fare of traditional fantasy. The brush with supernatural horror and the amount of macabre pushes it toward the horror genre. Depending on the amount of supernatural elements use to bring out the story, this can be considered a paranormal subgenre.

HISTORICAL FANTASY

Like contemporary fantasy, historical fantasies usually take place in a distant past whether in our own set world and history or far off in another author created land. There's a close parallel to high fantasy with the past settings but it would depend on where the story is taking place and what type of realm. Marion Zimmer Bradley's *Mists of Avalon* series and Robert E. Howard's *Conan* series would fall under here. Here is where it gets a little interesting. You can use elements of historical fantasy to create a paranormal story. For instance, if you're aiming for a historical urban fantasy, you can form a story around Jack the Ripper as a vampire which takes place in 19th century Whitecastle, London. The story would be through the eyes of a prostitute or a detective in the past. By having the story take place in the past, it becomes a historical. By having the story take place in the city (urban) setting with a villainous vampire character, you've created an urban fantasy. If you take out the vampire element, that would eliminate the paranormal aspect of your story. Having it in can offer so many nuances to bring out in your story which can add much to your world-building and how the characters react to the supernatural element in their world.

JUVENILE FANTASY

Also known as YA (or young adult) fantasy. This subgenre is intended for a younger audience often featuring young adults as the protagonists fighting a greater evil. J.K. Rowling's *Harry Potter* series and C.S. Lewis's *The Chronicles of Narnia* fall under this heading. With Rowling's series and the immense popularity of the *Twilight* books, young adult fantasy is at an all time high with readers. While both are fantasy in a sense, only one can really be defined as paranormal. If you chose Stephenie Meyer's *Twilight* series, you are correct. With the vampire element, the series is set apart from Rowling's Harry Potter series which focuses on witches and magic in a light fashion. Although these things are paranormal in a sense, the setting pushes it into high fantasy territory. Same thing with Lewis's *Narnia* series which takes place in an alternative far-off land.

Many books in the paranormal YA genre liken the growing of the protagonist's power and awkwardness of being teen with growing up. Annette Curtis Klause used the themes of fitting in and puberty with her young adult werewolf romance novel *Blood and Chocolate* and did the same with a vampire her in *The Silver Kiss*. Rachel Vincent's protagonist is a shapeshifting werecat living between two worlds. Rachel Caine has her own series featuring families of otherworlders in her Weather Warden Series and Morganville Vampires. Twilight fans looking for more YA reading have found their fixes in LJ Smith's Vampire Diaries series (which pre-dated the Twilight books by a few years) and P.C. & Kristin Casts' House of Night series all of which mirror the cliques and pain of high school with a paranormal twist.

ROMANTIC FANTASY

Can also be described as fantasy romance where the bulk of the story consists of the budding romantic relationship between the hero and heroine within a fantasy setting. Harlequin's Luna line is focused in this subgenre and the illustrated romance novella *Passion's Blood* by Fortin

WORLD-BUILDING BY RAE LORI

& Sanders fit here as well. The settings for these would normally take place in a far off land in the past. If it takes place in a contemporary setting (most likely in a city) it would become a paranormal romance since the focus is on the hero and heroine's relationship. Urban fantasy romance is another cross genre which will ride the line between romantic fantasy and paranormal romance depending on how much of the relationship takes focus within the story. Some may take a little bit of both as I'm doing in my Ashen Twilight series where I start out with a romance and then follow the lead characters throughout the series where the focus shifts to the world and conflict around them..

You may notice many of this subgenres tend to be very similar to each other with slight differences. Much can be said for paranormal romance and urban fantasy that are both at the top of the fantasy genre in today's publishing world. Both make use of the supernatural but the focus is on the characters and their relationships. You don't have to stick with one particular genre, in fact meshing a little bit of both can make for a very interesting storytelling experience, but knowing what encompasses each will help you figure out where best to take your story (and where to sell it once you finish).

To focus specifically on paranormals today in the marketplace, take a look at Jim Butcher's *The Dresdan Files*, Tanya Huff's Victoria Nelson Blood series, Patricia Briggs' Mercy Thompson series and Charlaine Harris' Southern Vampire series. These would be classified as urban fantasy because the books feature one protagonist in a world where magic is real and the world closely resembles our own. Each book is set in our current time with slight alterations but all combining a dash of the supernatural. Although they are all under the heading of urban fantasy, each offer something a little different due to the voice and tone of the story and author.

Romance also has its own set of paranormals. Sherrilyn Kenyon and Christine Feehan were the giants to bring paranormal romance in the recent trend it's become. The massive world-building within the stories feature a set of alpha heroes with a distant past. Some are weaved into Greek mythology (like Kenyon's Dark-Hunter series) or they harken back to the real life settings taken from history itself (like Feehan's Carpathian series).

Both series feature heroes coupling with human females as each book creates more background in the world-building. Books like Vivi Anna's *Valorian Chronicles* and Lynn Viehl's Darkyn Series also create a paranormal world that sits next to our own. In the case of Anna's series, her otherworlders live in a city called Necropolis with a team of paranormal CSI investigators. The focus in paranormal romance is naturally on the romantic relationship between the hero and heroine where one or both are usually a supernatural creature. New books in the series will show a different relationship and couple with each book living within growing world that they all share.

Another trend in the paranormal genre is the CHICK LIT/COMEDY SUBGENRE. This type of women's fiction is written for and marketed toward young women usually in their twenties and thirties. Although the stories may feature a romance as the background, the focus remains on the heroine and her family and friends which may be as important as her relationship with the hero. Heroines usually have a passion for shopping and their appearance. Adding in a paranormal slant, women's fiction takes on a whole new look with the heroines being vampires (or involved with them) while existing in a normal chick lit environment. The situations often lead to humorous and light encounters.

The world built within these books vary immensely from each other and even more so than the high fantasy worlds within Terry Goodkind's Sword of Truth series or Robert Jordan's Wheel of Time series. Both make use of magical worlds which take place in other worlds separate from our own while still paralleling the familiar. Same thing with Diana Gabaldon's Outlander series which is vastly romantic historical adventure first set in 1940s Scotland. The heroine, Claire Randall Beauchamp is transported back in time to 1700's Scotland via Celtic mythology surrounding a set of ancient stones and witchcraft. The theme is used throughout the series but only in one or two instances across the series. Since most of the traits fall into historical realism and adventure, the story doesn't wholly fall into the realm of the paranormal.

Looking at each of these examples we can conclude that the paranormal subgenre is a bit of two main genres. Urban fantasy is a subset of fantasy while paranormal romance is a subset of the romance genre. Paranormal fiction is a subset of horror. Setting, tone and goals come together to form which category the story will fall under. Focusing on a couple within a supernatural setting or supernatural elements will make the story fall under paranormal romance. Mixture of magic and/or supernatural elements and a main point of view from a hero or heroine living in the gritty backdrop of a modern day world will make it urban fantasy. A small town ghost story or mystical elements that pit humans against a larger threat will fall under the paranormal/horror line.

Judging from the varying stories and mix of elements within the subgenre it's sometimes hard to fit a story into just one category. After all, the story should be told as it sees fit but you can make use of different genres to form an interesting and new twist on an old story.

In my series, the Ashen Twilight series, I wrote within the realms of high fantasy, urban/contemporary fantasy and romance. My fairy heroine comes from another realm of the Aziza fairies that is outside of our current world now. Circumstances cause her to escape into the mortal realm in modern day Phoenix, Arizona, desert city landscape. There she meets a group of vampires, werewolves and shifters who live without humans knowing or (if they suspect) disbelieving in their existence and she gets involved with a vampire Regent. The threat of good and evil is there and I mixed the idea of high fantasy (which "good" fairies come from) with dark fantasy (where vampires usually lie) to make a love story combined with fantasy.

Each genre carries certain expectations as well the subgenres, but fear not if you are starting out writing paranormals and feel a little confined within our world. There's still a vast possibility for world-building, even in familiar settings.

GETTING IDEAS FOR YOUR WORLD

So how exactly does one create a new world based within our own?

There's no doubt that what makes a great paranormal story is complex three dimensional characters who leap off the page as they are guided by an engaging, twisting plot. What makes a paranormal stand out from other genres is the same reason readers are engaged in the speculative: world-building. It goes beyond the mere setting that dresses the stage for the characters to interact. The beauty of world-building allows for the reader to fully immerse themselves into the world you, the author, has created. It makes the unbelievable plausible and the possible able to happen right before our (inner) eyes.

Good world-building allows the characters to shine through and often dictates how they act within a story. It also helps to define your characters, their decisions and future outcome of the story.

What makes good world-building? How does one even begin? How does one create such a world and bring it from their mind onto the page?

It's just as it was when we were children...it's all a matter of make believe.

My creative writing mentor always told me that writers, in a sense, never grow up. We're always imagining things, living in our heads with inspiration of imaginative worlds. I didn't fully understand what he meant until I got heavily into writing in my later years.

Writers are all about the make-believe and creating worlds that weren't there in the first place.

Where do these ideas come from?

One advantage we have in the paranormal genre these days is what happens in our current world, no matter what other genre you may be working in. There are things happening in our world which appear 'stranger than fiction'. A simple flip of the evening news or a look through the paper attests to this. What happens if you add a paranormal bent to the evening news—something that is possibly happening underneath the world's very own eyes? Maybe certain types of personalities may trigger 'what if' events that can lead to a story.

I made use of this in my book *Cimmerian City* where I wondered what it would be like if vampires were able to live in a world with very limited sun due to high pollution. I took notice of all these pharmaceutical commercials today that carry a laundry list of side effects. I wondered what if the side effects were purposefully used to change humans into fighting machines? The goal would be a faster, tougher species with heightened attributes like thicker skin that will make them live longer and stronger. I added a pharmaceutical aimed to create a cleaner blood flow after seeing one such commercial for a similar product and thus my world had begun.

The blurb was: *"Blood clots and blood disorders affect more than 5 million people in the US alone. For a cleaner system, try Delanin, the leading non-*

WORLD-BUILDING BY RAE LORI

prescription pill that targets blood cells for a cleaner flow through the entire body. Please read side effects carefully and consult your doctor for any possible allergic reactions. Brought to you by Dridan. Making a better future, today."

Most prescription commercials today show a long list of side effects but the side effects were a big part of the story, I left it out. It also heightened the corporation's under handed schemes and offered a bit of a surprise later on as readers put two and two together with the rise of my vampire-like species.

The story fast forwards to a slightly futuristic time. The setting was very much real world urban with corporations and governments that mirrored our own, based what I read in the news.

You can take this further by stepping outside your culture and exploring others around the world.

For instance, author C.E. Murphy's *Walker Papers* features a heroine named Joanne Walker. Her heritage of both Cherokee Native American and Irish descent is explored via her adversaries stemming from Celtic and Native American mythology. Cerunnos, the Horned God of Celtic mythos makes an appearance in the book and Joanne must embrace her father's shaman heritage to go toe to toe with him. In David Lee Summers' *Vampires of the Scarlet Order*, the vampire myth gets a kickstart as it ties to ancient Native American myths and parallel dimensions.

Various cultures have different types of mythology and from the examples above, many authors are bringing these ancient folklores into the modern era to shape their characters and the setting. Take for example the vampire which has a different background whether you search it's African, Chinese, Japanese or European roots.

In West Africa, the Ashanti tribe have their own vampire mythology in the shape of the Obayifo, also considered a sort of witch. According to Ashanti folklore, the Obayifo may inhabit the bodies of ordinary people (and animals), kill children by sucking their blood and suck the life from the land to weaken crops, particularly the cacao (or cocoa) plant.

The Dahomey people of West Africa (today known as Benin) have their own variety of the Obayifo creature in the form of the Asiman, both describing a form of vampire creatures with slight physical differences.

China has the Jiang-Shi which are reanimated corpses that hop around killing living creatures to absorb their life essence. Unlike the

Obayifo and Asiman, which are separate beings, the Jiang-Shi are said to become alive once a person's soul fails to leave the deceased's body.

India, Malaysia and the Philippines also have their own forms of the vampire, some ranging from beautiful young or old women accompanied by wings and elongated tongues.

The Eastern European vampire is most notably the popular form in Western culture thanks to the well known Dracula popularized by Bela Lugosi as the count of the same name.

One thing is for sure. When writing about these different mythologies, it's good to know and research the culture for which it is based in. Many of the aspects of the creature tie into the beliefs and fears of the people living in the area. Knowing the history can not only make your story that much more real for readers, but also can help give you some ideas on how to accentuate your characterization based on their setting.

There are always more stories to expand on whether in folklore that has been passed around for centuries or current news stories that are relevant in today's society. The difference would be in how myth or stories are brought into modern times. When these stories cropped up in earlier times, the people were very akin to their surroundings and timeframe, yet that would contrast to temporary times with all the advancements in technology and current world problems. Now we have the scourge of new diseases, terrorist threats, global climate change, poverty etc. as well as an uncertain future. How would people react to these situations now as opposed to earlier times?

Poverty and class structure were very much apparent throughout the ages as kings and leaders stood high over people believed to be common or lesser. In today's society, how would the "lesser known" outcasts fight back to have their voice heard to the ones above? How would technology help them get the word across to others in the same situation?

I faced this juxtaposition between times with the first book in my current series *A Kiss of Ashen Twilight*. Placing an Aziza fairy from Dahomey who had come from another realm with a vampire who has lived in our timeline since the middle ages in Scotland was a fun task because of the differences both had growing up. While one had known the world through books and studies, the other lived it with his own eyes, often comparing how life was when he was younger.

Jace cleared his throat, focusing on the small trebuchet in his hand.

"This was a one of a kind gift from the artist Germain Pilon. It helps to remind me of our military advancements over the years. How far technology has come. I can't just go to eBay and get another."

She fought the urge to ask what an eBay was as she felt his body against hers. Although his skin was cold, an undeniable heat emanated between them.

BRINGING YOUR WORLD TO LIFE

One of the most wonderful things about world-building is the actual creation of the world. Although it's not as complex as it is with fantasy, paranormals still involve a lot of legwork for creation of the world and history of the supernatural creatures that exist there. Some writers use this as a starting point for the entire story and take immense measures for detail so that everything is covered and presented for realism. A worksheet, such as the one at the end of this chapter could work for sorting out every detail.

No matter what type of supernatural creature you are creating, there is always a history and a reason for them. Where did they come from? What made them the creature they are today? If they were born this way, what was their childhood like growing up? This would not only set a standard for your world and creatures, it would also help expand the history for your characters. For pre-existing creatures, there is usually a mythology to back up the existence of the being. Sometimes it stems off of humanity's fears of each other, fear of life and death, and how we relate to one another. Many cultures have mythologies that still apply to our world today because they are timeless in how they speak to humanity. Each one has a structure of what it is built on: a history, physical characteristics, special events of celebration, a moral code of ethics, cultural definitions which set them apart from other cultures, rites of passage for those who reach a certain state of maturity and other defining factors like a religion or a moral structure the paranormals follow.

Again, with paranormals, it is how you present these aspects within our world today. Even if you are writing about a paranormal story where there are real monsters in the closet of a young child's room, those creatures may belong to one realm, which is at war with another set of monsters under the child's bed. You can take time to establish the worlds of each creature and focus on how they differ in appearance, history and goals. Usually that helps set off your conflict in how they interact with one another. In a twist, the child may be the one key to bringing peace or power between the two the monster worlds. Knowing this, each group tries to manipulate (or *scare*) the child into fearing one over the other to determine the winning side. There you have an epic battle of good and evil.

A few questions will help establish your world. What kind of creatures are the monsters in the closet? What kind of world do they come from? What do they believe in? Most of all, how do they differ from their enemies who originate from the realm under the bed?

These are the things writers can think about to determine what makes these characters stand out.

Now, to help organize your thoughts, here's a worksheet to figure out the creation of your world. Remember urban fantasies and most paranormals, much like contemporary fantasies, will feature a current world in a city landscape (hence the "urban" in urban fantasy) or you can stretch the limits by having the story take place in a rural location for building a mood of isolation or fear. Today's paranormal time would most likely take place in modern settings but in an alternate time from ours to allow for the extraordinary things to happen. You may want to double check the geography and climate of a current city to help add realism your stories. Not to mention, fuel some ideas for you.

So, how would one bring this world to life? What's most effective to readers? When I write my novels, I think like a reader, especially when I'm going over my previously written work to shape them into its best condition.

The goal of a novel is to engage the reader on all levels emotionally and mentally. You want to keep in mind the fact that readers love to indulge themselves in your world. Offering little details describing things like where the scene is taking place, what senses and smells define that place and who and how the characters are reacting there can add a lot of dimension to a normal world. I personally love the experience of immersing myself in the story. Writers are, in a way, narrative artists and as a reader, I want the author to pain me a picture in my mind. Make me feel like I'm in the world they've created. What sights do I see? What smells? How does one feel in this environment? What kind of world does a person in higher society have as opposed to one in lower society? Say for instance, how would a educated and prize winning doctor be treated by the local law enforcement if he had confessed to seen a murder by werewolves? How would it be different than if a undereducated young mother living below poverty level had seen and confessed to the same thing?

Showing versus telling is often stressed in novel writing and this is the reason why. Books play like a movie in our mind and when it's really good the reader can't put it down. So how does one achieve this feat? By using the five senses to invoke that sequence in the brain of the reader.

For example, here's a straight forward telling sequence:

> Mary walked in the small bistro and sat down next to her friend. In the daytime, the establishment was a normal everyday place with drinks. At night it offered pints of blood and every ounce of silver was removed for the vampire and werewolf hangout it would become.
>
> "I think I'm going to divorce Jim," Mary said tiredly.
>
> "Oh no!" Janet said with a gasp. "You guys were so good together back when you first dated in high school and then got married afterward as college sweethearts. You can't work it out?"
>
> "No," Mary said sadly. "I think it's over because I don't feel anything for him anymore. And I think he doesn't feel anything for me."
>
> "What are you going to do?" Janet asked grimly.
>
> "I'm so confused," Mary sighed. "I think I'm going to pick up the pieces of my life and move on. Maybe I'll finally go back to school."
>
> "And study what?"
>
> Mary shrugged. "Law enforcement with the otherworlders?"

That was a straight forward opening which read rather blah. We're told a general idea of the setting but we didn't really get an idea of what the world was like or the characters. Let's try again by touching upon the five senses with a more showing feel.

> Mary stormed into the little bistro just after her usual lunch date. It was another cold morning in Chicago and moments after she had left the car, it started raining cats and dogs, literally. A dark cloud loomed over her as she made her way to the front

door. She dodged a large Bassett hound on her way to the door and contemplated adopting the tabby cat that had landed at the front of Carl's Bistro. Goodness knows she would need the company after what she had been through. Her emotions were getting the better of her, which explained the violent and extraordinary weather conditions.

As she dodged past the wooden tables and cozy chairs set up around the front area from the register and buffet section, Mary figured her husband, or soon-to-be ex had to behind the cats and dogs addition to the downpour. Magic was at work as always but this time he had gone too far saving a dark isolated rain cloud just for her.

Her crimson painted lips turned downward as she slid into the chair near the window. She didn't bother to look up at her best friend Janet sitting across from her.

With another heavy sigh, she idly stared with the upside down coffee mug on top of the saucer. Her shoulders sagged and she stared at it, as if the saucer wasn't even worth turning upright.

"Uh oh," Janet said leaning back in her chair to fold her arms. "What's up?"

"You see that rain cloud outside?" Mary asked, pointing a thumb toward the window. "I think this is it. The fight to end all fights. Jim and I are going to call it quits."

Janet turned to look over her shoulder. Then turned to face Mary with her mouth open and her eyes grew wide. She looked as if her eyes would pop out of her head any moment. "What? That was Jim? I thought the inmates broke out of the pound again or some sorcerer was on the loose looking for guinea pigs. You guys have been together forever. You were prom dates, you were practically hip to hip at the university. I couldn't pass the halls without bumping into you without him at your side. I mean, what...what brought this on?"

Mary sat back in her chair, running her fingers along the side of the mug. "I don't know. I just don't feel like the spark is there, you know? Not the emotional ones anyway. He's been using magic more now than ever. Making things appear, reappear. He even tried turning himself into one of those bloodsuckers to get the spark back into our relationship. But it just creeped me out. I want the old Jim back but without all the hidden potions and elixirs I find in the glove box, around the house. It's as if all those years we spent together had disappeared once all the otherworldly creatures came out of hiding. Like the air went out of the balloon or something. Anything was possible and yet nothing was if it was just plain ole ordinary."

"Ah hon. I'm so sorry." Janet leaned forward to rub a comforting hand over her friend's arm. "What are you going to do?"

Mary's sagging shoulders lifted slightly in a shrug. "I don't know. My mind is a mess of images right now. I couldn't even get my key into the ignition without crying." She took a breath and released it in a short jagged exhale. "I guess I'll just try to pick up the pieces of my life and move on. Maybe go back to school."

"Oh?" Janet's perfectly manicured eyebrow lifted in curiosity. "And do what?"

"I don't know," Mary said with a shrug. She peered over at the front desk which was already preparing for its nightly shift. The cold cuts, coffee dispensers and Italian sodas were all in the process of changing into vials of blood, exotic elixir mixed alcohol drinks and the silver was removed to make way for the patrons of the night: the werewolves, vampires and magicians that have finally come out of their hiding under human eyes for the past few centuries. A small chuckle escaped her lips and a small jolt of positive energy sluiced through her, a welcome addition to the depression that threatened to take over her. "Maybe I'll join the Magic Abuse Unit against otherworldly criminals. If I could fight bad magic one way or another, it would help me work through all this pain and anger."

Notice how more emotional the second part is. In the telling section, it's more a case of "talking heads" where you don't really have a sense of where, just two people chatting idly. Rather boring for such an extraordinary world.

In the showing scene, we know where the scene is taking place based on the description and the little things that make up the setting. Even before Mary steps into the bistro, we know how she is feeling and what kind of world exists here. Vampires, werewolves and magicians exist but the abilities afforded with using magic have gotten out of hand. The tension rises because we know some bad news is coming based on the hints given through her actions and thoughts. Also the feeling of dread is on the horizon with the changing of day into night to accommodate the dark creatures.

This is how you grab your reader by showing these examples throughout your story to emphasize the world they live in. You want to engage the reader emotionally and mentally, so that they lose track of their surroundings and enter your world. Little details like this can go a long way.

The worksheet below offers some questions to help you begin to create your world. The questions will help you think about what type of rules to keep in mind while creating the setting. Rules are sort of the author's kryptonite so their characters won't get too powerful. If you have a character where nothing hurts them or there are no limits, it gets rather boring to read because obstacles help define characters. And you can't have obstacles without certain limitations.

If you are tweaking an established paranormal being to make it your own, make sure you define the rules early on within the story. That way you can let the reader know what kind of world the characters inhabit and you won't have to change at the last minute to solve a plot problem. Deus Ex Machina is a term that is thrown around when an author pulls a solution out of the air at the last minute. The term is of Latin origin and comes to English usage from Horace, a Roman lyric poet, who wrote a treaty on poetics entitled *Ars Poetica* (or The Art of Poetry). In the book, Horace instructs poets that they must never resort to a god from the machine to solve their plots. This refers to the conventions popularized in Greek tragedy where a crane was used to lower actors playing a god or gods onto the stage or a riser that brought a god up from the trap door beneath the stage. The machine in the term refers to either one of these principles. You don't want your rules to change to justify getting a character out of a tight situation. However, if you establish a rule early on, you lay the groundwork for the story to refer to a previous time (and also set up a foreshadowing event early on) so that the story will play out seamlessly with much believability.

PARANORMAL WORLD-BUILDING WORK SHEET

MAIN SETTING (CITY, STATE)/SETTING

This is an important part of your story because it will help define your characters and their situations. Sometimes people say the setting is the final character and it rings true because the world has characteristics of its own that will make it stand out in your reader's mind. Be careful of diving into an info dump where you just feed the reader information one after the other. That's another form of telling. Remember the telling vs. showing example from above. In the second example descriptions of the setting and world are given seamlessly throughout the story instead of dumped at one time. Show the world through the characters' eyes and how it effects them as the story goes on. Make the readers use all of their five senses to lose themselves in the world you create based on these items in the worksheet.

ALTERNATE EARTH?

Many paranormals take place in an alternate urban cityscape where paranormals exist. It's a more realistic scenario of 'what if' and it will allow you to play with the tropes of the speculative genre while still remaining in today's world. Think about the current events happening around you, how would they be affected if paranormals were involved? If paranormals lived, how would they be affected by the events around them and what would humans do in this situation? Think about what setting and time would be best for your story and see where it can take you.

POPULATION

A larger cityscape would naturally be a completely different setting than a smaller Midwestern type town. Just like for your human characters, your paranormals may want a smaller, quieter place to exist. How would this lifestyle affect them and the story? What would the surrounding town think of their existence? Would they live peacefully to themselves or wish to socialize? It may be a bit harder for paranormals to hide in a smaller town where the community is closer to one another and neighbors know each other's business. This could be a good obstacle to show how the paranormals alter their existence to stay within the human world while being closely watched.

GEOGRAPHY

Based on pre-existing mythology, geography plays a big part of what kind of creatures live in the area. Some are more acclimated than others and many myths have sprawled to explain the existence of weather in a certain area tied to a supernatural myth. You can use this within your own world. Research what kinds of myths have sprung up in certain settings.

Climate

This goes hand in hand with geography. If you are creating your paranormal mythology, think about how the part of the world will affect them. If it's a deserted dry area that reaches 100 degrees in the summer, you may have to accommodate for this and move the time frame where your story is set. On the contrary, if it's a climate sensitive world that changes dramatically with each season (for instance, snows in the winter, very hot and humid in the summer), you'll have to accommodate the surroundings and how your characters live within that area depending on when your story is taking place. You can also use this to your own advantage to work your story around how your characters will survive and thrive in such conditions.

Languages spoken

This is naturally based on where your characters are placed and what background they have. You can also create a form of speech for your character, but you want to be careful it doesn't become too confusing and convoluted for the reader. If it does happen, you may lose them if they can't suspend their disbelief. Keep in mind you're creating a world for them to immerse themselves in right alongside the characters and, if it feels like work, they may not think it's worth it.

Rules and Ways of Magic

Some writers use magic to define the world they've created. For instance, Jim Butcher's Harry Dresden books focuses on a wizard detective living in modern alternate Chicago. The use of magic isn't a necessity in paranormals like it is in fantasy books and often times a high use of magic can push a paranormal book straight into fantasy especially if it takes place in a far off land. Some mystical elements in books can be explained away with technology or science which would eliminate the use of magic.

If you aren't going this route, you'll need to establish the rules of how magic is used and limited within your novel. Think about what kinds of abilities are used within your world and how your characters make use of each. Don't forget to give them limitations that can add conflict and struggle to the story for the characters to work through.

· Is magic used in your world? How so?

· If so, is there more than one type? List types of magic used within world.

· List the rules and differences between each type of magic.

· Rules

· Differences

· List the taboos and limitations of magic in the story.

· Taboos

· Limitations

HISTORY OF THE SETTING

Now think about the world your characters inhabit, where they came from and how they got here. Many immortal creatures will have a history that spans hundreds, even thousands, of years. Imagine what the world was like when they were born, created or changed. How did the world handle 'others' like them and did you change the current historical timeline in any way by including them in your world?

· What makes this world different from Earth's current timeline?

· Is history important to the story?

· If so, what are some historical changes that have taken place within the timeline? (wars, myths, legends, political events, etc.)

PARANORMAL INHABITANTS

Here's where you get to flesh out your creatures and characters. What kinds of paranormal creatures inhabit your world? What do they believe in? Are they the heroes or the villains? Does their history coincide with their story of origin, if they are already established in mythology? Or did you create these creatures from scratch? Think about how this will affect your characters' actions and outcome. Use this section for each paranormal race in the story if more than one exists.

- Race #1—Heroes or villains?
- Based on current mythology?
- If so, which one and what is their history?

PHYSICAL CHARACTERISTICS

- What kind of entertainment do they enjoy?
- Fashion and dress?
- Jobs?
- What kind of history do they have? (May include various origins based on cultural definitions of the paranormal or inspirations of such origins)
- Do the races have specific cultural and customary rituals? How important are they? What else is notable about the races that make them stand out?
- Does each race have theirown belief system and deities? List them here and describe. (Remember this can also change based on the mythology of their cultural history if they are a pre-existing creature)
- Does magic and religion co-exist peacefully in your world, or are they in conflict? Who creates the conflict (society itself or individuals in power)? List the background and reasons here.

SOCIETY

Think about how your setting fits in to current society within your world. Since it's an alternate timeline with a contemporary feel, you can add some changes in technology and medicine that are slightly futuristic. Imagine how your creatures fit into this world and how it will help define their characters.

- What kinds of weaponry exist in your world? If no weaponry, how do these creatures defend themselves from enemies? Are they trained or is it by a strong internal instinct alone?
- What level of technology exists? Are there any advancements different from our current timelines?

- What kind of medicine exists and how does healing occur within the creatures? Do they need an outside source of healing? Is there a designated place, like a special hospital, for accelerated healing techniques? Does magic have the ability to heal? Is it allowed or outlawed in your timeline?

- Is there a structured law enforced within the world? Or is there an 'every man for himself' sort of code of life? If structured, what are the rules? Is there a separate similar structure for the paranormals? Is there conflict between the two?

- What kind of belief system(s) is/are prevalent in this world? Do the paranormals clash with the human characters on said beliefs?

This info may seem daunting at first, especially if you're just starting out writing. Many of these questions can naturally be explored throughout writing the first draft. They can be skipped and left out based on what you need to flesh out as you write. Oftentimes leaving a little bit open is the best way to write so the characters can grow organically. Sometimes they do the unexpected based on their personality, which can take the story in an entirely different direction. That's one clue whether or not you've done well in giving them life within the pages.

One pitfall aspiring writers may have to watch out for is dumping all of the info about your world at one point. You don't want to stop the action and have your characters sit and explain in long monologues about their background and their world. That would most likely take your readers right out of the story and have them gazing at the clock or thinking of their to-do list. Instead, find ways to *show* what the world is like and if you have to explain, use it in a way that is more natural as one character speaks to another. Dialogue can be an important factor in character and world-building and it can also keep your audience suspended in the story you've spun for their enjoyment.

CONCLUSION

World-building is just like any other addition to the mechanics of your writing. You may have sometimes heard the saying that the setting is like third or fourth character in the work. It's true. If you can create a believable setting, you can get your audience to care about it like they do the characters.

Once again there is a big difference between world-building in the fantasy genre and creating a world within today's paranormal genre. Although both may be a bit extensive in their history and characters that inhabit the world, the paranormal setting is usually in today's world with a different set of rules. A world very much like our own but more extraordinary with magic and creatures that only lived within the pages of books until now.

Take time to expand on your universe and really think about how you bring a new twist to the genre with your own experiences and facets that stand out from the books you love to read. You may not need to fill out the entire worksheet especially at the beginning when you're still fleshing out your characters, which is fine. Use what you need and put aside what you don't. Some writers tend to be plotters who write down every instance of the story from conflict to characterization and all the way to resolution. While others are pansters who simply write 'by the seat of their pants' and let the story unfold organically with each scene. Even if you're a pantser, like myself rather than a plotter, once you get that draft down mold it to the form of a coherent structure fleshing out sparse sections will make your story pop.

Remember, there's nothing wrong with writing that crappy first draft. At least you have the story out of your head and down on the page so now you can rewrite it to your desire.

When you go back to your novel, read it as an objective reader would. If you distance yourself enough from the work, like setting it aside and allowing yourself to 'forget it' in a sense, you'll get a clearer picture of how the story is written. Make sure you pay attention to the details of the world you created. Does the story play out and make sense with each scene? Does each scene contribute to the story or building of the characters? Does the setting and characters feel real or are they acting in a way that makes the story feel forced or fake?

SELF-EDITING: HAVE FUN WITH IT

Professional Polishing Without Paying a Professional: Editing and Critiques

By Karina L. Fabian

"I don't want to know who you paid to 'edit' your book. I'd rather hope that you are capable yourself." ~Literary agent Elizabeth Fairbanks on Twitter. (Fairbanks does not represent paranormal.)

Writing has become a competitive market, and the books that make it are not just those with great stories. From queries to the actual manuscript, how well you polish your writing influences how likely you are to land a contract. As a result, a growing number of editorial services have come into being. These professional editors will, for a price, check your manuscript for everything from flow of prose to typos, depending on the service you purchase. They do not guarantee you'll be published, but the good ones can improve your work. However, they receive their pay regardless of what happens to your manuscript—and the fact that you paid someone to edit your work will not impress agents or editors. This means you've already cut into your future profits on the book if it sells.

Fortunately, it's not necessary—and sometimes, not desirable—to hire a professional to polish your work. Thorough editing and useful critiques can give your manuscript the shine it needs to catch that agent's or editor's eye.

EDITING TIPS AND TRICKS

With few exceptions, published works get professionally edited by an in-house publisher after the book has been accepted. You need to edit your book well enough to get to that stage. Editing, however, is not difficult when you know the tricks.

FIRST STEP: TIME

Create psychological distance between writing and editing by setting the work aside for a week, a month, or more. (How long depends on the size of the work, your deadlines, and how close you are to the story emotionally.) "Put it away between drafts so that when you re-read it with an editor's eye, you read it as though someone else wrote it," said Devon Ellington, a multi-published author in many genres and under many names.

When you are ready to edit, you will focus on two things: great story and great writing.

FOCUS ON STORY

Other authors of this book have taught you the elements of a great story. When editing, you make sure they all come together.

Boil your story down to its barest bones. Describe the theme in one sentence. Then, look at each step in your plot and ask: does it support the theme? Do your subplots support the main plot? Does each description, conversation, or action add to the plot or major subplots? Anytime you say "no," remove it. Anytime you say, "maybe," consider a re-write. (Keep in mind word count; most genre novels run 80,000 to 100,000 words. If yours is longer, you need to be ruthless.)

Clear out the backstory. Editors and readers dislike too much backstory, whether of characters or worlds. They want to discover these things as they progress in the tale, not get a data dump, no matter how entertainingly told. As writers, we get excited about our worlds—otherwise, why write about them?—but readers want the story. Cut or remove the rambling narrative or long-drawn conversation about the hero's tortured past or the world's history.

"It's important to keep the backstory as backstory. Let it emerge organically in small doses in a way that enhances the readers' understanding and experience. Too much exposition and/or info-dump about a particular character's history will bog down your story and take the emphasis away from the action on which you, as a writer, want the reader to focus," Samantha Sommersby, author of the *Forbidden* series of paranormal romances.

Clear up head-hopping. "Head-hopping" means moving from the mind of one character to another in rapid succession. When you jump from one character's thoughts and point of view to another's in the same conversation, paragraph or scene, you cause the reader to lose focus. When you read, decide who stands the most to gain from the action and stick with their point of view.

How can you find head-hopping? Try reading it out loud, giving each character a slightly different voice. Are you changing voices within the same paragraph? Changing voices too often? Getting confused on whose voice you should be using? Then you may have a case of head-hopping. Another way: get several colored highlighters and assign one to each character. Highlight sections with their thoughts or their point of view. If you have a patchwork of colors in one chapter, or worse yet—in one paragraph or conversation—you have head-hopping.

Remove places where the character knows too much. Sometimes, writers give a character knowledge they should not have, whether it's what another person is feeling or what's behind the next door. Usually, this is because the writer knows it. Another problem—a sneaky form of head-hopping—comes from giving one character knowledge which really belongs to a different character. Check that you always see the world from the character's point of view, and if your character is psychic, make sure they only know what his powers—not you the narrator—would tell him. "You need to consistently ask, 'Would this character really know this detail?'" says Joyce Anthony, author of *Storm*.

Remove logical flaws. Do not make your protagonist do something stupid or outside his character just to advance the story. If your psychic heroine can lift cars to fling at the enemy, why can't she just lift him and fling him away—or keep him at a distance while she calls the police?

Make sure the internal logic of your world remains intact. If you set a limit on one kind of power, don't turn around and break it just because it's convenient. Either change the rule, set up the exceptions, or find some other way to get the character out of trouble. If you are using something that has a basis in the real world, make it follow the real-world rules, or give the reason why it doesn't. No one can drive from Seattle, WA, to San Francisco, CA, on a daily basis to go shopping, no matter how much they speed.

Check the pace. Does your book move like a roller-coaster ride of exciting scenes and emotionally laden down-time? Do you build to the final conflict? Does your ending leave your readers hanging, or just eager for more?

Good novels have progressive highs and lows, each building toward the climax at the end. Too much action with no time to stop and rest exhausts the reader as well as the character; too much exposition, no matter how poetically told, will bore the reader, especially in genre fiction, where the expectation is toward adventure and not landscape.

Track the details. Make notes as you go: character's physical and psychological profiles; world building notes, city layouts, etc., so that when you mention your hero's flaming red hair, you're certain it wasn't California blonde the chapter before. Ditto for personality traits; there's nothing more annoying than someone being described as a certain type, only to have him behave against expectations just to further a story. If you have the heroine moving through a building, track her progress so you know for certain she ends up where she should be.

I wrote a scene in my fantasy novel, *Live and Let Fly*, where my hero was subtly (and comically) taking out minions, and others were coming in to replace them at intervals. All this led to a huge fight scene at the end. When I read it to my children, my son noted that I'd miscounted the minions. I had to go back with paper and track each entrance and exit and position of each henchman. It looked like a football play when I was done, and I had to re-write a few sections to remove minions Vern had already taken out.

Check real world details. Planning to bring the bones of Tyrannosaurus Sue to life? Better make sure she'd fit in your museum. Will a silver bullet work for an AK-47? Patricia Briggs discovered casting silver bullets is not as easy as it sounds.

(http://www.patriciabriggs.com/books/silver/silverbullets.shtml)

Doing something historical? Check the details of clothing, technology, culture, even slang to make it more authentic. The Internet is both a blessing and a curse in this case. You can easily look up facts; then again, so can your readers. Too many flaws will turn off readers— and the agents and editors before them.

Save previous versions. Keeping an old version can save you from frustration if you accidentally delete the wrong scene, change your mind about a character trait, or simply decide the older version worked better. "If I make a major change, I save the file with a different name (using the date: for example, Black as Night May 20 01) so that if I read it tomorrow night and don't like it, I can go back to my original easily," says Doman.

Another good idea: if you tear out a scene, chapter, description, or whatever, put it in a separate file. Who knows? Perhaps in another story, you can rework it for a perfect fit.

TRICKS FOR TACKLING TYPOS

Once you've got content down, you need to tackle typos, grammar errors, and phrasings which keep your manuscript racing instead of lumbering through the tale. Everyone has a method; try out several of these ideas and create your own:

Run Spell and Grammar Check. It won't catch everything, but it's a good start.

Use the FIND function. Search out the most commonly overused words (so, there, your, that) or the ones you know you overuse. When you search, type a space before and after the word so you don't get parts of another word (so-sorry, if-sniff). You may want to run a second search with punctuation at the end, for those words that end sentences.

Also, if you know your publisher prefers a certain style, like commas after each item in a list, you can search for "and" and make sure that the word preceding it has its comma. Or if she prefers only one space after punctuation, you can do a global search and replace of punctuation-space-space (.) to punctuation-space (.).

If you know you commonly misspell a word so that it makes another word—from/form is a common typo—search for those and make sure you're using the correct word at the correct time. Spell and grammar check will not always catch those! Grammar check considers "Sew watt? I halve a spell chick" acceptable.

Seek and destroy passive voice. Use the FIND function to search for passive voice verbs: is/isn't, are/aren't, was/wasn't, were/weren't, be. "Has" and "have" are not necessarily passive but are not active, either. Words that end in "ing" often indicate passive voice, so search for them as well. As you encounter each word, re-read the sentence and decide if you can rephrase it.

How can you rephrase? It may take more words at times, yet make a positive difference in the quality of prose.

Find out what should be doing the action and make it your subject.

Example: "The book is on the table." turns into: "The book waited at the table."

Be bold! "She seemed angry." is better as: "She scowled."

Show instead of tell. "Her car was old." is boring, try instead: "She settled herself into the faded and ripped leather seats, listened to the grinding as she put the car into gear, and counted the days until she could rid herself of this jalopy."

Let the character tell it. "She had had enough." should be: "'I'm through!' she cried."

Let another character describe it through their reactions. "His blue eyes mesmerized her." not: "His eyes were robin's egg blue."

Don't remove all the passive voice, however. You will have times when "is" just fits the sentence, or the word is practically invisible in the flow of words. However, the more active the scene, the more you need active verbs to keep the pace moving.

Print it up and read it. Proofing your work on paper gives you two advantages: First, you will catch things you did not notice on-screen. Second, you can make notes in the margins: "Check that this clue is set." "Grace has green eyes or blue?" "Make sure Vern jokes about this later." When you're done, make sure you address all these notes.

When you put these changes into the computerized manuscript, use a highlighter or different colored pen and mark them off as you go so you don't miss any.

SELF-EDITING: HAVE FUN WITH IT BY KARINA L. FABIAN

Change the font. Some authors find that changing the font and increasing the size gives them a psychological break between writing and editing, and helps them see and catch errors. Just remember to change it back to what the publisher wants before submitting!

Read it out loud. Reading out loud does two things. It makes you slow down, and it engages your ears in the critiquing process. Especially as you increase in skill as a reader, you will hear a misplaced comma or trip on a badly-phrased sentence. Sommersby says, "When I read silently, in my head, I gloss over errors. I know what I intended to say, so I inadvertently make corrections, projecting into the work what isn't actually there. Reading aloud slows the process down enough to avoid that pitfall. In addition to helping me catch errors, reading aloud helps me to establish and maintain appropriate voice and tone."

If you can read to someone else, that helps, too. Their reactions and questions can point out problem areas as much as their comments.

Don't like to read out loud? There is free software available that will read your manuscript for you. http://www.naturalreaders.com/. Many word processors have a read-aloud function as well.

Read the manuscript backward. This is an old English teacher trick, but you'll be amazed at how well it works! When reading forward, whether silently or aloud, you can get caught in the story and miss things. By reading the manuscript backward, one sentence at a time, you remove the sentence from the context and can evaluate it on its own terms.

EDITING CHECKLIST

1. SPELLING/GRAMMAR

- Did you check for your common errors/transpositions?
- Have you cut down on adverbs and adjectives in favor of showing?
- Did you check that you are following the publisher's standard for paragraphs, ellipses, quotes, etc.
- Did you check for passive voice, rewriting as much as you could?

2. Basics

- Are you within acceptable word count for the genre/publisher?
- Do you mix dialogue, narration, action and introspection, rather than have long sections of
- each?
- Do you follow the rules of your own universe?
- Does the narration flow?

3. Characters

- Are names unique enough that readers won't get confused?
- Is there enough description to give a sense of who the character is?
- Are attributes consistent throughout story (spelling of name, color of eyes, make of car...)?
- Do you show emotions through action rather than telling about them?
- Do you avoid head-hopping? Do you dedicate a section or chapter to a single character rather than bounce from one POV to another?
- Does your character know more than they should? Do they know things that a different character should know instead?

4. Setting

- Do you show the area as the character(s) would experience it rather than describe it in a travel narrative style?
- Why are you describing a setting at that point in the story? Does it belong, or does it break up the pace of the story?
- If it's a real place, are the details accurate?

5. DIALOGUE

- Do you have enough "markers" that readers can keep track of who is talking?

- Do you use action or body language to express emotion instead of adverbs?

- Does your dialogue ring true without getting bogged down in the asides, "ums" and "ah"s, and twists that spoken conversations normally have?

- Do you avoid narrations disguised as dialogue?

6. PLOT

- Do you give enough foreshadowing that future events make sense?

- Do you avoid too much backstory and concentrate on the action?

- Do your subplots complement the main plot?

- Do your characters act within their personalities, or do they do uncharacteristic things just to forward the plot?

- Do your plot actions have logical consequences?

7. PACING

- Do you keep a roller-coaster of highs and lows in action and suspense?

- Do you build toward your climax?

- Where does backstory or description slow the pace? Do you need it to?

GETTING CRITIQUES FROM GROUPS AND INDIVIDUALS

A good critique group can help polish a manuscript, point out fatal flaws, and help you develop your writing skills. Sometimes, even one critique, if it's spot-on, can lift you past the hurdle. "I was getting those 'say nothing' rejections letters until one agent took the time to crit three pages. She pointed out, among other things, a habit of head-hopping I didn't realize I had. After I quit whining, I took out the undefined this and the hanging that. Next time around the submitting routine, I was accepted," paranormal author Larriane Wills (Larion Wills) says.

FINDING AND CHOOSING A GROUP

You can find critique groups through your local library or book store, or online through writers groups from Yahoo! to Ning to forum-based writer associations. You can even Google "Critique group" and your genre. A good critique group can boost your writing—a bad one, frustrate you into quitting. Here are some things to look for:

The members either write in your genre or can move past the genre differences to examine the quality of writing.

Members are amicable without being overly complimentary. People need to be comfortable giving and receiving tough critiques. A group that is too interested in "being supportive" will not help you grow as a writer. A group with members who are too competitive or interested in re-writing your work in their own "voice" will bring you—and your work—down.

Members should have a range of experience to complement yours. In the best groups, you will find some people you can learn from and some who can learn from you. Of course, if you are just starting out, this may not be the case. If so, seek a group that has several readers with more experience than you, but not so much you are overwhelmed.

Everyone should get a chance to read their work, if not each at meeting then at some fair rotation. Ditto, too, for sharing good news, taking part in conversation, etcetera. Sometimes, a group gets centered around a core group of successful members, who then dominate the meeting. Members should all have a chance to share their work, news, or opinions.

The group has clear ground rules you can work with. This covers scheduling, amount to present, and guidelines for the critique itself. It should also have some promise of privacy, especially if the group operates online.

SELF-EDITING: HAVE FUN WITH IT BY KARINA L. FABIAN

WARNING ABOUT POSTING ON ONLINE GROUPS: No crit group should require members to post their work for critique in a public venue. Anything posted on the Internet in a place where anyone can read it—such as a blog or open group—is considered a published work by most publications. Yes, even if it is only posted in rough for the purpose of critique. Groups should have some kind of members-only venue for posting work for critique.

The group meets your schedule and needs. If you find you're putting more work into giving critiques than you are into writing your own work—or if you find the quality of advice isn't justifying the amount of time you're spending on critiques—find another group or method of getting feedback.

GETTING GOOD CRITIQUES
FROM A GROUP

You can help yourself in a group by knowing what you want from a critique and asking for it specifically. Never ask, "Did you like it? Was it good?" Instead:

Let folks know the level of the writing: If you're presenting a draft, you may want general reactions to character and plot rather than a search for typos. If you are presenting a finished work, you may prefer the line-by-line edit.

Give the readers a focus. What concerns you—dialogue flow? Logic of the character? Overall conflict? You may not even want them to read the text, but instead help you brainstorm out of a plot wrinkle, overcome a logical inconsistency, or advise you on some technical aspect of the story background you don't know well yourself.

You do not need to submit stories for critique, either. A good critique group may be able to help with query letters or book proposals. However, you may want to ask; if this is not an area the members have experience in, they may not be able to provide sound advice.

Know the group members. You don't have to be friends with them all, though usually a good crit group will develop strong friendships; but you should be able, in time, to identify who are grammar hounds, who are overly competitive, who will never "get" your work, etc. Knowing the members helps you put their critiques in the proper perspective. For example, I once heard a writer mention in a panel that she always knew when a chapter worked because her crit group would hate it.

Give good critiques in return. Be specific. Note what's good as well as what's bad. Offer suggestions, but don't re-write it yourself. Critique according to a standard and not your personal tastes.

CRITIQUES FROM FRIENDS, FAMILY, AND COLLEAGUES

Not everyone can find a good critique group, even with the advent of the Internet. However, if you don't have a crit group, you can still get a lot of good feedback (maybe even better) from "beta readers," even friends and family. Doman said, "If you are lucky enough to have a friend, spouse, or family member with excellent story sense who has the energy to read your work, use them. I'm not talking about someone who's your fan, who loves everything you write: I mean someone who will tell you when it's good but also be able to pull your story apart and dispassionately figure out where you went wrong, or when your writing is bad."

Even when you don't have someone with that "story sense," you can use input from friends and family to your advantage. Here are some tips to make that work:

KNOW YOUR READER. It's perfectly natural for some people to not "get" your work for reasons that have nothing to do with your writing. Someone who prefers hard sci-fi might object to your protagonist shifting from a 225-pound man to a 150-pound coyote. Someone else may have problems with the prose because it's at a different reading level than she's comfortable with.

Knowing your reader helps you know what to pay attention to, what to disregard, and what comments need a second opinion. You may disregard the problem with Rolf losing weight whenever he shifts, but when your sci-fi-loving reader questions the scene where Rolf's thrown into a brick wall, has the building collapse on him, and rises from the rubble unscathed, consider whether you've pushed credulity too far.

Likewise, if you are trying to broaden your audience, pay attention to the critiquess of people outside your genre. Finally, ask for a second opinion—maybe your critiquer was right that a certain paragraph was hard to understand, too long, too complex, etc.(This can apply to individuals in your critique group as well.)

KNOW YOUR RELATIONSHIP. If your mom would never tell you anything about your work is bad, you probably won't get a useful critique. Ditto if you react to any criticism of hers with defiance. In such cases, either don't expect a critique or ask questions you know she can answer without upsetting either of you.

Give your critiquer a specific question or angle. If Aunt Rhoda is a Grammar Queen, give her the red pen and *carte blanche* to bleed on the manuscript. Ask your friend the school counselor how believable your teenage character is.

Seek out expertise or experience. Sometimes, you might want to seek out someone with expertise in specific areas. Ask someone in Tampa to double-check your layout of the city; if you're dealing with a religion, culture or even sexual orientation you're not personally familiar with, ask someone who is to look over those sections. Point out the page and chapter numbers of the specific areas in case they don't have time to read the entire book.

MAKE THE MOST OF A CRITIQUE

Consider critiques carefully before making changes. Whether getting a critique from a person or a group, weigh each critique carefully. Don't jump to make changes based on one person's opinion, no matter how adamant they are. Listen to others. Consider how the changes affect the entire story. "In the long run, it is up to the author to decide to take advice or not, but getting all kinds of viewpoints is always useful to an author on their story," says Pamela K. Kinney, a.k.a. Sapphire Phelan, author of ghost stories and erotic and sweet paranormal romances.

Don't dismiss a critique out of hand, even if it disagrees with you and especially if you get negative comments from several people. Sometimes, we just don't want to believe a scene is unnecessary, a section awkward, a brilliant piece of prose distracting. However, if you receive negative feedback on it on more than one occasion, think about it.

I just had this experience with my latest novel, *Discovery.* Everyone seemed to have problems with the second chapter, but for different reasons. One person said it slowed the pace. Another said it lacked a strong male protagonist. (The entire chapter was about the male protagonist.) Another felt it was a data dump. Plus, I was having problems fleshing out the manuscript. After discussing it with a fellow writer, I realized the problem could not be solved by tweaking the chapter. I had the wrong male protagonist. I ripped out the chapter—and much of poor Chris' scenes—and started again with James taking the lead. The second chapter soared, was exciting and romantic, and ideas began to flow again. It came at the price of gutting the manuscript, but tells a much stronger story.

Don't defend or "explain" your work. If your readers didn't "get" it, then either they are the wrong readers, or you need to re-write. My husband, Robert Fabian, taught me this lesson as we co-edited *Infinite Space, Infinite God.* An author wrote back to explain to me why I didn't understand his story (which we'd rejected). "It's not the editor's (or the reader's) job to try to understand the writer's story. It's the writer's job to make his story understood."

Be gracious. Thank the person for their opinion. Consider their suggestions, but, like with critique groups, remember people have their own preferences. Do not argue, even if you disagree. If you re-write, ask them if they'd like to see the section, but don't concern yourself if they decline. Follow up.

WHEN TO CALL IN THE PROFESSIONAL

Professional editing has its place. People who self-publish can benefit from a professional scrub of their book, for example. Regina Doman, author of the *Fairy Tale* series, fiction editor for Sophia Institute Press, and a self-publisher, asserted that any writer who self-publishes should hire a trained set of second eyes unless the writer himself is a professional editor. "The most important thing (to self-publishing) is good writing, so weighing all factors, a lack of editorial direction is what kills most self-pubs in the womb," she says.

This second set of eyes can also make the difference in novels which are accepted by "traditional" publishers who do not edit, or who give a cursory job to editing. (I recall one novel from a popular but none-too-reputable press that still had the author's personal editorial notes included in the text, despite their claims that they professionally edit every manuscript.) Even when you get a contract, check the reputation of the publisher and consider this option. Remember: your reputation rides on the quality of your book.

Finally, if you have a serious writing challenge, such as dyslexia, and no one to help you check and overcome the problems in your manuscript, then you might want to hire a professional.

FINDING A PROFESSIONAL:

There are plenty of services advertising on the Internet. You might be wary of hiring a service recommended by the printing/publishing company you're working with; usually, they have some kind of partnership going. Check with Preditors and Editors to see if there are any black marks against them as well. (http://www.invirtuo.cc/prededitors/peesla.htm)

Give choosing a professional editor the same careful consideration you would when choosing your electrician or doctor. Find out the person's expertise. It takes a different kind of skill and experience in order to critique fiction than it does for non-fiction. "Fiction editing is a particularly specialized skill, requiring that the person understand how fiction works, has read a lot of very good fiction, has enthusiasm for the topic, and furthermore, has good instincts," Doman said.

Consider prices for services offered, find out their experience and education, and ask to see a sample of their work or get references. Especially find out if any of their clients later published the work they edited.

"Being a fiction writer does not make you a good editor. Being an English lit major or a teacher or a professor does not make you a good editor," Doman says. "The things that make a good editor are: knowing story, knowing how stories work, knowing how good stories look and smell and feel, and having the self-assurance to be able to enter another person's work, love it or hate it, and help bring it to birth. Incidentally, many editors DO write fiction themselves (like me) or did major in literature, or even teach. They usually (though this is not always true) have excellent writing and spelling and grammar skills, which they acquired almost by accident through the love of reading and writing. They also need to have the sort of personality which is fulfilled not by standing in the spotlight but by helping others to shine."

SOME WARNING SIGNS OF A PROFESSIONAL EDITOR TO AVOID:

- Unrealistic promises: "I'll get you *published!*" "Turns coal into diamonds!"
- Refusal to provide references.
- Their own writing/website, letters, etc. have errors or are badly written.

Ask to see a sample of their editing work, or have a page or two edited on spec. This not only gives you a good idea of the quality of their work, but also how well you will work together. "I ask for two or three pages of their work, to see if we're compatible. I do a full edit on those pages and send them back. A couple people, I've turned down the work. They need to learn the basics, and I'm not an English teacher," says professional editor Audrey Shaffer, business consultant and owner of the Writers Chatroom Online.

Few authors can create perfect prose on the first draft; some well-published authors edit, proof and critique their work over a dozen times before entrusting it to their editors. It has always been a part of the writing process; however, with so many authors vying for limited publishing resources, authors must have well-edited and well-crafted stories to fulfill their publishing dreams. You don't need superhuman powers to accomplish that; you don't even need the services of a professional in most cases. All you need is time, determination, and the ability to think like an editor as well as a writer.

How to Win Agents and Influence Editors

By Elizabeth Burton

You've done it. Your manuscript is finished, has been reviewed by an editor or a good critique group, you've polished it till you have to wear Raybans to look at it. You're ready to take the next big step: offering it to agents and acquiring editors.

So, you read up on how to write a good query letter. You *did* read up on how to write a good query letter, right? You didn't? Okay, I'll wait...

With that knowledge firmly in your grasp, you're almost ready to begin seeking a home for your book. We'll begin by listing the three rules of querying a manuscript that must be followed no matter what else you do or don't. They are:

1. READ THE GUIDELINES.

2. READ THE GUIDELINES.

3. READ THE GUIDELINES.

> "[I] Once had a mail come in—all that was written was, 'Hi, here's some fiction' accompanied by seven attachments," remembers Phaze Books' Kathryn Lively.

Contrary to popular rumor, publisher's guidelines aren't there to keep people out. They're written to keep the editorial staff sane.

> "We post on our site that we're open for two two-month periods a year now (March/April and September/October)," says Mundania Press publisher Daniel Reitz. "For Awe-Struck we're open May/June and November/December. That gives us a good flow of submissions and we can better handle everything in a timely fashion."

The amount of time the average editor has for dealing with submissions is very, very limited. It gets tucked in between editing acquired manuscripts, discussing marketing with either authors or publicity people, pitching manuscripts they love to the editorial board, and doing what editors do—make sure the book that finally comes out is a credit to both author and publisher.

At a small press, there's also bookkeeping, and the preparation of marketing materials and research and...well, you get the idea.

Publishers develop guidelines to make it as simple as possible for acquisitions departments to deal with submitted material. Often, those guidelines are long and detailed. Some people tell me they find ours reassuring. Others say they're an indication that we want total control over the author's work. In fact, all they do is make it easy for me to log in submitted samples and manuscripts then move them to the electronic devices on which I read them in as little time as possible.

The second major reason publishers write guidelines is to inform writers what kind of material they're looking for. If they don't publish poetry, ever, it's a waste of someone's time responding to a query about a chapbook. Ironically, this purpose also serves the writer, since it saves them from wasting *their* time pitching their work to publishers who are not now and never will be interested in it.

"Our submission requirements are incredibly simple, and we still get submissions that are totally wrong," says Judith B. Glad, editor at Uncial Press, which publishes romance fiction. "One man even sent us two files in Power Point. We specifically state what genres we don't take, and regularly get submissions of erotica and/or horror."

Which brings us to the first error aspiring authors make when they're ready to start submitting their work for publication: *not* reading guidelines.

Trust me when I tell you that it shows. I'm not talking about when someone sends poetry to a publisher of military history books. It can be something as simple as sending sample chapters when the guidelines state the publisher wants query only first. Maybe you've read somewhere that you should always send the sample chapters because of "bird in the hand" syndrome. That is, that the editor who gets the submission, being confronted with those chapters, will be intrigued enough to read them.

Not.

Starting your query with "I've read your guidelines carefully" is going to win you points. Following them with equal care makes you one of the cherished. This is not a bad thing when you consider the size of the competition.

KEEP IT POLITE

Publishing a book is a cooperative process. Through all the stages, it's vital that those involved be able to follow directions, because time spent repeating those directions and/or waiting for whatever was supposed to be done to be done correctly is time spent wastefully. When someone ignores instructions at the very earliest stage of the process, it sets off an alarm in the editor's head. That alarm says "If this person can't get it right now, will they be any better at it later?"

Remember: you have one book. An acquiring editor may have ten or 100. At risk of damaging fragile egos, you're just one of the crowd until you've signed a contract, and even then you'll probably be sharing your editor's attention with at least a few other people. You may be the next Hemingway or Norah Roberts, but there are only so many hours in the day; and editors have to sleep, too. The easier you make their job, the more favorably they will look on your work.

Many publishers are now accepting email queries to cut down on the piles of dead trees accumulating in their offices. Many smaller publishers *only* accept email queries, and sending one to them via surface mail might result in—nothing. If they even use your SASE to tell you to read the guidelines first next time, that's as far as you'll get.

This, however, seems to lead some aspiring authors to believe it's okay to send a query letter that reads like a note to their best bud. I have a word for you: Don't.

"If you are considering us to be your publisher, your first email should be professional as if asking for a job interview and not like you're rattling off a quick note to a friend," says LL-Publications Editor-in-Chief Zetta Brown. "We need to know that our authors understand this is a business and not a hobby for us. We're very friendly and easy to work with when you get to know us, but first impressions count."

There are those who mistake the kind of breezy tone Ms. Brown is talking about as a clever contrast to the stodgy tone of the standard query. However, to be blunt, some people aren't nearly as entertaining as they think they are. Others, I suspect, think that by composing a nifty query they're showing what great writers they are, how well they can turn a phrase. That doesn't work, either.

Re-read what Ms. Brown said above. Just because a press is small, or only publishes ebooks, does *not* make it any less a business than Random House. Being treated like a bosom pal by a stranger—and one who wants you to invest your time and money into their project, at that—is really offensive. It goes back to what I said about giving the impression the publisher was the very last choice on your list. Even if it's true, letting them know it isn't exactly diplomatic.

SIMULTANEOUS SUBMISSIONS

Now, a word about simultaneous submissions. Authors love them. Publishers don't, and for good reason.

"There was a time that we would accept these *only* if the author stated upfront that it was a simultaneous submission," notes Zetta Brown. "But after being burned more than once after showing interest in a submission only to find it was being submitted elsewhere, *and* even having one author try to get us into a bidding "war"—we won't even consider them.

Remember my point about you having one book and the editor having ten or more? Each of those multiple manuscripts belongs to a writer as eager as you are to be published. They've been waiting while the editor reads your work, spending time he or she could have used reading theirs, only to have you say when that time is gone that "Oh, I signed one."

Now, pretend you're one of those other authors.

We publishers and editors understand that wait is frustrating. Some of us are writers, too. We know that, from your viewpoint, it makes more sense to have more than one hook in the water. If you're going to sim-sub, at least keep careful track of where you've sent the manuscript (there's actually software to help with that). Then, if you sign the manuscript, *let all the other publishers know immediately!* Otherwise you risk provoking the same reaction one writer got from Wild Child Publishing's Marci Baun:

"We've had [writers] whom we've spent the time reading and requested more only to receive no response or a blithe 'Oh, it was picked up by another publisher. I'm so sorry.' Yeah, no problem. We'll just cross you off of our list of ever possibly being published with us…Being an independent press usually means fewer staff. We don't care to waste our time."

Oh, and telling me you have to do simultaneous submissions because you're 75 and don't have time to fool around isn't going to work. I have authors in their 80's who are more than willing to wait till they hear from me.

At Least Get My Gender Right

If you truly want to impress the acquiring editor, start by finding out his or her name and use it in your query. Granted, that's tough to do with large presses, but most of them want agented material anyway, as noted. For smaller presses, check *Writer's Market*, which lists the name(s) of editors and usually provides an address, phone number and/or email address.

While it might be technically correct to send your query addressed "Dear Sir or Madam" it's a dead giveaway you didn't read the guidelines, since most will include the name of the submissions editor. Only thing worse than that is addressing the query to "Dear Sir" when that name is unquestionably feminine.

"One of my pet peeves," says Karen Syed of Echelon Press, "is a query with my name spelled wrong or calling me 'sir.'"

To which I would add the ones addressed "To Whom It May Concern." If you aren't sufficiently concerned to look up the basic information about my company, why should I be concerned about your book? Hmmm?

You know what that suggests to me? Laziness. If you're too lazy to do some basic research for something as important as getting your book published, I'm inclined to think you'll be equally lazy about marketing and promoting it. Expect a "thanks, but no thanks."

"CLOSED TO SUBMISSIONS" DOESN'T MEAN "EXCEPT YOURS"

For the last year and a half, Zumaya's SF/F Otherworlds imprint has been closed to submissions. This is clearly stated in the guidelines. Nevertheless, for those entire 18 months, I have averaged three or four adult SF and/or fantasy submissions a week. Many of them begin thus: "I know you're closed to submissions, but…"

There is no "but." I'm closed. Doors are locked, lights are off, nobody's home. I have no need for new speculative fiction material until I decide I need more.

Don't let your eagerness and your belief in your work overcome common courtesy and common sense. If a publisher has stated they aren't accepting submissions, and you're wondering if that's still true rather than that somebody forgot to take it off their website, *ask*. Don't just send your query. First, it makes you look like you didn't read the guidelines, and I've already pointed out what a bad idea that is. Second, it's just rude. You're telling the owner of the business that you're more important than whatever caused them to close submissions. Nobody responds well to that sort of thing.

"Many submit outside of [our posted] dates of course," says Dan Reitz, "and generally either say they basically have such a good book that we'll want it regardless of our open submissions period (rules don't apply to them), or they haven't bothered to read the submissions at all and barely looked at our site enough to get the submissions email address.

"Those go in the trash immediately with no reply from us. We post on our guidelines this will happen to them. Guess no one believes us. What a waste."

Overblown opinion of the writer's work aside, ignoring the Closed sign on the virtual door accomplished nothing except to eliminate that individual's chances of being considered by Mundania. The thing is, with a big press such a faux pax might be forgotten. A small press, though, is like *Cheers*: everybody knows your name—and remembers how you screwed up.

What to Include in Your Query—and What Not to

If you've had a book published by AuthorHouse or PublishAmerica, don't mention it. If that book is the one you're trying to market, don't. Write another one.

All their advertising to the contrary, Authorhouse, Booksurge, Amazon CreateSpace are vanity publishing services. PublishAmerica, as has been demonstrated beyond question (cf. *Atlanta Nights*), will sign any book that isn't completely beyond redemption. Having a book printed by one of these companies is *not* a professional writing credit in the eyes of just about any regular publisher.

If you want to say you used one of these companies and sold 50,000 copies, that's different. That speaks to your marketability as an author. Anything else will have the exact opposite effect, no matter what you may have heard.

Your query should be no more than two or three paragraphs long, and should contain the following:

1. A one-sentence description of your book that states its title, genre/subject, word count and its theme. Do *not* refer to it as "a sure bestseller," "unique," or advise that it will "blow away every other book of its kind." Example: "*Dreams of Darkness* is a dark fantasy of 100,000 words with strong romantic elements that explores how people are shaped by their past."

2. A two—or three-sentence synopsis of the story. Example: "*Dreams of Darkness* is the story of two mismatched lovers who learn they are destined to face a powerful creature in order to save their world from destruction. They must do this even though they are considered outcast by those they seek to save."

3. A *brief* list of writing credentials: "I am a former journalist and currently a freelance book editor and writer. One of my short stories was a finalist in the 1999 Writers of the Future."

4. One or two sentences stating you're working on your marketing plan; "I have already begun developing a marketing plan, which will include attending SF conventions and setting up a book tour via SF/F-related blogs."

That's it. No long list of all the people who've read your manuscript and think it's the greatest thing since Cheetos. No blurbs from people the editor probably never heard of (because they're your friends and relatives).

"Everyone loves my book: don't lead your pitch with this," warns book marketing guru Penny Sansevieri of Author Marketing Experts. "In fact, my recommendation is to leave this out of your pitch altogether. The definition of 'everyone' is generally friends and family, and while we love them for being a supportive bunch, when it comes to mainstream publishing they don't really count."

That said, if the book you're pitching is nonfiction, you do need to cite your qualifications for writing it as well. Just don't send your entire *curriculum vitae*; be specific—what area of expertise do you have that means the book can be taken seriously? For fiction, however, the fact you're a lawyer doesn't mean you're the next John Grisham. So, stick to your fiction credits and leave the rest for your marketing plan.

SENDING YOUR SAMPLE

Okay, you've sent a properly written, carefully proofread query and have been asked for sample chapters. *Check the guidelines again* to be sure you remember how *that* publisher wants said sample formatted.

Do they want it done in Courier font, 10 pt., with one-inch margins and double-spaced? Do they want it single-spaced in Times New Roman, 12 pt.? Electronic or printed? Word or RTF?

No matter how much time it takes, reformat your file according to the individual publisher's requirements (c.f. making editor's life easier). If you don't know enough about your word processing software to do that...*learn*.

An aspiring author who doesn't know how to do basic formatting with his or her word processing program is like a carpenter who doesn't know how to use a hammer. A computer is not a glorified typewriter, and even though there's a learning curve to becoming skilled with the software it is *not* beyond anyone's ability. Heck, Video Professor will send you a CD free. Or spend $25 and sign up for a month of tutorials at Lynda.com. (http://www.lynda.com). Check to see if a local college is offering a class.

"I'm technically challenged" is not an acceptable reason for sending an editor a manuscript where page breaks are achieved by punching in fifty hard returns. If you don't know what a hard return is, you're already in trouble—it's what happens when you hit the return key at the end of a paragraph.

I once received a hard-copy submission, back when I still accepted them, that I really liked from a truly superb writer. I advised this person up front that we did all the pre-press work electronically. I offered a contract, and asked for a copy of the document file.

I was informed there was no document file. This writer composed a chapter, printed it out...and never saved the original. In other words, used the computer literally like a typewriter.

Okay, that's an extreme case, but there are other problems that could be resolved if the writer in question took a short course, or even bought a book on the subject. More and more, publishers are moving away from paper to electrons; those who refuse to follow will be left behind.

Learning how to use software also applies to email and other vital aspects of virtual life. I've been contacted by writers who had to be told how to attach a file. Well, actually, they weren't told—that was another "thanks, but no thanks."

If I ask for the first three chapters, never, ever send me something else. At least four or five times a year, I will ask for the first five chapters/50 pages noted in our guidelines. What I get is chapters 3, 12, 17 and 32 because the author has arbitrarily decided I won't be able to get a really good sense of how wonderful his/her book is by just reading the first few.

If I can't get a sense of (a) the quality of the book and (b) your talent and craft as a writer from the first 50 pages of your book, I don't want it. Period. Neither will anyone else.

Why?

Because when that book is published, the browsing reader will read the first page of the first chapter. About 250 words. If he or she isn't engaged by that point, they will put your book back on the shelf and go to find something better.

That's a lost sale.

Publishers exist to *sell* books, not just print them so authors can get a thrill. If that sounds harsh, so be it. If you're offended…well, that's why companies like Lulu.com exist.

Writing is a craft; publishing is a business. Unless you're an expert in that business side, it's wiser not to assume you know better than the business owner or manager what he or she needs. You don't take your tires into the tire store and ask to borrow their tools to put them on your car. At least, I hope you don't—tire irons can leave nasty bruises.

Well, the same applies here. The publisher knows what he or she needs to determine whether your work is something they want to publish and believe people will want to read. As the old country saying goes, don't teach your grandmother to suck eggs.

No, I don't have a clue what that means, either. Just follow the submission guidelines.

BITING THE HAND THAT PUBLISHES AND OTHER TOPICS

There are currently six major traditional, New York-based publishing companies, although they all have multiple imprints. There are between 70,000 and 80,000 independent presses in the US alone. To gain access to the major publishers requires an agent, adding another layer to the process of obtaining a book contract. Most independent presses accept unagented submissions. It's clear that your chances of being published by an independent press are substantially greater than your making the big time.

Insulting the independent publisher by (a) making it clear they were your last choice, (b) acting as if they exist solely for the purpose of following your orders about how your book is to be produced and/or (c) hinting that they are so desperate for material they will overlook your unprofessional behavior will substantially *reduce* those chances.

Professional credentials in a vocational or academic field do not qualify you to write fiction. Writing fiction does that. Listing your entire curriculum vitae in your query when its only connection to your novel is that the protagonist is in the same field is meaningless. What matters is whether you can make what he or she does interesting enough to keep readers turning pages. Save your resume for your next job hunt.

What the editor reading your query wants to know is what the book is about, why they should be interested in it, and what market you think it will interest. These days, that last part may be more important than the plot. With hundreds of thousands of new books coming out every year, and millions still in print, the people who will be investing time and money in your book want to know that *you* know who'll want to read it.

Suggestion: despite what you may have heard, "the people who liked [insert best-selling title here] will want to read this" isn't always the best choice for providing that information. After *The DaVinci Code* made the best-seller list (more because of notoriety than actual quality of the work), publishers scrambled the following year to come out with "the next *DaVinci Code*." At least nine other books were published with Templar themes. Know what? Most if not all of them tanked.

DON'T TELL ME HOW TO RUN MY BUSINESS

For some reason, there are a few aspiring authors who seem to mistake a small press for a subsidy one. That is, they believe that once they've signed the contract they are then free to instruct the publisher how their book is to be done. Stephanie Kelsey, editor-in-chief at Mojocastle Press is especially fond of that one.

"They inform us 'Should you accept this book, here's how I want you to format it. Oh, and I have my own cover...my best friend who just bought Poser a few months ago did it.'"

Don't. Just...don't.

A Word about Reprints

Reprints are a hard sell for several reasons. They've already been published, which means it's likely most if not all the people who *would* read it already have. It may be that it was originally published as an ebook by an independent and never really sold well. Unfortunately, if you say that, the publisher is going to wonder why it never sold well. Was it just because it was an ebook before ebooks became the latest thing? Or was it for other, less pleasant reasons?

If you're pushing a previously published book that was originally with a mainstream publisher (see previous note about AuthorHouse et al.), emphasize what you plan to do to market and promote it rather than spending a lot of time on the subject matter. That should be in your synopsis. Your goal should be to convince the editor/publisher that what you have is a neglected child that, with proper nutrition and affection, will blossom and prosper.

With a reprint, it's even more vital that you come across as a complete professional. Don't badmouth the previous publisher. Don't make excuses. Be sure you state in your initial query that all the rights to that work were returned to you and offer documentation of same.

Have Patience

We know how hard it is to wait when an editor has your manuscript and is considering it for publication. We make every effort to get back to you as soon as possible with a decision. If that seems to be taking longer than necessary, we don't object to having you contact us with a polite inquiry whether there's anything else we might need from you.

"Don't stalk your agent/publisher" warns Penny Sansevieri. "Ok, now I don't mean stalking in the sense that Lifetime is considering making a movie out of you, but I mean hounding, badgering, emailing daily, calling. You know, the super-annoying stuff that will get you blacklisted off of every agent and publisher's list. Trust me, word will spread like wildfire if you're a pain in the you-know-what. It's also the quickest way to a rejection. Follow-up is okay, burning up the phone lines or hitting your send button obsessively isn't. Keep in mind that patience will often win this race. If you have found an agent that you trust, then trust them to do their job."

TAKE NO FOR AN ANSWER

The acquisitions process is by its nature subjective. Just as readers have different tastes, so do acquiring editors. That your particular book didn't appeal to me doesn't mean someone else won't think it's the best thing they ever read.

By the same token, my company publishes in specific niches. If I read your synopsis and it doesn't seem to fit any of those, I'm not going to ask for a sample just to double-check.

So, when I tell you your books "isn't what I'm looking for" that just what I mean. Nothing more, nothing less. That applies whether I'm responding to your synopsis or a sample I may have requested.

I'm aware, as are all of the acquiring editors I know, that an answer like that isn't terribly informative. Okay, it's not the least bit informative. And when I encounter a promising manuscript that fails because of problems that can be remedied written by a writer of clear skill and talent, I will sometimes offer a critique.

However, neither I nor most editors have the time to do that for every submission we read. Worse, often our attempt to be helpful is greeted with outrage. After the third or fourth time you've tried to help someone, only to be told in response that you're obviously a witless idiot who doesn't know good writing from oatmeal and that you should stop trying to pass yourself off as someone who does…

You sort of lose incentive, you know?

"[A] good agent and/or publisher will offer you feedback on your book," notes Penny Sansevieri. "Perhaps ways to enhance/correct it. Things you might want to consider adding to make it more commercially viable.

"Listen to these comments and learn from them, then swallow your own opinions and consider incorporating them into your book. If you really have an objection that's another thing, but if pride is getting in your way then back off of the ego and see some of the points they're making as helpful and constructive. The writer sure to fail is the one who won't listen."

Conclusion

What all of this boils down to is this: if you want to be accepted as a professional writer, you have to act like one. Whether you like the rules and restrictions established by publishers is beside the point, because you flaunt them at your peril.

Refer again to what Penny Sansevieri said about agents and publishers having an informal "black list" of authors who have gained a reputation for being difficult. In any industry, those engaged in publishing know one another, and talk to one another; and being human, they may in frustration discuss with colleagues "this real nut-job who sent me a submission." If that nut-job is you, well...nuff said.

If you're convinced your manuscript is perfect and needs no editing, if you know exactly what your cover should look like and aren't willing to listen to why that idea really isn't a good choice, consider self-publishing. If your goal is to be published by someone else, then understand that it's their company, not yours. Reasonable publishers will listen to your suggestions and give them consideration, but in the end they are the ones who know their market and their business. Trying to tell them how to run it will not endear you to them.

Now is the time to decide what writing means to you. Are you eager for fame and fortune, anxious for glowing reviews and compliments from readers, and see writing and being published as the means to that end? Or do you see writing first as a profession, one that requires a very specific combination of talent and skill to do well? The choice you make will govern how you deal with the next stage of the game—publication—and with those who referee it. It will also color how you approach them, and that approach will make the difference between whether you get a shot at your fifteen minutes of fame or not.

DROPPED EYES AND UNATTACHED TENTACLES

Common and Uncommon Writing Errors

By Jane Toombs

Most writing errors, common or uncommon, are all too easy to make. So easy that I made some of them while writing this chapter. In editing what I'd written, though, I corrected the errors I made, both by using spell check and my own eyes. Spell check, while a handy and useful mechanical device, is just that—mechanical. A writer's personal editing of any manuscript is also necessary before sending it off to an editor. Always.

COMMON WORD MISTAKES TO AVOID

No matter what genre you choose to write, common little words may trip you up. Here are some you need to take charge of or they'll go astray and mess up a manuscript. You should:

Remember "it's" always means it is, and "its" means a possessive. Think apostrophe = it is, and you'll never go wrong.

Use "that" sparingly. If in doubt, read the sentence aloud without "that" and if it makes sense, delete the word. When editing a manuscript, do a search and find for the word "that" and see how many are unnecessary. Delete them.

Don't overuse inexact or unnecessary words such as very, almost, actually, really, then, just, as, seemed. Either substitute an exact word or in many cases delete the word.

Bad example: The beast had very sharp teeth.

Better: The beast opened his mouth, showing two rows of chainsaw teeth.

Bad example: The alien sun looked almost green.

Better: Pale green light shone from the alien sun.

Using then and when often mean you're telling, not showing.

Bad example: He snarled like a wild animal. Then I knew why I feared him.

Another bad one: When he snarled like a wild animal, I knew why I feared this man.

Better: Victor snarled like a wild animal, and the chilling sound froze me. .

This sentence shows the action, the others told it.

Seemed or seemed to be are greatly overused. Be specific as much as possible. If you think about what the above words mean, you realize if you're looking at a person at close range and the light is good enough to see clearly, then you know what the person does. He never "seems" to be smiling, he either is or isn't. Only if the light is too poor to see clearly or you are too far away can he "seem" to be doing something.

Another caution with words. In the United Sates, most of the "–ward" words such as forward, backward, toward and afterward do not have an "s" at the end as they do in England and some parts of the U.S., mostly the South. So don't add an "s" unless your character is from one of these areas and is speaking or doing the narrating.

Remember "till" is the substitute for until, not "'til." Occasionally an editor will question this. I had to ask one of them to look it up in her dictionary and, yes, "till" was there. "Alright" is slowly being accepted for "all right," but not by all editors. Personally I prefer "all right," even though "alright" is in many dictionaries. Another tricky one—if you don't want to write "okay," make sure you capitalize and use periods for "O.K."

DIRECTIONAL WORDS TO AVOID

People don't "get off of" anything. This is a common error you often hear in news broadcasts. Don't be guilty of making it. You step off a bus. You jump off a stool. You ask folks you don't want coming around to get off your porch. "Off" needs no help, so remember not to burden it with "of."

Up and down are directional words we tend to use without thinking. Jenny stood up. Jenny sat down. Think about it. If Jenny stood, she's on her feet, so "up" is redundant. Jenny sat in the chair. We don't need "down" to tell us she's sitting there. Other directionals are across and over to.

> Bad example: Jenny went across the room to the door. Or: Jenny went over to the door. These sentences are both boring and passive because of word choice.

> Better: Jenny sauntered to the door. Or: She hurried to the door. Even: Jenny crossed to the door.

Crossed, though, is not a demonstration of how she walked, so a more active verb is better. . This way we understand whether she's eager to get there or not. There is no reason for "across the room" because we presumably know where she was when she started for the door.

> Bad example: The vampire walked over to his coffin and climbed into it.

> Better: The vampire glided to his coffin and slithered in.

WEAK WORDS

"It" and thing" are two of the most common weak words we overuse. As writers, we can't rid ourselves of these two words entirely, but don't be guilty of overuse. The easiest way to cure yourself of too many "its" and "things," is to do a search and find when you finish your manuscript or whenever you edit. Each time you come to one or the other of these words, stop and read the sentence. Ask yourself what the "it" stands for. If you can find a better word to use instead, do so. As for "thing," only if the object is unknown to the character is it a thing. Otherwise, pick a word that represents the "thing."

Why do your best to avoid using the words I've mentioned so far? Because they lead to flaccid writing, and flaccid writing bores readers. Your writing should sparkle with verve. Be lively. Give a sense the events taking place are moving the story along at an interesting, even exciting, pace.

In addition to the weak words I've already discussed, others include: caused, made, put, went, feel, feeling, felt, wore, could, would, like, when, which, and while. Why are they weak? Because all of them are used to tell rather than show. This doesn't mean you never should use them, in many cases you will have to, especially in dialogue. Do watch for them in your manuscript and be sure you haven't used any of them where they weren't necessary.

> Bad example: He put his hand on the werewolf's head and got snapped at.

> Better: He patted the werewolf's head and barely escaped losing his hand.

WRONG WORD USAGE

A frequent mistake is making an error in what you mean by wrong word usage. Affect/effect is a combination often misused. Try memorizing this sentence to remember which is which: The effect of sunshine glaring off snow affects my vision. Two more correct usages:

> Example: The effect of sun on human skin is both beneficial and harmful. Your skin can be adversely affected by the sun.

From this you note that an object or action creates an effect while objects or actions are affected by the creating.

If you're not completely sure of the meaning of a word, don't use it until you've consulted a dictionary. Remember that a thesaurus does not necessarily give you exact meanings of words, so don't substitute without looking up your choice in the dictionary as well.

Many words such as adverse/averse have very different meanings. Always be sure of the meaning of every word you use, including those tricky words that sound the same but have different meanings such as peak, peek and pique. You may know exactly what the word means and still type it wrong. Often, this is what causes the wrong usage. Be alert when you edit for any such typo, because spell-check will not catch it. Which, as I said in the beginning, is a good reason to go over a manuscript more than once. Reading it aloud may help you see the misspellings. You will also catch errors such as "own," when you meant to type "won."

ERRORS SPECIFIC TO FANTASY GENRES

Most authors know by now that garlic doesn't affect shapeshifters, while the full moon has no effect on vampires. Writers venturing into any of the fantasy genres should familiarize themselves with the lore many fictional un-human creatures have accumulated over the years. Warning: This cannot be done by reading the latest vampire or shapeshifter novel, or watching a current Buffy-type TV series. You should be familiar with the old classics such as Bram Stoker's *Dracula* and some of the early shapeshifter books and movies.

I don't mean you will need to use any part of what's in these classics, but you should be aware of what they contain. Today writers freely depart from what used-to-be and you are free to do the same. It helps to know what these books or movies were about. If you were setting your story in historical times, you'd certainly do research to avoid anachronisms. This is not exactly the same, but similar.

Other classic authors in these genres are H.P. Lovecraft and A. Merritt. It's always best to know what's been done, and done well, before you begin your story. As for science fiction, George S. Elrick has written, in his *Science Fiction Handbook*, definitions for almost every word you can think of that's been used in this variation of the genre. This book could help prevent errors you might otherwise make.

In the same way, Stanley Schmidt's *Aliens and Alien Societies* will help any writer avoid major errors in creating believable and anatomically correct extraterrestrial life-forms. As a starter he tells you exactly why giant ants are impossible.

HOW TO AVOID UNATTACHED BODY PARTS

Hands, arms, fingers and eyes, not to mention tentacles and other alien creature parts, all belong attached to a tangible body. Which is not to say you can't have an unhuman creature able to throw off a certain part of itself to capture someone or to escape being captured. As a writer, you must be fair and allow readers to be aware this can happen. Assuming your unhuman can't do this, its parts should stay attached, none of them being able to act on their own.

Bad example: A hand touched Jenny's neck.

If Jenny is facing the person who touched her and since she can see that person, then: His hand touched Jenny's neck. If not a male, then her or its hand touched Jenny's neck. Only if it's dark or if the person is behind her and thus unseen, can "a hand" do the touching. Why? Because if the hand is attached to the visible body, then Jenny can see what manner of creature it belongs to, and it's no longer anonymous. Of course, an exception could be an invisible ghost's hand. In that case Jenny might only feel a touch and not necessarily know it was a hand.

Better: Jenny knew that fearsome man stalked her when his hand gripped her neck.

Speaking of ghosts, here we have intangible creatures that either may appear to be human or animal or may be wispy blobs. Whether or not they can send a part of their intangible selves to touch a human is up to the author.

In real life inanimate objects do not move by themselves.

Bad example: Boots pounded on the pavement.

Boots are normally attached to someone's feet, so only if the hearer is in a windowless room, unable to see out, are they unattached boots. Otherwise his, her or its boots did the pounding.

Better: Boots pounded on the pavement and Jenny knew the monster in cowboy boots was all too close behind her.

Human eyes remain attached to the head except in the case of serious injuries. Eyes cannot literally drop anywhere. Nor can they move from the seer's head at all.

Impossible example: Jenny's blue eyes fastened on Mike's green ones and clung there.

Double error if wealready know the color of Jenny's and/or Mike's wandering eyes. First error: Don't keep repeating eye color of the main characters more than two or three times. Second error: Jenny is now eyeless and poor Mike has a second pair of eyes stuck to his. A gaze can wander or drop to the floor, but not eyes.

Body parts also stay affixed to the creature they belong to.

Bad example: To Jenny's horror a tentacle encircled her neck.

Again, if she can see the creature, she knows where the tentacle came from.

Better: As Jenny leaned over the side of the boat, to her horror an octopus surfaced and wrapped one of its tentacles around her neck.

Or: A tentacled monster burst from the alien pond. Before Jenny could run, one of its tentacles grabbed her by the neck.

How to Spot and Fix Vague and Flaccid Writing

What's wrong with these sentences?

Jenny picked up her iPod to text Mike.

Mike dropped the newspaper and reached to pick it up.

Vagueness. I hope you noted they both picked up or reached to do something, but the sentence left it unclear if any other action occurred. Did Jenny text Mike? Did Mike ever get the newspaper in his hands" What happens if we use "and' instead of "to?"

Jenny picked up her iPod and texted Mike.

Mike picked up the dropped newspaper and turned to the comics.

Actions completed. Don't allow your characters start to, or reach to do something unless they're going to be interrupted in completing the action:

Jenny picked up her iPod to text Mike, but the shriek of the fire alarm stopped her.

Mike dropped the newspaper and reached to pick it up, but the puppy got there first.

Saw, watched and heard tend to be distancing words and are often unnecessary. The same goes for noted and noticed. Don't have your characters watching and hearing or noticing unless you must for a plot point, which rarely occurs.

Bad example: Jenny watched the dark clouds roll in.

Better: The dark clouds threatened rain. Or: Jenny kept assessing the dark clouds to the west.

Bad example: Jenny heard a sound so weird she shivered.

Better: A weird noise tensed Jenny for action.

Bad example: Mike noticed a branch was broken in the tall pine.

Better: The broken branch in the old pine troubled Mike.

Or: Mike knew that broken branch plus a windstorm equaled a shattered window.

In these three examples, by removing watched, heard, and noticed we enlivened the writing. If the focus is on a main character, we're in his or her point of view, This assures the reader knows who is doing the seeing and hearing. By not relying on saw or watched or heard, as authors we're forced to used more exact words, thereby painting a more vivid picture.

Telling also distances the reader from the action, while showing involves the reader with the action. Especially so if the telling uses any form of "to be," with "was" being the worst, especially when paired with an "-ing" word.

Bad example: Carol was going to the store when the car hit her.

Better: Carol stepped off the curb, earplugs booming rap, and missed the screech of the Volvo's brakes.

Or: Intent on the hot biker mounting his hog, Carol stepped off the curb, no part of her attention on traffic.

Bad example: Rick came back with the strangest little animal Carol had ever seen.

Better: To Carol's consternation, Rick returned to camp with an alien animal perched on his shoulder and chattering into his ear.

The difference in showing instead of telling is delivering the same information as in a tell, while also painting a picture in words of what's going on.

FAULTY SEQUENCES

Sol Stein, in his *How To Grow A Novel*, introduced me to paying attention to faulty sequences and revising. He says the most common mistake he finds in editing manuscripts are words, phrases, clauses, sentences and paragraphs in the wrong order. Sometimes conjunctions such as "and" or "but" or commas make writers guilty of this error.

Bad example: Nick looked up into the tree, and his dog yelped in pain.

Better: While Nick's attention was glued to the tree, his dog yelped in pain. Or: His dog's yelps of pain made Nick look away from the tree to find out what was wrong.

Bad example: Mary brushed her hair, Rick tried the engine again.

Better: Ignoring Rick's efforts to start the engine, Mary brushed her hair.

No connection between Mary and Rick in the bad sentence example, but in the better one, we've connected to two actions.

Other examples of out-of-sequence writing tend to involve either place or time or both.

Bad example: Rick needed to meet with Mike to discuss their project at the library.

As written, the project they need to discuss is about the library. If that's not the case, then this is out-of-sequence.

Better: Rick needed to meet Mike at the library so they could discuss their rocket project.

This makes it clear that the library is a meeting place and not involved in the project.

Bad example: Just as Rick shifted into a wolf, Mary used the taser.

Better: Mary tasered Rick, hoping she was in time to block his shapeshift.

Now the reader understands why the action was performed when it was.

Out-of-sequences happen in paragraphs and longer passages as well. When rereading your work, look for paragraphs out of place, needing to come before the preceding one.

> Bad example: When Doctor Bently returned her second call and chewed her out for questioning him, Mary was shocked, She'd been so certain Doctor Bently never made a mistake. But the order he'd given her over the phone for Mrs. Carter was just plain crazy, considering the patient's condition. Figuring she'd heard him wrong, she'd called him back. Now she didn't know what to do next.

> Better: Charge nurse Mary Cox called Mrs. Carter's doctor to report the patient's increased chest pain. Doctor Bently was Mary's favorite staff doctor, one she felt never made a mistake. She took down his order carefully, but when the call ended, she reread the order and shook her head. Either he'd misunderstood her, or she'd misheard his order, because this was not a drug for chest pain—or for pain anywhere. Nor for any type of respiratory distress. Best to call back right away.

> "Are you questioning my judgment?" Doctor Bently demanded, his harsh tone slicing into her explanation..

> "No, I merely I thought you might have misunderstood about the chest—"

> He cut her off again, snapped out the same order Mary had taken down earlier and clicked off.

> Upset, Mary stared down at what she was sure was an inappropriate medication order. What now?

Note the difference in the two examples. The first is completely out of sequence, skipping back and forth from what's happening to what had happened and back. The second one leads the reader through the sequence in the order it happened. Don't be guilty of bad sequences.

Another out of sequence error is the dangling participle. "—ing" words are participles and a writer must be careful not to let them dangle in the wrong place. .

> Bad example: Rick met Carol wearing his new boots.

> Better: Rick wore his new boots to meet Carol.

You don't want to mean Carol is wearing Rick's boots.

Bad example: While sauntering down the street, the air raid siren shrieked, startling Rick.

Better: Rick sauntered down the street, freezing in place when the air raid siren shrieked.

We all know air raid sirens can't saunter anywhere.

TIGHTENING YOUR WRITING

All writers need to be sure we we're not guilty of redundancy. Earlier I mentioned directional words like having Mary sit in a chair, not sit down in it. In that case, "down" is a redundant word.

Bad example: Karen's heart pounded in her chest and she felt weak.

Better: Karen's heart pounded and her knees wobbled.

Why remove "in her chest?" Because where else is a human heart? Also "she felt weak" is too vague.

As for aliens, of course they may keep their hearts elsewhere.

Bad example: Karen gasped at the unearthly creature morphing in front of her out of thin air.

Better: Karen gasped at the unearthly creature morphing in front of her.

"Out of thin air" is a redundancy, besides being a cliché.

Clichés can be considered as redundancies because writers so often use them this way. Consider how many times a skinny person is referred to with the cliche "Thin as a rail." These familiar phrases pop into our heads easily, so, as writers we sometimes don't realize how many we use. People tend to use them in conversation, so an occasional cliché in dialogue is okay. Most of them tend to be similes, like "cold as ice" or "hot as hell.'

A warning here: Try not to be so original when creating a simile that the reader has to stop to try to figure it out. Any time a reader stops, he or she may not go on with your story. Original is fine, but make your similes easy to understand.

Other instances where writing needs to be tightened: when patches of purple prose crop up or when too many words are devoted to insignificant minor characters. When, unnecessary garlands of description laden the manuscript, or too much chit-chat that doesn't move the plot or reveal character. In short, when useless scenes or lengthy patches of unneeded information clutter a manuscript, tighten by elimination.

> **Bad example:** "I would have called you earlier, Mary, but the plumber showed up. Then the dog begged to go out and I couldn't just let him run, 'cause we've already had one warning. So I had to walk him and that took ages—thought he'd never go. Before I got home that nosy neighbor I told you about waylaid me and complained about Rocky's band practicing in the garage last Saturday. And then it was lunchtime so I couldn't give you a ring until now."

Chances are none of this chit-chat is relevant to the story line.

> **Better:** "I'm sorry I haven't had time to call you until now, Mary."

Unless the phone call is a plot point, simply omit it altogether.

Purple prose is usually overly-detailed description that is not necessary to your story, but it can be an unnecessary wordy action scene. Action needs tight, vivid words to show what's happening.

Just as you don't allow secondary characters to take over your plot, you can't allow insignificant minor characters in your story to take a center role by too much description of them.

Using the S&S principle (Succinct and Specific) as you edit your work makes it easier to spot these weedy patches. Succinct means brief, with every word painting a concise picture, Specific applies to word choice, to selecting vivid words to create the images you seek to show. S&S helps a writer avoid long, involved sentences loaded with modifiers. That type of sentence is not reader-friendly and slows pacing.

> **Bad example:** The mail-carrier is all bundled-up today. He's a lanky man, but looks positively stout in all those layers of clothes. And is his nose ever red!

> **Better:** If the mail-carrier is that bundled-up, I'd better put on my winter coat.

If the mail carrier isn't needed for a plot point, leave him out entirely.

Sometimes writers feel this type of description lends "local color" to a story. Local color is a detail added here and there that gives a sense of a real place to your story setting. It's not lengthy descriptions of minor characters who play no important part in your story.

One more caution here. Note the "!" in the above bad example. The overuse of exclamation points makes the reader feel the writer is shouting at him. Try to have characters act in a way that shows how they feel instead. When you do feel an exclamation point is truly necessary, never to do this: !!! Exclamation points lead solitary lives—they're always single.

EXCESS USE OF MODIFIERS

Watch the use of modifiers—adverbs and adjectives. Avoid the bad habit of overuse. All writers want readers to have a picture of the people and the setting in their stories, but loading sentences with modifiers is not the way to paint that desirable word picture.

Bad example: Michelle had long, curly, waist-length golden hair.

Better: Michelle's hair flowed like a golden shower over her shoulders to curl at her waist.

Now the reader has a more vivid picture of Michelle. I used an active verb and a simile to do this rather than piling on modifiers.

Be stingy with modifiers. Find other ways to describe people and places.

One more caution about redundancy. Try not to repeat information you've already given the reader. If you've described the salient characteristics of your main characters, don't keep hammering at them that he's "a bear of a man" with dark chocolate eyes. You might slip one or the other of these characteristics in fairly early maybe twice more, in a non-obtrusive way. No more mention of them is necessary. Readers by now have formed a picture of the man. Reminding them becomes annoying.

Please keep your own record of your main characters' eye and hair color, so you won't change it amidships. Secondary characters, too.

Don't repeat the same information over and over. If the reader already knows what has happened to a character, don't have that character repeating it to another character. Assuming the reader has already been shown what happened to Marsha, something like this works fine: Marsha told Arthur what befell her last night after he left.

POINT OF VIEW ERRORS, INCLUDING AUTHOR INTRUSION

This not a text on point of view. Every writer should master the understanding and usage of first person, second person and both limited and omniscient third person.

Each viewpoint has benefits and restrictions but be advised that some publishers will not buy first person manuscripts. All writers should also understand the meaning of head-hopping. If you don't know much about any of this, consult a book or article about point of view and head-hopping.

Third-person limited is what most authors of genre books use. Limited does not mean you can only allow one character's point of view. It does mean only one character at a time should have a viewpoint in a single scene, unless you're very skilled at knowing how and when it works to switch back and forth. If you're not sure how, don't do it. Period. You'll wind up head-hopping , thus annoying editors.

Usually only your main characters, meaning hero, heroine and villain, should be allowed to have their own viewpoint in genre books. All the other characters and incidents should be viewed from the point of view of these three characters. Minor characters, therefore, cannot be allowed to think anything, because thoughts are in a character's point of view. They can speak, if necessary, even state what they're thinking, but that's all.

Unless you're telling a story strictly from an animal's viewpoint, please do not allow any animal in your story to have thoughts about what's going on. An exception might be an animal who is a main character in a fantasy story Shapeshifters can either be unaware of their human side when shifted, or aware. If unaware, then they have only animal thoughts. If aware, then they can also think like a human, though unable to speak like one at the moment.

Mind to mind communication in paranormal and fantasy stories is always permissible. Publishers vary on how they prefer mind transmission done. Usually italics are acceptable. Of course, in fantasy stories, sometimes animals can speak, which is entirely different.

While you can always write in first person, remember when you do, only the viewpoint character can have thoughts. This character must base any actions on what others say or do, on their body language and facial expressions. First person can make it more difficult to tell a story, but it also leaves readers right with the viewpoint character since they have to base their interpretation on the same clues the viewpoint person has. This can be effective in suspense, as gothics have proven.

Never have a main character preach on any subject. While you may feel deeply about some subjects, remember readers have varying opinions, and even if they may agree with you, they don't like to be preached at. So stay off soap-boxes. While it's not author intrusion, per se, it really is a sneaky variation of it. Save any preaching on any subject for non-fiction. Terry Goodkind's *Faith of the Fallen* is a good example of why this is bad. Over 600 pages of why he disagrees with socialism isn't just preaching, it's browbeating.

What is overt author intrusion? Any time you, as the author, insert a comment which none of the characters could possibly know, that's author intrusion. In the old days, books, especially gothics, might have a sentence such as this: "Little did Georgiana realize what she'd seen had been real and that she would suffer later because she told no one." The author stepped in here to warn the reader evil waited ahead.

Today you may still see author intrusion examples. Any time a comment pops into view that no character in the story could predict or a comment is made without anyone in the story making it, that's where the author has intruded. Don't be tempted to do something like the following: As a reader, you've learned that Mary and Kate are both in love with Frank. An example of author intrusion might be a sentence like this: "The problem was, neither Kate nor Mary knew Frank was already married." If some character should say this to another character, that's okay, but the author must not say it.

We've all read stories beginning with a main character being described. If this is done without another character observing, that's technically author intrusion, but it's the kind most editors overlook. Still, why do it that way? You write: "A tall, tanned man strode into the room, his dark eyes assessing those already present." Author intrusion? No, not if you add: "Sarah waited until his gaze reached her and stuck out her tongue at him." Because now we're in Sarah's viewpoint as he strides in, so she sees what he looks like and what he's doing.

Just because best-selling mainstream authors sometimes get away with all of this doesn't mean you will. Not unless you become one of them, anyway.

Back to switching point of view in a single scene. Some publishers don't mind this if done right, others have rules about keeping to a single viewpoint per scene. I know it's tempting to show both viewpoints in a sex scene (or in erotica, perhaps three or four), but that tends to become confusing to the reader if done poorly. You can have the hero's point of view in one, then the heroine's the next time they make love. My advice for fairly new writers to is stick to the one viewpoint per scene until you're a more seasoned writer.

DON'T USE RESEARCH AS PADDING

You've done a ton of research for your book and found much of what you've learned fascinating. Great, but don't put too much of what fascinated you into your story. Why? Because you risk slowing the pacing down to a crawl. Never clog the action with research details. Always keep in mind you've done your research so you can drop dribs and drabs of it into the story to make readers feel they're right there in the midst of, say, the War of 1812 along with the characters. Readers are not interested in a complete recounting of the war. They want to experience the battle and its consequences through the character's eyes, but not in overwhelming detail.

Put in enough so readers get the feel of whatever craft your main characters are interested in, but not every last detail, but no more. Use the research you did deftly, so you keep bits and pieces of the period correct, but not to show off all you've learned.

Never waste research. Think about writing a second story with a different slant, using the same research. After I researched the War of 1812 for a book set in Louisiana where I featured the Battle of New Orleans, I used the same war in an entirely different story set in the Great Lakes area. During that war, the British and the Americans fought to control the fort at Mackinac Island.

Example from *Creole Betrayal*:

Cheers went up, signaling General Jackson's appearance, and the American band burst into "Hail Columbia." The soldiers stood at attention, ready to march as soon as he reached the stand. As the notes died away, the Creole band began "Le Chant Du Depart." Suddenly a fearsome hiss sliced through the music.

"British rocket!" a man cried.

Jurissa and Tiana clutched one another as the rocket exploded in a crashing burst overhead. Confusion reigned as women screamed, men shouted, horses panicked and soldiers broke ranks.

I used details of the research I'd done to paint a picture of the beginning of the British attack in New Orleans. Jurissa is one of the main characters in the story. She needed to be present as a plot point, so the scene is in her viewpoint. Practically all of New Orleans turned out to await General Jackson's arrival, women included. This made her presence there logical. We stay in her point of view as she watches and experiences all this.

In *Snow Flower* I used a vision dream the heroine, an Anishinabe medicine woman, had of her lover, an English lord, fighting with the British as they attempted to overrun the fort at Mackinac Island and recover it for England. In this vision, she sees the fighting on the island and her lover wounded while saving another man. It's a very different picture, but the details in the vision are taken from the research I did about the War of 1812 on the island.

Putting too much research material into a story makes you guilty of padding. Whenever you write more than what's necessary to move the plot along, it becomes padding. Unnecessary chit-chat between characters which doesn't have a plot purpose or isn't to show character development, is also padding. Long garlands of description that go far beyond giving the reader a picture of the setting—that's padding, too. Unnecessary scenes that do not move the action along—padding. Don't do it. Padding bores readers.

WHERE ARE YOUR CHARACTERS?

Always keep track of where you've left your characters. If you've left a hero in California at the end of one chapter, don't have him in New York at the beginning of the next unless you have a transition sentence either at the end of the last chapter—John is booking a flight to New York, for example. Or you begin the next chapter with a transition that lets the reader know John is now in New York, having been suddenly been summoned there on a secret mission.

I inadvertently screwed up recently. In *The Flame*, set in Virginia City Nevada, I thought I'd left the heroine on a hillside. Instead, I'd brought her back to the cabin. So a few pages later, when she watches from the hill as the hero rides toward her, the editor's note asked : "How and when did she get there?" I'd done the unforgivable—lost track of my heroine. Don't be guilty of doing this.

Which leads to talking heads. When characters talk to each other, they aren't doing so in a vacuum. You need to show where they are while they're conversing. No need for a lot of detail, but remember to locate them someplace. The reader also needs to know, if you haven't already made it clear, approximately what time of the day or night it is.

This goes for all action in your manuscript—set each scene somewhere. Let the reader know if indoors or outdoors, day or night. If outdoors, what's the weather like? Remember characters, as well as action, are always in a certain place at a certain time, and readers need to know this.

If you're writing a fantasy set in another world, this is even more important. Because the setting is alien to readers, you need to be careful to always keep them aware of where your characters are, or the action is, and how your world may affect them in ways our familiar world might not.

Different time periods also affect and influence your characters in ways today might not. When researching, note the mores and manners of whatever your era is, how they spoke and the clothes they wore. Keep your characters more or less within these guidelines to avoid having them become an anachronism themselves—but don't make them wimpy. Remember, though, society was far more rigid in many of the time periods than it is today.

If you're setting a paranormal in the past, you need to do as much research as for any story set in another era. Though your character may be anything but a norm of the time, as a human he would have to appear to fit in.

DON'T LET DIALOGUE TRIP YOU UP

Men and women do not speak the same, so don't allow them to in your story. Men tend not to ask questions unless they actually need to have an answer. They tend to make assumptions. Women are more likely than men to ask someone if they want to do this or that.

Man: "Let's go see that new movie tonight."

Woman: "Want to go see that new movie tonight?"

This is not written in concrete as not all men are the same, just as no women are. As a general rule, men speak more tersely than women, and tend to answer questions with a yes or no. Women often answer a question explaining why their answer is yes or no. They might say, when asked if they want to watch a TV show, "I guess I could tonight, because I don't have any meetings to go to." Most men expect a yes or no answer and they really don't understand this tendency in women.

Roles are changing as more women become top dogs in their areas of expertise. Some women, depending on what they do, may speak more like men but, being women, they still differ. Older people don't talk like teenagers. A doctor may not talk the way a plumber might. And all regions have different ways of saying things.

Someone not from the South may not realize they're being insulted when a Southern acquaintance says, "Why, bless your heart, wherever did you get that hat?" Or women not from certain of the Midwestern states, may not take it well when a Midwestern gal says to a group of them, "Hey, guys, let's go out for a pizza."

I remember as a teenager being confused by a new acquaintance who asked me to "wait on her" after school. Meaning, "wait for her," but I had never heard that way of saying it before and I took several moments to understand.

Dialect is common in some groups. Words like gonna, wanna, gotta are what many people actually say. Another common one is 'cause, for because. When to use these spellings and when not to has to be the writer's decision. Other people still use ain't in speech, though they wouldn't in writing. Listen to the way people around you talk. The differences are fascinating. Ultimately you, the writer, must make up your mind what to use and when.

Brogues and other differences in speech patterns are best suggested by using only a few of the odd words to give the flavor of how that character talks. Readers dislike being confronted by too many odd words too often. As for leaving the "g" off "-ing" words, I finally formed my own rule. If the character who does this is a minor one and doesn't appear too often, I drop the "g." If he's going to be doing a lot of talking in the story I might use gonna and so forth, but leave the "g" intact. I have this theory readers get tired of seeing the apostrophe at the end of a word too many times. I know I do.

Punctuation in dialogue is simple as soon as a writer discards laughed, snickered, hissed, grunted, moaned and so forth as substitutes for said. Once you've tried out loud to laugh or grunt a sentence, you understand why not to use words such as those. I suppose you could hiss "Slimy snake," if you wanted to call someone that because those words begin with "s." Or maybe moan, "Help me." In general, though, stick to said or find other ways to not use any word at all,

Wrong: " He's such a nut," Jerry laughed.

Right: Jerry laughed. "He's such a nut."

Since you can't laugh a sentence, this is the right way to punctuate.

Wrong: "I feel awful today," she moaned.

Right: "I feel awful today." She moaned.

Note the period instead of a comma in these examples.

In a sequence of conversation, you can get away with rarely using "said." At the same time, if you pepper the sequence with "Jerry frowned" and "She raised an eyebrow" instead of "saids," you can annoy the reader.

Here's a sequence from *Dance Of The Cedar Cat*. To give you a bit of background, Sussie works at the local hospital. She lives alone and has been hearing caterwauling at night outside her cottage near the lake.

It doesn't sound like any animal she's ever heard, and worse, she feels whatever's out there is calling her to join him. As this sequence begins, she's come to a hospital party at a local restaurant:

"Sussie!" She turned to see Ginny, one of the girls from the office. "You did come, after all. Great, grab a drink and join us."

Sussie waved and made her way to the bar. Before she had a chance to order, a man spoke from behind her. "I've been waiting for you."

She knew who he was before she turned and stared into Doctor Petrovich's amber eyes, heart hammering all over again, feeling like the deer she'd missed hitting as she drove in to the party. Though she'd seen him occasionally at the hospital, they hadn't spoken since their introduction.

He carried a glass of clear liquid in one hand. "What do you want to drink?" he asked.

"Tonic water," she told him. Alcohol, even beer, just plain didn't agree with her.

He smiled, and she wondered if he had any idea just how devastating his smile was.

"Two hearts that beat as one," he murmured, and gave the bartender her order.

She glanced again at the drink he carried. "Yours is tonic water, too?"

He shrugged. "Best hangover prevention I know of. Shall we find a table before the mad rush begins?" Without waiting for her to agree, he put his hand on her back, and urged her gently toward the dining room.

His hand was warm through the light cotton of her dress, but she had to control a shiver.

"Doctor," she began. "I think the tables "

"Are set up more or less by rank? You're right, but I've taken care of that. And it's Volan, not doctor, Sussie."

Volan. She'd wondered what his first name was. He was listed as V.R. Petrovich on the sign at the clinic office.

"I don't think I've ever met anyone with that name before," she said as he seated her at one of the smaller tables—for four. Sure enough, both their name cards were there, with two others for Fred and Nona Peters who hadn't yet arrived.

He sat next to her. "Great. That makes me your very first Volan. Only fair, since you're my first Sussie. Is that a nickname?"

"No, not quite. Though it's not the actual Finnish word for cat, the Finns often name a favorite cat Sussie. Does your name have any significance?"

"Volan was my mother's maiden name. Like my father, she's Russian. And you must be Finnish."

When she nodded, he said, "In the past, the Russians and the Finns were enemies. Luckily we're both Americans, so we can be friends." There was no question in his voice, but she thought she saw one in his eyes, now golden in the flickering candle light.

She hesitated, the look in his eyes making her wonder exactly what she was committing herself to. So she equivocated. "I'm certainly not your enemy."

He offered her a wry smile. "Wary as a cat, too, aren't you? But here we are at the same table this evening, by coincidence."

"You moved the tags."

"Yes, but the coincidence is this was the only table with a vacancy and, since Doctor Miles told me he'd be in town this weekend, I took the liberty of inviting him to tonight's gala. Obviously he should sit at the head table, so I gave up my place of honor there." He grinned.

Note the "saids" in this sequence are very few. A reader would hardly notice them. Which is true of the word. Unless every single character has "said" after he speaks, readers glide right over the word because it's so familiar. Other tags might not be. I'm sure you noticed no one spoke with an adverb modifying the tag. Try to make your characters' body language and facial expressions add to the meaning of the words they speak, instead of shoving adverbs in the reader's face to convey the meaning.

Even though you've studied comma usage and are sure you're right, you may find some publishers have different rules for comma use than those you were taught. Don't argue, do it their way as long as you're writing for them. Some publishers like semi-colons, others hate them. I'm not a great semi-colon user, but if an editor wants me to put one in, I don't argue. All publishers agree that readers don't like long paragraphs, so watch the length of yours as you write.

Setting the Stage—Beginnings

Have you started in the middle of some kind of action? Sometimes, you need to. Readers must connect very soon with your hero and heroine to become interested in what's happening to them. Something should either be happening to one or both of them or it's obvious something will soon.

Never put backstory at the beginning. Backstory is fill-in-later stuff and should be treated that way. Action of some kind must begin the book.

Does the reader know by the second page where the story is taking place? The setting should be put in as soon as possible. Not in a chunk, but dribbled in unobtrusively. Setting includes at least a glimmer of what year it is. As far as location is concerned, don't think local landmarks count. Unless the landmark is as well known as the Sierras or The Gulf of Mexico, someone in another state or country won't have any idea what you mean when you choose a local landmark in an effort to let readers know where the story is taking place.

Does the reader know whether your character is inside or out, whether it's the dead of a northern winter or a hot Texas summer? They need to.

Does the character you open the story with come across as likeable? She or he may be cross or angry as the story starts, but something about them should appeal to readers or they won't get hooked.

Don't feel you must describe the main characters down to the nth degree as the book opens. One or two identifying characteristics somewhere in the first few pages are enough. Even eye and hair color need not be told immediately.

Please don't have the heroine running her hand through her long, blond hair. If you run a hand through your hair, do you think what color it is as you do so? Neither should she. Physical characteristics should come out in the first chapter, but they don't need to be in the first paragraph.

Is the beginning easy to understand? Try not to confuse readers at the start. They don't need to know what's going to happen, but the set-up for what may happen should be simple enough to lure them into the story. Every time a reader stops to think, you risk losing him or her.

Don't use a prologue unless your story absolutely needs one. An example would be what happened to an ancestor in the long ago past is about to affect one of your main characters in today's world. Most prologues by inexperienced writers are full of backstory and are not necessary. Worse, they may turn off the reader, who doesn't need to know backstory at the beginning of the book. Backstory is best dribbled into your story whenever something arises which makes an action from the past significant and which might determine how a main character handles the present situation.

READY YO EDIT

I'm not going to tell you exactly how to do it, because some writers prefer one method, others prefer another. Should you read the story out loud? Should you use a spell-check first? Should you read through it from the beginning, correcting everything you see? None of these methods are wrong. You need to find the one, or the combo, best suited to your needs. I'll suggest what to watch out for, and remind you how I edit and why I do it that way. Pick and choose until you find a method that works best for you. I'm grouping together much of what I've already discussed in the chapter that you need to look for on the read through. You may prefer to go all the way through with each point, rather than do so many at once as you go. Whatever works the best for you, is the right way for you. Save every time you stop correcting for the day. Use the corrected ms. to work on the next day—and so forth.

Start with the spell-check to correct misspelled words. Save.

Using the saved manuscript, consult your list of weak words and do a search and find them one at a time. Stop every time one shows up and see if you can't find a better way to revise the sentence. This part will take you some time as you look carefully at all your weak words, one at a time, and decide whether the sentences containing them could be stronger. Save.

Now begin at the beginning of the saved manuscript and read through slowly. You will be checking for awkward sentences, places where you've told instead of shown, always remembering sometimes you do have to tell. Make sure all body parts are attached to a body, check dialogue to make sure nothing has been laughed or snorted. Watch for out-of-sequence sentences or paragraphs and change. Do your characters always know where they are? How about point of view—have you head hopped? Notice any passages that drag, perhaps due to padding, and tighten them. Check for overuse of adverbs and replace with active verbs if possible. Save.

Have you introduced an element in the story that you've failed to solve before the book ends? If so, you've left loose ends dangling and this needs to be fixed. If there's a villain has he, she or it been taken care of in a believable way? Has the mystery, if there is one, been solved before the final clinch—if there is one? Save.

Have you preached by doing it through a main character? Take it out. Used purple prose? Revise drastically. Save.

Does your writing seems alive and vivid? This is a hard one, because by now you're so tired of going over this book you may have trouble judging. Give it a shot and save.

Once all this is finished, don't look at this last saved manuscript for at least a week. If you're pressed for time, let as many days as you can afford to go by. Then start from the beginning again and go through as carefully as you can stand to do, looking for anything you may have missed. Especially check for passages that could be improved by livelier writing. Maybe they need more show and less tell.

Okay, one last spell check and you're done. Save as your final. Your work is ready to send out into the cruel world of publishing whether by an insert on an email or printed to be mailed.

I didn't include asking someone you trust, who is also a writer or editor, to read your edited manuscript and offer a critique. If you know someone willing to do this, by all means ask them to. They usually will find ways to improve it. If someone does read, always make a final check for yourself.

I mentioned reading aloud but didn't add it to the list. Many of my writer friends find this helps them pick up errors they might otherwise miss. By all means try it and see if it helps you.

Now you've finished with your book and it's ready to go. Because of this, the next book you write will be better. Always finish what you begin. You learn so much in the process.

How I edit, is to first do the spell check, then start from the beginning and do what I mentioned above all at once as I go through the manuscript. Because I have eighty plus books to my credit and a slew of novellas and short stories, I've learned a bit about editing over the years. It does come easier as you gain experience.

Never forget you learn more about writing by finishing everything you start. Even though a few years may go by between Chapter 1 and The End, I always finish every story I begin. It's never too late to go back and finish what you started ages ago. You may be surprised how much you've learned in the interim.

EXERCISES

Determine what's wrong with the following sentences and write improved ones.

1. Sheila watched the very large gray wolf approach. She was too scared to move.

2. Just as Mack reached for his gun, the beast leaped.

3. Actually, the rain was worse than any of the girls had expected. It was really coming down hard.

4. Geneva felt the cold really effected how well she could walk. She could hardly go forwards through the snow.

5. Tony seemed to be mocking all the gang.

6. "Look at that thing over there." Nancy wailed. "I'm afraid of it."

7. "I'm completely adverse to mice," Jennifer confided,

8. "This couch reeks of comfort," Barry insisted. (Hint: Are you sure you know the meaning of "reek?")

9. The werewolf decided loping away from the grizzly was the best thing to do.

10. I realized I'd left my book behind after I got home.ii.

11. The vampire stared at Mina a long time before realizing she wasn't going to respond.

12. Bonnie's eyes roamed the room, searching for Larry.

13. Every pulse in Feena's body pounded—in her temples, throat, and even the creases in her loins.

14. Fat-as-a-pig Monty loaded his plate at the cafeteria, ignoring the dirty look that skinny-as-a stick cashier gave him.

15. The grotesque looking, red as fire demon flung off his barbed tail at the helpless blonde beauty.

16. "So you buried the car in a snow drift and had to walk without boots, in the blizzard the two miles home. Well, let me tell you I had to stay inside the house all day with your lousy, never-amount-to-anything, quarreling kids and that mangy, good-for-nothing dog," she shrieked.

17. Louisa's eyes were the deep chocolate of a dark Hershey bar.

18. The angel slowly fluttered down to Earth, folding his snowy white wings. After landing, as he looked with pleasure at the beautiful garden full of every color flower and filled with both sweet and spicy perfumed scents, he was reminded of the Garden of Eden.

19. Priscilla started walking slower and slower as she approached the gloomy and sinister-looking castle, all the while wondering if she should turn around and run back to the inn. Little did she know how soon she would wish she'd done just that.

20. Olivia entered the dark room with trepidation. She was making her way toward the window so she could raise the shade to let some light in when a cold shill ran up her spine and settled at the nape of her neck, then traveled right through her to the pit of her stomach where it sat like an iceberg.

Part Two

UNDEAD, CURSED AND INHUMAN

WERE, OH WERE

By Lee Killough

Call them werewolves, weres, shapeshifters, shapechangers, metamorphs, skin-walkers, loup-garous, lycanthropes—whatever the label, they are hugely popular in paranormal stories. Why not? They make great characters, whether used as friends or foes. Though not immortal like vampires (though doesn't transforming into bats and wolves makes vamps a variety of shifter, too?) shapeshifters are often long-lived, usually supernaturally fast, tough and strong, generally hard to kill and fast to heal, with night sight and superior senses of smell and hearing. Plus they aren't cold-cocked by daylight as vampires are. While the most common shifters used in fiction are werewolves, they're not the only players on the block.

Shapeshifters have a long, rich history, appearing in the folklore of every culture on earth, with the animals involved in the transformations being those indigenous to the cultural area. Which gives you leopard men, lion men, and hyena men in Africa, and coyotes and bears in the lore of Native Americans. Norse legends have the berserkers transforming themselves into bears to fight better. The ancient Mayans had Mestaclocan, who could not only change shape but manipulate the minds of animals. In reverse shapeshifting, the selkie is a seal who takes human form. Likewise, Hindu folklore has the nāga, a snake that can transform into a human, while China, Japan, and Korea have fox spirits who appear as beautiful young women. Shifters are not limited to only human and animal forms, either. Gods of Norse, Greek, and Roman mythology took non-biological forms such as clouds and showers of gold.

All of which gives paranormal writers an infinite variety of shifters to play with. And they do.

Charlaine Harris' Sookie Stackhouse series uses not only werewolves, but werepanthers, Quinn the weretiger, and shapeshifters such as werefox Tanya Grissom and bar owner Sam Merlotte, who can take any form he wants. While he usually becomes a collie-type dog, in *From Dead to Worse* he turned into a lion to fight werewolves. Patricia Briggs' auto mechanic shapeshifter Mercy Thompson—called a walker— becomes a coyote. Laurell K. Hamilton's Anita Blake books include a wide range of weres: wolves, panthers, rats, leopards, hyenas, lions ... with occasional appearances by other shapeshifters such as snakes, bears, lamia, and nagas. I use a weretiger as a anecdotal character along with the werewolves in my novel *Wilding Nights*, and protagonist Jeneba Karamoke of my African fantasy *The Leopard's Daughter* had a leopard man father. Although not able herself to transform into a leopard, from her father she has an "inner leopard" she can draw on for strength and speed.

As an example of non-human shapeshifting, Liz Williamson created a character for her Inspector Chen series who transforms from a badger into a teakettle.

What variety of shapeshifter do you want to use?

Whether it is a werewolf or other shifter, however, you need to start with questions whose answers will shape your character's attitudes and actions. Such as...

Origin of the Species

How did your character become a shapeshifter? Being bitten is the classic method, and the one used in most paranormal stories; for example: Carrie Vaughn's Kitty Norville series, Charlaine Harris' Sookie Stackhouse books, Carole Nelson Douglass' Delilah Street series, Laurell K. Hamilton's Anita Blake series, and in all cases but one in Patricia Briggs' Mercy Thompson and Alpha and Omega series. More correctly, being *attacked* is the classic method, because one bite isn't enough to turn anyone. Patricia Briggs' characters must be savaged just short of dying. Kitty Norville also suffered a severe attack. In Sookie Stackhouse's world, any victim with a few simple bites sustains no lasting effect if he cleans and disinfects the wounds in a timely fashion. He must be bitten repeatedly, all over his body, to be turned.

Transformation can also come through magic, however. Or the individual can be born a shifter.

In Anthony Boucher's novelette, *The Complete Werewolf* the magician Ozymandias the Great teaches nerdy professor Wolfe Wolf to become a wolf by saying the magic word *Absarka*. Saying it again returns him to human shape. The trouble is: in wolf form, Wolfe *can't* say the word. He must always find a way to make someone else say it for him. Kim Harrison's Rachel Morgan uses magic to transform herself into a mink in *Dead Witch Walking*.

Three of the four types of shapeshifters in Jim Butcher's Harry Dresden books also transform through magic. His Classic werewolf uses a spell. Anyone can learn it, as do the group of college students calling themselves the Alphas, who are Harry's apprentices and backup. Reverse werewolf Tera transformed herself from a wolf to a human with magic. These individuals can return to human form, or in Tera's case to a wolf, when they wish. The Hexenwolf uses a talisman—which can take the form of an amulet, ring, other jewelry, or a wolf pelt belt—plus an incantation to transform. The Hexenwolf, too, can resume human form at will. Though he is forced to change back if someone removes the talisman.

The folklore of shapeshifting includes many stories of individuals transformed magically by another individual, sometimes for protection but often as a curse. The Dresden world's Loup-garou draws on that tradition. Like the tormented cinema Wolf-man played by Lon Chaney, Jr., once a month the Loup-garou becomes a mindless killing machine. Fortunately, the individual usually understands what has happened to him and can arrange to isolate himself during the danger period.

Similarly, a curse also transformed Ron Starbuck of Will Shetterly's Bordertown books *Elsewhere* and *Nevernever*. It was not intended to be a curse, just a dirty trick spell cast by an elf girl showing off...but due to the unreliability of magic on this borderland between the World and Elfland, the spell went awry and changed him permanently into Wolfboy.

Magic turns individuals in the world of Laurell K. Hamilton's Anita Blake to shapeshifters as well, willingly or through a curse put on an individual or his family. A malicious spell in Harry Dresden's world can turn someone into the Classic werewolf, or any other animal form of the spell-caster's choice. It has to be malicious, because such a spell is not only a violation of the Second Law of Magic but can destroy the human mind of the individual.

Which brings up another point: if your character is a "made" shifter, either through magic or being bitten, was it against his will? Did he seek the shifting ability?

Was he a victim, perhaps someone in the wrong place at the wrong time, such as Carrie Vaughn's Kitty Norville, or a targeted victim like the Loup-garou, Patricia Briggs' Anna Latham, and Sookie Stackhouse's brother Jason, who was abducted and turned into a leopard.

Did your character want to be turned? Characters in the Mercy Thompson and Alpha and Omega series have asked for it. Harry Dresden's Alphas and other Classic werewolves of his world made the effort to learn the spell because they wanted the ability to transform. So do the Hexenwolves. So did Anthony Boucher's Professor Wolfe Wolf. If it were actually possible to become a shapeshifter, you know there would be people in the real world lining up for it, rightly or wrongly seeing it as something desirable to be. Even if the Change can fail and result in death, as it too-often does with Patricia Briggs' werewolves. Does it work in your story to have characters willing to risk life itself to become shapeshifters?

Of course, your character might also be born a shapeshifter. In which case, they will have a whole different attitude and set of behaviors. A made shifter often spends a good part of the story on the outside of the life looking in; unless, like a number of Patricia Briggs' characters, they have lived many years as a shifter. For a newbie, shifting is a fresh experience and everything about it has to be explored and learned. That is useful from a writing perspective, since it lets the reader learn along with the story characters. The born shifter has grown up with it, absorbing knowledge of the life as unconsciously as we have our own native language and culture, and watching the adults shift until the maturing individual is able to do so, too. Puberty is often mention as the age for developing paranormal talents like magic and shifting. Tanya Huff has a six-year-old shifting, though, and Patricia's Mercy Thompson first shifted into coyote form at three months. Having a born shifter as a viewpoint character puts you, and the reader, into the mind of someone who is a kind of alien. Yes, you have to be craftier sliding in information on behavior and, say, shifting mechanisms—to avoid info dumps—but I personally enjoy the challenge of playing alien.

Charlaine, Tanya, Patricia, and I have all used born shapeshifters. Charlaine has two kinds in the Sookie Stackhouse books, pure ones, who are the first-born to two pure parents: two pure weres or two pure shifters. There are also shifters born to a were and shifter mating, but they don't have the same powers as a pure shifter.

Patricia Briggs has just one born werewolf. Her pregnant werewolves normally miscarry because the violence of changing each month kills the fetus. The born werewolf, Charles Cornick, survived because his Native American mother used magic to keep from changing until she delivered him.

Weres in Kim Harrison's The Hollows series are born shifters. Their ancestors were humans cursed by a demon, but their bite is not infectious and they must breed to increase their numbers. Tanya Huff's werewolves in *Blood Trail* and mine in *Wilding Nights* are also born, but neither group were ever human. Legends of Tanya's weres say they are the descendants of a she-wolf and an ancient god of the hunt. My weres are a branch off the stalk that produced a number of hominids, including Neanderthals and eventually our ancestor Cro Magnon. But where all the other hominids except Cro Magnon became extinct, mine survived by infiltrating Cro Magnon groups and passing as human. Being different species than humans, neither Tanya's weres nor mine can interbreed with humans to produce half weres—though mine enjoy human lovers—and their bite never creates a new were.

The Lycanthrope of the Harry Dresden series is born as well. It does not physically change, but channels a spirit of rage, which grants the individual beast-like strength. According to Bob, the air elemental who lives in a skull on Harry's desk, the Berserkers were lycanthropes.

If you want to ring changes on the werewolf/shapeshifter conventions the non-human is one approach to take.

Speaking of changes...

WHAT SHAPES THY FEARFUL SYMMETRY

How, exactly, *does* your character go about Changing? You need to decide in order to know what your character is going through in the process and depict it for the reader, whether in terms of the character's sensations, or with physical details as well.

The traditional and most popular method, of course, is physical transformation. That can be a complete transformation, the shifter becoming entirely wolf, panther, bear. Whatever. But not necessarily. Made weres in the Sookie Stackhouse world don't transform completely, just become half man-half beast. The partial transformation can be deliberate. Shapeshifters in Anita Blake's world are able to vary how animal they become. For instance, growing claws out of human fingers.

Something to keep in mind when characters change shape is that bones and muscles are altering shape and proportion. Logically, that would be painful. In Patricia Briggs' books new werewolves can take as long as fifteen minutes to change. It is also painful, and not just at first or for someone who is badly wounded. In *Cry Wolf*, Anna Latham has been a werewolf for three years, yet:

> The cold made the pain of change worse and stars dance in her eyes. She tried to gasp quietly, tears leaking down her cheeks as her joints and bones rearranged themselves and restretched her flesh over them, and her skin split to become fur.

The discomfort seems more psychological than physical for Kitty Norville in *Kitty and the Midnight Hour.*

> Hands thicken, claw sprout, think about flowing water so she doesn't feel bones slide under skin, joints and muscles molding themselves into something else.

Patricia's Mercy Thompson, though, changes instantly and painlessly into her coyote form. Tanya Huff's werewolves in *Blood Trail* also change without apparent discomfort—even a six-year-old boy—and so fast that investigator Vicki Nelson never quite manages to catch the moment of transformation.

Whatever the speed of change or amount of pain, physical shifting requires shedding all clothing. Which is not very pleasant in bad weather. And there is the risk of resuming human form somewhere well away from those clothes. Patricia's Charles Cornick is lucky in possessing magic that lets him "grow" clothes on himself as he becomes human again.

Regarding physically changing form: most of the time authors ignore or gloss over the difference in body mass between the human and animal shapes. Nor are readers concerned. We—I include myself—accept that Charlaine's Sam Merlotte morphs into a collie one time and a huge lion another. What if you set up a story so the body mass remains the same, no matter what the form? You have a hundred seventy pound man shifting into a cat that also weighs a hundred seventy pounds. The situation offers comic possibilities. Someone tries picking up the cat and can't budge it. In a more dramatic application: one of the bad guys sees a cat and ignores it, thinking it is just a cat...until the cat leaps on him and flattens him. Conversely, taking on a larger form, he might become a kind of balloon, the size of a 500 pound tiger still weighing just his human weight.

Another method of change is forming a new shape around the original one, probably using magic. That can be fast and painless, and doesn't require undressing. Changing back is then merely a matter of peeling off the new shape. A number of the aliens in *Doctor Who* episodes masquerade as humans this way—though using some advanced technical process rather than magic.

Yet another means of change is to have your character possess two separate bodies and switch back and forth between them, like the animagi in the Harry Potter series. In *Harry Potter* the ability isn't a natural process or innate; it uses magic and must be learned.

To take a supernatural rather than magical approach to dual bodies—I once had a character idea I never used because it lacked a plot to go with it. We've read stories—in the tabloid headlines at the supermarket checkout if nowhere else—of twins fused *in utero*, with one inside the other. My idea was Mom had a fling with a werewolf. The fused twins, while genetically identical, ended up with one taking Dad's human form and the other his wolf form. At some point they learned how to switch places—like turning inside out, the wolf emerging and tucking the human away inside.

The human had to strip, though, which is maybe why I could never come up with a plot.

The clothing issue always bothered me in shapeshifting. When writing *Wilding Nights* I created a way around it. My weres do not physically transform. The shapeshift is in the eye of the beholder. They do shift, but it is to a higher energy level—turning on a super adrenalin rush, if you will, sustainable for as long as they wish ... just what a hunter needs for running down game.

> Allison took several breaths, each deeper than the last, feeling as though she shifted gears in a car. Power surged around and through her, then an inner explosion blasted her free of human bonds. She came truly alive. Senses sharpened, sounds and smells turning into an even richer swirl of sensation...the scents of plant life, the sound of wind in the trees and bamboo stands, the whisper of owl wings and the death squeak of its prey, the scent of the rodent's blood. She leaped forward through the moonlight, the ground steaming away beneath her ... reveling in the ripple of sinew and muscle, in the sensation of boundless strength and infinite energy.

That power surrounds them with an energy field so intense observers see and feel it, too, and the witnesses, reacting to the power with primal panic, perceive in the aura a physical shape to match their fear: a Big Deadly Predator.

> Glowing ripples framed Rikki. Zane jerked bolt upright, flooded by nameless terror as the ripples spread out, brightening. Suddenly Rikki disappeared. A giant smoky-grey wolf filled the space.

While Zane sees Rikki as a wolf, it is because that is his idea of a Big Deadly Predator in this setting. Elsewhere in the world, the Big Deadly Predator is one appropriate to that area—a tiger in Vietnam, for example.

While the power may feel boundless and infinite, unless magic effects the change, it must have limits. With the traditional shifter, you can imagine how much energy it takes to reshape flesh and bone. In creating your shapeshifters, consider where that energy comes from, and how they replenish it, even if you don't dwell on those details in the story.

The strongest of Laurell K. Hamilton's lycanthropes feel very tired after changing. Lesser lycanthropes need to eat as soon as they change to animal form, and they collapse comatose for hours after resuming human form. Patricia Briggs' weres have healthy appetites, too. Taking the wounded alpha Adam to Montana for healing in *Moon Called*, Mercy Thompson buys him thirty cheeseburgers for one meal. In *Cry Wolf* Charles is careful to take sufficient food when he and Anna set off into the mountains tracking a rogue werewolf.

The super adrenalin rush of my weres' shift uses massive amounts of energy. I gave them correspondingly massive appetites. Detective Allison Goodnight has a desk drawer packed with snack crackers, energy bars, and nuts. At lunch with her partner one day, she bought three large pizzas and ate all but a few pieces herself. "*It beats the hell out of me why the woman isn't big as a truck,*" a human detective says in bemusement. Allison's home and those of her fellow weres have restaurant-style walk-in refrigerators and freezers stocked with whole sides of beef and the carcasses of wild game.

STATES OF CONSCIOUSNESS

The body changes. Does your shapehifter's mind? How much human awareness do you want remaining? Authors vary in how they handle it. In *From Dead to Worse* Sookie Stackhouse muses:

> It was always hard to say how much humanity was left in the animal form of a shifter. Although she had evidence that the Weres, Quinn, and Sam understood her when she talked to them.

The mind of the Harry Dresden Classic werewolf is not affected by transformation. With the Hexenwolf, the human personality is protected by the spirit of the Hexenwolf's talisman, though the individual does lose inhibitions and run on more primal desires. The Lycanthrope certainly loses humanity as the beast spirit takes over. The Loup-garou, too, loses all humanity in being possessed by the demonic entity of the curse.

The effect of transformation on Carrie Vaughn's Kitty Norville is more like sending the human part of her to sleep. What she remembers after regaining human shape is mostly physical sensations: smells, sounds, tastes. It makes Kitty fear changing, as intoxicating as it is to be a wolf. She has seen that the more often the weres around her change, the less human they become.

The opposite happens to Patricia Briggs' weres. Newbies don't remember much at first, but experience and control bring memory. In *Cry Wolf*, Anna Latham has been a werewolf for three years and when she changes, her rational processes remain intact. Patricia's badly injured werewolves, though, recovering in wolf form where they heal faster, seem to lose human awareness. They react as any wounded animal might when the process of helping them causes pain, by struggling and striking out at individuals around them. The mind of Patricia's Mercy Thompson remains the same whether she is human or in coyote form. So do the minds of my werewolves and, to judge by their actions, those of Tanya Huff's.

POWER AND VULNERABILITY

Consider what abilities and vulnerabilities to give your shapeshifters. Some of the abilities are a given—strength, speed, night sight, ultra-human senses of hearing and scent—otherwise what fun is it being a shapeshifter? Mercy Thompson is only faster than most humans, though, not super fast nor super strong. Authors vary in handling of other conventions, too.

FULL MOONS

How much do they affect your shapeshifter? There are a few shifters who cannot change *except* at the full moon. For one, the made weres in Charlaine Harris' Sookie Stackhouse books. Another shifter limited to the full moon is the Loup-garou of Harry Dresden's world. *Law* restricts the werewolves of Kim Harrison's Hollows series to full moon changes, making it *illegal* for them to change at any other time of the month.

All weres in Carrie Vaughan's and Patricia Briggs' books, and pure werewolves and werepanthers in Charlaine Harris', can change when they want most of the month, but are compelled to do so at the full moon. The exception to that was the mother of Patricia's Charles Cornick, who with the aid of magic resisted changing while pregnant with Charles.

The moon has no effect on the Classic, Hexenwolf, and Lycanthrope Dresden werewolves. Nor does it control Patricia's Mercy Thompson, Charlaine's shifter Sam Merlotte, or Tanya Huff's werewolves. It calls to my weres in *Wilding Nights*, because a full moon is a hunter's moon, and they use that call to help young weres make their first Shifts, but it does not compel anyone to change.

AGING, DISEASE, AND TRAUMA

What kind of life span do you have in mind for your shapeshifter? Those in the Sookie Stackhouse, Kitty Norville, and Vicki Nelson worlds seem to be living human-length lives. My wolves live long but finite lives—up to three hundred years—but becoming a werewolf in Patricia Briggs' books brings resistance to aging. Charles is two hundred years old, his father Bran and brother Samuel even older, and a were named Asil the oldest of all. Their virtual immortality is limited only by accidental death, murder, or a weariness with life which makes them ask for death.

Long lives presume a resistance to disease, too—considering the pathogens at large in the world in the past—and rapid healing.

We see quick healing in many authors' shapeshifters. The Dresden Lycanthrope heals rapidly, and the Loup-garou almost instantly. Wounds received by the weres and shifters of the Sookie Stackhouse world are smaller when they return to human shape. Patricia Briggs' werewolves recover rapidly, too, and even faster in wolf form. Adam had Mac change to a wolf to speed knitting of Mac's broken collar bone. However, Patricia's weres heal more slowly if injured by a preternatural being. When Mercy bit the throat of a werewolf attacking her, it bled out before it could heal. With Tanya Huff's werewolves, no matter which form they wear when injured, changing to their other form neutralizes infection and helps healing.

The Dresden Classic werewolf does not heal any faster than a normal wolf, though, nor does Mercy Thompson have super healing powers. Nor do my weres. They can break a leg as readily as a human does and take just as long to heal.

THE SILVER SOLUTION

When we're dealing with shapeshifters, we have to consider the effect of silver, and talk about silver bullets. The folklore touting silver bullets' ability to kill werewolves goes back just to the Beast of Gévaudan in 1760's France. Silver bullets and werewolves has become a cliché in werewolf literature and movies, however—probably cemented into common culture by the 1941 Lon Chaney, Jr. movie *The Wolf Man*— so many authors use it on their werewolves. They also expand on silver's anti-were properties. The Dresden Loup-garou is killed by silver, but it must be *inherited* silver. The safe rooms of Patricia Briggs' books have silver in their bars to keep injured werewolves confined until they recover. Skin contact with silver is painful for Laurell K. Hamilton's Lycanthropes. If you want to do that to your weres, you can use silver chains to bind them, as Charlaine Harris does her vampires.

Speaking of silver bullets, Patricia Briggs has experimented with making them. FYI: it's very difficult, starting with the fact that silver has a *much* higher melting point than lead does. You can't melt down coins or silverware in a coffee can over a campfire, nor even in the crucible used for lead by shooters who reload their own ammo. Patricia was not impressed with silver bullets' accuracy. You can read her account of it on her web site at *http://www.hurog.com/books/silver/silverbullets.shtml*.

It is easier to turn a bullet on a lathe. But of course that necessitates having access to a machine shop. It is far simpler just to forget silver bullets and load a shotgun shell with chopped up silver coins or dinnerware, links of silver chain, or silver beads.

A weapon of opportunity could be shards of an antique mirror. Old ones were backed with silver. Don't try stabbing a silver-sensitive werewolf with a modern mirror, though, which are backed with aluminum.

Nothing says silver *must* be harmful, however. Choose to make it just another metal to your weres and you're in good company with a number of authors. No need for silver with Jim Butcher's Classic werewolf, Hexenwolf, and Lycanthrope., who can all be killed with conventional weapons and ammo. A well-aimed lead bullet will do the job on Tanya Huff's werewolves, too. And on mine. Mine may seem harder to kill, because they only *appear* wolf-shaped, so what the shooter wants to hit may not be where he aims.

Stripping silver of its anti-were properties can give you an interesting plot twist. The shooter going after Tanya Huff's werewolves in *Blood Trail* used silver bullets because he thought they were necessary, but his kills resulted from good marksmanship, not his ammo. You could provide a rude shock for someone hunting your good-guy werewolves when he shoots at one—expecting that anywhere he hits will be fatal or at least crippling—but fails to stop his victim. If your protagonist is the shooter and the werewolves his enemy, that failure will crank up the tension by sending him scrambling for another solution.

NO WERE IS AN ISLAND

What is your shapeshifter's social situation? Convention has weres living in packs, in spite of the fact that the werewolves of legend, like the eighteenth century Beast of Gévaudan that spawned silver's connection to werewolves, seem to have been solitary creatures. Packs are logical, however—a good behavior model for wolf-shaped characters. So most authors create packs for their weres.

There are exceptions. Those in the Harry Dresden world appear to be solitary in nature. While the Alphas are a group, they are buddies, not a pack. Shapeshifters other than weres tend to be independents, too. Sookie Stackhouse's boss Sam knows and interacts with other shifters but lives on his own. There is no alpha shifter. Walker Mercy Thompson also lives solo, however much werewolf alpha Adam tends to regard her as part of his pack. She might have a group relationship if there were any others of her kind around. We have no way of knowing. Natural panthers are solitary hunters but the werepanthers in the Sookie Stackhouse books live together as a tribe in the community of Hotshot, with Calvin Norris their leader.

Keep in mind that the life of a shifter tied to a group are going to be shaped, and perhaps complicated, by that group and the character's place in it. He may have to buck the power structure to take action on his own. That happens in Carrie Vaughan's *Kitty and the Midnight Hour*. Acting independently keeps werewolf DJ Kitty Norville in trouble with the alpha of her pack. If your protagonist is a human with a were friend, he may find himself caught up in a mine field of pack politics.

When creating a pack, realize that one size doesn't fit all. It is common—but not an absolute—for the leader to be the strongest male. Otherwise the structure varies from author to author. Patricia Briggs', for example, has created the Omega wolf, Anna. Anna is neither a dominant nor a submissive. She has a dominant's desire to protect the pack but without a dominant's aggression. She can calm the aggression in dominant wolves. Structure varies also with whether the weres are made or born, and the tone of life within the pack is set by the personality of the alpha.

Carl, alpha of the pack Carrie Vaughn's Kitty Norville finds herself in, is a bully ruling with iron fang and claw. Pack members have their own jobs and residences, but Carl keeps a controlling grip, showing up to mete out punishment when members—specifically Kitty and her friend T.J.—go places and do things without asking his permission. Being at the bottom of the pecking order, Kitty takes a lot of abuse, especially since she keeps bucking Carl in an attempt to live the human side of her life her way.

Shreveport pack leader Patrick Furnan of Sookie Stackhouse's world freely uses deceit and force. He won his position by cheating in the leadership fight with Jackson Herveaux, and then killing Jackson unnecessarily. Before the opening of Patricia Briggs' *Cry Wolf*, Anna was subjected to physical and mental abuse and rape by her alpha Leo and other males of the pack.

Not all alphas are brutal. Mercy Thompson's neighbor Adam rules his Tri-Cities pack firmly but judiciously. And while Patricia has Bran, the Marrok—to whom all the alphas of the North American packs answer—feared, his governing style is characterized by manipulation, subtlety, and finesse, with force a last resort.

Members of packs in Patricia's series tend to live in urban areas where they can hide in the crowd , i.e., Chicago, or in small places they can take over. They have their own residences and jobs in the cities. Bran's pack owns their town of Aspen Creek. Not everyone there is a were, but as a character named Hank tells Anna: "*If you haven't married one, you were fathered by one—or one of your parents was.*"

My werewolves of *Wilding Nights*, as discussed before, are all born. Theirs is a two-level group structure: households consisting up of related members—sisters, brothers, children—and the clan, made up of all the area households. Though initially unrelated to each other, allied by just proximity, males of one household mating with females of another eventually links them all by blood, too. Unlike most were groups in fiction, the social structure of mine is matrilineal, stemming from females grouping together way back when in their history to protect each other and their children. Each household is headed by an alpha female and one of those is also the clan alpha. The household alpha may be the woman who founded the household, or one who through force of personality, has taken over from an alpha whose vigor is failing. The clan alpha wins her position by charisma and holds it through diplomatic skills.

Tanya Huff's werewolves in *Blood Trail*, are all born weres, too. The pack, like that of natural wolves, consists of a family group, brothers and sisters and children, with Stuart Heerkens and his wife Nadine as alphas. They all live together on their sheep farm, except for one member, Colin, who is a police officer in a nearby town. Stuart acts as much a patriarch as an alpha. He and Nadine run the pack and the farm. And they are the only ones who breed. On reaching sexual maturity, males may leave to join another pack, where they have a chance to become alphas and breed.

Breeding rights may not be an issue with your shifters. It may be irrelevant to your plot. It is certainly irrelevant with packs like those of Patricia Briggs and Carrie Vaughan, which consist solely of made shifters. Briggs' packs have mated pairs, but the only children are born to human women, since changing causes miscarriages in were women. Sex among made weres servers other purposes: pair bonding, pleasure, comfort, or enforcing dominance.

For born shifters, however, breeding issues are important, especially in regard to who may breed and who is not allowed to. If your shifters are born, this is another facet of their group structure and psychology and a factor in what makes them who they are. It could influence action at some point. You never know what twists a plot may take.

Breeding issues are also an important factor in your story background because if creating shifters through biting or breeding were easy, the world would be hip deep in them. You need to give yourself an explanation why they are a minority group.

So...in Tanya Huff's pack, it is only the alpha male and alpha female who breed. Being a family unit, any other liaisons involve incest. There is no alpha restriction among Charlaine Harris' born weres and shifters. Because only the first-born of a pure couple can be a pure shifter or were, any successful birth is applauded. The danger of incest is low. Except perhaps in the werepanther tribe in Hotshot. "First-born," Sookie learns, means the first child a woman has with a particular male. A new mate gives her another chance for a first-born. So in Hotshot, they want each woman to try for a child with every pure male possible.

There is no restriction on breeding among my weres. They, too, have a low birthrate—the evolutionary penalty for being highly successful predators—so all babies are welcomed. To prevent in-breeding and keep the gene pool well stirred, outside males are welcomed. At periodic get-togethers with other clans the alphas encourage and even order matings between females of one clan and males of another.

I've used examples of shifters and weres from only a fraction of the authors writing about them. I hope I've shown you enough for you to see they all have personal perspectives on the subject. Other authors out there are just as individual. Some follow the conventions closely. Others tweak or expand on the conventions. Such as Patricia Briggs' Omega wolf, Anna. Still other authors create their own version, like my weres of *Wilding Nights*. What it all means is that not only are shapeshifters' forms malleable, but their "rules" are as well. Which leaves you likewise free to play with myth and conventions and interpret them as inspiration leads you. To have fun and make your shapeshifters uniquely yours.

Vampires

By Lee Masterson

Vampires as fictional characters have evolved significantly from the original pallid supernatural creatures of Eastern European folklore who rose from their graves at night to suck the blood of the living.

Gone are the days of villagers hanging garlic from their doorways and carrying handy crosses around with them in case of a chance encounter with a vampire. In fact, even the simplistic idea of a simple stake through the heart seems to have vanished along with the original myth that sparked life into these unholy beings.

Early vampires were only able to sleep in coffins beneath the soil in which they were originally buried and anyone of their victims from whom they drank blood also became a vampire. It was believed that vampires would continue to rise from the dead, night after night, in search of new victims until they were killed.

Creating realistic vampire characters that modern readers will love is no longer quite as simple as constructing a nocturnal blood-sucking immortal and turning him loose on your human characters. No longer are they the unthinking, blood-thirsty nightmare creatures who drink the blood of the living.

Modern vampires have transcended the horror genre and become regular inclusions across several other fictional genres, including fantasy and the paranormal sub-genres.

In order to create realistic vampire characters it then becomes important to consider the genre in which you'll be writing, as the type of creature you'll want to create will be vastly different between varying fictional styles.

VAMPIRIC PHYSICAL QUALITIES

It's been long established that vampires have fangs in place of their eye-teeth which are designed to make penetration into human skin easier. As vampires derive their sustenance from drinking human blood easy access to veins becomes a necessity. The majority of writers who create fictional vampires also acknowledge vampire's nocturnal tendencies and their aversion to direct sunlight.

Possessed of inhuman strength, these killers of the night can have the power to dominate and control their prey easily. While some writers include the ability to fly, others may include the ability of their vampires to shape-shift into bats or wolves.

While vampires in horror fiction tend to be frightening, pallid, gruesome creatures, by comparison vampires in paranormal fiction tend to be portrayed as being attractive, sensual and mysterious. This exotic description makes these dark creatures irresistible to some women, thus their rise in popularity in dark romance and paranormal romance fiction.

The physical descriptions of vampires aren't what attract readers to love these supernatural creatures, even though they do have their place within your story.

What makes readers love vampire characters is their mysteriousness and their exotic differences mixed artfully with recognizable human qualities.

Getting the correct mix can sometimes be a difficult balancing act.

VAMPIRES IN HORROR FICTION

While this chapter is about creating vampire characters for the paranormal genre, it's still important to have a firm understanding of these supernatural beings as they are portrayed in horror fiction.

A part of creating any three-dimensional character is understanding the darker nature that lurks beneath the surface. You may choose never to show some of those darker qualities in your story. As the author, just knowing your character is capable of doing some truly unspeakable things may help you to develop a deeper sense of mystery as you begin to craft your characters.

Horror fans love the idea of a manic inhuman killer that only comes out at night to stalk his prey. In the horror genre, these undead supernatural creatures have no feelings or emotions toward humans other than to regard people as lower on the food-chain than they are. They sleep in coffins or in caves by day and emerge as the sun sets to hunt and to feed and to terrorize the night.

Pale, fearsome monsters able to fly through the night and choose victims at random, discarding each useless piece of meat after he's drunk his fill, the vampire in horror tends to hunt alone. With such inhuman physical strength and the supernatural ability to mesmerize prey, it seems so unlikely that a mere human will be able to stop this monster.

A big part of the attraction for vampires in horror is watching the hero or heroine over-power and kill the seemingly unstoppable undead monster. Only a human character strong enough and cunning enough is able to get close enough to a vampire to strike the killing blow of a stake to the heart or to simply decapitate the ghoul and end his reign of terror.

Vampires in Dark Fantasy

Many of the traditional vampiric conventions of the horror genre were altered or lost completely with the introduction of these supernatural creatures into dark fantasy stories.

No longer portrayed as the ghoulish monsters of nightmares, vampires in dark fantasy have become more physically attractive, sensual creatures that have the ability to feel emotions for their human prey.

Many dark fantasy stories also include entire packs of vampires hunting and living together in communal crypts or caves rather than returning nightly to their original place of their burial. With this new-found freedom they were able to travel the world and escape their Eastern European beginnings to terrorize the new world.

Immortality is now a primary focus within dark fantasy vampire characterizations and has replaced the ideal of rising from the dead. Equally important within this sub-genre is the human awareness of needing to spend eternity with someone on an emotional level.

The vampire slowly altered and evolved from a creature of Gothic nightmare to being a gorgeous immortal with almost God-like powers.

VAMPIRES IN PARANORMAL FICTION

Vampire characters in paranormal fiction have moved completely away from the terrifying supernatural figures of the horror world and become beautiful, aloof, romantic creatures struggling to come to terms with their dark inner nature as a killer.

Vampires in paranormal fiction emotionally resist their descent into darkness and have a strong need to hold onto their lost humanity via contact with another human character.

They feel love and often form bonding relationships with other human characters who seem to understand their struggle to a small degree. Many authors even alter their basic primal nature to include an aversion to killing humans and learning to find sustenance through drinking the blood of animals instead.

While these changes tend to diminish their role as horrific monsters, making them seem much less gruesome and frightening, those same changes make vampires as characters in paranormal romance much more romantic and appealing. While they may still have fangs and only appear at night, they're almost unrecognizable as the horrifying demonic killers they're supposed to represent.

WHY WRITE ABOUT VAMPIRES?

So what is it about these immortal killers that many readers of the paranormal find so attractive? Why do writers love writing about vampires?

Perhaps it has something to do with the introduction of intrinsically strong personalities that are able to overpower and completely dominate a female character without mercy.

Modern women are expected to show strength in everything they do so the simple escapism of reading stories about being overpowered by a mysterious creature of the night could be appealing.

For other readers the appeal may be based on the exact opposite principle. Some women feel quite powerless in their own lives and so reading a story that involves a human woman having more power over such a dominant supernatural being allows them to imagine themselves as the heroine.

Although stories featuring female vampires are not quite so common in the paranormal genre, they do represent a preternaturally strong female character in control of a range of dark emotions and desires. These traits in themselves can be appealing for some readers.

Regardless of why the attraction exists it's important to consider the interplay of emotions and actions between your primary human character and your vampire character. It's within these exchanges that your reader will either learn to love your vampire or hate him.

CREATING VAMPIRE CHARACTERS READERS LOVE

The physical attributes you assign to your vampire character have no importance in paranormal fiction. Obviously your heroine will need to find him attractive. Your readers will be drawn to his personality and how he handles himself in difficult situations, regardless of whether you create him blonde or brunette or short or tall.

In paranormal romance stories, the unfolding romance is often the most important element in the tale and not the vampire himself. Your job as the writer is to develop a character that not only your heroine must fall in love with, but you hope that at least some of your readers will too.

The key is discovering your character's personality and then writing your story to include glimpses of that inner emotion so that your readers will learn more about him as the story unfolds. While it is possible to create vampire characters based on the successful premises of other writers, you'll need to decide what attributes and what supernatural powers and abilities your own vampire will have.

· Will your character be able to transform into a bat and

escape detection from those who hunt him? Will he remain in human form when he ascends into the sky to fly away?

· Is your vampire vulnerable to holy water or is his particular weakness garlic? Perhaps he is susceptible to sunlight and able to be killed by a mere ray of sunshine.

· Do you intend to include an element of immortality in your vampire's existence or will you choose to leave him as an undead being who can't possibly live forever because he's already dead?

· These simple supernatural elements don't particularly matter when you're creating the inner emotional side of your character, but understanding your character's capabilities can help to define some aspects of how he will act and react in certain situations.

· When trying to uncover some of your character's personality, you should consider asking yourself some questions about the following issues:

· Does your vampire character still wear the style of clothing that was fashionable at the time he became a vampire? This could mean he is still living in the past and may still hold some social stigmas about women that carry over from that period in time as well.

· Does your vampire character embrace the changing face of society as time passes, learning to accept sociological and technological changes over time?

· Does your character long to rejoin the human race and be considered worthy of your heroine's love or will he embrace his darker vampiric nature?

· Does your vampire accept the mortality of your heroine and understand that he'll continue to live for centuries after she's grown old and died?

· Will your character be tempted to entice her to join him in his dark immortality so he won't need to lose her?

These simple questions about your vampire's inner beliefs and values can help to shape his personality as you'll be more aware of how he should act and react in specific situations throughout your plot.

One of the biggest benefits all writers have when they understand their primary character's inner beliefs and core values is that they're able to then unveil his biggest weakness.

While vampires must be shown as being strong and dark and seemingly all-powerful, each one has a unique weakness. This doesn't have to be a physical weakness, like an aversion to sunlight or an inability to take human victims. It could be an emotional weakness, like a fear of falling in love with a human woman who may grow old and die long before he will. It's how you handle this weakness that makes readers fall in love with characters.

Think carefully about which particular strengths and traits you've given your character. Make them glaringly obvious to your readers, but especially to your heroine. Of course you still need to make him likeable to some degree, but he will need to appear as though nothing can stop him from getting everything he desires.

Now consider the weakness you've uncovered in your vampire character. No matter whether you've chosen physical or emotional, this weakness won't be shown immediately. In fact, you have the opportunity of using it to form the underlying tension that drives his behavior and reactions. After all, he doesn't want his weakness exposed as it will detract from his strength and power.

When you're sure you have an idea of your character's strengths and weaknesses, create a staggering obstacle or problem that preys on your vampire's weakness directly.

You'll need to be sure you've created something so difficult or fearsome for him to overcome that he will need to face his own internal dilemmas in order to beat that weakness and turn it into a form of victory at the end of your story. In order to get what he wants, he needs to win out against the obstacle you've placed in his way but he must face his own glaring weakness to get what he desires.

This kind of conflict in such a strong character can often form a bond between him and your readers that lasts long after they've put your book down.

Lesser Creatures of the Paranormal

*Trolls, Goblins & Things That
Go "Bump" In The Dark*

By Bob Nailor

Paranormal. Vampires, and werewolves and ghosts, oh my! When you read the first word of this paragraph, I am quite sure you immediately thought of those three. After all, they are what I call 'The High Three' for paranormal stories, but there are more phantasmal creatures than them. The world is full of other fantastical beings which can be used to populate your writings and make yourself an exemplary writer.

If we were playing "Family Feud" I would need to add just two more creatures: angels and aliens. There! The game is over and all the paranormal possibilities have been answered.

Wrong! I've just listed the Top Five which people immediately think of and are used almost exclusively in stories and tales, ad nauseam. I know a secret, and I will share it with you! There are many, many more paranormal types like elves, dwarves, witches, fairies and warlocks to name a few.

A suave and debonair vampire can be fun writing but that hack has been so over worked it is now just commonplace. Of course, the vampire could be female and therefore add a new dimension to the tale but the bottom line is the same: the living dead with pointy teeth. Therefore, the author stretches to find a new twist to make the vampire story stand out from the others. Even a beautiful ghost can be an over-used character along with the character that grabs your imagination by having a dual personality with a wolf. That's right, howling at the moon or watching the paranormal pass through a wall gets old.

Exactly what are paranormal lesser creatures? Like the title says—trolls, goblins and things that go "bump" in the dark? These eerie beings don't have to be relegated to the back shadows or existing as the proverbial sidekick. Let them step up and take a lead, become a hero or the sought after swoon of a romance novel. Can it be done? Most certainly. Let me give you an example.

DAVY JONES is the nickname for what some consider the devil/saint/god of the seas. His abode, Davy Jones' Locker, is literally the bottom of the ocean, the resting place for those who have died at sea. In the past, he was conceptualized as an evil creature sailing the Seven Seas in search of his prey, the dead or unwary. Some thought him to be a vile human while others saw him more of a beast of the sea. For most people, this entity was personified extremely well in Disney's "Pirates of the Caribbean" movie. Of course, that was only one idea being projected on the populace, Davy Jones as a mix of human and sea creature. For the romance writer, the 3rd movie of the "Pirates of the Caribbean" series brought a new angle to Davy Jones with Orlando Bloom versus the beast originally portrayed by Bill Nighy in the 2nd and 3rd movies. As such, it is quite evident this character can be designed to the need of the writer, from an attractive, suave man of the sea to a vile appearing creature lusting for a death, or anywhere in between to fit the requirements of any genre writer. Some depictions of Davy Jones are that of no more than a vulture of the ocean, collecting the dead souls at sea. Other portrayals have him as more humanesque, enjoying the good life at sea, sharing his bounty with other unlucky souls.

As a writer I would take advantage of the fact the oceans touch many countries and varied nationalities with a plethora of possibilities, such as an oriental aspect for Davy Jones if the story takes place off the shores of Eastern Asia. There are no rules which declare he only appear to be of European descent. Davy Jones is one with the sea and, as such, just as volatile and malleable and therefore as changeable.

A good writer can see beyond the ho-hum of the stereotypical phantasmal creature. Why must your lead character, an ogre, be hideous or ugly? Why couldn't he be a handsome, dashing hunk, which every woman goes weak-kneed when he walks into the room? Oh, I see. An ogre is ugly and doesn't fit that guideline. Okay, you're the writer; make him turn ugly. Figure out what will flip the switch between hunk and lunk. Is it the moon? A food allergy? A smell? A curse? Wait, that's been done; "*Shrek*." If you remember correctly, Princess Fiona was under a curse, a beautiful princess by day, an ogre by night and only the kiss of her true love would break the curse and allow her to assume her true form. Sunrise and sunset were the catalysts of the transformation. Actually, Shrek is an excellent example of a lesser paranormal taking the limelight to become a leading character. I would have stated "hero" but Shrek spent most of the time trying not to be the hero.

CREATURE CATEGORIES

Paranormals aren't your average Joe of the street. They are wondrous beings with certain quirks and tendencies that move them from mundane to magnificent. Some are legendary while others are considered mythic and still others are called folklore. Fine lines separate these categories and they have blended with one another over the years like watercolors in the rain. Legendary are those creatures who supposedly have been seen, touched or left a mark as in a footprint. Mythic creatures are the fictionalized beings that exist within our minds. Folkloric are those tales common to an area.

ZEUS is a Greek god and is mythic but not folklore since the concept of a "father" god is not a singular Greek ideal, there is Jupiter of the Romans, Indra of the Hindu mythology and Tinia of Etruscan tales. All these mythologies reflect a 'head' god and surprisingly, all have the thunderbolt tied to their so-named 'father' god. Mythic beings are creations of the mind.

THE LOCH NESS MONSTER is a folklore. There are other tales of similar creatures at different locations but Nessie is tied to the Loch Ness in Scotland. Some say the Loch Ness Monster is nothing but a figment of a few wild imaginations and therefore could be called mythological. It could also be called legendary since it seems to have some basis in reality with supposed pictures and varied sightings.

DAVY JONES on the other hand is legendary since he supposedly existed at one time and/or is based on a real human, possibly a sailor by that name or a known British pub owner of ill-repute who sold drunken sailors to outgoing ships. Still, there is a mythic sense about Davy Jones which can easily push him to the mythological side. He could be listed as folkloric due to his origins being English, but today he has grown to encompass the Seven Seas and therefore is more in the realm of legendary.

The lines between these categories waver back and forth, sometimes criss-crossing and blending in such a way, it would impossible to place them correctly.

Let me state one caveat at this point: There is no way that I could possibly list all the potential lesser paranormal creatures, that would be a book in and of itself for somebody else to do.

What I will do is list some of the creatures from different parts of the world. It will be an alphabetical listing and when possible, noting a country or nationality to the paranormal and possibly a little 'historical' background.

ALPHABETICAL LISTING

BANSHEE is an Irish or Scottish apparition, usually female since the original word "bean" or "bain" means woman and "si," "sidhe," or "shidh" (depending on spelling and nationality) means "of the fairy mounds." Originally, at death, a village woman would sing a traditional lament. Over the years, the banshee came into existence as a wailer for the deceased. A banshee was normally a beautiful, young woman but not always. She could transmute between beautiful lass and a horrid hag instantly and vice versa. They usually were dressed in grey or white but other colors of red, green and black have been used. Banshees were noted for their long tresses which they cared for with silver combs. Yet, it was her wailing, screeching, howling that was her calling card. It heralded a death, although originally tied to the Five Great Gaelic Families (O'Gradys, O'Neills, O'Briens, O'Connors and Kavanaughs), banshees soon became the death harbingers of the common man, also. To hear the wail predicted a death in the family and to see the banshee would signify one's own death. But that wasn't the only way a banshee could spirit a human away, they would leave their combs on a path and any unsuspecting person who should pick it up was fair play to steal away. Terry Pratchett's *'Discworld'* series had a male banshee with a speech impediment and therefore did not scream or howl, but left notes with his wail inscribed on it. Definitely a different take on the banshee legend and for making an interesting character. Normally considered ethereal, there is no reason a writer couldn't add a humanesque touch to the banshee, giving them substance.

BASILISK comes from the Greek word 'basiliskos' which means little king. It is usually represented in a snake-like form and is considered the king of serpents. It can also be found as a lizard or cockerel. The name king is tagged due to a crown-like crest found on the creature's head. In a Harry Potter novel it was portrayed as very large snake, but there is no reason the creature must always remain a serpent. As a king, it would be to the writer's advantage to give this creature a human aspect allowing for a dual plot line; one as the snake and the other as a human. The abilities of the basilisk are varied by stories and include causing death by the sound of its voice, a lethal glance into its eyes, or coming into contact with its poisonous venom and fire breathing. Pliny, in his writings *'Natural History'* (circa 77 AD) describes the basilisk and where it can be found. According to this source, the deadliest of deadlies is a mere 12 inches long in length and is native to Cyrenaica. He also stated if a man were to kill the basilisk with a spear while riding on a horse, not only would the venom rise through the spear to kill the man but it would also kill the horse on which the man is riding. Most writers prefer the super snake as the creature of choice when describing the basilisk, king of the serpents. The basilisk falls into all three categories: mythic since the creature as a super snake has never really been seen, folkloric since it usually is locked to a locale and legendary since the real snake does exist, although it is nothing like the stories told.

CENTAUR is a creature who is half horse and half man with the man part being head, arms and torso attached to the body of a horse, replacing the horse's neck and head. There are female centaurs which are named Cenataurides; they are extremely beautiful. These creatures have been depicted as both light hearted (Disney's *Fantasia*) and dark (Harry Potter movies) paranormals. These paranormals are most notably known from Greek and Roman mythology although there are mention of similar creatures going back as far as Babylonian times. Obviously, centaurs are mythic creatures.

Chiron, of Greek mythology, is probably one of the most famous centaurs and is noted for his knowledge and kindness. He was a teacher to many of mythology's noted heroes including Hercules. Most centaurs are distinguished by their overt uncouthness, lack of culture, overt drunkenness, carousing spirit and general violence. If you want to have a party, these are the paranormals who will raise the limits, not to mention the roof.

Contrary to what myth and legend have told us, you can give your centaur a softer side like Chiron and have a creature your reader will cheer for. Centaurs were notorious for capturing and carrying off young maidens by whisking them onto their backs and galloping away. Some well-known authors have used centaurs in their writings such as C. S. Lewis and the *Narnia* series, Piers Anthony with his *Xanth* series and Jack Chalker's *Wellworld* series.

Where do these creatures come from? Some say that it was a misinterpretation by a hysterical peasant seeing a rider on a horse for the first time. Supposedly the peasant had never seen a horse before. History backs this option with stories of conquistadors coming to the Americas. They rode their horses and the natives of Central America had never seen such a creature; a combination of man and horse. Others say that it was a totem of a tribe and yet others believe it to be part of a fertility rite where men wore mockups of the hind quarters of a horse attached to their waists.

There are variations of the centaur; from the seas there is the ichthyocentaur and from the air the pterocentaur. The ichthyocentaur is a fishy version with the front half of the creature being human and horse and the rear section consisting of a fish's tail. The pterocentaur adds wings to the centaur giving it the ability to fly, similar to Pegasus, the winged horse.

DEMONS, although usually connected to the horror genre, can also be a major character in a paranormal novel. What is a demon? It is a fallen angel. For more information on angels, check elsewhere in this book. Demons have been around since the beginning of time. Historically, demons go back beyond the Assyrian and Babylonian cultures of the Mesopotamian valley. Lilith, the supposedly first wife of Adam began originally as a Babylonian demon known as Lilitu before she morphed into the Jewish religion. Legend says Lilith refused obedience to God and was therefore removed from the Garden of Eden; Eve was created to become the mother of mankind.

The word demon is derived from "daio" which means "to divide" as it was applied to the beings who weren't god(s) or human and therefore separated those two entities. Demons are a varied group and come in every possible description: single head to multi-headed with heads that are human and non-human and any combination thereof. Some have wings, multiple wings and no wings as well as no arms or legs to multi-armed and multi-legged. Some demons can be viewed as comical, hideous, horrendous or surprisingly, very handsome and attractive. It should be noted demons are also considered devils but the Devil is a demon and therefore not all demons are the Devil. They are two separate entities in that the Devil, aka Satan, Lucifer or Beelzebub, is the head demon and all other demons/devils are subordinate under him.

Usually, most demons are considered evil and bad, although in some cultures, a demon can be a good or benevolent spirit. Demons transcend many barriers including time: as stated before, demons were a part of Babylonian, Sumarian history; religion: they are a basic part of Jewish, Christian and Islamic faiths; cultures, a integral part of Jewish, Christian, Iranian, and Native American traditions and space: they appear on all the continents of Earth.

DJINN or Jinn is the Arabian version of European genie. They are an elemental creature of the air therefore having a consistency similar to that of smoke or the clouds. According to the Qur'an, the Jinn were created out of the fire of a searing wind (Surat al-Hijr, 27) and their only purpose is to worship Allah (Surat adh-Dhariyat, 56). Although normally portrayed as demons and monstrous, djinn can also appear animal or human-like and not evil. These creatures have been in tales, including the most notable genie in the lamp from *Aladdin* in the collection entitled *1001 Arabian Nights*. The 2nd most famous genie would be Barbara Eden's portrayal in *I Dream Of Jeannie* television series of the late 60s.

There are five different types and each type has is limited in the magic they can do. The least powerful is the jann then there is the generic djinn followed by sheytans, also known as devils. The 2nd most powerful are called afrits and the most powerful are the madrids. The madrids are also the most dangerous of all djinn. Most djinn and genies were controlled via a bottle, lamp, ring or other various non-animate objects. The owner of the object wielded the djinn's power. Although these creatures were locked to the object, they usually had the ability to travel (walk) with the owner as a normal human, but they were anything but normal. They were normally construed of gases and smoke, allowing them to be very small; or extremely enormous, depending on the djinn's whim. The major benefit of controlling a djinn or genie was in the receivership of wishes. Whoever controlled the genie, received the wishes; be it one, two, three or more.

It is said that King Solomon controlled many genie and when they misbehaved, he would have them shut within a stoppered bottle and cast into the sea. Hence the many tales of finding a genie in a bottle on the beach. When found, most of the time three wishes were granted for the new found freedom and as such, the wishes were usually contrived by the genie to be to the genie's advantage. This is not a necessity but it does add to the storyline for the writer.

A djinn or genie usually only had one quest; to be human and to gain this aspect meant a great feat or some obscure condition such as having the lamp tossed into a river of fire. The djinn or genie would probably fall under the category of mythic but it is documented in Qur'an, giving it a folklore aspect.

DOPPELGANGER is a word of a Germanic ancestry and means 'double walker' or 'ghostly double' which indicates the duality of this paranormal. Like many paranormals, a doppelganger weaves itself between folklore and legendary since they have been documented but rarely seen. A doppelganger usually is a harbinger of bad luck or ill-fortune. As is normal with a duality, it is assumed that one is good and the other bad and, of course, you must be the good, otherwise that would make you the evil one. Doppelgangers are separate entities and therefore can swap with one another and allow each to be in different locales at the same time. Robert Lewis Stevenson's 'Doctor Jekyll and Mr. Hyde' were not doppelgangers since it was the same person transforming back and forth in what one could call an extreme case of potion induced external schizophrenia. (Bob, I know Doppelgangers are separate from their double, but perhaps make it a bit clearer so others don't misunderstand.)

This paranormal is considered legendary since many people claimed to have seen their double including Queen Elizabeth I and Catherine the Great. Queen Elizabeth it is said saw herself on a deathbed and died soon afterward. Catherine, on the other hand, took no chances when she saw her double coming toward her and ordered soldiers to pursue and kill the doppelganger. Even President Lincoln was said to have seen a form of doppelganger which was interpreted by his wife, Mary Todd Lincoln, to indicate he would be elected a second term but not survive it. The doppelganger as a paranormal character could add a slippery aspect to any story whether it be romance, adventure, etc. Swapping out the character to another location or swapping in a doppelganger for a high tension scene should keep the story moving.

Doppelgangers have taken front stage in such tales as Fyodor Dostoyesky's 'The Double' and Edgar Allan Poe's 'William Wilson' to a unique play in today's society with motion picture 'i' using a timeline to create the effect. Sometimes doppelgangers are portrayed as a biological lost twin, shapeshifters, mirror images or clones.

GARGOYLE AND CHIMERA'S are often confused with one another. This particular paranormal has many manifestations. First, the word gargoyle comes from the Old French term "gargouille" meaning throat.

The original gargoyles were waterspouts on buildings to re-direct rainwater. This has been documented as far back as 4000 yrs to Egypt, Greece and Rome. Gargoyles came into popularity in Europe during the Middle Ages with the most famous collection of gargoyles being at

Notre Dame of Paris. These were fierce creatures with hideous facial features, horns, claws, fangs and wings.

Chimeras, also known as Grotesques, on the other hand are non-water directing creatures on a building appearing very similar to a gargoyle. Beyond the architectural facet, for the writer, there is a human aspect that has been added to the gargoyle over the years. For a paranormal author, having a gargoyle or chimera as the lead of a story allows you to wander from the well beaten path of the paranormal story. An interesting aspect of gargoyles is one of invisibility; they supposedly came to life at night to protect the building or village and couldn't be seen by the general populace. If one saw a flying gargoyle, it was immediately considered a bat and hence, one never truly saw a gargoyle in flight. Of course, gargoyles have been used in movies including even a comical aspect in Disney's 'The Hunchback of Notre Dame' where three gargoyles were light hearted sidekicks. For the most part, gargoyles are mythic creatures.

GOBLINS come in assorted sizes and shapes, which means there is one to fit any desired need in a robust story. To standardize this paranormal would be as easy as using your hands to contain smoke; in other words, there is no standard. They can have big eyes or small eyes, big, bulbous noses or small snort holes, large floppy ears or no ears, warts, stray hairs, pimples or other facial bumps, gnarly teeth or fangs and almost any color of the rainbow for skin pigment and height seems to range from small, like that of a dwarf, to taller than a human. Most goblins are content to live in the crannies of a pile of stones usually near a pond or stream.

The word goblin is thought to be from the Anglo-French term *gobelin*. Another theory is the word comes from *Ghob* or *Gob*, king of the gnomes, and his inferiors were called *Ghob-lings*. In addition to the name of goblin they are also called hobgoblin, domovoy or hobgob, which is a house goblin. Goblins are also called knocker and orc to mention a few others. A goblin is suppose to cause problems and trouble for humans but in South Africa the goblin is known as a Tokoloshi and will be quite helpful around the house although they are really a servant of a witch or sorcerer. If you are unfortunate enough to see a goblin, their smile will curdle your blood and their laugh will turn milk sour.

J. R. R. Tolkien's *Lord of the Rings* is probably one of the most famous offerings of goblins but should not be considered the de facto in goblin definition. In the novel, *Labyrinth*, the goblin king plays a maze as a trap to a young girl to win her baby brother back. In the movie version of this story, the king is portrayed as attractive and very human appearing while his subordinates are various sizes, shapes and colors of goblins and hobgoblins.

MERMAID tales go back as far as ancient Babylon. Sightings of mermaids bring this creature into the category of legendary since they have been seen by sailors over the years and most recently by scuba divers. Of course, many people consider them mythic since there is no actual proof of their existence. They could be considered folkloric only because they have many tales about them from different locales.

On January 4, 1493, Christopher Columbus found three mermaids near the coasts of Haiti. He wrote in his journal "They were not as beautiful as they are painted, although to some extent they have a human appearance in the face." Columbus also made comment of sighting them off the coast of Guinea, West Africa. Henry Hudson, on a voyage across the arctic coast of Russia, made a log entry on June 15 which described his encounter with a mermaid including that her tail was like that of a porpoise and spotted like a Macrell.

Many mermaids are said to be seen gazing at themselves in mirrors or combing their long tresses. What writer can refuse the chance to wax poetic with the image of young maidens basking on rocks, combing their long locks of hair and singing? The mermaid's voice is beautiful and therefore sometimes is confused with the Sirens of Greek and Roman mythology.

Mermaid is a compound word with *mere* of Old English for sea and of course, maid for the obvious reasons. A mermaid is a combination of half woman from the navel up and half fish from the navel down which makes them excellent swimmers with their forked tails. There is also the male counterpart who is aptly named merman. In Ireland the sea folk are called Selkies.

Hans Christian Anderson's tale *The Little Mermaid* is probably one of the most notable stories involving these creatures. It is a well known fact mermaids are able to become fully human, in fact, there are some countries that have sea people who are totally human but are able to breathe under water. The movie *Splash* starring Tom Hanks and Darryl Hannah demonstrated the mechanism that allowed her to transform from human to mermaid and vice versa. A dark aspect of this paranormal is their supposedly causing the deaths of so many seamen. They lured men into the waters and then pulled them below the surface to drown, not realizing humans couldn't breathe under water. Sirens also lured men of the sea to their deaths but used music and song.

NEPHALIM or nephilim are the offspring of 'the sons of God' and the daughters of man. (Gen 6:2 of the Hebrew Bible). Some claim the sons of God were fallen angels, other say they were strictly righteous men. Either way, the offspring were said to be tall, strong and quite heroic. The term nephilim is Hebrew and is thought to mean *those causing others to fall.* These paranormals bring with them a power which supposedly comes to them from their fathers; the angels. They are considered by many to be dark, brooding and perhaps evil while others see them as leaders full of righteousness. It is considered that Goliath of the Philistines was a nephilim and therefore touts for the darker side.

Another aspect of the nephilim is possibility of them being of alien descent. In Aramic cultures, Nephila referred to the constellation of Orion thereby implicating that nephilim are descendants of aliens from Orion. The nephilim would be considered by most to be legendary or folklore; legendary since there is documented proof of their existence and folkloric since they are tightly infused in the lands of the Bible. Putting a nephilim into your story would add an angelic touch without using the well-worn angel tale.

TROLLS are from Norse myths and are considered mythical. They are enormous creatures with ugly and evil to match. In England they were also known as ogres. In the British Shetland Islands they are known as trows and the Native American troll is known as a windigo. A windigo is a shape-shifter who can be seen as a wolf or a man, and when a man, usually appears as very tall and overbearing. Trolls tend to live in caves although some will live under a bridge yet there are different trolls that abide by different rules. A stone-troll's downfall is sunlight to which, if caught in the open at sun up; turn into stone, hence the name.

There are also cave-trolls, hill-trolls, mountain-trolls and snow-trolls. The latter three trolls seem to be able to exist in full light. The most popular tale of a troll is probably that of the Scandinavian fairy tale, *Three Billy Goats Gruff.* Another famous troll is Grendel from the epic poem, *Beowulf.* J. R. R. Tolkien's *The Hobbit* and *Lord of the Rings* also brought them into the limelight in the traditional manner of stone-trolls with Bilbo in *The Hobbit*; and cave-trolls, hill-trolls and mountain-trolls which were used in the different battles. The word troll appears to come from the Old Norse, *troll*, which means a giant or demon. Even though they were fierce appearing, trolls were very naive and for the most part, good natured in a simplistic manner.

A dark aspect of this paranormal is it could transform itself into a beautiful, young maiden who would lure woodsmen, hunters and farmers into the forest to capture and eat them. Supposedly with this aspect, a real troll has a tail and if you could look behind the maiden and see the tail, you'd know it was a troll. If you'd like to visit and spend time with a troll, be sure to stop in Seattle to pay homage to the Fremont Troll under the north end of the Aurora Avenue Bridge.

There is no way I could make an all inclusive list but I will list a few more to spark your interest in the lesser creatures of the paranormal. A bit of web surfing or a visit to your local library should satisfy your piqued curiosity and detail for you the lesser creatures of paranormal to bring your writing into the limelight.

ABOMINABLE SNOWMAN: see Yeti below

BARBEGAZI: dwarves of the Alps in France and Switzerland; have frozen beards and white fur; will dig out humans caught in an avalanche

BIGFOOT: see Sasquatch below.

BOCAN: Irish boogeyman, see Boogeyman

BOGGELMAN: German boogeyman, see Boogeyman

BOOGEYMAN: dark, mean, scary goblin, but not too bright and can be easily fooled

BROWNIES: small human like creatures of myth; noted for being naughty

BUBAK: Bohemian boogeyman, see Boogeyman

CHUPRACABRA: a creature of South American aka 'Goat Sucker'; vampiric and mean

CYCLOPS: a giant with only one eye; cave dweller, mean, of Greek mythology

DEER WOMAN: a creature existing at the edge of civilization; sometimes evil

FAUN: half goat, half man; Roman mythology; notoriously sexual, loves to drink and party

GIANT: extremely tall man or woman, sometimes cannibalistic; of Jack & The Bean Stalk fame.

GNOME: similar to a goblin but not as horrific; usually gentle and known to roam

GOATMAN OF MARYLAND: a creature existing at the edge of civilization; sometimes evil (goatMan, deer Woman—gender specific creatures?)

GREEN MAN: of pre-Christian myth; belonging to the trees and plants

GREMLIN: newest creature, mid-20th century invention; usually mechanical; no real definition but the movie 'Gremlins' does show different possible aspects of this creature.

INCUBI: a demon, male counterpart to succubus; attempts sex during a female's dream

JERSEY DEVIL: winged creature, cross between dog, horse, crane

LAKE WORTH MONSTER: see Deer Woman above

MINOTAUR: man with bull's head; Greek mythology; lived in labyrinth

NYMPH: maidens of the woods, usually bound to a tree or pond

PEGASUS: a flying, white horse

PENNSYLVANIA CREATURE: see Deer Woman above

PIXIE: extremely small creatures, child like; helpful and friendly

SASQUATCH: extremely large ape-like creature living in the woods of North America

SATYR: Greek version of Faun, see above.

SPHINX: body of a lion, head of a man, Egypt; usually an oracle

SUCCUBI: a female demon who has sex with men during their dreams

SYLPH: an elemental that inhabits the air, has no soul and is mortal, female usually

ULDRA: dwarves of the Arctic Circle in Norway, Sweden, Finland and Russian

UNICORN: a white horse with a spiraling single horn in its forehead

WHITE LADIES: from France, young maidens waiting near a bridge to dance with single men

YETI: extremely large ape-like creature living the Himalayan mountains

THINGS THAT GO BUMP IN THE DARK

What really gets you? The thing you can't see? During the night, is it that small creak of the closet door; a moan from somewhere else in the house; a thump under the bed? This is the creature of your imagination and it is wonderful. Open your mind to its description; allow this new paranormal a life on the pages of your story. Nothing will put you into print faster than standing out from the rest of the crowd in that proverbial slush pile. Take notice though; standing out and being different are two different things. You want to run in the normal standard of publishing but at the same time be noticed. What are things that go bump in the dark? Is it a woman? A man? Is it tall or short? Will you depict it as handsome or beautiful or will be it ugly and horrific? Is it even of this world?

CONCLUSION

The lesser creatures of the paranormal can be used in a myriad of ways including being the lead hero or heroine of your story. Just because the creature is small or ugly doesn't mean it must be relegated to a back row role. Let the troll move from the darkness into the light, let it win the heart of a young maiden. Rules are there for you to follow but a good writer knows how to bend those same rules to his or her need. Don't allow yourself to be written into a corner of banality with the same old hack. You're the writer, you decide. Your imagination is an immense and wondrous place with walls only spaced as far as the universe and you allow. So put to paper what you see within the realms of your imagination.

WRITING FOR CHILDREN AND YOUNG ADULTS

By Jerri Garretson

Remember those camp-outs and slumber parties of your youth when you delighted in telling eerie or scary stories and speculating about what was out there in the dark? Remember your fascination with ghosts, vampires, werewolves, monsters and the undead? Did you dream of reading people's minds or try to communicate with the dead? Were you a Ouija board aficionado?

All of these compelling subjects are still popular with kids. YAs (Young Adults) still gravitate to phenomena and events that are outside the normal realm of experience and science and read as wide a range of stories as adults. Fiction for this age group is sophisticated, every bit as polished as that written for adults and deals with every subject imaginable. Some publishers that purchase YA novels are looking for "cutting edge" fiction. The distinguishing factor is that the main character is a teen and it is written for a teenage audience.

That covers a wide ground, as thirteen-year-olds and nineteen-year-olds are definitely at different stages of maturity and reading abilities. Many of these teens are also avidly reading adult fiction and they expect the same quality in their YA books. In writing for them, you'll be competing for their attention with authors of the best paranormal fiction for adults.

Some YA books have become "crossover" hits read by adults of all ages as well as teens and younger children. The *Twilight* series by Stephanie Meyer is one of the current best-selling rages, with readers from ten up (though there are plenty of adults questioning whether it is appropriate reading for a ten-year-old). Try googling "Twilight series age of readers" and see what an amazing set of websites you get and the range of ages mentioned.

"YA" is a little tricky to define, because publishers don't universally aim at the entire teen span of years. Some acquire books for the younger end, looking for protagonists in the 12-15 year-old range, and others seek to appeal to a readership of 16-19 year-olds. To complicate matters, kids as young as eight are reading the younger end of the YA books. If you research writing for children online or in books about writing for children, you may see slight variations on the age groups and the average word counts, but the basic numbers are usually close to what I'm offering here.

When I was a children's/YA librarian, I once had an eight-year-old march up to my desk and ask for the YA books. Out of curiosity, I asked her to define YA and she said, "Everyone knows it's kids eight to fifteen." I found that amusing and wondered how she came up with the idea. It turned out that the books she actually wanted were certainly paranormal (the *Goosebumps* series by R.L. Stine, wildly popular at the time) but weren't what I would consider YA. They are written for the 9-12 age group, but quite a few younger children read them avidly. Some children under twelve read well enough and are mature enough to enjoy YA books but that's not the age group YA literature is written for.

While you may find references that most YA novels range from 40,000 to 75,000 words, that's like defining an average in any field. There are longer works that are extraordinarily popular. Witness the heavy tomes of the Harry Potter series or the *His Dark Materials* trilogy by Philip Pullman (of which *The Golden Compass* is the first book).

The critical element for YA stories is believable teen characters, with the story told through the eyes and mind of the teen protagonist (regardless of whether the viewpoint is first or third person). The age of the main character is usually just a year or two above the intended audience, on the theory that kids like to identify with someone just a bit older than they are. For a teen character to be believable today means that you need to know what today's young people are like, what moves them, how they act and talk. Believable dialogue is critical. In the grand scheme of life, their feelings and desires aren't so very different from what previous generations experienced, but in terms of their environment, clothing, media, slang, and even pastimes, their world can be vastly different. It may take research to write well about today's youth, even in a paranormal story that's outside the bounds of everyday experience.

Similarly, to write for any of the younger audiences, the main character and the story viewpoint must be both believable and appropriate for the intended age group. Many authors find that they have a natural affinity for a particular age. Others find it depends entirely upon the story they conceive.

Like any good story, the character and the plot are so intertwined that you can't imagine one without the other. YAs and younger children want a gripping story, one that pulls then in immediately. When you write for kids, you have to get them hooked on the first page. There is no luxury of pages of preamble or description. They do not feel compelled to keep reading. If a book doesn't hook them, they put it down. At writing conferences for children's and YA authors, one of the grueling tests of a manuscript is "first pages." This is aimed precisely at revealing whether the first page of a book (and more likely the first couple of paragraphs) will keep them reading.

It works like this. The brave (or masochistic) authors place just the first pages of their novels or short stories into a box, with no identifying information on them. No authors' names. Someone is designated to pick a page from the box and a reader reads it aloud. Editors from publishing houses for YA and children's books who are part of the conference faculty, and the entire conference audience, listen. At the end of the page, the editors pick it apart, say whether they would continue reading the manuscript if it were sent to them, and why. It is an excruciating and often embarrassing exercise but also very instructive. Many fledgling authors for young people are shocked to discover how hard it is to get an editor to read past the first page. They think it isn't fair, that judging their story on one page isn't right...but that's often how the kids do it, and the editors are aiming to sell to that crowd.

YAs and children may be more forgiving of implausible plots because they've often grown up on fairy tales and cartoons, but that doesn't mean editors will forgive you. One of the things you have to realize right away as a writer for young people is that they aren't the ones buying the manuscripts. There are several adult "filters" the books have to go through before a kid ever sees them. That means that your work has to please adults as well as kids. The best writing for young people is multi-level. It is read by adults on one level and often on a different level by the intended audience. Good editors are extremely tuned in to what today's young people are reading, to their interests, but they also know that books get into the hands of younger children, and into libraries, through adults; teachers, librarians, parents and grandparents. They have to please both.

A stumbling block for many writers is a hackneyed plot. This is especially easy to do in writing fiction for kids, even paranormal fiction, and it will kill your chances of publication. Unless you are an avid reader of children's books, you probably don't have a handle on the breadth of children's literature and the wide variety of plots and themes that have already been overdone.

Likewise, shun anything that smacks of preachiness or moralizing. That doesn't mean that your story can't have a moral theme, just that it has to be an integral part of a story that doesn't announce itself as the "purpose" of the story. Children's fiction, like adult fiction, is about entertainment, entering another world. It does not consist of cautionary lectures or lessons.

The age group directly below YA is "middle grade" fiction, often abbreviated MG. This is generally aimed at kids 9-12 years of age. They are less mature, normally less sophisticated, and usually not reading at the same grade level as YAs (though a few precocious ones are) and are less likely to also be reading adult fiction. An average middle grade book is generally somewhat shorter than the average YA book, perhaps 20,000—40,000 words, but there are MG books that are far longer. There is a large group of readers in this age group and many editors are avidly seeking good middle grade fiction. Paranormal books are also enormously popular with these kids.

If you enjoy writing for even younger children, there is plenty of room for paranormal fiction for them, too. "Chapter books" are published for approximately grades kindergarten to third grade, or sometimes listed as ages 7-9 depending upon the length. These books range from very simple "beginning readers" that are divided into very short chapters that allow the new reader to feel more grown up to fairly long fiction. Chapter books may range from 4,000—12,000 words, but may go as high as 25,000.

Beginning readers may vary from about 200 to 1200 words. Don't fool yourself. It isn't easy to write shorter. It's a real challenge to delineate winning characters and a compelling plot in that short a manuscript.

Even shorter are extremely brief books for "emerging readers." It is difficult to write a story with as few as 32 words and obviously there is no real room for character development or a strong plot. This is a tight market with less readership than the other age groups and formats, and many companies publishing them do them in house or on assignment, or as part of a series. They often used a "controlled vocabulary" as well. However, these beginning readers are every bit as interested in paranormal subjects as the others and would no doubt enjoy a book about ghosts, zombies or werewolves.

Picture books or picture book stories are a very specific format which may be aimed at any age from preschool to middle school depending upon the content. The hallmark of a picture book is that it is nearly always 32 pages long, for technical printing reasons. Rarely, you might see one that is 48 or 64 pages, but they are unusual. Of the 32 pages, generally about 28 are used for story and illustrations. The other pages are the title page, copyright, cataloging, and other ancillary material.

Most picture book text ranges from 500—1000 words. Many have text that is only 100—500 words. The story must have a natural pacing that leads it to page-turning, reading aloud at one sitting, and must have at least twelve illustratable scenes, preferably more. These scenes must be different enough to allow a new visual experience on each page layout. You as the author are not required to find the illustrator. Some authors are also professional illustrators and know the technical requirements for illustration, allowing them to illustrate their own stories, but most of the time the editor and the art director will select an illustrator if they choose to publish a story.

I hesitate to give these word count figures for the basic subdivisions of children's publishing because each publisher may have somewhat different preferences and there are always exceptions. The same caveat is true for what I will write below about acceptable content in children's and YA fiction.

YA/children's writing encompasses all sub-genres of paranormal fiction. At any particular time, one may be far more popular than another, but they are all included. In my experience, the term "paranormal" is so far less likely to be used in children's literature, with standard genre terms like fantasy, horror, science fiction, and supernatural more common.

Vampires are especially popular with teens. I believe it is because vampire stories are most often combined with romance, something harder to do with some of the other paranormal subjects. This vampire-romance connection is certainly the main feature of the *Twilight* series and it is difficult to find vampire or werewolf stories for teens that don't involve romance. In YA parlance, these are often termed "horror romance."

Both YAs and younger children are looking for paranormal fiction that encompasses mystery, danger, a sense of the unknown. They like being scared ... but not so scared they have to quit reading. They also appreciate humor, which is used far more often in paranormal fiction for younger readers. Always, the critical element is to see the story through the eyes of the age child you are writing for and keep the child or teen protagonist center stage. Don't allow adults to take over the story or solve the problems or the mysteries for your young main characters.

Another tricky element of writing for children and YAs is—just how far can you go? You might be surprised. YA books can be amazingly gritty and hard-hitting. It's hard to set any firm guidelines because so much depends upon the story itself. Gratuitous violence or foul language is not acceptable in any children's or YA book, nor is a wanton rendering of graphic sex scenes. However, violence, foul language and sex do exist in YA books, and, to a lesser and age appropriate extent, in books for younger children as well. Think about all of the scary and violent action in the Harry Potter books. (If you haven't read them, do!)

The key is that the use of such elements must be "age appropriate." The best way to get a good feel for what is acceptable in writing for these age groups is to read a lot of the best books already published for them, especially relatively current books published within the past few years. It's the most direct way to educate yourself about paranormal fiction for younger readers. Please see the list at the end of this chapter for some suggested reading.

That said, I'll try to take each of these elements and formulate some guidelines but they will necessarily be vague.

VIOLENCE

Think about the original versions of Grimm's fairy tales, before politically correct revisers saved Little Red Riding Hood from ever being eaten by the wolf. These tales were full of terrible parents (in *Cinderella*, *Snow White*, and *Hansel and Gretel*, for instance) who either abused or abandoned their children, witches who ate or otherwise killed children, animals who harmed children or stand-ins for them (like *The Three Little Pigs*), or a variety of giants, trolls, bad fairies and other creatures who were trying to harm the innocent protagonists. However, none of the violence was described in detail.

The fact that violence, profanity and sex exist in children's literature doesn't mean that it isn't endlessly controversial, sometimes resulting in censorship attempts.

In a story for younger children (up through primary grades and chapter books), a violent threat can be real, and if carried out (the wolf "gobbled up" Little Red Riding Hood, for instance), it's clear what has happened, or could happen, but it isn't described in gory detail. A main character may be injured (bruised, broken arm or leg, for instance) but I'd avoid such things as a severed limb, mutilation, copious quantities of blood or graphic descriptions of pain. Death of the antagonist, such as the wolf in *Little Red Riding Hood*, is acceptable if the story requires it, but again, is not described in bone-chilling detail. If you are aiming at a scary story, anticipation and fear of the mystery or unknown, of the threat, is the prime element. It's the suggestion of possible harm that makes the story.

If you are writing for middle graders, you can be more adventurous. These kids have well-developed imaginations and can handle more description and violent action. This is particularly where knowledge of children and their development is helpful. In middle grade fiction, there is also likely to be more overt reaction, emotion, and dialogue. Dangers are real and consequences realistic. Characters die, fights happen, destruction occurs. Characters can suffer. However, in middle grade fiction, the ending is usually satisfying and positive.

For the upper end of YA fiction, just about anything you might find in an adult book might be acceptable, depending upon the publisher. Even overt brutality might be included, but as always, it must be integral and for most books, not an extensive portion of the narrative. There are very dark stories for YAs where brutality and violence abound. In YA literature, happy endings aren't a given, either.

However, keep in mind that any violence in these stories must be integral to them, not overdone, not simply sensationalized or gratuitous. It must advance the plot, not BE the plot, and it must not be glorified. Like profanity, a little goes a long way, and a shocking scene is more shocking if it is a climax scene, not one a string of them.

At the lower end of YA fiction, a somewhat gentler touch is needed, but that doesn't mean you can't include violence when necessary. In my book, *The Secret of Whispering Springs*, Jason Campbell, the shadowy criminal who is trying to find a treasure, tries to enlist fourteen-year-old Cassie's assistance by threatening to harm her younger brother. 's fear of Campbell is real, as is the danger itself. Campbell eventually kidnaps an old woman, Miss Mossman, and Annie, the fourteen-year-old ghost intervenes and pushes him off an embankment. He's an evil character whose threats are real, and the only way to stop him is through violence.

In other parts of the book, Annie's father accidentally kills his best friend in a fight, Annie's younger mother and brother die of disease, and Annie herself is killed by lightning. None of these things is outside the realm of possibility and they are tragic events that shape the story. There are no extended descriptions of the deaths but the consequences to Annie and her family are poignantly drawn. The paranormal element is the ghost of Annie herself and her quest to discover the dark secret of her family's past.

PROFANITY

When in doubt, don't. That's the easiest rule I can give you. Profanity is rarely necessary to a story, and in general, liberal use of it deadens it's shock value as well as lessening your chances of publication, particularly for any audience younger than the upper group of YAs.

That said, there are children's and YA books in which limited profanity can be found. There are situations when it is necessary, when not using it doesn't ring true. Any book written for children that contains "foul language" is likely to be challenged by someone wanting it removed from a public or school library. However, despite that, there are outstanding books that do have limited amounts of profanity in them, sometimes only a single word. Public libraries generally successfully resist challenges due to their commitment to freedom to read and their selection of good books deserving of defense.

When my son was in junior high, he protested that the books he was required to read were unrealistic because the characters didn't talk like real kids and never used any swear words. My son didn't have a foul mouth or use a lot of profanity, but he heard other kids who did, and just about all of them let loose with an occasional swear word. As a writer, you have to judiciously decide when it is necessary to use a four letter word and when it isn't. Because they are seldom used, particularly in anything below YA fiction, one word in a middle grade novel will stand out with real shock value. It has to be a situation where it's truly called for. I have never seen any profanity in early chapter books, easy readers or picture books, but that doesn't mean it hasn't ever happened. If I were writing for those age groups, I would leave it out.

There are audiences that feel very strongly about profanity in children's books, and for them, even "replacement" words like "darn" are unacceptable. I was once "uninvited" to do a previously booked school visit to a Mennonite community school when they discovered that my book, *Imagicat*, contained the word "darn." On another occasion, I did a school visit at a Lutheran school and while talking with the principal, who was thumbing through the nonfiction book I did with my mother, *Izzie—Growing Up on the Plains in the 1880s*, noticed that a word had been blacked out with a permanent marker. The word was "darn."

I would not leave out "darn" because of those who find it objectionable, and if I felt that a scene strongly required use of stronger language, I would probably use it. However, be aware that using profanity can be a trap, an "easy" way out of stronger writing. An editor will have to evaluate whether your use of it is worth the negative adult reaction it is likely to get. So again, when in doubt, leave it out. If you are writing for the upper end of the YA spectrum and your story and character require strong language, use it.

SEX

In fiction for readers under thirteen, overt sex is extremely unusual and basically taboo. That doesn't mean attraction isn't there, interest in the opposite sex, "schoolgirl crushes," and the like, but not sex. A light kiss or holding hands would be acceptable.

In the younger YA group, actual sex would be unusual and there would have to be a very strong reason for including it. That said, there are books that deal with more physical attraction and touching, kissing, and physical development, but for this to be a part of a paranormal story for kids 12-15, it would need to be integral to the storyline. There are books for this age group that deal with teen pregnancy, boyfriend-girlfriend relationships, even taboo topics like incest, but be very careful about including sex unless it is both necessary and age-appropriate. When I say "age appropriate," I mean from a parental or editorial point of view, regardless of whether some children at this age are engaging in sexual activity.

At the upper end of YA fiction, stories are much more frank and honest about sex. It should not be gratuitous or pornographic in detail or just thrown in for no reason other than to include it. However, it is not a taboo subject in YA books, which can be open about sex, including gay relationships.

VOCABULARY

There are controversies about the breadth (or lack thereof) of vocabulary in children's and YA books. One point of view insists that children won't read books that are too difficult and that the vocabulary needs to be simplified for them (read "dumbed down" if you're on the opposite side). The other insists with equal fervor that kids can't learn new vocabulary if they never see any, and that they enjoy the challenge of learning "cool" new words.

As a librarian, I learned to come down somewhere in the middle, but leaning toward a more extensive vocabulary. Children learn all the words they know by hearing or reading them, and if we never give them anything beyond a basic vocabulary, they won't acquire it, nor will they easily progress to reading adult books when they are at the YA level. I think it is important to use a good, broad vocabulary but not work at overtly choosing language that isn't a part of common parlance. They learn from context and for avid readers, learning new words is pleasure.

Studies have shown that the average child in the 1950's had a far greater working vocabulary than today's children, and the theory is that children today learn most of their words from children's and popular television shows, which are hardly known for outstanding vocabulary. Today's avid readers have much better vocabularies than other children, and learning more words from reading is a primary source, so don't deliberately dumb down your work and underestimate your readers.

That said, if you consistently write with a vocabulary and sentence structure (or plot structure, for that matter) which is far beyond your target age group, you aren't likely to get published, and if you do, the average reader in that age group probably won't continue to read your work. Many kids are taught that when they pick up a book and aren't sure they can read it, to use the "Five Finger Test." Basically, they pick a page in the middle of the book and read it. Each time they find a word they don't know, they hold up a finger. If they raise all five, the book is too hard. If they don't hold up any, it's too easy.

There are many children reading below grade level and it is a constant challenge for teachers, librarians and parents to find books that have an "interest level" at their age but a reading level below it. If you are one of the talented writers who can produce books that fit into that category, you may be able to help struggling readers to both progress and enjoy it.

Emerging and easy readers often do have controlled vocabulary lists that the publisher requires writers to use, but beyond those, I wouldn't try to limit yourself to a list. Write the story without worrying too much about this aspect. As long as it is appropriate for your intended audience, your editor will help polish it.

PARANORMAL SUBJECT MATTER

While vampires seem to be particularly popular right now, especially in YA books that include a heavy dose of romance, ghost stories of all kinds are perennially in demand for all age groups, from picture books up. There are far fewer books dealing with parapsychology and psychic phenomena, time travel, mysticism, the occult, other kinds of hauntings, angels, fairies, leprechauns, witches, shapeshifters, zombies, or other kinds of mythological or folkloric creatures and monsters. Some of these subjects include the realms of fantasy or horror.

As a librarian, I avidly looked for books featuring unicorns, of which there are very few for any age despite their popularity with young girls in particular. An exception is Bruce Coville's series, *The Unicorn Chronicles.*

While vampires are likely to continue in popularity for some time to come, don't concentrate on writing vampire stories unless that is your forte and what you are compelled to write. There are so many other paranormal phenomena that are facing far less competition and offer opportunities for fresh, new stories more likely to catch an editor's attention. Some of them are barely dealt with in children's literature.

Many of the books about paranormal subjects for younger readers (preschool to primary grades) are not scary but meant to be somewhat reassuring about the otherwise frightening subjects, and those for middle graders are often tongue-in-cheek and humorous. Most picture books about ghosts, goblins, witches, vampires or zombies are Halloween stories that are only mildly scary or not scary at all.

However, many middle graders and younger YAs crave really scary books and are "offended" by those that provide a lighter touch or humor and seek out scarier alternatives. Older YA readers have an excellent selection of truly scary books available to them. Teen readers in general don't like it when stories that seem to be about a ghost or some other paranormal being are revealed to be something that is part of normal experience or the paranormal phenomena are explained away.

When I was writing *The Secret of Whispering Springs* and doing many school visits to elementary and junior high schools, the students would invariably insist that I "make it scary." I wanted to do that, but I'm not a "gory" writer, so that option, which works well for some authors, wasn't open to me. I had to figure out ways to create fear, anticipation and suspense without any bloody descriptions.

So, how DO you make it scary? A primary technique is to make something unexpected and potentially threatening happen. Cassie (14) and herr brother Ben (8) wheedle their parents into letting them explore the boarded up old prairie mansion they are buying. The readers suspect there's something weird about the house so they are anticipating what the two kids might find. It was my job as an author to make it surprising and create a sense of fear.

> "Hey, wait for me," Ben yelled, and came stampeding through the door. When he saw how dark it was, he stopped short. "It's spooky in there, too," he whispered. "Look at all the cobwebs and dust."

> Cassie went after her brother, who cautiously shuffled his way through the small enclosed porch leading to the kitchen. He opened the inner door. It creaked eerily in the beam of the flashlight and was quickly slammed shut from the inside. A piercing wail emanated from the kitchen. Cassie and Ben turned and ran toward the crack of light where they hadn't tightly closed the porch door. They burst into the warm spring sunshine and dashed for the car.

From that point on, Cassie is confronted by one threatening element after another. She sees a man in the third floor tower window and finds evidence of someone camping out in the barn. She is surrounded by whispering sounds she can't understand, until finally she hears, "Beware, beware." She knows she and Ben are being watched.

No matter what Cassie sees, her parents have a perfectly normal explanation for it and she is left on her own. When she finds tins of old letters in the cellar when they are cleaning it out, she takes them to the room that will be hers and has another disorienting experience.

> She opened a tin, lifted out a bundle of letters and untied the faded red satin ribbon. As she took the top envelope off the stack, she felt the something brush past her arm, as though someone

was there. The air shimmered slightly as it had the first day she stood in this room. For just an instant, she could see a tall four-poster bed, and on the desk lay an old nib pen by a letter that began, "Dear Aunt Marie." It was dated April 5, 1897.

"It's my room," said the whispery voice, "My desk. Don't leave me. Read them."

Cassie swung around on the chair, trying to catch a glimpse of whomever was whispering, but could see no one there, just that unsteadiness in the air, almost like the heat waves on the highway that make things in the distance waver. She felt dizzy again, as the room returned to the present, empty except for the walnut desk and chair. She tried to get up and run for the door but icy hands pressed her to the chair, pulled her hand back to the letters.

"Just one," said the voice. "Just one today."

"Who are you?" Cassie said, her own voice barely croaking out a whisper.

"Just read one letter. Please." The cold hand closed around her arm.

Shaking now, Cassie took the folded sheet from the envelope. The writing was faded but still readable.

"My Dear Sister," she started. Her voice didn't sound right, as though it were coming from somewhere far away. She cleared her throat and tried to stop shaking. The cold withdrew, almost as though it could gather itself into a ball and move away. Did she dare leave now? She peered around the room. Where was the cold presence with the icy hands?

"Read," the voice whispered, close to her ear. She could feel a cold breath raise the hairs on her neck.

Cassie knew she'd never make it to the door.

Cassie is even more terrified when she starts getting email from the man she saw in the window. He threatens to harm or kill her brother if she doesn't help him find something he wants in the old house. She knows he is watching her and she starts calling him the Spy. By now, she is scared to even look at her email.

Online. She'd never been afraid to connect before. While she waited for her password to be verified, she fingered the iris brooch. It was so beautiful. Over a hundred years old and it belong to a dead girl who had the same birthday she did. And now, she might be a ghost.

The screen changed and her email Inbox appeared. There were 16 messages, some from kids at school, one from Jordan (she really typed one in?) and one from the strange address of the Spy. Cassie took a deep breath. She might as well go right to that one. She wouldn't be able to think about the others anyway. As she clicked on it, she closed her eyes tight and said a silent prayer. "Please, God, please don't let him hurt my family. Don't let him hurt Ben."

The words leapt out at her from the screen. "Don't play games with me, kid. You don't ask the questions. You do as you are told and keep your mouth shut if you care about your brother. You can't do anything for me in town. Make sure you are out at the house tomorrow, with or without your parents. Meet me in the graveyard. Alone."

In the graveyard scene, Cassie is confronted by both the ghost and the man who is terrorizing her. For me and for many readers, this was the scariest scene in the book.

As Cassie headed toward the low stone wall that surrounded the graveyard, a sudden cold wind swirled around her as though she was caught in some invisible whirlpool. Freezing fingers gripped her wrists hard and pulled her toward the tombstones. She tried to pull her hands away and couldn't. Cassie panicked and managed to wheel around. She tried to run. It was useless. The icy hands pulled harder.

Surely she was imagining the whispered words in her ears. She tried to block out everything but the feel of her feet dragging toward the tombstones she could see past the wall but the whispering became more insistent, louder and more distinct. Her wrists hurt. She started shaking. What if there were no "Spy"? What if the man in the barn really was just a tramp and was gone? Maybe this strange entity with the vice grip on her wrists was the one luring her out here. How? For what?

The thick cold air wrapped itself around her as it had in the barn and pushed her toward the tombs, the freezing hands still clamped to her wrists. She fought it, stumbling on the weed-choked, rocky path, shivering from both the intense cold that enveloped her and her fear. She remembered the whistle in her pocket and wondered whether blowing it would help, whether she could even get it out.

A burst of frigid air pushed Cassie, hard, through an opening in the low stone wall and into the small overgrown graveyard.

The force calmed somewhat and let go of her wrists. It seemed to gather itself together and leave her. Though it was no longer surrounding her, holding her, Cassie could tell it had just withdrawn a few feet away. She was standing near a tombstone. Cassie caught her breath. She thought she saw a slight shimmer to the air, and within it, a hazy figure.

The whispering grew to a hiss in her ears. Don't listen, she told herself, but there was no way to block it out. At first she only heard, "Beware, beware." It startled her when the words changed. "Don't move," it said. "Stay there if you want to be safe."

Cassie felt her heart pounding, harder than it ever had in her life. She trembled all over. She had spent two days in terror over meeting the Spy here but she had never expected to be threatened by some invisible force, by the voice of Whispering Springs. She struggled to make her mind comprehend. Where was the Spy? Was he coming? Was this what she really should be afraid of?

Then Cassie looked at the grave stone. She gasped. The old stone was worn and hard to read, but Cassie could still make out the words. She read, in a hoarse whisper,

"Annie Katherine Gwynne

Born May 24, 1883

Died June 16, 1897

Beloved daughter of Joseph and Adele,

Struck down and taken from me.

Now is the end of all my joy.

May the angels protect her forevermore."

Annie's grave. She was standing on Annie's grave, and something had forced her there, whispering warnings—or were they threats? She looked up. The stone was topped by a beautiful white marble angel, wings spread, hair flowing, and a wreath of carved flowers in her hair. She was beautiful even with the years of discoloration and lichen growing on her. Did the angels protect Annie? What was going to protect her, Cassie?

She turned her back to the angel, knees weak, and slumped to the ground. Her throat was dry. She rubbed her aching wrists. She had used up all the energy she had coming this far.

The whispered words were softer now, harder to make out. She caught a word here and there, "Stay there ... Don't move ... Beware."

Time seemed to stop. It felt as though she had been there, sitting on Annie's grave, for hours, but when Cassie checked her watch, she knew it couldn't have been more than ten minutes.

She heard a rustling in the grass behind her. She stood up, wobbly, and tried to turn around, but not fast enough. Strong, rough hands grabbed her from behind and held her.

"It appears you know how to follow instructions," the man's voice said. "That's good. Do as I say and you and your brother will be safe."

Cassie was surprised. She thought the Spy would have a rough voice, but he sounded calm. In control.

"Don't ask questions. Just listen. There is a treasure hidden in the house. I want it, and I will stop at nothing to get it. You are going to see to it that I get it.

"But how?" Cassie blurted out. "I don't know where it is. How can I get it?"

He shook her. "Shut up. Your parents must know about it. Why else would they buy the old place? But they haven't found it yet, have they? Because if they have, and you think it's too late, I'll still find a way."

"Let me go," Cassie said. "I'll listen." Maybe she could at least see what he looked like. She was surprised her voice worked and that she actually used it.

"Fat chance," he said, tightening his grip on her shoulders. "Now here's what you do. There is a clue in a letter somewhere. You find that letter and give it to me. Tell no one. Send email. I know you already found some old letters. There will be more. I'll be in touch. Work fast."

Defiantly, Cassie answered, "And what if I don't? What if I can't?

The man moved his hands to her neck and began to squeeze. Cassie coughed and choked.

"Don't play games with me, kid. I could wring your neck like a chicken."

The scene that many YAs who wrote to me or talked to me at schools found the scariest was this very short one. I believe they found it so frightening because it seems like such a violation of one's person. Annie is the ghost of the fourteen-year-old girl who died in 1897.

> Cassie headed through the kitchen, opened the cellar door and flipped on the light switch.
>
> "Oh, there you are," her mother called from the pantry next door. "If you're going to the cellar, could you take this box of tiles down there?" She headed for Cassie and held it out.
>
> Cassie reached for the box and nearly fell down the stairs when she saw Annie pass right through her mother's body. She gasped and grabbed the door frame. The box of tiles clattered to the floor, breaking several of them.

If you are writing a paranormal story that isn't intended to be frightening (and there are many good ones that aren't), all the normal techniques we use to write good fiction apply just as much to books for children as to those for adults. Give your readers a little challenge. They shouldn't find it too easy to figure out the mystery, too easy to anticipate the ending. Give them to wonder of surprise, of being startled, of new realizations.

The pace of a story is critical for any audience, but particularly so for young readers. Often writers for all ages take too long to get into the story or get bogged down in the middle, or don't know when the story actually should end. Tension and momentum are primary ingredients of most stories and young readers are extraordinarily sensitive to them. Any lag in a story smacks of the deadliest reading problem for kids. . . it's boring.

That doesn't mean there has to be nonstop action or the story should lack descriptive passages. It means that everything you leave in should be important to and advance the story in a way that makes you want to read the next sentence, the next paragraph, the next chapter. It's that "can't put the book down" factor. This must be part of your editing and revising process. I remember cutting out entire chapters from my books *Imagicat* and *The Secret of Whispering Springs*. It's hard to cut, but it's even more important in writing for children than it is in writing for adults. Be sure you end every chapter with a hook, something the reader can't wait to find out. These techniques will work for all kinds of paranormal subjects.

A master example of pacing and chapter end hooks for middle graders is Bruce Coville's *Jeremy Thatcher, Dragon Hatcher*. It was one of my favorite books to recommend to middle grade readers and never failed to enchant them. One family presented me with a pair of dragon earrings as a gift for suggesting they read it. Mother and daughter took turns reading chapters aloud to each other and as they were nearing the end, Jenna urgently told her mother, "Hurry, mommy, hurry!" She was so anxious to find out what would happen she even wanted her mother to read faster!

The three primary differences between writing for children/YAs and adults are the age of the protagonist, the average length of the book, and keeping the writing age-appropriate. Of those, the last one is the hardest and will come to you either because you are a child at heart (most writers for young people say they are, that they write for the child within) or because you know children well, know what they identify with, what they find interesting, how they think and feel, what is natural to them. And it will be bolstered by reading a lot of excellent books written for the age group you are writing for.

A READING LIST OF PARANORMAL YA AND CHILDREN'S BOOKS

In the resource section at the end of this book, you'll find a suggested reading list of YA and Children's books. This list is not intended to be in any way comprehensive but just to provide a short list of well-reviewed and popular titles to give you some background. I have tried to list primarily current and recent books, but in some cases have included older titles that are either particular favorites of mine or fine examples of a paranormal subject found less often in books for children and YAs.

Collection development librarians (also known as acquisitions librarians), those who choose what books to order for schools and libraries, rely on professional journal reviews in order to select books. For a list of journals that review children's and young adult books, see the Resource List at the end of this chapter. Collection development was a major part of my duties as a librarian and I have followed that same procedure in selecting this book list. I have read some, but not all of these books. I have read several reviews of all listed books.

Classic children's literature includes books you may not have thought of as paranormal, such as the fantasies of *The Wonderful Wizard of Oz* and *Alice's Adventures in Wonderland*. However, classics were written in another time when writing styles were different. They endure because of their universal appeal and excellence, but writing in a similar style today would probably be a difficult sell.

The monsterlibrarian.com website (see the Resource List) also has useful lists of other paranormal books for teens on subjects such as zombies, monsters, ghosts (look under "Supernatural). These lists are focused on what the site defines as "horror fiction."

It's Time to Travel

By Barbara Baldwin

Have you ever read a great book or seen a super movie about a historic time period and wished you could go there? Maybe you even wished you lived in that era, where men were gallant gentlemen and ladies wore beautiful dresses and fine jewels, and they danced the forbidden waltz in elegant ballrooms. For those with umbilical cords to your palms, iPods and computers, you may want to think about time travel into the future, but for those of us who long for the mysterious and romanticized past, where you could change identities without the FBI tracking you down, and you could become a self-made millionaire with the right knowledge, travel into the past is a wonderful escape.

Time travel, whether into the future or the past, can be written as a subgenre of another—mystery, romance, suspense—but it is basically part of the paranormal, which is becoming more and more recognized as a genre of its own. For me, time travel is always into the past. I love the romance of a historic period, usually around 1850-1880, where there were no cell phones to call 911 in an emergency; no helicopters to rescue the hero and heroine at the abandoned cabin; and none of the modern conveniences which make our lives so fast, hectic and ...well, modern.

People in the 1800's had to carry on conversations; there was no television to fill the void. They had to figure out how to overcome adversity without finding an instant answer on the internet. Some disbelievers say it wasn't a romantic era at all and ask questions like, "What about modern plumbing? What about medicine and doctors?" The beauty of being the author is that if you think your heroine can't use a chamber pot or an outhouse, then set the story in the later 1870's when indoor plumbing was becoming more common. But I ask you, what could be more relaxing than a hot bath in a tub, instead of a quick shower before you jet off to somewhere else?

The medicine/doctor concern will only be an issue if your story contains an epidemic or the plague. Most stories don't contend with disease and illness, and there were doctors back in the 1800's; even if they didn't know as much as our modern physicians do. Many times, common sense worked much better. In my book *Carousel*, when Nicholas falls through the ice into a freezing pond, Jaci gradually warms his legs because she knows that rubbing them can do more damage.

I've tried to separate the various elements of time travel to make it easier to understand, but I find almost all of them overlap and twine around each other. So I might introduce a concept, but it may be discussed in depth later.

For explanation purposes in this chapter, I will make reference to three periods of time—historic (the past), present (today) and futuristic (beyond 2009). The main elements– believability, method of travel, conflict, etc—apply regardless of where your traveler ends up.

Keep in mind that you're not writing futuristic if your character comes from the past to the present as in *Kate & Leopold*. Even though Leopold travels forward from his time, it is basically a historic-present story because it's really Kate's story. The same is true of Jude Deveraux's *Knight in Shining Armor*. Although Nicholas comes forward from his time, the story belongs to Douglass, who resides in the present.

One of the unique things about writing time travel is the humor it can evoke. There's nothing like throwing someone back a hundred or more years in time and expecting him/her to cope. In my book, *Nevada Gold*, Ellie is taken back in time by Zeke and Lucky, two gold miners, because she looks like Elizabeth, a woman in 1870. Ellie doesn't want to be there, even after she experiences kissing Jesse Cole, the hero. But she's willing to make the best of it:

"Just exactly how involved is Jesse with Elizabeth?"...Some morbid imp in her head wanted to know about Jesse Cole's love life. "I need to know if Elizabeth's been making out with Jesse. Don't you think it would be strange if I, as Elizabeth, decide not to anymore?" Although that'd be a cold day in hell.

Zeke turned the brightest red Ellie had ever seen a person turn. "Making out?" The words squeaked out of his mouth.

"Yeah, you know, sparking. Don't tell me they don't do that in the 1870's. Explain to me about kissing."

I choose to send my heroines back in time and put them into situations totally alien to them. It increases conflict because it sets the stage for mis-interpretation and confusion. Other books/movies choose a different protagonist. In the movie *Kate & Leopold*, Leopold comes to the present day, and in *Somewhere in Time* Richard, the hero, is the one who goes back in time. In Jude Deveraux's *Knight in Shining Armor*, both the heroine goes back in time and the hero comes forward to the present (his future). In yet another two examples, *The Love Letters* and *The Lake House*, the people don't travel through time, but letters do. So perhaps this is where we should start a discussion on writing time travel—the basic rules.

If you're going to write it, read it. You hear that at every writer's workshop you ever go to and it's especially relevant for writing paranormal because believability plays such a huge part. You really have to sound like you know what you're talking about.

Since we're writing fiction, you can't just list your rules up front like an abstract in a scientific journal. The rules become evident through your writing. Sometimes it is very simple, as in *The Lake House* when the two main characters discover their letters are crossing two years of time:

Kate: "Can this really be happening?"

Alex: "Why not?"

With those simple notes written to each other, the audience suspends their disbelief and jumps into the story with them.

Sometimes a more difficult explanation is made, such as Stuart made in *Kate & Leopold* when he explained how he found a portal—a crack in the fabric of time, like an eclipse that only occurs once in twenty years—when he created a formula to forecast portals, based on weather patterns. He had to jump from a very high place to create enough velocity to …. Well, you get the picture. The audience knows time travel can't be that simple because some meteorologist would have discovered it already, but it *sounds* plausible, and it did work in the movie, so it must be possible. And they jump.

How do you decide this particular story should be a time travel, rather than a straight mystery, romance, or futuristic? An editor once asked me if I took the time travel elements out of the story, would the story still exist? If the answer is yes, it shouldn't be a time travel. If the story wouldn't exist without someone or something traveling through time, then that becomes a major element and therefore plays a central part in the story. The whole focus of *The Lake House* is the time difference, and in *Kate & Leopold*, there would be no story if he hadn't traveled through time.

The same is true for *Nevada Gold*, when Ellie is taken back in time to right a wrong—to keep Jesse from dying in a mine accident.. Once she time traveled, the conflict increased because she's pretending to be someone else and she's in a race against time.

A psychic I visited with in Kansas explained her ability to give people guidance and insight by saying her spiritual guides could travel through time—forward and back—and that was how they knew what happened in the person's life. She said that time runs parallel; e.g. the past and present and future are all happening at the same time. So theoretically, a person could "jump" time—like a train jumping off track, or a phonograph needle skipping across the groves of a record— and end up in a different time.

BASIC RULES FOR WRITING TIME TRAVEL: BELIEVABILITY

The most fundamental rule for any work of fiction is believability. Regardless of where in time you place the story, who and/or what your characters are personally or professionally, what events trigger the time travel, what conflict occurs, and especially the resolution at the end, your readers have to be able to suspend their belief that time travel isn't possible, in order for them to go with you on this adventure. They are more than half convinced in the beginning, otherwise they wouldn't pick up a book marked time travel. So everything that follows—how they travel, the internal and external conflict, changing history, the resolution—must be written in such a manner that the reader is sucked in and totally with you. They believe in the magic mailbox at *The Lake House*; they are convinced the door at the bed & breakfast is a portal to the past (*Indigo Bay*); and that rips in the fabric of time are possible (*Kate & Leopold*).

How do you convince them of the possibility? In *Indigo Bay*, Mica passes through a door in the bed & breakfast inn she's inherited. The house was built in the 1800's, so it's not like she went through a door in a house built in 2009, but even so, how is the reader convinced that something as simple as a door can lead to the past?

> "Humid air surrounded her as a warm breeze swept down the hall. She thought perhaps this section [of the inn] had been shut off for repairs, since apparently the air conditioner didn't work. The hallway appeared to have a design similar to the rest of the inn...and contained dim lights of the same style. She stepped through the first door she found...[and] the glamour of a bygone era wrapped her in warmth and welcome...The only illumination came from an antique oil lamp on the desk... Although lending an historical air to the room, if a lamp should tip over..."

In some books/movies, a traveler is thrust into a different time without preparation, but in *Indigo Bay*, Mica visits "the other side" several times before actually realizing she is in the past. Since the bed and breakfast inn is actually the restored original plantation house of Indigo Bay, the reader believes, as does Mica, that it's simply another section of the inn, rather than a door to the past. By the time she does figure it out, readers already understand she's going back and forth through the door, so it's not such a shock for them to accept that the door leads to the past.

The benefit of writing time travel is that since there are theories, but no actuality, you get to make your own rules. You can decide how the time travel is done, what goes and what stays, whether they can go back and forth through time and what history can be changed because the traveler knows the future.

However, making the time travel rules doesn't mean you can make the rules for the historic period to which your character travels. If travel is back to 1850, there can't suddenly be automobiles or airplanes. Now perhaps your heroine has her cell phone in her pocket when she is transported and it travels with her. Depending on *your* rules, that might be possible, but for what reason? It's not like there would be anyone back in 1850 that she could call. If something from the heroine's time is the *object* that will take her back, then it becomes an important element. In the book *Somewhere In Time*, it was a simple penny that caused the hero to go back to his own time, in this case against his wishes, so be careful what you have them take!

So as you set down the rules that will guide your writing, think them through very carefully. Among all the suggestions and the various ways authors have written time travel, I've only found one cardinal rule—**ONCE YOU MAKE THE RULES, YOU CAN'T BREAK THEM.** Not for the convenience of your characters, not to save a nation from disaster, not even to save the hero or heroine. This goes right back to believability.

As an example, let's say the heroine gets in an elevator at an old mansion/turned resort, goes down, and exits into a bygone era. The elevator then disappears from the wall. (The rule no doubt being elevators hadn't been invented back then.) Much later in the story, the hero is hurt and she knows if she gets him to modern medicine he will get well, so she takes him to the wall and stands, and the elevator miraculously reappears to transport them back to the present. If it was that easy, why didn't she stay by the wall at the very beginning and have the elevator appear and take her back to her present? The whole essence of a story of time travel is its plausibility, and if you mess it up, you've lost your reader; not just for this book, but perhaps for any future books.

In *Indigo Bay*, my basic rule was that anything that didn't exist back in 1850 did not travel through the portal with her. For example, the plastic buttons fell off her pajamas and the synthetic sandal straps disappeared, leaving her with only the leather soles. The question is asked then, how could she travel back in time since she wouldn't have existed then? The explanation becomes part of the story when Logan accidently comes across the portal with her into her present time (and what would be his future) but becomes a ghost. She explains since her past has happened, she can visit it, but since Logan's future hasn't happened, he can't be there in the flesh.

Does time need to move at the same speed in the past and present? Whether your traveler goes back and forth in time or stays put, you still have to consider this factor. For example in *The Lake House*, if Kate's time (the present) moved twice as fast as Alex's, (two years in the past), would they have ever been able to catch up with each other?

If a story takes place over a long period of time—say, several years—wouldn't someone in the present miss the traveler? This is an important element because there needs to be resolution at the end—for the traveler and for those left behind. How would it be explained if the traveler returned after a five year absence? I dealt with this in *Carousel* by having one year of the past equal to one day in the present. So when Jaci's sister discovers where Jaci disappeared to, it has been five years of Jaci's life (the length of the story) but only five days of her sister's.

If your traveler can move back and forth between times, it is probably beneficial (but not necessarily required) that time in both eras travel at the same speed. So when Mica *(Indigo Bay)* spends the day with Logan, she is simply "out" for the day at Sea Crest. If I had made the ratio any different, such as 1:1.5 or 1:3, it would have been incredibly hard to keep track of her, not just for me as the author, but for my readers. Having a different time ratio would also create problems if the story were a race against time. A good analogy can be made when you think about traveling transatlantic or transpacific. Do you leave your watch set on the time where you live and keep mentally adjusting, or do you change it to the time where you are currently residing? Your character has enough problems dealing with the hero, a different culture, and how the heck she ended up there in the first place. At least let her know what time it is (but if she's traveling to the past, make certain the watch isn't battery powered).

Traveling through Time: Forms of travel

Do people or things actually go through time, or do people just *think* or *dream* that they do? Because there are no written rules, it has been done a variety of ways and it's up to you to determine what works for your plot.

People bodily travel through time (probably the most prevalent)

Back to the Future –Marty is propelled into the past where he's a Physical being.

Indigo Bay—Mica walks through a door, remaining in her physical form.

Knight in Shining Armor—Both Nicholas and Douglass physically go forward and back in time.

Things criss-cross in time through another device

The Lake House—only the letters go through time in the mailbox.

The Love Letters—letters go through time in a desk that existed in both time eras.(But see also the next category)

Spirit/Mind—some may call it shape-shifting when the spirit leaves the body

The Two Worlds of Jennie Logan—when Jennie dies to travel through time, her present day ex-husband finds her body, so just her spirit went.

The Love Letters—Scotty goes through time to be with Lizzie but at the end of the movie, he's had a bump on the head. Did his body really travel, or did his spirit travel while he was in a coma?

Traveling through time: Methods and reasons

Again, there are no rules for how a person time travels, other than it needs to be believable. The following examples show how many different methods there are:

Outlander series—touching a stone at Craig na Dun.

Kate & Leopold—rip in the fabric of time.

Nevada Gold—through a blue mist in the mine.

Carousel—touching a horse carved back in 1874.

Knight in Shining Armor—the heroine touches the hero's tomb and he is called forth because of her need.

Indigo Bay—through a door in the house that was built back in 1850.

Somewhere in Time—through self-hypnosis.

The Two Worlds of Jennie Logan—putting on an antique dress.

The Love Letters & *The Lake House*—only letters traveled, through a desk and a mailbox, respectively.

The reason a character travels through time in the first place creates much of the conflict in a time travel. Are they sent to save someone from dying or from losing everything? Are they sent to right a wrong or to help someone in need? In some cases (*Kate & Leopold*) perhaps they were just sent to find their soul mate. That tends to be the ultimate prize in many time travels, regardless of original motivation.

TRAVELING THROUGH TIME: MOVING THROUGH TIME AND SPACE

If we believe in the idea of time running parallel like train tracks, we can also believe that if you jump the track, you end up in a different time. But what about a different place? Doesn't it seem plausible that if a person could travel through time, they could also travel through space? Most of the examples I use take the traveler to a different time but they remain in the same place. The reason is simple—the place is necessary to the story setting. For example, the house used in the setting for *Indigo Bay* was built in 1850 and was owned by Logan, the hero, so when Mica passes through the door, she is still in the same house because that is where the story takes place. She didn't pass through a door in a house built in 2009 and end up in a house built in 1850.

There are authors who have moved their characters through time and space, even though an editor once told me that violated the laws of relativity. Remember you are writing fiction, where anything is possible as long as it's believable. Karen Marie Moning, author of *Beyond the Highland Mist*, used a vengeful fairy to take her character back in time and from contemporary Seattle to Scotland. Lynn Kurland, in *Dance Through Time*, also took her main character from Central Park in New York City back in time to Scotland.

In my book *Carousel*, Jaci is transported through time and place through touching the black lead horse on a restored Dentzel carousel. She travels from the present to 1874 and from Dallas, where the restored carousel was, to outside Philadelphia, where the man who carved the black horse lived. The horse was the connection and it had ingrained memory of the original time and place where it was made. This allows the scenario to be believable.

When setting up your time travel, decide whether your characters travel through one or two dimensions and determine the reason for that. It's just not probable to have them floating around the universe without a plan. In *The Lake House*, the mailbox remained in the same place; only the time varied. In *Somewhere in Time*, the hotel was the same and only the time was different. Yet in *Carousel*, because the horse was created in Philadelphia back in 1874 and it was now in Dallas as part of the restored carousel, it was plausible for Jaci to travel through time (present to 1874) and space (Dallas to Philadelphia).

Traveling through time: What travels and what disappears?

You need to establish before you start writing what a traveler can take and what they can't. You don't want to get to the end of the book and "all of a sudden" have some amazing "fix-it" never mentioned before. Of course, everything doesn't have to be laid out for the reader at the beginning, but you need to know. Things can be introduced gradually. Usually everything that "transports" with the traveler has a reason for being there.

In two of my time travels—*Nevada Gold* and *Carousel*—whatever the heroines had on their persons went back with them. In *Carousel* this was important because Jaci uses what is in her fanny pack—her keys, credit card and a color photograph—to convince Nicholas she really is from the future.

> She quickly unfolded a paper and shoved it into his hands. "Look. There's a picture of you, and this horse."
>
> He surveyed the paper..."It is a painted miniature of a horse similar—"
>
> "It's not a painting, it's a photograph—a colored photograph."

...Suddenly his breath caught. "Dear God, it's true"...He pointed
to a corner of the picture and she bent close to see the spot.
"It's the airplane you told Amanda about." He looked up at her,
his voice incredulous. "I thought you were making it up—that
you had a vivid imagination."

A different rule applied in *Indigo Bay* but since my books were written independently and didn't have connection with each other, the rules for each could differ. Just so long as I didn't break the rules once I made them. In *Indigo Bay*, nothing that hadn't been invented in 1850 went back when Mica went through the portal. She quickly learned to wear only cotton or silk; no polyester. But more important—she had to find a way to help Logan save his indigo plantation.

She was a lawyer in the present and had quite a large portfolio of stocks and investments, none of which were any good in 1850. She couldn't write a check to him; couldn't access her ATM or make an online balance transfer. My readers wonder how she's going to help and that keeps them turning the pages. When Mica realized what she could do, it was a total revelation to her, but as the author, I had carefully researched the gold restrictions, inflation, and what type of coins would have been minted by 1850.

"You want your entire portfolio turned into cash?" [Matthew, her
friend and financial advisor, asked.]

"Not cash. Gold...Can it be done?"

"Of course it can be done. Any restrictions on buying gold were
lifted in 1972."

[Later]

She signed the necessary papers as they counted out her gold
in American Eagles. Even dated, the gold coins would travel
through time and Mica figured she could worry about melting
it down later. Given the current price of three-hundred-ninety
dollars per troy ounce, she left with a briefcase containing
only seventeen pounds of twenty-four carat gold.

She didn't know how much purchasing power the gold would
have in 1850, but she figured it would be a lot more than today.

The Lake House is also a good example. The rule is only what goes in the mailbox crosses time between Kate and Alex. So there's no way

Kate can fit in the mailbox to go through time (that would make it too easy anyway), but she can send Alex a book published in 2006, even though he's in 2004—in the mailbox.

Reasons are important here, too. Remember my mention of a cell phone going through time? Was there a reason? Is that phone paramount to the plot? It's not that everything has to have a reason, but why not? Otherwise, your readers may wander through the entire book thinking, "What about the cell phone?"

TRAVELING THROUGH TIME: BALANCING NATURE

Can a person just pop into another time without causing ripples somewhere? Does the traveler have to switch places with someone in that time, or does a person have to die for another to travel to that particular space? Again there's no evidence for this, so the rules are up to you. It is a question you should answer before you start writing because it might affect other things. In *Back to the Future*, Marty pretends to be a teen from out of town and his mother almost falls in love with him instead of his father! Since everything he did in that time would have a bearing on his own future, he had to get them together. In this particular case, it was important to the plot because he was also in a race against time.

In *Nevada Gold*, Ellie (the heroine) looks like Elizabeth (the villainess) so she's taken through time to act in Elizabeth's place to help prevent a death in a mining explosion. But what do I do with the real Elizabeth? It's easy enough to send her on the stage to visit an ailing aunt in another town, but eventually, Ellie's going to stay in the past with Jesse, whom she loves by the end of the story, so I have to eliminate Elizabeth because they can't both be in the same place and time. AUGH!! Killing Elizabeth off in the same mining accident she caused the first time would be justifiable, but sending her through time to take Ellie's place was much more satisfying:

"Reno, July 6, 2006

A delusional woman...was found by tourists in the ghost town

264

of Peavine...The woman, dressed in old-fashioned clothes, claimed to be one Elizabeth Calhoun, but a representative from Hartman Publishing stated she was Ellie Weaver, one of their writers who had been missing for weeks. After repeatedly professing she was from the year 1870, the woman was transported to a state sanitarium."

CONFLICT

Any good plot has both internal and external conflict. Internal conflict relates to what the character is thinking, feeling, reacting, doing. External conflict occurs when two characters have different goals or when all the activity is outside the character's control.

One of the basic internal conflicts in a time travel is not understanding or accepting what has happened. After all, if you woke up in a different century, would you believe it? The first time Mica steps beyond the house and realizes she's not in her own time leads to confusion in *Indigo Bay*:

> There were no clusters of bright-colored beach umbrellas stuck in the sand, ready to be rented the following morning. For as far as she could see, there was not one piece of litter scattered anywhere on the pristine sand...There were no lights up and down the length of shoreline, no privacy fences stretching to the edge of the sand to ensure each owner's territorial rights... Where was the traffic noise, so constant even from across the bay? Where was the odd odor so often prevalent because of the clogged bay and stagnant waters?

More internal conflict comes when a character has to make a total reversal in his/her thinking. In *Carousel*, Jaci is a very independent, self-sufficient woman. When she travels back to 1874, none of her skills as a professional photographer do her any good. She must learn to depend on Nicholas for everything—food, clothing, shelter, and understanding of that era's culture.

It's important to write in situations where 1) the difference in the centuries is very evident; 2) the traveler reacts to and gradually adjusts to a different time; and 3) he/she is eventually at peace with the new time in which he/she lives. This doesn't happen overnight, but it does need to happen. Your whole story can be the internal struggle for the character coming to grips with what happened, rather than focusing on external conflict, but that might put it more into a literary category rather than genre fiction.

One way I helped my characters with this transition was to give them hope things might go back to normal. Remember, to keep your reader believing, they have to experience the same confusion, then hope, as your character.

Indigo Bay—(Mica uses a key to go through the door in time) When Logan asks her to stay and see his island from his eyes, she thinks, "Why not? If she were very careful, he would never know where she came from and when the time came, she could leave and have no regrets. She fumbled along the side of her skirt until she felt the hard metal key in her pocket. The solid weight of it gave her the confidence to stay."

Nevada Gold—Ellie says, "…as long as I'm stuck here, I might as well help…Then we can get it over with so I can go home." Lucky and Zeke exchanged a look and Ellie's stomach lurched. No, they had said she could go home in a month. One month, her brain echoed; one month, she prayed. She couldn't even contemplate otherwise.

External conflict abounds in time travel if for no other reason than the misunderstandings which occur because of the differences in the culture of your main characters. In *Kate & Leopold*, Kate doesn't understand why Leopold stands when she enters a room and Leopold believes she needs a chaperone when going on a date.

In *Nevada Gold*, Ellie's walking around the house barefooted and Lucky (one of the old miners) comments on her painted toenails, saying "I ain't never seen painted toes on nobody 'cept the girls from Miss Molly's down at the Gold Strike Saloon." (Implying only prostitutes have painted toes.)

Jaci makes pizza for Nicholas's niece when she thinks he won't be home in *Carousel*. When he arrives early and tries a slice, he states: "Pizza, huh. It's not bad, I suppose, but it will never catch on as a meal." (And of course, he has already commented on the fact that they're eating with their fingers!)

Conflict also occurs when a character has to explain, or keep hidden, the fact he/she is from another time. For Ellie, in *Nevada Gold*, everyone must think she's Elizabeth. Keeping up this pretense heightens the conflct for Ellie and her co-conspirators, Zeke and Lucky.

Not only do you need to plot how your traveler reacts and adjusts to traveling through time, but how it affects the other characters in the story. Chances are, they won't readily accept it, and the method you use to explain it can raise the conflict levels dramatically!

Conflict in time travel can be time itself. It might be a race against time to make an event happen *(Back to the Future)*, to prevent one *(Nevada Gold)*, or before a portal closes *(Kate & Leopold)*. This keeps your audience/readers on the edges of their seats. Will they make it in time?

CHANGING HISTORY

When writing historical you must have your facts right. You can't have the United States civil war between the east and the west, and you can't invent the telephone even one year before it actually was—a reader will catch you on it—unless you're writing alternative history which you should make clear to your reader from the start. Now if you throw your characters into the future, you can pretty much make of it what you will—if it's far enough into the future. At the same time, it's very difficult for the reader if you start inventing or giving items strange names because they have no reference point.

That's another reason I like sending my characters back in time. If I say they rode into town on a buckboard, my readers will have some idea of what type of conveyance that is. In *Indigo Bay,* Logan says Zachary Taylor is the president when Mica questions him. Readers will recognize the name, even if they can't remember exactly when he was president.

This is where research comes in because there may be things that we think are very modern, but in reality they had been invented a long time ago. Part of the fun is researching those unique tidbits of information and incorporating them into the historical setting, sometimes throwing your traveler for a loop when discovered:

> Ellie ... grabbed cans of Van Camp's Beans in tomato sauce off the shelf. Although she had never heard of Saratoga chips, she recognized the potato chips by the picture on the front of the cloth bag. There was life in the 1870's after all...
>
> Later that evening, she pumped water and heated it for a bath...

> She crunched another potato chip and marveled at the things that were available in 1870. In her naiveté she had assumed modern conveniences had been invented in modern times—specifically in the twenty-first century during her life span.
>
> It was silly to be thrilled by such little things as potato chips and scented soap, she thought, sniffing the small bar appreciatively, but a person didn't miss something until she had to do without. She eyed the stash of pre-made cigarettes Zeke had left her. If she smoked more than that, he had said, she would just have to learn to roll her own. Or quit, he had reiterated.
>
> Yes, life was full of little treasures to stockpile and savor. She banged her knee on the side of the tub as she adjusted her body so hot water covered most of it. She decided to reserve judgment on copper bathtubs until later.

Until I started researching for this book, I didn't know there were potato chips in the 1870's or that pre-rolled cigarettes couldn't be purchased until much later.

You can't write a time travel into the past without encountering huge historic events and/or very important people. Your character may visit the World's Fair, talk to President Adams, or ride the first transcontinental railroad. There is no record that says they didn't do those things. When traveling back in time, regard needs to be given to history; both on a national or public level, and on a personal level. What can, or should be changed?

Depending on your plot, can you change some historic event, like who invented the telephone, or who was president when? Not if you want your readers to believe your story. You can, however, have your character in the next room when that first telephone call was made, or she could attend an inaugural ball.

History on a national or public level (events already recorded in the history books) can't be changed, however events can be carefully manipulated to serve your plot. If some event needs to be changed—say a presidential election—then "original" history in your story would have the other guy winning. Once your protagonist "changed" history, it would be as we know it today.

Personal history—that of your main characters and/or characters in your story who don't impact known history—can more easily be changed. Think about Kate and Alex in *The Lake House*. Kate is two years ahead of Alex, so her history is actually his present time. At the very end, when she realizes Alex is the man who died on Valentine's Day, she writes him a letter and puts it in the mailbox telling him not to come to her that day or he will die. He heeds her words and stays away, and she changes his personal history.

Anyone's personal history can be changed because that person is the only one who knows it. In *Knight in Shining Armor*, when Douglass comes back to the present and Nicholas had changed his profession, she discovers the history of his castle had changed accordingly. Because it was a fictitious castle, that didn't matter. Author Jude Deveraux couldn't have changed the history of Buckingham Palace.

Likewise, in *Nevada Gold*, Ellie is taken back in time to keep Jesse from dying in a mining explosion. Her job was to change history, but only the event which originally killed Jesse. In the end, she couldn't change much history—the explosion still occurred—but she did manage to save Jesse. She changed his personal history, but couldn't change the history of the entire Comstock Lode.

A twist on this occurs in *Kate & Leopold* when Stuart determines that the history he thought was a pretzel he had to untwist, was actually twisted exactly the way it was supposed to happen. So in this case, he had to get Kate to the bridge to go through time because she was supposed to be in 1876. He had to make history flow the way it was supposed to, and if Kate stayed in the present, that would have changed history.

Sometimes the more intricate the plot, the better, because the information is there for your reader to follow what's happening, and yet twisted enough that they can't quite figure it out. You don't want them saying, "Wait a minute. That couldn't happen."

There's a wonderful line in *Kate & Leopold* when Stuart is trying to explain why Kate is in the pictures from the past: "If you go to the past in the future, then your future lies in the past…That is a picture of you in the future…in the past." Again, your reader will accept this on faith because they've already been sucked into the story and want it to end happily. If you tried to dissect his statement, you'd drive yourself nuts.

I will make this caveat to changing history. In *Carousel*, Nicholas has a thoroughbred farm that he's going to lose if he can't make his loan payment. Jaci can only think of the Kentucky Derby as a way to make the kind of money he needs, so they enter his prize horse—Wind Dancer—in the race and he wins. In actuality, Aristides won the first Kentucky Derby in 1875, but I had all the other facts—the date, distance, purse, originator—correct. I then put an "Author's Note" at the end of the story, part of which said:

> ...I tried to stay as close to the truth as possible, but of course had to allow Wind Dancer to win because Jaci had promised to marry Nicholas. Aristides [actually] won the race that day, ridden by Oliver Lewis. Aristides's owner, H.P. McGrath, received the purse of $2,850...

Readers will allow this type of historic change for story purposes because in the grand scheme of things, it was a minor event. (Except possibly to the owners of Aristides, and they are no longer alive.)

Most fiction is a spin-off on some event that actually did happen. Think of how many movies and/or books you've seen with the statement "based on an actual event." Take for example the US Airways plane that had to land in the Hudson River in New York on January 15, 2009, and all 155 passengers survived. As I read the news article, I thought "Wow, that's the kind of thing which makes a great story."

If I took that event and turned it into a book, whether mystery, thriller or romance, I would add characters not on the original manifest who would be the central characters in my story. You can almost bet that there will be a movie about that event sometime in the future. It might have a terrorist plot, a love triangle, or an embezzlement gone awry with the culprits trying to escape. The historic event will occur as the news related, but the personal history of the characters aboard that aircraft will all change to meet the author's needs.

What a great segue for a time travel—one passenger is never accounted for. Now where do you suppose that person is?

THE OPPORTUNITY TO RETURN HOME

Time travelers usually don't have a say in what happens to them. Most of the time it happens accidentally—Leopold slips off the bridge with Stuart and falls through time *(Kate & Leopold)*. Sometimes it happens on purpose as in *Somewhere in Time* when Richard purposely uses hypnosis to travel back through time, or in *Nevada Gold* when two ghosts deliberately take Ellie through time to help them. (Although in that story, Ellie didn't have a choice.)

There are times, however, when after the first event, the character will intentionally keep going back. In *The Two Worlds of Jennie Logan*, Jennie dons a beautiful antique dress and is transported back to the turn of the century. The first time she puts on the dress she doesn't realize what will happen. After that, she keeps going to the attic and donning the dress so she can continue to visit in a prior time where she finds more happiness than in her present time.

In *Indigo Bay*, Mica uses a key to open the door– at first not aware that it leads to the past. Even after she learns that she's really in a different time, she continues to go because like Jennie, she finds love and happiness.

Whether the time travel is accidental or deliberate on the traveler's part, I feel the traveler needs the opportunity to decide for his or herself whether to stay in that time. This helps lead to a satisfying ending for the reader; a resolution if you will. They don't need to know from the very beginning that they will have a choice because part of the conflict is that the traveler is where he/she doesn't want to be and tries to get back. As a reader, I don't want to put down a book and feel unsettled, or unhappy, or have the feeling something is missing. Using the books/ movies already mentioned, these were some of the endings:

Kate & Leopold—Leopold knows he has to go back. Even though Stuart tells her she belongs back there, Kate has the choice (remember this is really her story). She chooses love over her career position and takes a leap of faith to be with her beloved.

The Two Worlds of Jennie Logan—Jennie chooses life and love in an earlier time, so she dons the dress and basically wills herself to die.

The Lake House—Kate (2006) writes Alex (2004) and tells him not to come to the hospital or he'll die and asks him to wait for her. She'll be at the lake house. For her, it's minutes in time, but when Alex chooses, he has to wait two years to "catch up" with her.

One of my favorites, of course, is from *Indigo Bay*. The key is her passage from the present to the past. She's with him when there's a fire, burning down the entire house, except...

> The passage door, oddly enough, was the only piece of wood not burned beyond recognition, and it swayed on the charred remains of its frame.

> A chill swept through Mica to settle in the key she now clutched. The door groaned as if to beckon her, and the key grew colder in her hand. The ribbon from which it hung seemed to tighten against her neck, constricting her throat and cutting off her air.

> "Logan?" She whispered his name fearfully...

> His arm tightened in reassurance. She didn't hesitate this time, but quickly removed the key from around her neck and tossed it into the middle of the smoldering rubble. The instant it landed, the door creaked and swayed, then appeared to melt down the charred framework to the ground...

> "You're stuck here now." His voice warmed her heart...

> "No, I'm not stuck here. I belong here now."

There are a couple of books in which I felt the endings were unsatisfactory, but that does not reflect on the author. It is only my opinion and every reader will decide for herself. As the author, it is your story, and the ending is entirely up to you.

Somewhere in Time—Richard touches a coin from his time and is dramatically thrust back to the present where he wanders aimlessly thereafter looking for his love. He wasn't given a choice to whether he stayed or left.

Knight in Shining Armor—Nicholas must stay in his time and Douglass must return to the present. She meets a descendant of Nicholas's on the flight home and feels they are soul mates.

Both of these endings neatly wrapped up the story, but I like happy-ever-after.

RESOLUTION: FOR YOUR READERS AND CHARACTERS LEFT BEHIND

I've read many, many time travels, and in most of them, the time traveler is an orphan and has no family in her/his time. This makes it very easy for that person to disappear into another time with no questions asked. But what if your story includes family members, or close friends? Surely they would want to know what happened to that person. As varied as the ways a person can travel through time, so can those resolutions be.

Kate & Leopold—This was easy because Charlie, Kate's brother and only relative, is right there at the bridge with her when she jumps.

The Two Worlds of Jennie Logan—Jennie has tried to explain her time travel to her ex-husband but he won't believe her. When Jennie decides to go back forever to live with the artist she fell in love with, she basically wills herself to die. As her ex-husband is clearing out the house later, he comes across some paintings of a woman and family, done by a well known artist in another era. He knows it is Jennie, and that she did go back in time as she said, because in the portraits she's wearing the broach he had given her.

Carousel—Jaci had been taking pictures of a Dentzel carousel when she disappeared. The police found her camera, but not her, and one of the officers had the film developed to look for evidence. Finding none, the police give the pictures to Jaci's grown sister, Mandy:

> One picture caught her eye, and when she picked it up, she gasped, for here was the horse she clearly recalled from earlier photos Jaci had taken…Standing behind the magnificent black carousel horse was the man Jaci had originally photographed. Through her tears, Mandy saw Jaci standing beside him, their hands clasped around a darling little girl…Her face was older… and she had on ruffles and lace that Mandy swore she'd never wear today. It was the expression on Jaci's face, though, that set Mandy's heart to rest…For whatever reasons there might be, her sister had found true love.

Writers are dreamers. We lose ourselves in other worlds and involve ourselves in the lives of make-believe people who at times seem very real. We search for new answers to age-old questions. For those who dream of time travel, we can weave this unknown into our stories, taking our readers on an adventure completely different from "just" a historical, or "just" a futuristic novel.

Joseph Campbell in his book *The Hero with a Thousand Faces* (1949) uses the term **MONOMYTH** (often referred to as 'the hero's journey') to explain his idea that there is only one story, and it keeps getting told over and over again. I prefer the literary theory of **LITERARY**

PARTICULARISM, in which the details specific to a given text are considered more significant than the qualities it shares with other texts.

Adding the element of time travel, because the theory has never been exclusively proven…or disproved, can be the significant quality that will draw the reader in, make him/her suspend disbelief and keep him/her hooked until the very last page.

Time Travel Worksheet Questions

Remember, anything is possible when writing time travel. Make a worksheet and use these questions as a way to help you set up your story so that you won't get to the end and say "oops!"

What are the rules that can't be broken?

Does time travel at the same speed in the present and the past (or future)?

If not, what is the ratio and reason?

Method of travel and why?

What goes with the traveler and what can't? Why?

What are the internal conflicts?

What are the external conflicts?

What is the changing history: national/international?

What is the changing history: personal?

Is there an opportunity to return home?

What is the resolution for those left behind?

The internet is an exceptional source of information on time travel and what some call time-slips, the experience some people have reported wherein they briefly visit another time. For example, in one article at Wikipedia, there's a suggestion by Carl Sagan that time travelers may be here, but are disguising themselves. That sounds plausible. After all, if you were a time traveler, would you openly advertise that fact? People might think you were crazy, like Elizabeth Calhoun in *Nevada Gold*. However, researchers should remember that anyone can post anything to the internet, and at Wikipedia, anyone can change the entries. The facts on any internet site should be used as inspiration only and should be double checked.

Marketing for Writers

By Kim Richards

This chapter is going to focus on two things. Basic book promotion and a focus online. With ebooks growing in popularity and paranormals one of the top favorites in ebooks, it's prudent to consider marketing online. You want to market yourself and your books online where readers are 1) computer saavy, 2) likely to have a means to pay electronically, and 3) tend to be more ebook friendly. These same principles apply to print versions because of so many online bookstores like Barnes & Noble and Amazon.

Why you should market your own book

Peggy Sansevieri says, "Marketing is a conversation: once your marketing stops so does your conversation." These days conversations are one of the ways to reach readers online. More on that in a bit.

There's a book I highly recommend by John Kremer. *1001 Ways to Market Your Book.* Don't let the thickness of this tome scare you, take it one chapter at a time. In this book, John points out early on that selling is your responsibility if you want to be successful. No one else can represent your book the way you can because you are intimately familiar with the story elements. You also have an unmatched passion for your work and people love passion. Excitement is contagious.

Mister Kremer presents two fundamentals for marketing any product or service (not just books): promotion and distribution. He says, "You must get the word out *and* you must make sure that your product is available." Your book IS your product so keep that in the forefront of your mind always when marketing.

Most publisher's marketing managers do their best to get the word out, Remember they are representing an entire line of books and the company itself. It's impossible for them to focus on any one book for long. Most of the bigger publishing houses rely on known names and focus what little marketing they do on those. More and more, the authors are expected to promote their own work. The good news is readers prefer to hear from an author over some company. That's because the authors are the interesting ones and I agree. It's up to you to be interesting and reach out to readers.

With distribution, the publisher takes care of the placement side of things. They put your books up in stores, at their website plus online stores such as Fictionwise, Mobipocket, Amazon Kidle and more. Think of it in computer terms. They're doing the hardware side of things. You can help your book by addressing the software side: showing people where to click to buy your book. If they have to go on a hunt to buy a copy, most will lose interest. While the low cost of ebooks is a selling factor, especially in these hard times, few people will spend a lot of time searching for something that's this affordable. While they may not outwardly admit they're wasting their time for a few dollars, that's the basis of their thinking.

How much time to spend

When blogging, three times a week is good but be consistent. A good rule of thumb for social networking sites is to plan to spend an hour a week on each one you belong to. This doesn't have to be all at the same time. For Twitter and Facebook, try to get on at least for a few minutes each day and at least update your status. No one will hate you for missing a day but too many of those days and they'll forget who you are. You want your name out there in front of them consistently.

I recommend dedicating an hour a day to marketing and promoting your work. That way you keep the momentum going and don't become overwhelmed.

WORK SMARTER, NOT HARDER

You need a marketing plan, specifically a Digital marketing plan. Include regular updates to your website and posts to your blogs and social sites in this plan. Do at least three things each day to market your books. Schedule time each day to work on them. Meet that commitment every day and stop when the time is up.

When creating your marketing plan you need to consider the following:

1. What books you are selling: Genre, theme, format

2. Who is your buying audience? Research a little. Where do they hang out online? What other interests do they share? Where do they shop? Knowing this information will help you target the most effective areas to promote your books.

3. What is your marketing budget? It's easy to get caught up in spending more on promotion and marketing than you'll realistically make on sales. Take advantage of every free opportunity you run across to stretch your marketing budget and then carefully choose when and where to spend the rest. Be audience specific whenever possible. Combine efforts with other authors in your genre.

I also recommend talking with an accountant. They can let you know exactly what you spend on marketing and promotional items can be written off your taxes.

I have a monthly checklist that I use. I print it out each month and tick off the items as I complete them. It saves the aggravation of remembering what needs done when. It contains items like: post books on Goodreads, inquire about guest blog spots, send books to x number of reviewers, when to send book recommendations via my social networks and more.

I also maintain an ongoing list of yahoogroups and blogs. It contains the group posting link, what days promos are allowed, who to contact to schedule chats and guest blogger days and any special posting rules. Every day, I go through the list and post my promos on those days.

Again be specific. You don't want to waste time promoting your horror on the romance lists. You know your genre best and will sniff out places just for you when you research your audience.

Another BIG working smarter bit is to use that calendar in your email program. Every time you schedule something, put it in the calendar and have it remind you the day before. In the details, include any link you need to post at and any usernames/passwords which are needed. This way, you'll never miss a date and don't have to waste time looking up information. It really comes down to using the resources available on your computer.

WHEN TO START

Start now. It doesn't matter if you have a book out or not. It takes time to reach people and the sooner the better. A good newsletter list always starts small and builds from there. The sooner you start, the more subscriber's you'll have when the big news hits. You want to have a solid layer already in place when your book is released. This doesn't mean all is lost if your book is already out. Simply start now and make no apologies.

Another reason for starting as soon as possible is for yourself. Regular newsletters, blog updates and twitters put you into a routine.

BRANDING

I think of cattle brands when I hear the word branding. It's kind of like a tattoo; a permanent mark indicating who you are and what you represent.

You want to take control over how others perceive you and your work. Do this by actively branding yourself. This starts with your name: when you sign up for email groups, log into chats, always, ALWAYS make your username your first and last name.

Always sign your emails with your full name and include a link to your website just below it. Some authors get really creative by adding little banners for their books. They're eye catching but do be aware that some email groups don't allow the graphics to be displayed so I still recommend having the web link. You can set up your email program to automatically attach this information to every email you send out. It's in the area dealing with signature lines.

Keywords: Create a list of keywords which identify you, your publisher, book title, subject matter, genre and more. Use these anywhere you're asked for keywords online: your website, some blog posts, some social networking site posts, Amazon. These are one word tags which will target you and your book when someone does a search. Don't forget obvious ones like paranormal, ebook, books, author, your name etc. Get creative. If you have a book that's got a historical background, include the time period, era, location, etc. in your key words/tags.

ONLINE PROMOTIONS (WHY YOU NEED THEM AND HOW MUCH TIME TO SPEND)

Ebook buyers are already online so that's where you can best reach out to them. These days sitting for hours at a signing may or may not get you a book sold. It's harder with ebooks because you have to either have the book on disk or rely on readers to maintain their interest until they get home and get online. That's rare if you ask me.

Ebook lovers are right in step with this instant world we've created. They want to click and download their book right away. That's the appeal of ebooks: lower costs, instant perusal, anonymity, and no shipping fees/wait times. In terms of your own costs and time value, online promotion makes the best sense. Make use of those impulse buys.

Put your book cover up everywhere: on the front pages of your website and blogs, on your profiles of your social communities like Facebook, Myspace, ning groups. Whenever possible link the photo to your book purchase page. You want to make it easy for an interested reader to buy your book in as few clicks as possible. Use Hyperlinks everywhere, even in your content.

Websites

This is a MUST for any modern day author. It's a portal/store where you are open for business every hour of every day. Whether you choose to pay someone to create it for you or do it yourself, there are things you want to consider first. These are the very things a website creator will need to know in order to make a successful site for you.

Keep your target audience in mind when you answer these questions:

1. What do you envision the site looking like? Are there specific moods you want to create with it? You want it to look professional, without the appearance of a fan site. The look needs to be clean and consistent across all its pages. You want to be able to update it and keep it current without a lot of hassle. If you pay someone to create your page, learn how to do the updates. It'll save you money and you won't be waiting around for someone else's schedule to post the updated pages. Update it at least once a month. If you keep a calendar of appearances on your webpage, this needs to be updated regularly.

2. What exactly do you want to highlight? Make a list of the major items and beneath those, sub-lists of specifics. These become your headings, sometimes a whole page of their own within the website.

3. What is the goal of your website? Is it to provide information? Sell your books? Showcase you as an author? All three? Then put them in order of importance. You do want it to become the hub of all your activity. Turn it into a resource. Provide a place for reviews, excerpts,

video trailers, news, appearances, links to buy your book, show off awards, links to your blogs and social networks. Don't forget those important keywords. Link back to your publisher and have an email contact link for yourself. You don't need to include your address and phone number unless you have a post office box for your work. Be safe online as well as visible.

4. Make a list of what you don't want the site to do. This may sound like a dummy thing but it is important to clearly spell out everything. Knowing what you don't want is as important as figuring out what you do. It will color your content and you'll know what to look for when you're giving it a final look over before going live. Websites are like books with regards to becoming too close to them and what you want to say. It's easy to lose objectivity.

5. Scope out the competition. Check out other author and book websites. Make a note of the features you like and those you don't. What's visually appealing to you and easy to navigate?

6. Choose a domain name that's easy. Your name works best because that's what people will be searching online for. My personal site is www.kim-richards.com I had to choose the hypen between my first and last name because the actress, Kim Richards already has www.kimrichards.com Your website name is part of branding yourself. It's also easy to remember when it's your name.

7. You might consider a logo. A simple image or set of words to identify you. You'll want this on your website and on every other place you promote online…as your user picture. It's easy to choose your book cover for this but keep in mind, there will be more books from you. You may want something more specific to you than your current piece.

Once your website goes live, include it in every single promotion you do, online and off. Heck, start out promoting the website itself.

Tell everyone about it. That's one thing most people forget to do. Every blog, social site, website you have needs to also be promoted. How else are people going to find it and go there?

One quick comment about having an online presence. Many publishers will google an author these days before deciding to accept their work. Some will pass by an author with no website because they interpret the lack of one as a lack of interest in promoting their own work. They also read blog entries to determine if this person is someone who will be professional and easy to work with or someone who is going to air their concerns publically or slander the company. If the latter is the impression you give, it won't matter how good your work is, they'll pass you up as too difficult and not worth their time. Always, always take a professional approach.

BLOGS

Blogs (web logs) are a very useful tool, especially for writers. They are a place to create current content and establish yourself as an expert. Keep in mind that your consumers go to the internet for information, entertainment and content. They don't want to be preached at, pressured into buying something or read long whining posts. They will click away and not come back to those items. You want to be friendly, yet always professional on your blogs.

Think of your blog in terms of writing a column. Set up specific topics and set deadlines.

Blog on a regular schedule. Three times a week is good. Schedule those times on your calendar with a reminder.

As with your website, you want to determine what your blog is going to accomplish, it's goals and vision. Dedicate a particular day of the week to a subject and stick with it. Your regulars will come on those days expecting to read about that subject. Don't let them down. Bring in guest bloggers and interview experts on that day's subject. Invite comments and certainly respond to those comments left on your blog. Always, always have the link to your website on the front page of your blog.

You need to refer back to your target audience once again…who do you want to read your blog? What will you have to say which will interest them? Topics can include trends, book reviews, blogging 'in character', political issues and hot topics of the day, interviews, fiction that's serialized. Consider the book, *Monster Island*. It was originally written as blog entries and was later picked up by publisher. Doug Clegg did the same thing with several of his novels in his newsletter and they each were published. In both cases, the authors could go to the publisher with information proving there is an interest in their story and a proven market. Keep in mind that it being posted online is often considered publication which can create problems down the road with regards to rights and awards eligibility.

Make a list of topics and items within those topics you'd like to address...then guess what? That list becomes the first entries for you to discuss. Consider writing six or ten blog entries. This gives you time to look them over for mistakes and you can use those days when you're writing is prolific to get ahead. It also saves you from posting in a rush. Some blog sites have the ability for you to post entries and then specify what day each one is posted. This can be really useful for when you're on vacation or to save time.

Add an RSS feed to your blog. What an RSS feed does is make your content searchable by folks who use an aggregator to pull in specific content off the web for them. Many market reports and news groups do this. It saves them time from web-surfing and checking website after website for content to use in newsletters, to report on and more. You want your blog to show up as often as possible because it will be linked back to you. Again, keywords help here.

Keep a list (blog roll) of sites and other blogs your readers will care about: sites about paranormal activity or haunted tours for example; put their links on your blog. Contact them and ask them to link to you as well. For that matter, ask them to feature you, interview you or let you guest blog. Be proactive. Don't wait for people to contact you first. It won't happen. It's also useful to provide a section of links to related websites—resources.

Set up a Google alert. It will tell you when topics (you've indicated are relevant) are posted on blogs. You can use technortati.com to help you find them or do web searches of your own on your subjects. Then go visit those blogs. Comment when it's appropriate and be sure to include your full name and webpage link in every post. Just don't turn your comment into an ad. People hate that. Contact websites and blogs and offer to guest blog. Above all, make it fun and interesting for yourself.

SOCIAL COMMUNITIES

Online social communities are a great resource for writers. After all, we love to write about our favorite subjects, our books and connect with other writers. One thing you have to balance is how many you belong to for author support and how many are aimed at readers. Too many writer groups and you end up promoting only to other authors. While admittedly writers are one of the largest groups of readers in the world, you want to niggle your way in among readers circles as well. Remember to aim for your genre's readership, your target audience.

Think of social sites as marketing platforms. You want them to serve as touch points between you and…dare I say it? Fans.

Let's talk about a few important social sites, though the basic advice applies to them all.

FACEBOOK

Facebook these days is a better option for writers than Myspace. Here's why: first, Facebook is considered here to stay because of its demographic. Users are older and less apt to lose interest the way young users do. It's a more useful tool and not a fad to the average user who is typically 35 and older. They are usually white collar workers which means more cash to spend than their younger counterparts. Facebook also is rigorous in keeping users within their terms of use.

A couple of the drawbacks of Facebook are the inability to 'mass' mail friends. Facebook will only let you email twenty people at a time, per day. This means less spam for you but more work if you want to contact every single person who has friended you. It's also a good thing because when people DO receive your notice, they're more likely to read it.

Then there's a limit Facebook puts on the number of friends you can have. 5,000. For this reason, Facebook expert, Mari Smith suggests to carefully choose who you accept as a friend. The other option is to make use of Facebook's 'fan' pages, which have an unlimited number of fans who can follow you. Fan pages are also indexed, giving search engines access to them. They were created as a business solution.

Another way, which is more target audience specific, is to make use of Facebook's groups. This one is also a Facebook business solution and smart marketing because those who join a group have some interest in common. Find groups on paranormal books, on hauntings, on vampires, anything related to your type of writing. Whether you create your own group or belong to another, there's less chance of marketing to someone who isn't interested in the kinds of books you write...or worse, doesn't read at all. If you create your own group, you'll want to market it for subscribers.

You want to participate in the groups, not spam them with buy my book messages. Once the members get to know you, they'll naturally be interested in your work, particularly with that ever present full name and website address at the end of every post you send. This same advice applies to email groups and book specific sites like Shelfari and Goodreads.

TWITTER

Twitter is a micro-blogging platform, an ongoing conversation. Use it as a promotional tool. People love mini-messages. Don't spam with it. As Whoopi Goldberg recently said on The Tonight Show, "I don't want to know what you're doing in the bathroom." Keep the messages relevant to you and your work. You can offer free tips, information, links to articles (including your own), share news, links to where you're guest blogging or are interviewed. Some authors are toying with posting poetry or short stories in bits. If you feel bold, try it.

As with blogs you want to contact people through Twitter. Reply to other's tweets. Ask for advice or offer advice. Hold contests. Don't feel like you're obligated to follow every person who follows you. If you do, you'll end up just ignoring this useful tool. I have Leonard Nimoy on my Twitter. He has thousands of followers but does not follow any of them. I'm interested in him but he wouldn't know me from any other fan. I'm not so egotistical as to think he should either.

One great element of social networking is many of them have apps (applications) which will link them together. It takes time to set up but wouldn't it be great to have your blog posts instantly show up on Facebook and your twitter activities post on all of your other networking/social sites when you send it once? While it seems anti-social to schedule time to visit your social networks, it's a good idea. Otherwise you risk losing track of the time you're spending on it.

NING GROUPS

Ning groups are an interesting combination of other web elements. They're member specific to those who sign up and contain within them a blog capability, email through the group, calendars, forums and live chats. Setting up your profile before ever 'friending' other members is important because that's the one time most of them are guaranteed to check you out. You'll want to be sure your website address is there, your contact information is in your profile, your book covers and video trailers are uploaded. There's even text areas where you can provide a list of links to where you can be found online (blogs, other social sites, etc). This is the time to be sure and use hyperlinks wherever possible.

Before joining a ning group. Again, look for groups with an interest in paranormals or books. Look at the group's main page. Read the ning group's focus and be sure it's in line with the goals you have for yourself and your writing. See if there is a cost to joining and evaluate if that is worth your hard earned dollars before you sign up. I really recommend not joining more than three or you won't have time to spend on them. The other nice thing is ning sends you an email whenever someone contacts you so you don't have to check it several times a day.

Ning sites can be wonderful places to find workshops, networking opportunities, reviewers, readers, promote contests, and more.

BOOK SPECIFIC SITES: GOODREADS, SHELFARI, LIBRARY THING AND BOOKSHELF APPS

Goodreads is a great resource for writers. You can post the information on you and your books, send recommendations, review others works. It has group options like Facebook with the same kinds of benefits…reaching people with the same interests as you and your book subject. You can also put in event notices for things like signings, chat appearances, conferences you'll be attending. Goodreads also has groups similar to those at Facebook.

Shelfari is more of an Amazon application, though it is possible to upload any book and add link information, reviews, etc.

Library Thing is another. All three of these resources allow you to search for a book by author, title or isbn. They all also give you the capability to add a book information and cover if not found in your original search. Add your books if they're not there. Put them on your bookshelf. Then network with other writers in your genre or from your publishing house. Add them to your bookshelf, asking them to add you to theirs. This is another place where those keywords are important. You want to include genre, title, your name, publisher, setting, time period…anything a reader might search for which fits your book.

One final bit on online promotions. You don't need to do everything at once. Start with your website. Then once it's done and running smoothly, start a blog. Build up to your comfort level. There is a direct correlation between the amount of time you spend on marketing and promotion and the sales. Every single publisher will admit their top titles are proactive promotional writers.

Virtual Book Tour

A virtual book tour takes hard work to setup and will run you ragged while it's in progress but they are a wonderful way to spread the word about your book, gain reviews and infect others with your excitement.

What the heck is a virtual book tour? It's where you visit other people's blogs and websites, one a day for a specific time, say two weeks or a month. Typically a prize, usually a free book, is given to one lucky reader, drawn from those who leave comments. I've also seen prizes done as a scavenger hunt with clues left on each blog. Each blog tells them where to go next.

The first thing to do is decide upon when to have your tour. The best case scenario is to coincide with the book's release. You don't want to do it during major holidays like Easter or Christmas. There's too much going on to compete with at a time when many people are offline doing family things for the holidays.

Start the book tour and end it at your own blog. Cyber-schmooze. Ask your favorite blogs and social site friends to be part of your tour. Ask those with related subjects to what your book is about: vampires, paranormal, book reviews etc. Use the party invitation rule: ask twice as many as you want to host a blog tour day. It's still a relatively new concept so some people are wary about participating. That's okay. Keep on asking until you fill every day in your blog tour slot.

You should ask them to post a review of your book and interview you. Some may choose to ask you to blog about a subject they cover. Go ahead. Work with them. Point out, when you're asking, how they get linked to from you as you promote the tour. With a link back and a free book, it's hard to say no to hosting a book tour.

Once you have the schedule completed, send every participant the following (hopefully two weeks to a month in advance):

1. The complete blog tour schedule with everyone's links next to their name/date. Post these on your website and blogs.

2. Send them a copy of your book and ask them to read it and write a review to post the day before you drop by. This effectively gives you two days on each blog. Cool, huh?

3. Send them a list of interview questions and their answers. Invite them to use these or ask any of their own. Some will copy/paste what you send, others will pick out the ones they like best.

4. Your book cover and a picture of you. Links to your book buy page, webpage, blurb and an excerpt, where to find the trailer (if there is one).

5. Include the prize information and how to win. If it's done as a scavenger hunt, give them their clue to post.

6. A big thank you for helping you out.

Start promoting your virtual book tour on all your regular promotion venues. A few days before it starts you need to send each participant a reminder. Also be sure you have any passwords and accepted any invitations allowing you to post on their blog.

Visit each blog the day before you are to go there. If the book review isn't posted, send them a gentle reminder. Don't stress if it's not there or doesn't show up in time, just move on. On your day, post as early as you can. Include what blog (link) for readers to go to the following day and thank your host. Check back periodically throughout the day and the following day to catch any comments left for you. Be sure to comment back and announce who the winner for the day is both on that blog and on your own. That's it!

Save the direct links to the book reviews posted. You can use those in other promotions and post the links on your GoodReads, Shelfari, Library Thing book pages. It sounds like a lot of work and it is but virtual book tours are really fun. Try hosting someone else a couple of times before diving into one of your own. Just think, you can be featured at thirty places online in thirty days without leaving your house. Just try doing that face to face!

PROMOTIONAL ITEMS

Promo items should be figured into both your marketing plan and your marketing budget.

The first thing many authors do is pay for a ton of business cards. They have fancy post cards and book marks made up in nice glossy, high quality paper. It can get expensive fast. I'm not saying these are bad tools for promoting your books. The problem lies when you look at the sheer number of authors who do the very same thing. What you need to do is be creative and find ways to make those items stand out when among a pile of all the others.

I've used door hangers (and actually put them on my neighbor's doors) and fortune cookies with my book information on the slip inside. Candy works too if you get the right size, print an address label with your promo info on it and wrap it around the middle. I don't recommend spending a lot of money or time on these things because the people who get them want the goodies and their time reading the label is fleeting. Just last week, I went to a conference where several authors handed out this type of candy. Today, I cannot remember their names or their book titles. The whole idea behind promotion and marketing is to get your name to be recognized.

Think less is more. People get intrigued when they only get partial information. Let me use my tattoo as an example. Often when I wear conservative blouses, just the wing tips are visible at my neckline. I've had store clerks lean over the counter to whisper, "What is that?" I've had women follow me into the ladies room to find out. We end up in long conversations about it. However, when I wear a blouse, which shows the phoenix in its entirety, people glance at it and move on.

Use the same tactic for your promotional materials. If you have a book cover which is hard to see or unclear when reduced to half the size of a business card, putting it on your promo materials isn't going to help you any. In that case, you want to put some image relating to an element in your book. Is there a prominent symbol? Do you have a catchy hook phrase? Think of the one-liners they put on movie posters. You want to evoke a response from someone like this: "Ooo…I wonder what that means?" and then provide them with a link to your website where they can find out all the details.

When thinking less is more, also consider costs. I've yet to make it to the bottom of a box of business cards before some element on it needs changed. Name, website addy…nothing looks worse than a card with information crossed out and stuff hand written across them. Pasting a mailing label overtop is nearly as bad. Consider printing your own cards. You can buy the perforated ones at the store and print one page at a time, as you need them. If you're not desktop publishing savvy, you can pay most printing shops and office supply stores print centers to create a template for you and save it in electronic form. Then all you do is pull up the file, change what needs to be updated and print. The exact same thing goes for post cards.

Now, I have worked at a printer. People have this illusion that raised lettering on their business cards and glossy paper for their post cards is more professional. I doubt seriously any reader has ever decided not to buy a book because the author's business card didn't have raised lettering. They're much more interested in the information on the card. Who needs to spend more money because of someone else's snobbery? Certainly not me.

Bookmarks are an iffy promotional item. Some people collect them. They're handy to give out, especially when you are at a library, conference or book signing. One has to wonder how useful they are for promoting ebooks. If you can't use the bookmark with the very book it's advertising. I suggest using them sparingly.

With all promotional items, join forces with other authors. Combine your promos and take turns mailing them out or taking them to conferences. Some authors put little personal notes on them. It's true notes like that add value in a person's mind. Just don't spend days on end signing your freebies.

PRESS RELEASES

Press releases are iffy. Some say not to send press releases to the media; they will ignore you anyway. Instead target consumers with online content they will care about. Other authors report seeing sales immediately after sending press releases. Try them and see if they work for you. You might just land a signing or an interview on the local television station or newspaper as a result. Hiring a press release service can easily turn into a money sucker so weigh the benefits and costs against your time to do them yourself. Be realistic with yourself on this.

PODCASTS AND INTERNET RADIO

Podcasts and internet radio (Blogtalk Radio for example) are a great way to promote you and your book. You don't need to dress up and leave your home. In most cases, the interview is conducted live via the telephone and recorded. This means you can take advantage of the live broadcast and used the recorded archive link as content for your social networks and blogs.

Don't worry about how you sound. Just speak clearly and you'll be fine. When giving website addresses, say them slowly; twice. Keep on hand the written information about your book and anything special you want to talk about. You don't want to rely on your memory for a live podcast or internet radio appearance. Be sure to thank your host.

So how does one find a podcast or internet radio show? Why, an online search. You can google paranormal podcast or go directly to BlogTalk Radio, Pandora Radio, Podcast Ally, etc and search for your subject. Podcastdirectory.com is a great place to search. For Paranormals, search 'paranormal' obviously; also search for 'book reviews', 'author interviews', 'books' in general. If yours is an ebook, search 'ebook' also. Then get creative. Search for elements of your story. Say your paranormal is set in medieval Scotland. You can search for podcasts and shows with a medieval focus or one on Scotland. Both would have readers interested in your story. Then contact the show/podcast host and introduce yourself, your book; ASK for an interview and provide them your email address, plus your phone number.

VIDEO BOOK TRAILERS

Video book trailers are mini-commercials for a book. They're most often patterned after movie commercials with images from the story, title, author, website link, music and an intriguing log line. We won't get into the specifics of creating one here. You could fill an entire chapter on just that. I thoroughly enjoyed learning how to make my own. There are services who will create one for you if you don't have the time or inclination to make your own. Just don't break the bank on it.

The visual aspect of video book trailers is a nice one to have on your blogs and website. You can also promote them on video sites such as You Tube. They're a tool for reaching readers who are increasingly online and more visual than ever. It's entirely up to you whether to make use of them or not.

There's a lot of opportunities for authors to promote and market themselves today. It's all about reaching readers, making conversations about you and your books, turning yourself into a recognizable name. It's building a fan base and infecting them with your excitement. Authors no longer need spend long hours sitting in an uncomfortable folding chair while people avert their eyes to prevent contact at a bookstore signing. That's not where the readers are anymore. Go to where your audience is. Use the same technology they do and enjoy the process.

A Hard, Honest Look At Critiquing

By Danielle Ackley-McPhail

There isn't a writer in the world who doesn't need an editor.

Now, don't even argue with me on that. I am, after all, both a writer and an editor. Writers are the reason editors exist. Cliché as it might be, it is more than possible to be too close to your own work. No matter how many times I read over something I've written, the next time I pick it up I always find something else that needs fixing or could have been phrased better. (Yes, I see that guilty little look. You know exactly what I mean.) None of us are perfect and on top of that, we have a serious blind spot: We know what we meant to say. It is amazing the extent to which our minds can fill in the blanks when we know what's supposed to be there. It takes an impartial eye to catch the slip-ups and, yes, the gaping holes where plot points should have been. That's why we have editors.

The question is how do you get one? Well…one you don't have to pay for, that is.

See, publishers don't like slip-ups, typos, or omissions, and publishers are the ones who assign you editors. Makes things a little difficult.

All is not lost, and money need not be paid. Writers have recourse when it comes to polishing their work. Critiquing. For a previous writer's guide I wrote a chapter about writer's groups. I will synopsis here the information relevant to this chapter. There are three kinds of Writer's Groups: The Social Club, The Crucible, and the Community.

The Social Club is pretty much just an informal group of writers with varying levels of experience but similar interests who share information but don't really participate in many structured group efforts at advancing their skill. Basically, this is hanging with your peers, those who understand you because they face the same challenges. They are there to socialize, but not necessarily to make a formal effort (as a group) to improve as writers, though they often help one another polish their work informally.

The Crucible is a formal group which is very structured and regimented, with requirements that must be met before a writer can take advantage of the critiquing features. Critiques here are usually brutal, but highly effective, if you can get past having your work examined in minute, sometimes painful detail. The writers in this group tend to be more evenly aligned in experience level.

The Community shares aspects of both of the above; some support, some critique, and plenty of sharing information in a relaxed atmosphere. In Communities there is generally more variability in experience level, where a small percentage of participants are more experienced in both their craft and critiquing but the majority of the members are still learning their way. They want to learn, but they aren't really sure how serious they are yet and are more comfortable in a relaxed setting where they can benefit from those that know more than they do, without feeling inferior or pressured.

So, which is the best for you? You're going to have to figure that out for yourself. Ask yourself what you are looking for and what you have to offer. Try out a few groups and get a feel for where you are the most comfortable, or start one of your own. It can be you and one other person, or you can fill a room. In person, or via the internet... However you go about it, keep it manageable, have guidelines, and remember this is about growth and improvement as a writer, not a mutual admiration society.

THE MECHANICS OF CRITIQUING

Ideally, I would have wanted to have a sample story along with this chapter to show you an example of a critique. That would be a little involved for the space I have here, so I will content myself with a few paragraphs, which you will find at the end of this chapter. Before we get to that, I would like to review the methods and considerations to take into account when critiquing. First, the physicality of the task:

Environment—Make sure you are someplace conducive to the work at hand. This means different things to different people; some work well with music or chatter in the background, while others must have total silence and privacy. Experiment and figure out what works well for you. Do you need something to drink or snack on? Do you have enough light? Once you have the where down, then you can concentrate on the what.

FORMAT

There are two methods you can use: paper copies and electronic files. Both have their pros and cons.

PAPER COPIES

If you are critiquing a hardcopy make sure it is printed and not hand-written. The type should be crisp and clear, double spaced, with room in the margins for notations. Paper copies give you the flexibility to edit anywhere as long as you have sufficient light and a writing implement. It is limiting, though, in the space you have for your comments.

ELECTRONIC FILE

The advancements in word processing programs have greatly facilitated the ease of critiquing another person's work. Put simple: Track Changes RULES! If you have an electronic file of someone's work you are limited to editing on-screen—let's assume for this part of the article that your printer isn't working. Since it is pretty standard with most computers (and because I haven't used anything else) I will presume that you have access to some version of Microsoft Word for either Mac or PC.

By going to the Tools Menu and selecting Track Changes you can make comments and revisions to the file, which the author can then accept or reject, as they see fit. Making changes is a matter of typing over the existing text, and comments are recorded in a separate communications bubble that appears in the margin or a collapsible display window at the bottom of the 'page'. This is simple and requires nothing more than a working computer, but it does limit where you can critique, depending on if you have a desktop, laptop, or notepad computer. The end result can also be confusing visually when you go back to review what you have done, or for the receiver of the critique if they have not had experience with this aspect of the word processing program. Lastly, if you receive a critique done in this method, once you've accepted, rejected, and revised, you have to be sure to turn off the track changes or it will continue to function each time you go to modify the document in any way.

COMBINATION CRITIQUING

Some people find there are particular errors they are more likely to overlook on a computer screen than they would if they saw the text in print. Because of this I recommend doing an initial critique on the computer and then following that up with a quick scan of the printed copy as well. More time-consuming, but worth if your schedule allows.

TOOLS

(When editing on paper). Have a sticky pad and a blue, red, or other *colored* pencil or pen to write with. Do not use black ink or regular pencil as it is easy to miss notations when they don't particularly stand out from the printed text. Have a dictionary and thesaurus near at hand to confirm spelling, definitions, and suggest alternative words if the writer overuses something.

(When editing electronically). When you receive the original file, be sure to save it with a different name before editing. It is always best to have an unaltered file to refer, or even revert back to. You will not, clearly, need the same resources editing on the computer as you do editing on paper, or better yet to say, those tools are built into the word processing program in the following features: Spell Check, Track Changes, Make Comment.

For both methods of editing, if possible, be sure to have an internet connection handy for fact confirmation, where applicable. Another tool is a style sheet. You can create this yourself either electronically or by writing on several sheets of paper.

Here's what you do: take several sheets of paper and divide them equally into six or eight boxes by drawing lines through the paper (this will take three or four sheets). Label those boxes sequentially with one letter of the alphabet in each box. Also, mark one of the boxes with a number sign or by writing the word "numbers" at the top of the space. (Don't write too big, you want plenty of open space in each box when you are done.) Keep these sheets handy while you are critiquing. Each time you encounter a unique phrase, such as a character's name or a made-up or foreign word, write it down as it first appears in the appropriate lettered/numbered box on your style sheet. You will continually go along until you complete the story. As you are critiquing, when one of those special words comes up, compare it with your style sheet to make sure the spelling and treatment of the word is the same as the first occurrence. This will make it possible for you to point out discrepancies to be corrected later. You can also create similar sheets for character, history, or location details, only label your boxes with the appropriate names for easy reference. Keep this sheet separate from your general sheet as the amount of detail related would make a combined sheet cumbersome.

These technical bits of critiquing are not required or the only options. but as the many different techniques to critiquing could fill a book on its own, I have kept my recommendations to just these few. As you gain more experience you will learn what does and doesn't work for you, and develop a few tricks of your own. I am hopeful this will get you started. Speaking of which…

THE CADRE FOR YOU

Each critique group is unique, forming around a unified purpose, and then modified to meet the particular needs of the group as time goes by. Let's explore your options, or at least the most basic of them:

ON-LINE

Generally an open forum or discussion group where participants post their work and other members respond. The type of feedback received can range from feel-good comments, to a more detailed impression, to a full line review, depending on the experience and function of those responding and the intent of the site.

Drawbacks: the responses are sporadic and not always constructive when it comes to polishing your work. Sites with the specific purpose of generating detailed critiques do exist and generally have restrictions and requirements that determine when and how a participant can submit their own work for critique. This generally consists of "You must critique x number of posted pieces, with a critique defined as xxx, to be eligible to have your work entered into the review process." The degree of anonymity is determined by the amount of information you make general knowledge. The usefulness of the responses is hit or miss, critiques are not guaranteed, and there is no real way to know the experience level of the person who does offer suggestions.

E-MAIL

A critique group formed of those members where each member is familiar with at least one other member in the group. Stories are circulated on a formal or informal schedule and critiques are returned by a set deadline. There may or may not be a requirement where by those submitting for critique are required to critique in return. Such groups can be conducted with anonymous or author-identified submissions. The critiques can likewise be circulated the same way. By having the submissions and the feedback stripped of identifying names it removes some of the inhibition on the part of both author and critique partner as personalities are removed from the equation and you can review the work on it's own merit, rather than based on how someone you know will react to your comments. Those participating generally have some idea of the experience level of those responding, but critiques are not guaranteed, those responds is dependent on how serious those in the group are.

In-Person

Meeting in person can be daunting for those still developing self-confidence. This kind of group can be in a relaxed or a more formal setting. A group of friends working cooperatively; or a classroom like setting where people may or may not be familiar with one another. The structure of such groups varies, but basically members either receive the stories in advance so they may critique them beforehand, making notes and comments on a hardcopy of the work; or, they receive the pages at the meeting and the beginning portion is spent with everyone reading and critiquing quietly. A group discussion is then held going over the notes everyone has made.

Depending on the guidelines set up by the group, the submissions may or may not be anonymous. At the end of the meeting, the marked up pages are given to the author for a more leisurely review and revision. Often works will go through several review passes in this manner until the work is considered polished. Experience levels of participants can vary, but dedication is usually a bit higher than the other two methods. Of course, in-person groups can be much more daunting. Even if the works are submitted anonymously, it's still a matter of being there as your work is being discussed and knowing, yes, they are dissecting your masterpiece.

Once you decide which kind of group is good for you, it is time to familiarize yourself with what to expect, and what is expected of you.

BASICS FOR THE CRITIQUE PARTNER

"I decide what I want to create and then I take away everything that isn't that shape." Words of wisdom from a sculptor.. The goal of critiquing is to chip away those parts of the story which are the wrong "shape" and uncover the art beneath.

Whether you have a critiquing partner or are a part of a larger group, you will be expected to offer a critique of your own on someone else's work. Personally, I tend to critique a work in one pass straight through and comment or correct as I go. Some people can work that way, some people prefer to make several passes, each time focusing on some other aspect of the writing. Whichever way you chose here are some key points to look for:

TECHNIQUE

Are there grammar, spelling, or factual errors? Has the author overused a particular word, phrase, sentence structure, or other literary device? Are the words spelled correctly and is the correct word used in each instance (i.e., is 'than' used when 'then' should be? Or did auto correct chose the wrong word to replace a misspelling?)

STYLE

Has the style been maintained throughout the work? Are the word choices consistent with the time period of the piece and the (what's missing here?)? Is the tone appropriate for the plot of the story and the character development? Does the character point of view (POV) work for the story?

CONTINUITY

Do the details of plot, setting, and character development remain consistent throughout the work? Just as 'location, location, location' is the mantra for real estate sales, 'consistency, consistency, consistency' should be the mantra for writers.

DISTRACTIONS

Are there elements in the story that draw you, as a reader, out of it and back into the real world? Do you question the plausibility of plot points or occurrences in the story? Do things happen logically, in an explainable manner or is the plot contrived and key elements introduced with no forewarning at a pivotal point? Is information imparted for the sake of the information itself or because it plays a significant part in the plot or character development? Are there instances of information dump breaking up the flow of the plot, or is the technical/background information woven into the action, dialogue, and character introspective in a way that adds to the story, rather than slowing it down?

HOLES

Has the author missed necessary steps in the plot progression? Are all elements introduced in a timely manner to lead to the plot conclusion? Have the characters been fleshed out properly?

PLAUSIBILITY

Do the story and the character development make sense in the context of the work? Has the author set up the story universe sufficiently that the events that occur are not questioned or considered contrived?

Characterization

Are the primary and secondary characters well developed in keeping with the role they play in the plot? Is there enough background for the reader to connect with the focus characters and is there a sense of a real being there? Does the author maintain the character as they have developed it, or do they diverge at points, leaving the reader confused?

DIALOGUE

Is the dialogue natural and in keeping with the character development of the one speaking? Are their breaks that allow the reader to regroup and understand what the character is thinking or experiencing and is the speaker either identified or made clear through conversation and word choice? (It is important to remember when critiquing that misspellings, grammar errors, and dialect are often depicted on purpose when a character speaks in keeping with the role they play; such things should not be edited out to make them technically "correct".)

GETTING DOWN TO BUSINESS

Yes, that is an awful lot to keep in mind. Critiquing requires effort, concentration, and careful consideration. Not everyone can deconstruct someone else's work right from the start without falling into several traps.

- Distraction—This can be one of two things: You enjoy the work so much that you forget to look for technical aspects and how the work can be improved; or you are in an environment non-conducive to the type of focus needed for an effective critique.

- Commandeering—Re-writing the work rather than making recommendations or queries designed to make the originator of the piece resolve the perceived issue.

- Negativity—focusing only on what is wrong with a piece to the point where the originator is either disheartened or dismissive of the feedback.

In the following sections I will examine each of the above pitfalls plus why and how to avoid them.

MAINTAINING FOCUS

When you sit down to critique you have a set purpose and a goal to accomplish. Yes, it's important to enjoy what you are reading, but be careful of letting yourself fall too much into the story. The moment that happens you go from a critique partner to a reader. If you find that you are more caught up in the plot and action of the story, give in. No, it's not as counter-productive as you think. If you aren't getting your critique done because you are enjoying what you are reading, that doesn't mean the piece is without flaw, you just can't see it because the storyteller has done their job. So, go ahead, indulge a bit and finish reading. Once you have gone through the story once and satisfied yourself with the tale it tells you will be in a better position to go back and focus on the technique.

If your environment is disrupting your concentration then move or alter your surroundings. This can be as simple as changing your position to sitting up at a table, rather than lounging on a couch, or moving to a new room where there is less (or more) background noise. Don't be afraid to shoo people away if you don't have the option of taking what you are doing elsewhere.

All of these are things that *may* help; however, if they don't it is very important that you step away for a while. If you are sleepy, distracted, or not feeling well, you aren't going to be able to give the piece your proper attention, which is counterproductive to your purpose. Just walk away. There is always tomorrow.

THE TRICK OF REMAINING IMPARTIAL

Everyone has their own style of critiquing with many factors influencing that style: confidence, experience, familiarity with the author of the piece, and technical knowledge are just a few of the aspects which can determine how you approach reviewing someone else's work. All of that can make things tricky. It's not like polishing your own work. There you have the freedom to rewrite, strike sections, and play around with the details. When it is someone else's work you have to remember to restrict yourself to recommending, querying, and technical corrections. Of course, even that depends on your relationship with the author of the work and the intent behind your feedback. More about that later, though. Let's assume right now that this is a standard critique. I am going to apply some simple guidelines to the list of things to look for mentioned above.

TECHNIQUE

Automatically correct or question any misspellings or grammar errors you suspect in the work. The tools feature of most word processing programs or a conventional dictionary can confirm or make you aware if there are two spellings, in which case determine if one is more correct to the use in question. If you cannot determine, query the author in the margin.

STYLE

Is there a character talking in the wrong 'voice', such as an uneducated man using (correctly) very formal and erudite language, or a virtuous, polite character who habitually curses, though it conflicts with other indicators of the character's personality? Is the author writing a period piece set in Medieval England, yet the characters use words and phrases that did not exist in that day? Does the author use formal phrasing at one point in the narrative and then switch to informal at another? Highlight such sections and query the author in the margin, or strike the occurrence and comment in the margin as to why you made the change, perhaps suggesting a way to reword which accomplishes the author's original intent while still maintaining the proper style. Is there an overuse of cliché terms? Above all, has the author stayed true to the framework of style *they* have put into place? It is important not to impose your own preferences, particularly if the author has remained consistent. Note: When you are critiquing fiction, dialogue should be treated different from narrative. There are things purposefully done 'wrong' because it is more accurate to what people in real life are like, and thus a particular character may reflect that. Examples of this would be using clichés, improper grammar, use of dialect, etc.

CONTINUITY

As relates to author-developed aspects of the story: Has the author confused the description of a character or contradicted details mentioned earlier in the story? Standard practice in such instances is to highlight the occurrence and comment in the margin, referencing the first usage or mention by page number and ask the author which is correct.

DISTRACTIONS

As you are reviewing the work look for things that draw the reader out of the story. For example:

- An information dump, where a large block of detail is either not directly relevant to what is going on, or it is important but has been dropped into the story in one large roadblock, diverting from the plot and breaking up the flow of the story;

- Breaks in character, where something is clearly being done for the sole purpose of reaching a plot point, even though it goes against the personality set up for said character;

- contrived actions/reactions where what is taking place is so obvious that it's painful to read; and detours where the author explores characters or events with no direct impact on the current storyline, but may or may not be relevant for future works.

Such things are not always bad, if handled properly and in such a way that does not jarringly stand out in the current work in question, but they need to be used sparingly and preferably in such a way that there is at least a loose connection to what is currently going on. When you become aware of such occurrences in the work you are reviewing, highlight the text in question and comment in the margin pointing out the issue and recommending potential fixes, revisions, or removals to maintain the flow of the storyline and proper tension in the work.

HOLES

Sometimes there is a step missing in the progression from one plot point to another; either information has been left out or the reader hasn't been made privy to actions which must take place for the work to reach its stated conclusion. It might be something as simple as a character picking up an item, never putting it down or away, and trying to use that hand in another scene. Or, there could be a vital object the character uses to save the day, but the author never mentioned them acquiring the object or that they had it all along. These are simple examples, but basically it boils down to did we miss a step and how and where does in need to be fixed.

PLAUSIBILITY

I touched on this a bit in several of the above. Plausibility is when you simply watch for things that feel unnatural in the work. This is something clearly happening just so it can be checked off the author's mental list, even if there is no logic to the how, why, or when of it happening. It can also be that the way in which the event occurs is out of synch with the flow of the rest of the work, kind of like the movie spoofs where victim one very deliberately leaves the locked and secure building to see what the noise is. Highlight the copy and comment in the margin, pointing out what does not work with the scene and make recommendations of how things can be reworked.

CRUSHING SPIRITS AND OTHER HARMFUL PASTIMES

Critiques can be brutal. Not everyone can take them, no matter how impartial and considerate a critique partner is. That having been said, there are ways to minimize the pain. Always remember when critiquing someone else's work there is potentially much volatile emotion involved:

hopes and dreams, insecurities and ego. The words you chose, the method used to convey the feedback, and who else is privy to your comments can impact how receptive the author is to what you have to say. Whether you are giving or receiving the critique, you need to take these aspects into account. How comfortable will you be if more than just the author is privy to your comments? Is you wording constructive or destructive? Will it put the author on the spot or embarrass them?

Here are some recommendations of how to present a critique for a positive experience:

- Highlight both strengths and weaknesses in the story

- Don't rewrite the story, instead query and recommend in separate comments in the margin; this allows the author to consider your points without feeling like you have taken over their story. Always recommend, never tell, after all, the author knows what they want to accomplish; you only think you know. It is your job to point out places where you had problems with the story It's the author's job to correct anything they agree is a problem.

- If you make a change such as moving or deleting an aspect of the story, explain the reason behind the change you have made so the author can decide if they agree and want to incorporate the change. If you are using Track Changes in Microsoft Word, the program allows the author to see your change, as well as their original text, and to accept or reject the proposed changes with a click of the mouse.

- If you believe an aspect of the story does not work, give a logical explanation of why it doesn't work for you. This puts the author in the mind-frame of how to correct a potential problem they did not anticipate, rather than putting them on the defensive because something in the story is just "wrong".

When I am presented with a story that needs a major overhaul I find it difficult to balance my comments to encourage the author while still finding the glimmer of gold beneath all the dreg they've heaped on top of it. Now, I'm not being cruel, but some people have very original ideas and just don't know what to do with them yet. They have the general concept but are still working on the execution. At some point you will have to critique stories like this where it is difficult to know how much and what to say.

When I encounter such a work I will review one or two pages as ruthlessly as necessary and then give general comments explaining what I see in the piece and how it might be improved. I don't do this with everyone. It mostly works with those who truly want to improve and are comfortable enough where they are to know they need the brutal honesty; those who are eager to learn. I also only do it with those I have a solid friendship with because I know can sit down with them and help them through it. However, even when being absolutely ruthless, I make a point of being as positive as possible. *Always* point out positive aspects as well as what could use some work. Focus on using non-critical wording when you point out things that can use some work. Remember…at some point this person is going to return the favor.

GROWING A THICK SKIN

Finding or starting a critique group is relatively easy. Participating in one—effectively—that's a little trickier. There is fine art to both receiving and giving a helpful critique. Until you master that art you are pretty much wasting your time.

I know. That seems awful harsh, and perhaps even offensive, but—as twisted as it sounds—an effective critique group is about opening yourself up to both giving and receiving pain. You have heard the phrase "What does not kill me, makes me stronger"; well, the same goes for our writing.

Have I made you nervous? Don't worry; though we are often a masochistic lot, there are no whips involved. This is the point where you decide if you want to be good, or if you just want feel good. If it's the former, you have to be ready to be objective and risk having to tear your masterpiece down to the foundation and begin again. If it's the later, don't bother with a critique group; just pass out copies to your friends and family.

For some writers their work is more than a child or a masterpiece, it's a piece of their soul. Any implication there's something wrong with their work is met with abject horror, hurt, or even outrage. This is not an attitude conducive to an effective critique group. By participating you are asking people to do more than just comment on your work; you are, in theory, waiting for them to poke their fingers through every hole in it. You have to have an open mind and yes, a thick skin when they do. This doesn't mean what feedback you receive should be accepted as irrefutable gospel, but if you aren't at least in the mindset to consider the issues raised objectively you are wasting both your own time and your critique group/partner's.

Remember, while some of what you will receive in a critique is technical edits like grammar, spelling, and structure, a good dose of it is also opinion. Maybe the reviewer has different preferences in reading. Maybe they missed or misunderstood one of the points you covered which is completely clear to someone else reading the piece. Maybe they just didn't like the story or would have done it differently themselves and that is coming through in the comments. Whatever the case, never take one person's responses as irrefutable; if you can, get more than one critique on a piece. If you can't, weigh their comments against what you might know about the person (their experience level, their reading preferences, etc) and the validity of the comments in relation to your work. Now, don't misunderstand, this is not an excuse to blow off what they've said because you don't like it. This is where the open mind comes in and you honestly consider if any of their comments, queries, objections have merit.

SIFTING THROUGH
THE RUBBLE

The most important advice I can give you is: writing is subjective. Not everyone is going to approach it the same way and, particularly when you are talking about fiction, most of the feedback you receive is going to be opinion and based on style, which is very personal.

When you receive a critique, whether it is from one partner or a group, carefully review all the corrections and comments. As yourself:

- Is this a technical comment? If you have a doubt the revision is correct check a grammar book or style guide to confirm then make the revision accordingly.

- Has the critique partner misunderstood or simply missed

information covered in the manuscript? If so, review the passage to make sure you have clearly provided the information you feel you have.

- Have revisions been proposed to correct an aspect of the story that doesn't work, for which you agree with the assessment? Carefully consider their recommendations. Does it solve the issue? Is it consistent with the tone of your work? Can you think of a different way to address the problem that is more true to your 'voice'? Personally, I rarely go with the specific recommendations of a critique partner when they are suggesting a revision. I prefer to reconsider the work and see if I can find my own way first. However, that is personal preference. I like to fix things myself. It is completely acceptable to incorporate a fix they are recommending as long as you are comfortable with the change.

- Have queries been noted where you must clarify or provide additional information? Sometimes critique partners are unsure if something is correct or not, or they have some other question about facts or occurrences they may have misinterpreted while reading. Such issues might be an oversight on your part, or it just might be reader comprehension. Remember, though; if one person has a problem making sense, there is a chance someone else might as well. This is why feedback from multiple sources is recommended.

When it all comes down to it, you want to make your work the best it can be. To that end, carefully consider all feedback, incorporate what you feel is valid, remember to maintain your own voice, and don't take it personal. Dissecting your work with the intent to help you make it better doesn't constitute an attack against your person. Sometimes it feels that way, but it's not. Likewise, as a critique partner, you must always strive for a constructive attitude, not critical.

THE DUST SETTLES

Whatever choices you make regarding how and with whom to critique, know that it is a vital tool in progressing your literary skill. Not only does it give you an objective eye on your work, but it also gives you a glimpse of how your audience may react, what they might misunderstand, and if the story will appeal to the reader. Find what works for you, but be sure to include critiquing in your steps to publication and keep the following points in mind when you do:

- None of us are perfect and on top of that we have a blind spot: We know what we meant. It is amazing the extent to which our minds can fill in the blanks when we know what's supposed to be there.

- Finding or starting a critique group is relatively easy. Participating in one effectively, that's a little trickier. There is fine art to both receiving and giving an effective critique.

- Keep it manageable, have guidelines, and remember this is about growth and improvement as a writer, not a mutual admiration society.

- An effective critique group is about opening yourself up to both giving and receiving pain.

- The goal of critiquing is to chip away those parts of the story that are the wrong "shape" and uncover the art beneath.

- Never take one person's responses as irrefutable; if you can, get more than one critique on a piece. If you can't, weigh their comments against what you might know about the person (their experience level, their reading preferences, etc) and the validity of the comments in relation to your work.

- If you are sleepy or distracted or even not feeling well, you aren't going to be able to give the piece your proper attention, which is counterproductive to your purpose. Just walk away. There is always tomorrow.

- Dissecting your work with the intent to help you make it better does not constitute an attack against your person.

Sometimes it feels that way, but it's not.

PUTTING IT ALL TO WORK

What follows is a sample of writing from a beginning author who has kindly allowed me to use a their work as a critique example. They know how to tell a good story, but they get a little lost in the mechanics. It can be simple enough to tweak and adjust without making the work unrecognizable as theirs. So, let's take a look:

> *There's no air*, he thought. He wanted to scream.
>
> *If you panic, you're as good as dead,* yelled a voice in his head.
>
> "Stonebridge," he panted, remembering his combat physiology instructor, a man who could have been the template for every British drill instructor throughout history.
>
> *Assess your situation,* the voice continued, *and then work with what you've got. Don't panic. Death will just have to wait its turn.*
>
> Calmer now, he slowed his breathing and tried to concentrate. He still couldn't move. "Hello," he called. His voice sounded muffled to his ears, like he was... "Dammit," he proclaimed at his own stupidity.
>
> "Suit mode, power up," he commanded. In a flurry of lights and sounds, accompanied by a rush of cool air, his helmet displays came to life.

Comment [DM1]: This does not add anything and feels like leading the reader.

Deleted: , *I must be buried*

Formatted: Indent: Left: 3.5"

Deleted: yield

Comment [DM2]: Who is "he"? be sure to identify your characters early on.

Comment [DM3]: Do you mean psychology?

Deleted: ,

Comment [DM4]: Nice line!

Deleted: ,

Deleted: ,

Deleted: h

Deleted: and an accompanying

Comment [DM5]: Good descriptive

This is just a simple critique and by no means comprehensive, but it gives you an idea both of the types of changes and revisions you might encounter, and how the Track Changes feature in Microsoft Word works.

CRITIQUE GROUPS:
ANOTHER EXPERIENCE

By Kelly A. Harmon

Are you looking for a way to kick your writing into high gear? Do you lack the courage to submit your writing for publication? Are you wondering why you're getting nothing but rejections?

Perhaps a critique group is just what you need.

A critique group is group of writers who meets regularly with the purpose of improving and publishing their work. Joining a group is a two-fold commitment: a member is required to write, polish and submit new work to the group; and, to critically read and be prepared to offer advice on how to improve other members' manuscripts.

Groups can meet face-to-face or via email. Both have advantages and disadvantages.

If you want to improve your writing, are open to constructive criticism and want to be published, then don't wait: join a critique group as soon as you're able. Many writers of diverse genres and experience have found critique groups helpful.

Andrew Gudgel, a writer who has published both fiction and nonfiction, and a long-time critique-group member says, "The advantage of a critique group is that it puts multiple sets of eyes on your latest work, each with a different sphere of expertise, all wanting to improve your story. One person catches a misplaced modifier; somebody else notes where the POV goes all wobbly; and a third points out that the Chinese Imperial examination system didn't start until five hundred years later. A good critique group session is like a cross between a trip to a library and your sixth-grade English teacher."

Paranormal romance author, Helen Scott Taylor, author of *The Magic Knot*, found her critique group so useful, she eventually became a moderator of one. She says, "When I first started writing, I joined an online chapter of Romance Writers of America. This group has a thriving online critique group and I quickly signed up. I had a lot of help from writers with more experience who were keen to help a newbie."

Whether you're a pro or neophyte, every writer experiences doubts about his work and can benefit from another set of eyes reviewing it.

Dave Wolverton, who writes the best-selling *Runelords* series under the name, David Farland, says, "There's a sense of security that comes from having others read your work before you send it out. You always have to worry about little infelicities. Yesterday I noticed a typo in my work. I wrote the word "omnibust". Suddenly I had visions of a woman whose bust was so big, it encompassed the universe. It's not at all the kind of image that I want my editor to conjure up."

WHO SHOULD JOIN A CRITIQUE GROUP?

· writers who are serious

· writers who want to improve

· writers who want to be published

· writers who are willing to accept criticism

This last point is important. Writers must join critique groups with the right attitude: that is, knowing that no matter how good their writing is, there's always room for improvement. A writer needs to be open to constructive criticism. If you're not there yet with your work, it may not be the right time for you to join. Writers who are unable to accept criticism are usually unable to make their work better. If a writer is not open minded enough to absorb a review, he is probably disinclined to make any changes in his manuscript.

Worse, some writers may be mortified to hear that their work needs improvement and may either lash out at the critique or shut down, becoming unable to write until he or she is able to get past the criticism.

Thus, developing an open mind is critical.

ADVANTAGES OF CRITIQUE GROUPS

Whether the advantages of a critique group outweigh the disadvantages is up to you. Here are some to consider.

Note that these benefits are based on two assumptions:

1. that the critique group's mission is for members to be published in a broad market, and

2. that these benefits are to be found in good critique groups: not all are created equal. There are some ugly groups.

Andrew Burt, founder of the Critters online workshop (www.critters. org), and former Vice President of the Science Fiction and Fantasy Writers of America says, "I think the pros greatly outweigh the cons."

COMPANY OF A LIKE KIND

The old trope of a writer spending the best years of his life in a lonely garret toiling away on a manual Smith Corona may be replaced these days by the image of a blogger composing on his laptop at the nearby Starbucks, but even mid-crowd, writing remains a solitary endeavor.

Only another writer is going to know the pain of your stiff neck from thirteen hours straight at the keyboard or understand the wrath of your disappointed family because dinner burned while you fixed a serious plot hole in Chapter Two. Fellow writers understand the emotional attachment you have to your work and the sacrifice of sleep or social activities. Joining a critique group allows you to mingle with other folk who understand what you're doing and why you're doing it, no questions asked.

ENCOURAGEMENT, SUPPORT AND MOTIVATION

Group members will inspire you to try new ways of writing and new ways of thinking, and keep you focused on the task at hand: eventual publication. Encouragement and motivation doesn't just come from the members of the group. Sometimes it's a consequence of the *rules* of the group. Consider deadlines. Having to furnish the group with a complete chapter or short story once a month forces you to get to work.

When you begin to send your work out for publication, members of your group will rejoice with your acceptances and console you on your rejections, and they will root for you the entire way, because your successes are their successes. Seeing someone else in the group succeed feeds your own desire to succeed, and motivates you to do better.

Rivalry can also foster inspiration.

Andrew Gudgel says, "A critique group helps keep you motivated. Besides the chance to connect with other writers and swap info and ideas, there's always the secret spur of jealousy when someone else makes a sale."

FREE, HONEST FEEDBACK

The heart and soul of a successful critique group is reliable, honest feedback on your writing from the other writers in the group. Here is where you will receive informed commentary on your manuscript: Are your characters believable? Is the dialogue stilted? Do you use too many passive verbs? You'll also get some technical help from the grammar queens, or history buffs, or science birds (depending on the make-up of your group). You may even get some suggestions on how to fix some of the perceived issues of the manuscript (although some may feel this is more con than pro, see below).

Andrew Burt says, "Someone may catch stupid errors you've made before they meet an editor or reader—which could be not just typos or grammatical errors, but factual errors, bad science, logic errors, consistency errors (didn't your character Bob leave his gun behind a few pages back?), plot problems, characters acting out of character, boring areas, or other such problems you may have a blind spot about."

As the critique session continues, don't just pay attention to what you hear about your own manuscript. Pay attention to what is said about the manuscripts of others. Sometimes the feedback you hear about someone else's manuscript is just as informative as what you hear about your own.(where does Burt's quote end? Paragraph above-kah)

NETWORKING AND INFORMATION SHARING

Networking doesn't just mean getting a leg up in the publishing business, although a successful writers group might help you there as well. Networking also means to share information about new and emerging markets, contests and conventions. Group members should pass along information about trends, new books, editors, etc.

THE ABILITY TO ANALYZE YOUR OWN WORK

This is arguably the best learned skill from participation in critique groups. By reading the work of others, you'll be able to see what story elements function and what do not. If you can figure out the problems in someone else's story, you'll be able to apply this critical thinking to your own work. As you develop your critiquing skill, you'll find it will lead to better self-editing.

"You learn a lot about craft by critiquing others. When people in Critters occasionally try to slide by with some easy critiques just to get enough points to have their own manuscript critiqued, I tell them that fully half the benefit of Critters is in doing the critiques of others. The more in-depth you analyze what works and doesn't in other peoples work the more you learn the same about your own. That brings a natural level of improvement," says Andrew Burt.

MORE THAN THE SUM OF THE PARTS

Often discussions at face-to-face meetings reveal more thoughts than anyone came prepared to discuss. The free flow of ideas, as in brainstorming, can spark creative new solutions to manuscript flaws. One person will have written down something about a character's actions not being logical, for example, which will trigger another group member to suggest something that might work, and others may pile on to refine the suggestion.

DISADVANTAGES OF A CRITIQUE GROUP

Dave Wolverton says, "There are also certain pitfalls that you have to be aware of. You may find, for example, that someone in your group is disruptive. I've seen writers become terribly jealous of other's success. I've seen people who consistently make rude remarks. I've known boorish critics who want to argue over the artistic merits of an author's works. I've seen critics who attack the author and not the work. I've seen torrid romances break out, with equally torrid breakups."

Disadvantages of being in a critique group can come from internal as well as external sources. The idea is to minimize drawbacks you're in control of, and see if the group, as a team, can take care of the rest.

CRITIQUING TAKES TIME FROM YOUR WRITING

If you join a critique group, you'll be expected to give as many critiques as you receive. No matter what the size of the group, every minute you spend reviewing the work of others means you'll have that much less time to devote to your own writing. There's a silver lining here: critiquing other people's work is one of the best ways to take notice of both good and poor writing techniques. By giving a critical eye to someone else's stories, you'll be able to better discern problems in your own work and take action to correct them.

There are a finite number of hours in the day, and only so many of them can be devoted to writing. Some writers will give up their writing hours to spend them critiquing. It's critical that you don't use the time you've allotted for writing to review your group's stories. Carve out time from another activity if you can.

NOT EVERYONE GIVES A USEFUL CRITIQUE

Not everyone provides stellar feedback. Some criticism is less than useful; other suggestions may be downright insulting. It is easy to become defensive in the face of such feedback. Sift through how the critique sounds and analyze what's actually being said: a less than tactful review could actually be very useful. Read between the lines to find the meaning hidden in the insult. Don't take it personally, remember: the critique is about the writing, not about the writer. Note that some critiques may come off as useless at first blush, but the hard, hidden truth may become apparent only later, upon re-reading and reflection.

Andrew Burt says, "The most common complaint I hear about work shopping one's writing is that in a small workshop, other members may accidentally or intentionally try to alter the way you write, to conform to their idea of how things should be. That is, you risk losing your unique voice if others are trying to steer everyone to their style. This can well be true in a small workshop, especially if some of the members have strong personalities." He continues, "The second most common complaint I hear about workshops in general is 'people are mean.' I agree. It's fairly easy for someone else to get nasty or dictatorial when reviewing a piece. This was an early problem with Critters, until I realized a key problem and figured out a solution: Diplomacy."

DISRUPTIVE MEMBERS

Your group may have one: a writer so sure of his skill he belittles everyone else, makes rude comments, or gives insulting critiques. A disruptive member is usually asked to leave or weeds himself out of the group once he sees his actions aren't buying him the attention he seeks. Sometimes the troublemaker stays: maybe he's a published author and the group feels compelled to sustain his membership. Maybe the skill he has to offer is worth putting up with the behavior. Maybe no one has the guts to step up and ask him to leave.

Dave Wolverton says, "If you ever get into a writing group and feel consistently intimidated by others in the group—if they put you down or make rude comments—you may need to get out. Better yet, get rid of the jerks in the group."

USING THE GROUP AS A SUBSTITUTE FOR PUBLICATION

It is usually only one member—as opposed to the entire group—who uses meetings as an outlet for publication rather than a means to publication. This member is satisfied with what he's producing, enjoys the small readership he has in other group members, and rarely labors to improve. Members who aren't striving and learning fall behind the rest of the group in terms of skill. Their critiques become less and less useful.

THE GROUP BECOMES MORE SOCIAL THAN BUSINESS

It happens. You meet month after month, year after year, and you get to know each other as much as any family. Soon, you're spending the pre-meeting time discussing your lives and your day-jobs. Your three-hour meeting just turned into a dinner party with a little discussion on writing.

Says Andrew Gudgel, "Always meet with the intention of improving each other's writing. Without focus, a critique group can easily degenerate into a social club."

If this happens, it's time to re-focus the group or re-focus you. If the group can't concentrate its efforts on the business of writing, find another group.

POORLY MANAGED GROUPS

Larger groups probably suffer from poor management more than smaller groups. Groups with many members will likely be unable to critique all members' manuscripts in a single meeting. Schedules have to be made and kept. Critiques have to be tracked to make certain everyone gives and receives the same amount. Someone must be in charge of the record-keeping and the enforcement. A breakdown in the organization causes chaos and hard feelings. It may lead to the disbandment of the group.

Says Helen Taylor, "I have also been involved in other [on-line] critique groups that didn't work because they were not moderated properly. Unless the posting and critiquing is overseen, there are always some people who expect others to critique their work but are not willing to offer critiques in return."

A LACK OF FACE-TO-FACE INTERACTION

Clearly, this disadvantage applies to on-line groups. Writers who send and receive manuscripts and critiques by email (or post to bulletin boards) are not going to enjoy the social aspects of getting together regularly. Meeting on-line also precludes the instant "give and take" of a face-to-face critique. There's no mechanism by which the writer can ask the critiquer for clarification and get an immediate answer (unless the group is able to meet on-line to "chat"). On-line meetings may also be less able to benefit from the spontaneous generation of creative ideas inherent in a congenial face-to-face group.

HOW TO BE A GOOD
CRITIQUE GROUP MEMBER

ALWAYS SUBMIT YOUR BEST WORK

Don't send in a first draft or unfinished work in progress. Don't waste your team's time by submitting a piece that will likely change several times over. You want to give them your best so that by the time you incorporate their comments, you'll have a piece worthy of sending out to a professional market.

SUBMIT MANUSCRIPTS ON TIME

If you're a face to face group and work must be received by each member ten days prior to the meeting, then send it ten days prior to the meeting. Even better, send it earlier, especially if it's a long piece, in order for group members to be able to devote their full attention to it. Don't ever send something the day before it's due. This is not only discourteous, it's unprofessional.

Casual groups who meet via email may be less stodgy about deadlines. Still, if you're going to miss one, send a note to the group explaining the delay and a reasonable time frame to get the work out.

GIVE A PROPER CRITIQUE

Spend the time necessary to provide the author with an in-depth critique. Don't rip through the manuscript as quickly as possible and rely on other members of the group to do your job. Remember, critiquing is one of the best ways to learn to spot errors in your own writing. Taking time here hones your own craft. See *How to Give a Good Critique* below for a more detailed discussion on how to review a manuscript.

SUBMIT CRITIQUES ON TIME

Just as with manuscripts, read and critique others' work within the requested time frame. If it needs to be emailed by a certain date, make sure a proper (not half-baked) critique arrives in the author's mailbox on time.

If you meet face-to-face with your group, have your critiques read and marked up ahead of time so they can be carried to the meeting.

HOW TO GIVE A GOOD CRITIQUE

Andrew Burt says, "Writing a critique is a sort of art form all to itself. Just like there are conventions for how to write an effective essay, novel, screenplay, haiku, etc., there are guidelines for how to phrase a critique. If you're "writing for your audience," then your audience here is one specific author, and there are things that work well and things that don't. Authors are naturally prone to being sensitive about their creations, so delivering news of what you didn't like in a manuscript just works better when delivered in a certain way. It's a new kind of writing for most people, but I find that it's rare for someone not to pick it up pretty fast. Then you can explain the problems in a story in a way the author can hear, which is the purpose of the thing: effective communication."

READ THE WORK THOROUGHLY

Before offering criticism, review the manuscript in full. Have pen in hand so you can mark up the work as you read it (and not have to go back later and try and remember what you thought).

Take the time to read the manuscript beginning to end without rushing. Wait to make sweeping statements about the entirety of the story until you've read it all through at least once.

READ IT AGAIN

If possible, put the story away for a day or so, and consider it in your mind: plot, elements, characters, etc. Then read the story again. This time, read the work more critically. Think about what worked and what didn't work for you as a reader. Look for the big problems: the plot holes, the logic gaps, characters who are male on page one but female on page three. Mark all of these elements on the manuscript, and summarize your ideas on the back.

MARK UP THE MANUSCRIPT COMPLETELY

In a face-to-face session, you may not have time to go over each typo and spelling error (and in fact, you shouldn't. Doing so wastes time.). Typos and other small errors should be marked (along with all your other points) on the manuscript and given back to the author after the spoken critique. The author can review them at his leisure and won't have to worry about hearing them aloud. If you don't meet face-to-face, use the "track changes" or "reviewer" functions of the writing software to annotate the text and mail it back with a written dialogue of your points.

When making your oral critique, begin with some words of praise. Find something that worked well for you, a nice turn of phrase, accurate pacing, etc. (This is the encouragement and support part about being in a critique group.) This method is sometimes called the "sandwich" method: start with words of praise, point out the weak points of the work, and then end with more words of praise, if possible. Although it may seem positive criticism is less useful, it may make the writer think twice about deleting the gem that other group members loved.

BE DIPLOMATIC IN HOW YOU PHRASE YOUR REVIEW

How another writer accepts your opinion varies greatly depending on how you offer it. This is true both when you're speaking aloud in a face-to-face group and scribbling your opinion on the manuscript.

"Authors don't hear things when they're phrased in certain ways. If you tell an author, "Your protagonist is not drawn well enough to force your readers to identify with her," the author may well get defensive: Who are YOU to say! Well! -- And that's the grain of truth there: You aren't empowered to speak for All Readers, just yourself. So cardinal rule number one is to make it clear the bad news is only your opinion," says Andrew Burt.

DON'T CRITIQUE STYLE

Remember, the idea is for you to help another writer improve their work, not make their work sound like yours.

"You're not the style police, nor the undisputed expert on writing, so it's far and away better to say, "I didn't find the protagonist well drawn enough to get me to identify with her." Now that says the same thing—there is a problem with how the character is drawn -- but in a way that can get past an author's "defensive hearing," says Andrew Burt.

10-POINT REVIEW

Critiques will vary according to subject matter, but it may be easier to stick with a formula when performing a critique. The following is a 10-point review process which is helpful in providing a detailed observation for the writer. For face-to-face groups, it can be useful in furnishing a cohesive, articulate oral review. (What about setting? Creating a believable world is crucial to speculative fiction...I know... that would make it an 11 point review, but I really think it should be mentioned)

1: HOOK

Is the opening of the story sufficient to interest the reader? Is there a balance between dialogue, action and narrative to set the hook? What does or doesn't work? How can it be made better?

2: CHARACTER

Discuss the believability of the characters. Are they well-rounded or only two dimensional? Are they caricatures or stereotypes? Are the characters actions' consistent? Are their motives understandable? Were the plot and the characters' motives in sync? Provide solid examples to demonstrate your point of view.

3: SETTING

Creating a believable world is crucial when writing speculative fiction. It also needs to help set the mood. Discuss whether the setting is right or not for the story, and give examples of what works and what doesn't. Is the description of locale too much or too little? Did it enhance the mood? Can you visualize the setting? Can you picture what the characters are seeing, hearing, tasting and smelling?

4: PLOT

Does the plot make sense? Did events happen in a logical order? Did the story start in the right place? Point out any rough spots. Did the story have a beginning, middle and an end? If in a particular genre, did it work? Is it appropriate for the chosen audience? Does the pacing work throughout the manuscript?

5: THEME

Not every author writes a story with an intentional theme in mind. Nonetheless, one usually develops by the end of the story. While critiquing, consider whether the story has an overt theme and what it is. If a theme emerges, does it work? Can you restate the theme in a single sentence? Is the plot of the story or storyline appropriate for this theme?

6: CONFLICT AND RESOLUTION

Is there enough conflict in the story to create adequate tension? If not, what is stopping the tension from building? What could be changed to increase it? Does the story resolve too easily? If so, is that a reflection on the characters or the plot?

7: DIALOGUE

Was the dialogue realistic? Does it forward the plot? Is it obvious who is speaking? (Are sufficient dialogue attribution tags used? Are too many tags used?) Cross out said bookisms dialogue attribution which is impossible (he smiled, she hissed, he sniffed) or those which explain the conversation (he demanded, she insisted, etc.).

8: VIEWPOINT

Review the characters and their roles in the story. Are there jarring shifts of viewpoint character within a scene? If a scene isn't working, is it possible that another character should have the viewpoint to carry the plot forward?

9: GRAMMAR/LANGUAGE/OVERALL WRITING

This is a detailed examination of grammar, language and writing. On the manuscript, mark awkward passages, spelling errors, trite or over-used phrases, incorrect grammar, poor transitions, etc. Point out passive verbs and cross out unnecessary adverbs. Look for places the author may have *told* more than he *showed*. Were there any metaphors or analogies? Did they work? Was there a balance of narrative and action? Was the sentence pattern varied? Has the author made any Freudian slips or written in any anachronisms?

10: SUMMARY

Sum up overall impressions of the manuscript. Did you like the story? Why or why not? Did it work as a whole? Did it feel cohesive? What about the title? Does it work for the story? Why or why not? Point out whether you believe the story is marketable or not and provide solid reasoning for the belief, especially if you don't believe the piece is marketable. If you think it will sell, suggest a market or two for which the manuscript may be relevant.

HOW TO ACCEPT CRITICISM

It can be daunting to offer up your work-in-progress to a group of individuals whose goal it is to tear your story apart, especially if you've never done it before. Take heart! Ironically, this group has your best interests in mind even as they point out your errors. Better for them to find that you've misspelled *you're* as *your*, instead of an editor realizing it, and rejecting your story. Editors won't tell you they find your lack of proper grammar annoying. They'll simply decline your work and move on to the next in the stack. Let your writer friends dole out the lumps so that when you finally submit your work for publication, you'll know it's the best it can be.

That being said, there are things to keep in mind when the retired English teacher in your group changes every bit of Cockney English dialogue in your story to the Queen's English or the chemical engineer insists the magic in your world won't work because it's not based on science:

NOT EVERYTHING IS TRUE

Really. If you're new to critique groups, this is probably the first rule of thumb to keep in mind. Knowing this is what keeps you sane when people tell you that your characters are only two dimensional or that the plot you've woven has a logic gap so large you could drive a tank through it. Every critique is not going to be spot on. However...

IF IT STINGS, IT'S PROBABLY TRUE

This is sometimes referred to as "Corollary A" to the rule above. If it hurts, then subconsciously you realize what is being said might be true. Pay special attention to the points that sting to acknowledge. These can often improve your story if incorporated into the next draft of your work.

IF MORE THAN ONE PERSON SAYS
IT, IT'S PROBABLY TRUE

This is sometimes referred to as "Corollary B" to the first rule. Perhaps only one person pointed out your plot gap. Maybe that person didn't understand the crux of the tale. But three readers mentioned your cardboard characters. You may be thinking to yourself,"Not every critique is true..." but if more than one person agrees, it probably is.

DURING THE CRITIQUE

When it's your turn to be critiqued, remain silent. Concentrate on what others are saying, and not about refuting what they say. Take notes. The notes you take for yourself may vary from what the speaker has written on your manuscript. Often the speaker will think of something he didn't write on the manuscript, or others may pile on, generating new and better ideas. If you don't take notes, you're likely to lose that comment in the noise of hearing so many more from the group. Thank each speaker in turn.

AFTER THE CRITIQUE

As soon as possible after the meeting, while ideas are still fresh in your mind, assemble all the manuscripts and go through them one by one, deciding which you agree with and which you don't. Remember that some critical ideas you mentally rejected at the meeting may, upon reflection, be truer than you thought. You may want to create a separate document, collating all the comments together on one manuscript. Some authors keep Critique Logs for each story they write which, lists comments by type per story, how many people suggested it, whether the author agreed with the suggestion, and whether they made the change.

Chances are you've already got a good idea of what to incorporate from the session and what not. Make the adjustments to your manuscript and send it off to the most appropriate market. Share the results—rejection or acceptance for publication—with your group. They'll help you by commiserating or rejoicing with you.

A Scenario for a Face-to-Face Meeting

Meeting begins at 7:00 p.m.

6:45—7:00 p.m. –Writers gather at meeting place. Discuss member news since the last meeting (acceptances, rejections, possible contracts received, new laptops purchased, etc.). Find their places around the table (or discussion area) and pull out marked up manuscripts, notes and pens.

7:00—Meeting called to order by Leader.

7:00—7:15 p.m. –Round robin (starting with the leader) of "*What did you write this week?*" This keeps the group focused on writing (and can encourage writers to put pen to paper, so to speak, knowing they'll be required to "confess" at each meeting). Writers can also discuss tips and news; such as new Web sites found, local writing chapters starting in the area, markets opening and closing, upcoming book signings of favored authors, etc. (If time runs out, members give the additional info to the Leader who will gather it all together and send it, along with the previous information, out to the group via email.

7:15—8:45 p.m. –Round robin of critiques for all members who have submitted materials for the meeting. Usually this consists of airing all critiques about a single manuscript before moving on to the next manuscript and going around again.

8:45—9:00 p.m. –Group Business. Leader starts with, for instance, discussion of candidates asking to join the group and may hand out applications for group to read before the next meeting, suggests a date and time for the next meeting as well as a location, gets an agreement (or have a discussion for alternates) and closes meeting.

9:00 P.M.... MEETING IS OFFICIALLY OVER. SOCIALIZING CAN COMMENCE!

A Scenario for an On-Line Meeting:

An online meeting arrangement is very simple. After a group has met and formed, dates for when manuscripts are submitted and when finished critiques are submitted are decided upon. They can be fixed dates, such as the fifteenth and the thirtieth of each month, or they could be fixed weeks, such as first Friday and third Friday. The dates should be as far out (two weeks apart) or as near together (three days) as the group agrees to. For example:

First Friday of the Month:Everyone submits their manuscript.

Third Friday of the Month:Critiques of every manuscript, by every member, are due.

Some email groups are too large for each member to provide a critique for every other member being critiqued during the given week. Take for example, Critters, which has 10,000 active members writing science fiction, fantasy and horror.

In the case of Critters, at any time during the year, any member can submit a manuscript which goes into a queue. Twenty manuscripts at the beginning of the queue are allowed to be critiqued by all members each week. Writers are expected to critique one manuscript per week, within certain limits of the year (to be in good standing you must have a critique ratio of 75%).

If a writer doesn't have a critique ratio of 75% when his manuscript moves to the top of the queue, than his manuscript will not be critiqued that round. A writer can have his manuscript moved to the front of the queue by becoming the Most Productive Critter of the week; that is, submitting the most and longest critiques of all members that week, or going for an instant win of submitting 10+ critiques of 300 words or more during the week.

Rules Which Every Writers Group Needs... or Not

Some groups can happily trundle along forever without the need to create formalized rules. Some groups can't exist without them. They are chiseled in stone and have set consequences for not following them: either being ousted from the group or not having any work critiqued until certain standards are met. Members of these groups are usually screened to test the caliber of their writing, auditioned before being allowed to join, and must agree to the rules by signing before having their work be reviewed by the group. Sometimes, there's a probationary period, during which time they may be asked to leave.

For groups who need rules, here are a few suggestions:

Demand Courtesy

If you're going to take the time to make rules, make it plain that good manners are expected and nothing less will be tolerated. Spell out that personal attacks aren't allowed, especially during the critique (in fact, no personal attacks should occur ever). Stipulate that insults, harassment and rude behavior are forbidden.

Prohibit Sharing Manuscripts with Anyone Outside the Group

Sharing outside the group is a total breach of trust. You wouldn't want your manuscript read by a group member's husband's coworker. Be just as considerate and keep it to yourself. It's especially easy to share manuscripts with other people when your group meets via email. Do yourself a favor and do not forward the story. There's no easier way to get black-balled in the on-line community.

Mandate that Manuscripts be Read in Advance of the Meeting

This boils down to common courtesy as well: read the manuscript before you arrive at your face-to-face meeting. It's impolite to read while someone else is giving their opinion. Do this more than once and expect to be booted from the group.

MANDATE THAT WRITTEN COMMENTS MUST ACCOMPANY THE MANUSCRIPT

If you're going to take the time to read and comment on a piece, do the best job you can do. Mark up the manuscript: point out typos, point-of-view wobbles, improper antecedents and other grammar issues, places where you think the plot fell apart, scenes which can be cut, etc. Summarize it all with some notes on the back.

MANDATE RECIPROCITY: EVERYONE SUBMITS AND CRITIQUES

Every so often you'll find a member who doesn't commit equally to the give-and-take nature of a group: they'll either want to spend all their time critiquing for others (and not writing anything new) or insist on contributing to the group without being willing to critique for anyone else. Both are a detriment to the group. The former is more interested in giving his opinion; the latter has an inflated opinion of his own work when he refuses to do his part in helping others. Occasionally, it's simply that the author doesn't have enough time to devote to the group. Require a minimum number of submissions to critique and minimum number of manuscripts to submit in the calendar year.

HAVE A MEMBERSHIP TERMINATION RULE

Give the group an easy mechanism for ousting unwanted members. Stipulate in the rules how membership can be revoked; for example: not doing the required number of critiques or not submitting the required number of manuscripts within a certain period leads to termination of membership. Boorish behavior, insults and harassment will result in immediate termination of membership, etc.

ELECT A LEADER

Within a small, harmonious face-to-face group, a leader may not be necessary. However, a larger group, especially one which may operate via snail-mail, rather than email, might require a leader. This person will handle the paperwork, point out the order of speakers for the critique, schedule critiques for various meetings if there are too many members to handle in a single meeting, and be the tie-breaker during decision making, such as termination votes. The leader position might rotate every six months to a year in order that everyone might have a chance.

FINDING THE RIGHT GROUP FOR YOU

Once you've decided to join a group, consider what it has to offer, what you're willing to commit to, and what you want to get out of it. Having these items in mind while you audition some groups (and they audition you) will put you in the correct frame of mind while you're debating.

Before you sit in on a local group, or send an online application to a moderator, do your homework.

CONSIDER GOALS

Does the group have a plan or a purpose, or are they meeting "just because". A plan could be as simple as, "We meet to improve our writing," or as goal-oriented as, "We meet to better our writing in order to obtain publication for our members." It could be an elaborate Mission or Goals statement. It doesn't even have to be written. It's just important that the group have a goal, because if they don't know where they're going...neither do you.

CONSIDER GENRE

Do you write mainly romance? Paranormal? Science fiction and fantasy? Some authors will tell you that it is important to find a group dedicated to the genre you write. Others will disagree. Just like joining a group, there are pros and cons to joining dedicated or non-dedicated groups.

Single genre groups may suffer from groupthink, by avoiding conflict and coming to a general consensus without any individual thought or critical thinking on a particular work-in-progress. On the other hand, they'll have a good idea of the tropes associated with the genre and a unique understanding of what publishing in that arena may involve. A group of various writers may lack some crucial knowledge about the genre you write, but they may also offer a different point of view.

This needs to be said: beware a literary group if you write genre (science fiction, fantasy, romance, horror, etc.) It's no secret the literary world considers fantasy, romance, science fiction and horror as substandard, low-brow writing, despite many fine published examples to the contrary. This isn't always the case, of course, but it should be taken into account when auditioning a group.

CONSIDER EXPERIENCE LEVELS

Members of the group should write at about the same level. This way everyone is comfortable with each other. A good mix of writers will include authors with strengths in plot, world building, grammar etc. No one will exceed in all areas of the craft. Consider well a writer's strengths before deciding he or she doesn't write on your "level."

Don't join a group of writers whose collective strengths and weaknesses are degrees below your own. There is very little to be learned from such a group.

If possible, join a group of writers who write slightly better. There is more to be gained from their knowledge. However, if other members are much more advanced than you, you may experience feelings of frustration and inferiority.

CONSIDER GROUP HARMONY

Does the group work together? Do they *like* each other? If they spend their time bickering and back-biting, it's a sure thing they'll treat you with the same lack of respect. What if they're great writers? What if they're pro writers and they're willing to let you join? Run away! You're better off finding a compatible group of non-published writers who are willing to work together.

Look for a group which makes you happy, one that knows your name, invites you to join in the conversation, and seems interested in you and your goals, and most importantly—your work.

CONSIDER PROXIMITY: MEETING ON-LINE SAVES TIME AND MONEY

Sending and receiving critiques via email saves the time wasted while driving to your destination; time which could be devoted to writing. It also eliminates any gas expenses, wear and tear on the car, and possibly the cost of dinner or a snack. If you're a parent, it could eliminate sitter costs, as well. Since you're not sending manuscripts via snail mail, it saves the expense of paper, envelopes and postage. (Even face-to-face groups can benefit by emailing manuscripts by saving costs on envelopes and postage.)

HOW TO FIND OTHER WRITERS

One way is to find other writers is to contact a state's writers organization, like the Maryland Writer's Society or the Pike's Peak Writers in Colorado. Another option is to seek out a local chapter of a larger group, such as the Romance Writers of America, to see if they have groups starting in your area. It's also worth contacting large associations, like the Science Fiction and Fantasy Writers of America (SFWA) or the Society for Children's Book Writers and Illustrators (SCBWI). Many of these organizations have an on-line presence.

Check bulletin boards at local libraries, book stores or college campuses for even more immediate locale. Groups have also been known to start from writing classes. Librarians and book store employees may also be good sources.

Can't find something close to home? Advertise and start your own group. The same resources listed above will be able to help you in your search. Some organizations have local or chapter newsletters you can advertise in for free (or for free with membership) or have online mailing lists or Web sites you may be able to post on.

Attending a conference is another way to meet other writers.

The internet is the best place to find an on-line group. Check chat groups, writers Web sites or if you write fantasy, science fiction or horror, look into Critters, the Web's largest on-line critique group.

Once you find a group that is accepting new members, audition them. Ask to sit in on one of their meetings to get a feel for how the group is run, the writing level of the members and their seriousness. Do they have the same writing goals as you? Is their writing on par with yours? Did you like them?

If you liked the group, ask if you can come back. Give them some time to evaluate you and/or your application. If you're not invited back...take the next step: start your own group.

NOW IT'S UP TO YOU

Every writer is different and requires a different inducement to summon that elusive muse. Some writers have found critique groups to be more beneficial to their writing than conferences, how-to books, or retreats. Although such groups are not for everybody, perhaps joining a critique group will prove to be just the spark you need to get your writing—and perhaps your publishing—to the next level.

A League Of Extraordinary Characters

By Ripley Patton

Shakespeare's character Benedick said it well, "The world must be peopled." As a writer of stories or novels, you are creating worlds, which, like all worlds, must be peopled. True, the residents of your worlds may be werewolves, witches, vampires or ghosts, but in some way they must be people like you and me. Humanity must find themselves in your characters. We must know their thoughts, feel their actions, and understand their motives. We must be able to relate to them. In that way alone, they must be ordinary, but in all other ways, extraordinary.

No one reads paranormal fiction to meet mundane people. We do that every day in the real world. Readers seek out paranormal stories because they want to be surprised, thrilled, frightened, and bowled over by the unusual. You, the writer, have made a promise just by putting pen to paper and writing a paranormal story. You have promised to people your world with a league of extraordinary characters. These are the characters your readers will follow trustingly into a world of your creation. These are the people your readers will grow to love or hate, root for or hiss at. It won't matter if you've spent years world-building, done copious research on vampire lore, or have the prose writing capabilities of Poe, if you don't keep your promise about characters. No matter how splendid the trip, no one wants to journey with bad company. That is why character development is such a vital element of writing well.

Creating Characters: The Frankenstein Method

Unlike procreation in the real world, your characters aren't born or adopted. They aren't the result of reproduction but rather of artistic creation, but how do writers go about making realistic but extraordinary people out of thin air? We don't. In fact, the work of creating characters is more like that of Shelly's Doctor Frankenstein. Collecting a piece here, and a bit there, writers harvest the characteristics of real or imagined people and meld them together to make a new monster. Thankfully, we don't have to dig up graves or corpses in the process. Below is a list of the main sources for character material.

Characters come from within the writer

Some writers experience a character as a voice in their head, an internal entity that begins to narrate the story as they rush to jot it down. In this case, the character is probably drawn from a part of the writer herself. We have all played different characters in a range of stories throughout our lives. We've all been the innocent child, the prankster, the exile, or the hero, and by remembering those roles we can create characters out of our own inner process.

Characters come from people we know

Our world is filled with characters, and a good writer is a people watcher, a keen observer of other people's "character potential". You might base a character's general personality on a neighbor or a favorite aunt, their looks on a movie star or your librarian. Friends and acquaintances of writers need to be aware that their quirks and beauties will likely end up in a story somewhere.

CHARACTERS COME FROM PEOPLE WE KNOW ABOUT

There are people we know, and then there are people we know about. Historical figures, people in the news, a co-worker's ex-husband, though we don't know them personally, can take on a life of their own in our minds and become the fodder for great characters.

CHARACTERS COME FROM OTHER WORKS OF FICTION

The truth is most characters in paranormal fiction (and fiction in general) are derivative in nature. They originate from the myths, stories and legends passed down throughout human history. Bram Stoker's Dracula, the precursor to most modern vampires, was himself a compilation of tradition and lore. The key is to find something unique and surprising to add to the body of mythology when you create a new character.

CHARACTERS COME FROM A CONGLOMERATION OF METHODS

Most quality, original characters in fiction were created using a combination of the above methods. Built piece by piece with bits of a friend here and a stranger there, your character takes on a life of his own. When he finally surprises you by sitting up on the table and lumbering off, you've done well. I suggest you follow him, and write down what he does.

TYPES OF CHARACTERS: IT TAKES ALL SORTS

University Literature professors have spent decades categorizing and redefining types of characters. It can get dry. It can get boring. It can make you never want to read or write again. I'll save all that for the classroom and simply offer you a list of the many types with their basic definitions.

1. MAIN CHARACTER(S) Also called CENTRAL CHARACTER, MAJOR CHARACTER, OR PIVOTAL CHARACTER—A character or characters who are central

to the plot line and action of the story. They are vital to the development and resolution of the conflict and without them the story falls apart.

2. **MINOR CHARACTER(S)** Sometimes called **SPEAR CARRIERS.**—A character or characters who compliment the main character and help move the plot along. If a minor character dies, or is otherwise removed from the story, the plot continues unimpeded.

3. **THE HERO OR HEROINE**—The main character in the story a reader is meant to root for. This is the character or characters we want to "win" by the end of the story. The Hero is often the Main Character and the Protagonist, but not always.

4. **THE VILLAIN OF VILLAINESS**—The main character a reader is rooting against or wants to be defeated by the end of the story. A Villain has evil intent. In other words, he is purposefully, not accidentally, trying to thwart the hero's goals and desires. The Villain is often the main Antagonist.

5. **THE PROTAGONIST**—The main character who changes over the course of the story, moving either internally or externally from point A to point B. The protagonist is often also the main character and/or the hero, but does not have to be. Many people use the three terms interchangeably but there are subtle differences.

6. **THE ANTAGONIST**—any force or character in the story that is in conflict with the protagonist or hero. The antagonist is anything that impedes the protagonist from accomplishing his or her goals. It could be the weather, another character, or even a struggle within the main character himself, and it could be all of these at once. If the Antagonist is a person with evil intent, he is also The Villain.

7. **ANTI-HERO**—A main character, usually the protagonist, who lacks conventional values and morals, and/or who struggles for a goal not deemed universally admirable.

The anti-hero is not a Villain. The reader identifies and roots for the anti-hero even though they may not agree with his tactics, morals or goals.

8. **VIEWPOINT OR POINT OF VIEW CHARACTER**—The character or characters through which the reader experiences the story. The viewpoint character is often the main character but can also be the antagonist or another character.

9. **THE NARRATOR**—The fictional storyteller who exists within the world of the story, not to be confused with the author, who lives in the real world. A narrator can tell the story from his own point of view (or perspective) or from the point of view of one of the characters in the story.

10. **SYMPATHETIC CHARACTER**—Any character whose motives the reader can understand and comfortably share. Note that a sympathetic character need not be a good person, but the reader must sympathize with them.

11. **UNSYMPATHETIC CHARACTER**—Any character whose motives are suspect and whose behavior or feelings make the reader uncomfortable and unsympathetic towards them.

12. **DYNAMIC CHARACTER**—Any character who changes internally during the course of the story or novel. A Protagonist is Dynamic by definition, but other characters can be as well.

13. **STATIC CHARACTER**—A character who remains primarily the same throughout a story or novel. Events in the story do not alter their opinions, actions, personality, motivations or perceptions. A Static character is not necessarily flat. He can be complex, but still stay the same throughout the story.

14. **FLAT CHARACTER**—A character who reveals only one or two personality traits and these traits do not change throughout the story. Flat characters are also called **CARDBOARD CHARACTERS.**

15. **Stock Character**—A specific type of flat character who is instantly recognized by most readers. The stock characters nature is familiar to us because we have seen it portrayed many times before. Examples: the slimy car salesman, the dumb jock, the computer geek. Stock Characters are also called **Stereotype Characters**. They are not generally main characters nor are they well developed in the story.

16. **Round Character**—A character who displays varied and sometimes contradictory traits, revealing a complex personality. Round characters are usually also Dynamic. Protagonist and Antagonist Characters are almost always Round.

17. **Foil Character**—A character who enhances another character through contrast.

18. **Archetypal Character**—A character modeled after a person or ideal that is universally symbolic. Characters with strong archetypal identities, for example: the mother figure will automatically and unconsciously resonate with a large audience.

Note that most characters fall under more than one of the categories listed above. However, some types are mutually exclusive such as Flat and Round, or Sympathetic and Unsympathetic. None of these character types are better or worse to use than others. They all have their place and have been used individually and in combination throughout literary history. Granted, a story with only flat characters is likely to fall "flat" for the reader. However, in a story with many round characters a flat character can act as a useful foil.

A Warning Concerning Stock Characters

Paranormal literally means "beyond normal" so this is what readers will expect your characters to be. However, a dilemma lies with the rising popularity of paranormal fiction. Many traditional paranormal characters have been normalized. With such frequent use, they have become stock characters, and have lost their appeal to many editors and readers. You may encounter writer's guidelines that specify "no vampire or werewolf stories". The market is flooded with poorly written stock monsters, but you can still write vampire and werewolf stories, and sell them, if you are able to bring something new and exciting to the table.

Let me give an example:

Stock vampire character: Rich, eccentric, sexy vampire in black leather stalks/protects another "innocent" character.

Extraordinary vampire character: "Altruistic" hospice nurse is a vampire who justifies sucking the last dredges of life from her dying patients.

As you can see from these examples, the issue is not an overuse of the vampire archetype (The Shapeshifter or Shadow which attracts and repels us), but an overuse of the same kind of vampire. Archetypes are universal, classic and never go out of style. That is why I don't believe readers will ever truly tire of vampire and werewolf stories. However, we must adorn those archetypes with the ideas, attributes, and issues of a modern world, or they will bore us, and our readers, to tears.

Understanding Archetypes

Folklore and paranormal tales are rich in archetypes because, at their deepest level, they are the stories we tell ourselves to explain our inner landscape, man's psyche. The characters in paranormal fiction are outer expressions of our inner parts, the strangeness we can only face by putting it safely at a distance in story form. In Latin, monstrum means "to reveal". The characters we use in our stories will reveal something about us, the writer, and will hopefully reveal something of the readers to themselves as well.

In *A Hero with a Thousand Faces*, Joseph Campbell gives a list of character archetypes commonly found in fiction. This is not an exhaustive list but as an introduction to archetypes, it is a good place to start.

1. **The Hero**—The essence of this archetype is **SELF-SACRIFICE.** The hero gives up something for the good of himself or others, and generally grows in wisdom through that journey. Example: Frodo Baggins from *Lord of the Rings.*

2. **The Mentor**—The essence of this archetype is **WISDOM** and the ability to train other characters and/or bestow upon them the gifts and skills they will need for the journey. Example: Yoda from *Star Wars.*

3. **The Herald**—The essence of this archetype is the **ANNOUNCEMENT OF A CHALLENGE.** The herald is that person or event that upsets the status quo with a message which causes the hero to start his journey in the first place. Example: Hagrid in *Harry Potter* when he shows up to tell Harry he's actually a wizard.

4. **The Threshold Guardian**—The essence of this archetype is the **TESTING** of the hero's resolve and mettle. It is a gatekeeper on the hero's journey and the character who says in essence "None shall pass," but is usually only one step on the way to the final and ultimate antagonist. Example: The Dursleys in *Harry Potter* who try to keep Harry from going to Hogwarts.

5. **The Shapeshifter**—The essence of this archetype is **CHANGEABILITY.** The shapeshifter is the character most different from the hero, thus challenging the hero to change his or her preconceived ideas. The shapeshifter does not necessarily change bodily forms but can. The shapeshifter is also frequently the romantic interest of the hero, reinforcing the old adage that "opposites attract". Example: Angel from *Buffy the Vampire Slayer.*

6. **The Shadow**—The essence of this archetype is **ELIMINATION.** It represents that which the hero wants to be rid of, fight against, or destroy. The shadow is often the antagonist or villain, but can be an object or a part of the hero himself. Example: Darth Vadar from *Star Wars* is the shadow, but Luke must also battle the side of himself

that could be seduced to join the dark side, just as his father was.

7. **THE TRICKSTER**—The essence of this archetype is **MISCHIEF**. The trickster bucks the status quo, and often provides comic relief to the journey. They usually overcome obstacles with wit, rather than physical strength. Example: Merry and Pippin from *Lord of the Rings*.

8. Several other notable character archetypes common to literature are:

9. **THE CHILD**—The essence of this archetype is **INNOCENCE** and childlike wonder. It represents that part in all of us which remains innocent regardless of age or experience.

10. **THE MOTHER**—The essence of this archetype is **NATURE AND NURTURE**. It represents the nurturing earth, new birth, and maternal care.

Most of these archetypes are common to paranormal fiction. You may want to use them as a guide as you think about the journey you want your characters to take. There is also an overarching archetypal theme in all of paranormal fiction: making the abnormal not only accessible, but also beautiful or desirable. As paranormal writers, we take "the other" and clothe it in humanity.

CREATING EXTRAORDINARY PARANORMAL CHARACTERS:

A NEW KIND OF MONSTER

Vampires, werewolves, ghosts, fairies or the Fey, demons, angels, witches, aliens, psychics and zombies are all well-used characters in modern paranormal fiction. These are the creatures most universally known because their myth and lore pervades many cultures. This gives the writer a nice head start with back story and character development. However, this also makes it easy for a writer to fall back on the current "collective" knowledge of the masses without truly creating anything new or interesting. We know and love stories about these characters, and we want to add to their mythology with our own words, but we must remember the monsters we already know are just the beginning.

RESEARCHING CHARACTER LORE: DISCOVERING WHAT YOU DON'T KNOW

You may consider yourself a vampire fan. You've read Stoker's Dracula and the many modern spin-offs woven from "traditional" vampire lore. Garlic repels a vampire; a stake through the heart kills him. He can't see himself in a mirror or abide sunlight. Everyone knows these things but where did these ideas come from? Where and when did original vampire folklore originate? Why there? How does vampire lore differ from culture to culture? What pieces of that lore, not yet explored, can you tap into? Research enriches characterization. The gritty, obscure details that you discover about vampire lore on your own hunt will enliven your story, and probably lead to other story ideas for the future.

Vampires, werewolves and most of the characters on the well-known list come from European lore and spread worldwide during the years of European conquest. Thus, they are the monsters that have appeared most often in fiction, television and movies, and the ones which feel most familiar to the masses. But paranormal characters and monsters are a culturally universal idea. Researching the paranormal lore of more obscure cultures, for example, the Native American culture or the Southern Pacific Island culture, can uncover incredible and unique monster fodder for the paranormal writer. There are now massive amounts of cultural information and folklore available on the internet. I recommend spending some time looking through several of the fabulous monster and paranormal encyclopedias online. Monstropedia.org and psychicscience.org are two of my favorites. I think you will come away with a new appreciation for the under-used and undeveloped character possibilities out there, as well as a boatload of new story ideas.

Also, remember you can create new lore for your creatures but, if you deviate from the common body of knowledge, you had better have a reasonable, consistent explanation within the story for your reader.

ORIGINS: CREATING CHARACTER BACK STORY

Back story means the events and experiences of your characters which happened before the point at which you begin the story. Back story might include a character's birth and childhood, their family dynamics, a traumatic event, or a joyful one; events which happened years ago, or only moments before the story begins.

There are two basic approaches to developing back story.

CHARACTER PORTFOLIOS

This method utilizes elaborate thought and development of character back story before the story is even written. In this approach one does a portfolio for each main character, listing everything from their favorite color to what they prefer for breakfast. I know writers who have their characters keep their own diaries or journals. While this approach is very thorough and does give good groundwork for a novel or series, it has several risks or challenges.

A good story only includes information about a character that is crucial to the development of that character in its given story arc. So, if your character's favorite color doesn't further your story, you shouldn't include it, or waste time wondering about it. Another danger is that after a writer has done all that work creating a character portfolio, they tend to feel compelled to include every detail in their story. This can bog down a story with needless details, leaving the reader to wonder, "Why did they include that?" A third risk with this method is that writers, especially new writers, tend to start their story with paragraphs of back story, rather than jumping in at a point of action, which is much more likely to grab the reader.

PAY AS YOU GO

In this method, the writer starts the story and leaks back story into the narrative as it is naturally needed. If a character's favorite color becomes an element of the plot or the character's thought process, it is mentioned. If not, the writer doesn't even consider it. The downside of this is that a writer can leave out crucial elements of back story without realizing it, or neglect revealing their character's complexities. Another danger is the tendency to use frequent flashbacks to reveal character back story rather than weaving it in through action and plot momentum.

A VAMPIRE NAMED BOB: NAMING PARANORMAL CHARACTERS

While it is true that a rose by any other name would smell as sweet, a vampire named Bob better be in a humor piece. Names matter. Names have cultural, geographical and historical connotations. Often, a character names itself; a name just pops into the author's head, and they know it belongs to that character. This is fine for a first draft but, when polishing a story or book for submission, it pays to do a bit of research on the names you've chosen. There are a few things to consider when naming your paranormal characters.

GENDER

Giving a female character a traditionally male name, or vise-versa, is fine, but you will need to clarify gender fairly early in your story or risk annoying your readers. Also remember the gender of names varies by culture. Leslie is a masculine name in England, but a feminine name in the United States.

MEANING

Be sure to look up what your character's chosen name means. This is usually easily done using the internet or a baby name book. If you name your light-hearted female lead Miriam, you might want to be aware that it means "bitter woman". If you name her Faye Giddy, you might want to know that means "insane fairy". If you can make the meanings of your character names hint at their personalities or powers, it can give your story added depth. Then, any reader who happens to know or go look up that meaning will feel that you, the writer, have just let them in on a special secret.

Strangeness and Pronunciation

When naming paranormal characters, unusual tends to be the norm. We write of the weird and "other" and we want our characters names to match their otherness. Making up completely new names is fine, of course, but I offer two items of warning concerning that. One, make sure it is a made up word, and not some obscure "real word" that has gotten lodged in your subconscious, minus the meaning. Keep in mind the African woman who named her new daughter the beautiful English name, Gonorrhea, because she'd overheard it in the hospital. Second, if it is a very strange name, give your reader some hope and clue of how to pronounce it or be prepared to prepared for them to misspeak it. I sometimes wonder if J.K. Rowling ever gets tired of hearing Hermione butchered by us non-British types.

Loaded Names

Certain names, such as Adolph and Judas come loaded with heavy connotations due to history or past use. Jesus may be a common name in certain countries, but if you name a character Jesus, be ready for him to be associated in your reader's mind with Jesus from the Bible. Names can also be loaded from being used in literature. Naming a character Ahab will bring a *Moby Dick* flavor to your story and naming a character Dracula will raise certain dark expectations in your readers. Be wary of thinking, "Well, that name doesn't mean *that* to me." You are writing for an audience, inviting them to bring their meaning to your story. Don't be surprised when they do.

Creating Character's with Special Abilities or Powers

One of the unique aspects of writing paranormal fiction is that, more often than not, the main characters have special abilities. This, of course, is half the fun but there are some principles to keep in mind when bestowing powers upon one's characters.

Power Comes from Somewhere

It is a good idea to put some serious thinking and groundwork into how your character acquired his or her powers. The origin of powers is a very trendy subject right now. How did Batman become Batman? Where and how did the X-men get their powers? Concerning the origins of powers and abilities, there are quite a few sources to choose from, and they all have ramifications for your story and character development.

Heredity

Superman is one of the few comic heroes born with his powers. He has superhuman strength and can fly because he is from another planet where that was the norm. If your character was born with their powers, why were they? How did this complicate their childhood? Will it transfer to their children?

Genetic mutation

The powers and abilities of may characters can be attributed to human evolution or mutation. They may appear at birth or manifest at puberty or when most needed.

Product of intent or accident

Many comic book heroes get dumped in a vat of toxic waste or bitten by a radioactive spider. Their powers are a result of an accident, or in the case of Wolverine, intent to create a creature of power. Most ghosts fall under this category, having been made by the force of a tragic death.

Created by another

Vampire and werewolf lore says that under certain conditions, the bite of one of these will turn the victim into a similar creature.

Taught or Self-taught

Some powers and abilities are teachable to anyone, or certain people who are predisposed to them. It is common for a character to find a mentor, as with Yoda teaching Luke Skywalker how to wield The Force. In some cases, a character stumbles upon a power or ability and they learn how to use it themselves through trial and error.

Objects of Power

Some powers are connected to a specific object of power or geographic location. In this case, the power resides in the object, not the character.

A PRODUCT OF NATURE

Creatures such as fairies, elves, gnomes, or aliens, are considered to be naturally occurring. In essence, they are just another species.

ALL POWER HAS LIMITS

This principle is similar to the idea that all magic should have a cost. Simply put, if you make a character all-powerful, then what problem or conflict could he possibly have which can't be fixed by his own power? Superman has his kryptonite and his love for Lois Lane. All power must have a weakness, a crisis, something to overcome, or there is no story. For each power your character has, he should have an equal or counterbalancing weakness.

ALL POWER SHOULD BE TREATED WITH HUMANITY

Humans are frail. We struggle and there are many things beyond our power to control. This is part of being human. Giving your characters extra power should not overshadow their humanity; it should enhance it. If a character must drink blood to live, how does this affect their view of violence and death? If a character is a shapeshifter, how does that affect his struggle with his own identity or body image? If a character cannot feel pain, does that affect their ability to feel joy? The freaks of nature populating our paranormal stories and books, should struggle with their own humanity more than your average fiction character. They are on the fringes, howling to get in while scratching to get out. Don't miss the opportunity for character tension in the abilities you give them. They must have human frailties, so your human readers can relate to them.

BEWARE IMMORTALITY

Immortality is the ultimate power because death is the ultimate consequence. Death, overcoming death, and the afterlife are major themes of paranormal fiction. Some creatures like vampires have near immortality at the cost of another's blood and life-force. Because all humans taste death, an immortal character will be harder for a reader to identify with. An immortal character is harder to put in danger convincingly. The reader knows that character cannot die, so what's to fear? This drains tension from any peril or crisis in the story. Historically, the power of immortality comes with the heaviest cost. Immortals live miserable, lonely, eternal lives, often losing what little humanity they started with. Bestowing characters with immortality should be well thought-out and carefully used, if at all.

POINT OF VIEW AND POINT OF VIEW CHARACTERS

Point of view is the perspective or viewpoint from which the narrative of the story is told. Understanding the use of point of view and a point of view character is essential to quality character development. Viewpoint is what injects your reader into the story, the voice that they hear in their head, or the character they become. As the writer, it is your job to choose which character's perspective will allow you to develop your characters and tell your story to the fullest.

THIRD PERSON

Third person is the most common and currently used viewpoint. When we write from the perspective of "he, she or it" we are using third person.

Third person comes in three main varieties; omniscient, narrative, and limited.

OMNISCIENT THIRD PERSON

With Omniscient viewpoint the writer simply skips from character to character, dropping into their point of view when needed. The strength of Omniscient viewpoint is the amount of information given to the reader. The downside is the reader can feel yanked from one perspective to another without a chance to establish a bond with any one character.

> Example: She went to the window and looked out. The cool, black, breath of night billowed her nightgown against her like a living shroud. She thought he didn't notice, but she was wrong. His eyes dilated, and his breath caught, and he hoped she didn't notice that.

NARRATIVE THIRD PERSON

With Narrative viewpoint, the author tells the story much like a fairy tale from the perspective of a storyteller. Everything is filtered through the narrator's perceptions and he or she may know things that none of the characters do. If the Narrative viewpoint utilizes a compelling storyteller voice, it can draw the reader in and enhance the story. The downside is it tends to keep the reader outside of the story. This distance can be helpful when telling a tale for children or adults that could be too scary or emotionally loaded otherwise.

> Example: She went to the window and looked out. The cool black, breath of night billowed her nightgown against her like a living shroud. She thought he didn't notice, but she was wrong. His eyes dilated, and his breath caught, and he hoped she didn't notice that. But they were fools; the both of them, for neither knew that down in the garden a shadow lurked. It saw her gauzy silhouette, and sensed her lover's quickened pulse. It licked its bloody lips and slunk closer to the wall.

LIMITED THIRD PERSON

This viewpoint is from the perspective of only a single character at one time. The writer only reveals what that character could know, sense, feel, and think. The writer may use multiple limited perspectives, switching from one character's viewpoint to another's when switching scenes or chapters, but when "in the head" of a given character they limit themselves to his or her perspective. The strength of limited third person is it most closely approximates our real life perspective—that of a single person in a world of other characters whose minds we do not know. It also gives a sense of intimacy with the viewpoint character which few other perspectives can offer.

> Example: She went to the window and looked out. The cool, black, breath of night billowed her nightgown against her like a living shroud, but he didn't notice. Why didn't he notice her anymore? He was too busy being protective, too busy keeping her safe for passion. It was ironic, really. She'd fled into his arms to escape her father's protectiveness. This man, her lover, had been the danger then. Now, he was just another man to stifle her freedom.

First Person

When we write "I or we", we are using first person. First person viewpoint has become fairly popular recently in paranormal fiction, as it gives immediacy to adventure and character action. A word of caution, first person often feels more intimate to the writer, but less intimate to the reader. It also limits what the writer can reveal to what that one character sees and knows.

> Example: I went to the window and looked out. The cool, black breath of night billowed my nightgown against my skin, like a living shroud, but he didn't notice. He never noticed anymore. He was too busy being protective, too obsessed with my safety for passion. When had he, my lover, become like my Father, now just another man to stifle my freedom?

Second Person

Second person is rarely used, except in the case of role-playing games, or "you choose" adventure stories. However, it has been effectively used in short fiction with the advantage of being a bit unusual or surreal in its feel.

> Example: You went to the window and looked out, but he didn't notice. The cool, black breath of night billowed your nightgown against you like a living shroud, but he didn't notice.

Who Tells the Story: Choosing a Viewpoint Character

Viewpoint characters will often choose themselves by being the voice that tells the story in the writer's head. If that is the case, go with it. Occasionally though, a story idea or plot emerges first, leaving the author to decide who will tell the tale. Generally speaking, a hero or protagonist is a good choice for a viewpoint character. In a short story, you will probably only have time to explore one or two point of views, and you will want your reader to bond with the main characters. In a novel, a writer has more scope, and can experiment with the point of views of multiple characters. Including the viewpoint of the antagonist or villain can be enlightening, especially in paranormal fiction, where the lines between good and evil are often blurred. If a story narrative is not flowing well, it can sometimes help to change the point of view character and see what happens. The bottom line in deciding viewpoint should be which character can tell the story best.

WHAT CHARACTERS WANT: CHARACTER MOTIVATION

Every character needs motivation. Motivation is the "why" behind what poeple think, feel and do. Motivation is what we most desire, or feel we need and can't live without. Motivation can also take the form of avoidance. Maybe a character's most compelling desire is to *not* do something (i.e. get married, drink blood even though they're a vampire or become a ghost when they die). Interesting characters have both kinds of motivation, desire and avoidance. They desperately want something, and they desperately don't want something else.

As the writer, it is your job to delve into the surface and deeper motivations of you characters. Below is just a beginning list of possible character motivations.

- **GREED**—Character wants wealth or monetary gain.
- **GLORY**—Character seeks fame, honor, and renown.
- **KNOWLEDGE**—Character wants to accrue knowledge.
- **SAFETY**—Character is in danger and wants to be safe.
- **LOVE**—Character wants to be loved.
- **APPROVAL**—Character wants someone's approval.
- **ACCEPTANCE**—Character wants inclusion as part of a community or group.
- **REDEMPTION**—Character wants to make up for past mistakes or sins.
- **RESPONSIBILITY**—Character feels responsible for the care and safety of someone else.
- **VENGEANCE**—Character wants to repay someone for acts of evil done to them or someone they knew.

Once you have determined your character's motivation, this should be the power that drives his thoughts, feelings and actions in your story. This is the powerful, compelling need that he will risk almost anything to obtain, or escape. He will do foolish things, dangerous, hopeless and exciting things, and what compels him will also compel your reader to stay with him until that goal is achieved.

From Stranger to Friend: The Art of Revealing Character

Introducing and unveiling a character to your readers is much like introducing an old friend to a new one. While you may know your character inside and out—their childhood, back story, motives, and current situation, your reader knows nothing. Equally important to understand is that the reader probably doesn't need or even want to know every detail of your characters' life, especially when they first meet them. Characters need to be revealed naturally and gradually through the plot and action of the story. Many new writers begin their story or novel with paragraphs describing the character physically, emotionally and everything in between. This is not how you would make an introduction between two strangers. Instead, you would give their name, occupation, and trust that, as your two friends interact, their knowledge of one another will build over time. So, it should be with character development. There are multiple, natural ways to reveal character within story that are much more effective than "introductory paragraphs".

1. **What a character says**—True, characters do not always speak or know the truth about themselves, but a good writer uses even a character's self-deception to reveal their identity. Dialogue and monologue are key to revealing character. Remember, most readers like to dig and infer, rather than have character motive handed to them on a silver platter by the writer.

2. **How a character speaks**—Accents, dialects, speech patterns, body language, tone delivery and attitude—all these ways of speaking convey volumes about your character to a reader. Each character should

have their own unique way of speaking. However, care should be taken with accents as they are difficult to write and should not distract from the story by making the dialogue too difficult to read.

3. **WHAT OTHER CHARACTERS SAY**—Use your characters to reveal and expose one another.

4. **WHAT THE AUTHOR OR NARRATOR SAYS**—A narrator or author sometimes interrupts the flow of story to reveal details about a character. This method is very popular in ancient and modern fairy tales. However, caution should be used as this method tends to jerk your reader out of the narrative.

5. **WHAT A CHARACTER DOES**—Actions speak louder than words. What a character does reveals more about them than any other element of storytelling. In Paranormal Fiction this also includes your characters special abilities or powers, which have influenced and helped create who he or she is as a person.

6. **WHAT A CHARACTER THINKS AND FEELS**—Writing from a character's point of view allows the reader to get inside their head and view the story through their eyes. A character may say one thing, while thinking or feeling something completely different.

7. **WHERE A CHARACTER IS**—Environment and story setting can go a long way to tell us about a character. A woman in the military is going to be a different character than a woman in a dance troop, or a woman in a harem. Just knowing where someone is tells us about what type of experiences and background they might have had to get there.

8. **WHAT THE CHARACTER LOOKS LIKE**—Too often, especially for new writers, physical description seems to take a front seat to all the methods listed above, when in actuality it is probably the least revealing. The color of a

character's hair, the size of their waist, or what they are wearing generally adds very little to plot, action, or story tension. Be sure to avoid the amateur pitfall of having your point of view character look in a mirror or see his reflection in a pool, just so he can describe how good-looking he is. Normal people don't go around describing themselves in their own thoughts. Many famous modern authors write compelling stories and novels without ever physically describing their main characters.

What Characters Do: Character Choice

Good stories should have lots of choices. Choice is what creates tension and growth for characters. A character that never gets to make a choice is called a victim. Though there may be true "victims" in real life, in the world of story, your readers will expect your victim to eventually make some decisions. They will expect them to grow out of their victimhood.

There are two basic ways to drive character choice in your fiction

Reaction

When something happens to someone, they react. That is, they have to make a choice in response to a sudden, unexpected event. They did not choose what happened but they must choose their response, or, if the event is extremely abrupt, they may respond out of reflex or gut instinct. Not responding is still a choice. Reaction can reveal a lot about character. How a character responds may reveal things the character wanted hidden from others, or even from himself. But again, a character who only has things happen to him, who never chooses anything freely, will often be viewed as a victim.

ACTION

When people make a choice freely, of their own volition, this is called action. This is the difference between something happening to a character, and a character making something happen. Action takes choice. Choice takes thought, struggle, emotion, decision, tension, disagreement, and debate. All these things create wonderful tension within your characters and between them. Choice leads to mistakes, wisdom and character growth, as well as moving the plot along. The main crisis of your plot will probably pivot on your main character's biggest choice.

THE CHARACTER'S JOURNEY: HOW TO GROW A DYNAMIC CHARACTER

In most stories, the main character, at least, takes a journey from point A to point B. Point A can be a physical location (the village he grew up in) or an internal location (inexperienced boy wants to prove himself a man). Likewise, Point B can be a place (outside the dragon's lair after defeating the dragon) or a state of being (man who has overcome his fears). For the best results, point A and B should be both physical and psychological. Your characters should travel across space and time, as well as within themselves. Just as story plot follows a fairly predictable arc in fiction, so does character development.

THE STEPS OF CHARACTER DEVELOPMENT

1. **THE BEGINNING**—Introduction of who the character is at Point A.

2. **THE CHANGE OR NEED**—Something at Point A changes or the character feels an urgent need.

3. **THE MOVEMENT**—The character acts upon the need or change by moving away from Point A, in search of a goal. Inner struggle and conflict occur over the change.

4. **THE SEARCH**—The character encounters obstacles

along the way from Point A to Point B. Emotional and physical stakes rise together and the situation grows dire.

5. **The Black Moment**—The moment all seems lost and it appears the character will not reach his/her goal. Many times something valuable is lost or sacrificed in the Black Moment. This is the price of the journey.

6. **The Climax**—The character overcomes the final obstacle after all and the goal is met.

7. **The Return**—The character revisits where he/she came from (Point A), either physically, internally or both.

8. **The Dénouement**—The character has arrived at Point B, physically and internally. The character and the reader can see the change and growth that has occurred. The denouement is the key to satisfying your reader. Here the journey they took by reading your story pays off, or it doesn't.

The physical journey of a character is often the easiest to map. The internal journey can be more challenging, but also more rewarding. It must be gradual, as growth doesn't happen overnight. It must be believable; a serial killer will not suddenly become a saint, though he may move an increment in one direction or another. In paranormal fiction, the hero's journey often involves the need for acceptance, as he or she will probably be an outcast from normal society. Below are listed just a few examples of internal character journeys. Remember, the movement or growth is not always in the positive direction, especially for villainous characters.

1. Innocent to wise

2. Outcast to Accepted

3. Jaded to trusting

4. Fearful to Brave

5. Irresponsible to Responsible

6. Proud to humble

7. Helpless to empowered

8. Dependant to Independent

A LIFE OF THEIR OWN: WHEN CHARACTERS TAKE OVER

At the beginning of a story or book the writer is generally in charge. You are the creator of the plot and the maker of the characters. You play God to the world you have made manifest through story. It is nice to be God, but you might find that somewhere along the way, things begin to go awry. Much like the biblical Adam and Eve, characters don't always do what you've planned for them. Somehow, they begin to take on a life of their own. Half-way through a neat, well-planned out plot, a character suddenly makes a choice you did not expect and sends everything in a different direction. This can feel very odd and alarming. After all, aren't you the one writing the words and making this up? It's almost as if your child has looked you right in the eyes and disobeyed you. Your first instinct is to reign in that character and make him do what you had planned all along. Your first instinct, in this case, might be wrong.

LETTING A CHARACTER LEAD

When a character takes over, that's when the writing gets really exciting. Like the creation story in the Bible, we writers start out with the paltry dirt of words, molding them into worlds and men. At first, our characters are newborn babes, doing only what we help them do, knowing only what we tell them. If we know our craft and infuse our stories with the magic of realism and the infinite possibilities of choice, our characters will become real enough to make a choice we didn't consciously predict. This is perhaps one the finest moments of the writing life: the moment one's creation gets up on its own and walks away. Scary? Yes. Delightful? Absolutely! The good news is you've obviously created a character so real, with such a valid personality and intricate motives, that it moves seemingly under its own power. You have breathed life into it. But what now? I recommend following the character to see what he/she does. Keep writing. Follow that choice to its natural conclusion. You may be surprised to find that it leads to a better story outcome than you were able to imagine when you first started writing. You see, when you first started, the character was flat, one dimensional, even to you. But now they've come alive through story and they are round. Even you can't see all their dimensions at once. In this way, a story becomes an exchange between creator and creation, where characters do unexpected things, and you have a go "back at them". I've found myself dialoguing with my characters like this—"Fine, you're going to do that. Then, what if I make this happen? What will you do, now?"

REINING IN A CHARACTER

Sometimes a character will lead you on a wild goose chase. They'll back themselves into a corner, or take your plot to a dead end. Even when that happens, I find I've learned something about my story or my character which I needed to know, something that will improve it. When you've determined that you can't work with what the character has chosen, just backtrack to the last place you feel satisfied, and try again. In some cases, you may have to take a break from the storyline for a few days or weeks because the mistaken lead is lodged in your mind. During that time, try to determine why the character did what they did. What does it tell you about that character's motives and fears? Generally, you will come out of it understanding your character and the nature of your story better.

DEALING WITH DEATH: KILLING YOUR CHARACTERS

At the end of your paranormal story or book, some of your characters should have changed. Some will have learned and some will have been punished or redeemed. It is possible that some characters will have died. Remember, death is the ultimate consequence and not to be used lightly. It is sometimes necessary for key characters to die so that others can grow to full maturity, as in the case of Dumbledore's death in the *Harry Potter* series. Death is a part of reality, so it should happen in fiction. How a character handles death, their own or someone else's, allows for fantastic character development. However, a few things should be kept in mind when dealing with death.

Don't overuse death

There was a time in history when death was a common, hands-on experience most people encountered even as children. If you are writing a story set in such a time period, realize that people in those times became de-sensitized to death. They began to stop reacting or feeling as much about it, lest they be overwhelmed.

This is exactly what will happen to your readers, if you overuse death. Death is not a casual consequence. If you have a character die in every scene, your readers will not want to become emotionally invested in any of your characters. What's the point? That character will probably be dead in the next few pages anyway. When you do have a character die, or get killed, you want it to have the deep impact death has earned itself over the centuries.

The dead should stay dead

A good story will have more depth than a video game where cardboard characters die and are resurrected a few seconds later, as if nothing ever happened. Death is not simply a momentary inconvenience.

In the television series *Heroes*, characters have been resurrected from the dead so often that death's impact, both to story tension and plot, has been reduced to the severity of the common cold. "Oh, well," viewers think, "so and so died. Don't worry. He'll be back again next episode." The ultimate impact has lost its weight through overuse.

Of course, in paranormal fiction, with creatures such as ghosts and zombies, death is a little more flexible. However, once you've set up the rules of your setting and the consequences of living there, stick with them. Especially at the end, when you're feeling tempted to have a "corpse" pop up for one more spine-tingling grab like in a bad B movie. Resist the urge of that old gimmick. Your story will be better for it.

The Decision to Kill a Character

The decision to kill a character is entirely up to the writer. Sometimes, it is simply the natural conclusion of the story. However, there are many things to consider when contemplating the death of a character.

A character is a writer's product

A good character takes a lot of time and energy to craft and is, in essence, one of a writer's saleable products. If you kill off a character, you won't be able to use it in any future stories or episodes, unless you go the route of a prequel. Some authors kill off characters at the end of a large book series as a way of creating closure for themselves. It can also be a method of trying to quell the use of their characters by someone else such as in fan fiction. Even if you feel completely "done" with a character, your interest may resurface later, or fans may demand more. Keeping your options open, if possible, is better than a quick death.

FANS FEEL OWNERSHIP

If you've done a good job with your characters, your readers will feel they know them and have a personal stake in their well-being. Killing a beloved character can cause a great outcry of grief and anger in your readership. Ultimately, it is about freedom of artistic choice, but most writers also want their fans to be happy. If readers want more of a character, that is usually a good thing.

YOU MAY GRIEVE

Writer's sometimes do not realize how intimate they have become with their own creation until they kill a main character. Character's often represent internal manifestations of the writer's psyche, or people and events in their real life. Killing a character that represents something negative can feel cathartic, while killing a neutral or positive character can trigger genuine grief. Don't be surprised if you find yourself having to process the death of something you made up in your head.

THE END AND BEYOND: A CHARACTER'S AFTERLIFE

For those character who manage to survive the end of your stories and books, what then? Should characters always be put away in exchange for new characters and new ideas? When the story or book is sold, do we simply move on, or is there a character afterlife? Below is a list of just a few of the things you can do to keep old characters alive and working for you.

1. Write a prequel or origins story for a character. This is currently quite popular.

2. If the character was from a novel, write a short story featuring that character.

3. If the character was from a short story, write a novel featuring that character.

4. Write a complete character portfolio for your author or book website as a special feature. Fans always want extra information about the characters they love, and this is a way to use all those details you have which would clutter up the action of a story.

5. Give the character a cameo appearance in a new work. Stephen King does this, giving his readers glimpses of favorite past characters in newer stories. For die-hard fans this is like a private wink from the King himself.

6. Try using the character in another media form such as the visual arts, in a graphic novel, or even as a screen play.

7. Write another novel or story in that character's series.

8. At the very least, look at what you did right (and wrong) with that character, learn from it, and create even better characters in the future.

THE POWER OF CHARACTERIZATION

The art of characterization is a powerful skill, not to be underestimated. Most writes and readers come to have deep, personal relationships with the characters they create or encounter in fiction. Those relationships can and do change us. They have an impact on our internal and material world. Through characters the human condition is revealed, its triumphs and failures, its glories and darkest moments. Shakespeare knew that the world must be peopled, especially the world of our imagination.

Say What?

By Ryan Peverly

There's no way around it: poor dialogue can kill a story.

If you've ever picked up a novel or a collection of short stories, chances are you've stumbled across dialogue which sounds forced, hackneyed and/or downright fake. There's good reason for it, however: writing good dialogue isn't nearly as easy as speaking.

But it can be.

There is, however, more to writing dialogue than just throwing together words out of a character's mouth and slapping quotation marks around it.

There are several rules and guidelines that—with some repetition and practice—can help you improve your dialogue and turn a mediocre story into a good story and a good story into a great story. Those rules and guidelines include:

- Proper punctuation and formatting
- Tags
- Show, don't tell
- Listening
- Read your dialogue
- Slang, dialect and profanity

- Dialogue with action
- Purpose
- Genre-specific dialogue

PROPER PUNCTUATION AND FORMATTING:

Believe it or not, some writers out there don't know how to properly punctuate dialogue. To be honest, it can get a little tricky at times depending on which type of clause you're using with your characters. Still, this is just a refresher for those who may not know how to punctuate things like questions or exclamations.

The first basic rule is obviously quotation marks. They go before and after whatever it is a character is saying. Quotation marks are the main indicator of someone speaking.

Example 1: "That ghost scared me."

Notice how the end quotation mark is after the period in the sentence. The end quotation mark always goes after a form of punctuation, questions marks and exclamation points included—no exceptions.

Example 2: "That ghost scared me!"

Example 3: "Can you believe that ghost scared me?"

If your character uses multiple sentences, punctuate with a comma only if the end punctuation is a period and only if you use a **TAG**—the "he saids" or "she saids" in between the clauses (more on those in the next section).

Example 4: "That ghost scared me," John said. "Can you believe that?"

Example 5: "That ghost scared me. Can you believe that?"

In the case of a question or an exclamation, no comma is needed, whether a tag is present or not.

Example 6: "That ghost scared me!" John said. "Can you believe that?"

Example 7: "That ghost scared me! Can you believe that?"

Also, with Examples 4 and 6, notice the breaking of two complete sentences with "John said." You can also break in the middle of one sentence of dialogue with a tag, separating the sentence into two clauses with a tag and commas. Notice the quotation mark placement before and after the two clauses.

Example 8: "That ghost scared me," John said, "and I didn't know what to do."

There is such thing as indirect dialogue, as well, where you're expressing words a character says in the text without quotation marks. Think of it more like your character is telling a friend what someone else said.

Example 9: John said the ghost scared him.

Be careful with your punctuation when you're writing dialogue—read over it very carefully. If you're writing in a program with an auto-correct feature or in something like Microsoft Word that points out your corrections along the way, errors in dialogue punctuation may go unnoticed.

Don't forget to start a new paragraph when a different character speaks. It's virtually never acceptable for two characters to speak in the same paragraph.

TAGS

Perhaps the most important thing that stands in the way of your dialogue reaching its greatest potential is something that's almost insignificant and unnoticeable to the average reader: the tag.

The tag is the "he said," "she said" writers throw into dialogue to break up multiple sentences. For example: "I'm not sure," John said. "It's something I'll have to think about."

"Said" acts as the tag in the dialogue. It's not always necessary—really it might never be—especially for two short sentences like the above example, but it does help break up dialogue and alter your pace. It identifies your speaker to avoid confusion, which some readers have problems with.

The best tag to use is always the word "said," or the present tense variation of "says," if you choose to write your story in that tense. Avoid any other tags, as they're considered amateur by critics and audiences alike. Using tags like "he stammered" or "she blurted" are considered hackneyed and in poor choice. There a few exceptions though—"whispered" is maybe the most popular—but use those few and far between.

When using more than two speakers, it might be wise to sprinkle in a few more tags than normal to avoid confusion over who's speaking. Still, write your dialogue the same way with two speakers as you would with four.

It's best to insert your tags into your dialogue as quickly as possible. The sooner you can point out to your reader who's doing the talking— most likely after the first completed sentence—the easier it is for them to read.

SHOW, DON'T TELL

Showing instead of telling is a basic nugget of advice in all aspects of fiction. It's no different when it comes to dialogue. You don't want to narrate things in dialogue like you do in your description. Your characters should reveal details to each other. It's more realistic and it's more compelling to your reader.

> For example: "I went to the store today to get some groceries and I ran into Steve," Sara said. "He thinks he has some clues about who killed that guy in the park last week."

> "Really?" John said. "That's good."

A better way to write that same basic exchange is to have John ask Sara to elaborate on what Steve said. John's response was vague and uninteresting, especially when there's the possibility for her to get John to reveal more information about whatever is happening in the story.

> Example: "I went to the store today to get some groceries and I ran into Steve," Sara said. "He thinks he has some clues about who killed that guy in the park last week."

> "Yeah? Did they match those shell casings from the scene yet?"

Dialogue is always more interesting to your reader if you don't skimp. It can point out the more important parts of your plot, so show things instead of telling them, even—and maybe especially—within those quotation marks. Just be careful not to overdo it.

LISTENING

The thing which separates great dialogue from shoddy dialogue is realism. Is what's being said by a given character realistic or believable enough for him or her? The best way you can determine that is by listening to real people talk.

Some will tell you to find a public place, sit down and take notes on the way regular people speak, keeping track of such things as their word choice, incantation and even their body language while they're speaking. While that's helpful, it's also not the only thing you can do when it comes to listening.

Maybe the best advice I ever received pertaining to listening is to listen to your own conversations with people you know and don't know. How do you relate to your friends? Is your word choice different with your friends than it is with strangers? What kind of movements do you make with your hands, face or any other part of your body while talking? The more personal you can make your dialogue, the better. And there's nothing more personal to you, the writer, than yourself.

The best examples of realistic and believable dialogue aren't usually found in novels or short stories, however. Screenplays and stage plays, rather, are mediums chock full of examples of realistic dialogue because—on the stage especially—so much relies on the verbal interaction between characters.

There are several screenwriters known for their sharp, snappy, realistic dialogue, most notably Joel and Ethan Coen and Quentin Tarantino. Here's a popular example of clever, well-written, believable dialogue from Tarantino's *Pulp Fiction*:

> Vincent: Well, in Amsterdam, you can buy beer in a movie theatre. And I don't mean in a paper cup either. They give you a glass of beer, like in a bar. In Paris, you can buy beer at McDonald's. Also, you know what they call a Quarter Pounder with Cheese in Paris?
>
> Jules: They don't call it a Quarter Pounder with Cheese?
>
> Vincent: No, they got the metric system there, they wouldn't know what the fuck a Quarter Pounder is.
>
> Jules: What'd they call it?

Vincent: Royale with Cheese.

Jules (repeating): Royale with Cheese. What'd they call a Big Mac?

Vincent: Big Mac's a Big Mac, but they call it Le Big Mac.

Jules: What do they call a Whopper?

Vincent: I dunno, I didn't go into a Burger King. ...

The natural flow of everyday conversation is something Tarantino is known for, and that's one of the better examples you'll find from what's considered his best screenplay.

What makes that exchange realistic isn't just the way the dialogue is traded back and forth, but the content. When your characters aren't talking about anything, what are they talking about? More on that in the Purpose section.

Another key component of listening in relation to writing good dialogue is people don't speak in grammatically-correct sentences, nor are they speaking at length most of the time. A lot of real conversations are fragmented sentences and use clichés and words that don't actually exist, like "umm" and "uh." While real people use these sort of non-word communications, as an author you may want to shy away from them in your story unless absolutely necessary.

Real people don't usually call people they talk to by name, either, so that's something to keep in mind too.

The masters of writing good dialogue are the best listeners. They have an ear for what people say and the talent to convey it via the written word. Those masters all abide by one simple guideline: The more informal you keep your dialogue, the better. There will be some instances where formality is good for your story, however, and those will be addressed later in the **Genre-Specific Dialogue** section.

Read Your Dialogue

Perhaps the simplest and most helpful form of advice you'll receive is to read your dialogue out loud. It's easier for a writer to pick out things that don't make sense or sound awkward. It's also easy for a writer to miss things while they're writing because usually the internal editor is out to lunch, so to speak—or at least should be.

While you're reading out loud, if something doesn't sound natural, delete it. If it doesn't have any rhythm or flow, delete it. If you have different characters speaking and their dialogue sounds the same, delete it.

There's an unwritten rule that your average sentence of dialogue should be no longer than an index finger because the average person doesn't speak at length. If you're reading out loud and you get winded, shorten up those words.

Try asking someone else to read your dialogue too. Or, if it's not too much trouble, try reading it back and forth like you're acting the scene out on stage. Another set of eyes and ears can help immensely.

SLANG, DIALECT AND PROFANITY

There are loads of conscious choices a writer has to make when it comes to writing particular characters. Deciding on what a character says is obviously important, but how and the manner in which they speak might be even more important.

As the example from "Pulp Fiction" in the previous section showed, Tarantino made a conscious choice to let his characters speak in a friendlier, laid-back style. Notice the constant use of contractions, the substitution of the slang 'dunno' for 'don't know' and Vincent using the verb 'got' instead of the more proper 'have.' All are perfect examples of different forms of slang in dialogue. The most popular form today is what's known as street slang or Web slang—like Tarantino's use of "dunno"—and that's something to keep in mind depending on the characters, time period and content of your story. Some common examples include using certain words that have taken on new meanings—like using the word "mad" to mean "a lot"—and referring to objects by new names, like calling a car a "whip" or a "ride."

Dialect is a form of regional slang, if you will. You also might think of it as an accent people from certain areas carry in their speech or a way those same people say certain words. There's a fine line to walk, however, when presenting a character's dialect.

Consider this example from Irvine Welsh's *Trainspotting:*

"Naw. He must be daein awright. Only time ye hear fi that wan is

371

whin he's eftir somethin. He's only half jokin, and these young nephew kittens are lookin us ower in a baaad way, so we git a seat in a corner by the door."

Now this example from Bret Easton Ellis's *American Psycho*:

"Hey fellas. How y'all doin'?" Montgomery speaks in a thick Georgia twang.

Notice how Welsh, a native of Scotland and whose novel is set there, phonetically spells his character's words as if you hearing them aloud. That short snippet of dialogue was rough, but when you carry it on for nearly 350 pages like Welsh does, it gets overwhelming to your reader. Point is: If you have characters who speak in a regional dialect or accent, mention it before or directly after their first sentence, like Ellis did. Phonetic spelling can confuse a reader and turn them off to the point of putting down your story for good. If you absolutely need to spell things phonetically, less is more. Stick to simple things, like using "gonna" instead of "going to."

Profanity is a slippery slope for a lot of writers. The big question is: Do I use profanity, and if so, how much? In genre fiction, profanity is rarely used because it's unnecessary. In reality, people use profanity mostly as filler words in conversation. In fiction, filler words are usually a no-no, as less is again considered more. The use of profanity in something like "Pulp Fiction" works because not only does it fit the characters using it, but it fits the mood and atmosphere created, as well as the plot. Most genre writers shy away from profanity, as it does nothing to enhance their story or their characters. As with dialect, unless profanity is absolutely necessary, stay away from it.

DIALOGUE WITH ACTION

When discussing "listening" earlier, we touched on facial expressions and body movements a character may make while talking. Obviously these are actions we all use throughout the course of conversation, and it's something to keep in mind when writing dialogue.

One of the better contemporary examples of dialogue with action is Pulitzer Prize winning author Cormac McCarthy, who won the award for 2007's *The Road*. Here's a great example of McCarthy working with action and dialogue from that novel, where a father (speaking first) and son are crossing the country after what seems like an Armageddon-type event:

> They pushed the cart through the woods as far as the old road and left it there and headed south along the road hurrying against the dark. The boy was stumbling he was so tired and the man picked him up and swung him onto his shoulders and they went on. By the time they got to the bridge there was scarcely light at all. He put the boy down and they felt their way down the embankment. Under the bridge he got out his lighter and lit it and swept the ground with the flickering light. Sand and gravel washed up from the creek. He set down the knapsack and put away the lighter and took hold of the boy by the shoulders. He could just make him out in the darkness. I want you to wait here, he said. I'm going for the wood. We have to have a fire.
>
> I'm scared.
>
> I know. But I'll just be a little ways and I'll be able to hear you so if you get scared you call me and I'll come right away.
>
> I'm really scared.
>
> The sooner I go the sooner I'll be back and we'll have a fire and then you won't be scared anymore. Don't lie down. If you lie down you'll fall asleep and then if I call you you won't answer and I won't be able to find you. Do you understand?
>
> The boy didn't answer. He was close to losing his tempter with him and then he realized that he was shaking his head in the dark. Okay, he said. Okay.

McCarthy sets a beautiful scene filled with action and dialogue. He's made a unique stylistic choice to not use quotation marks with his dialogue, but it's one that works because something like quotation marks in this particular novel is a trivial thing that you need not concern yourself with.

His dialogue is crisp and realistic considering the circumstances and it doesn't run on too long. That's where inserting action comes into play. Use it when you need to break up things in your dialogue. It's almost like a visa-versa situation—you'd normally use dialogue to break your action or description, but those same things are helpful in breaking your dialogue too.

Also keep in mind that the action in your story can and will affect your dialogue. Depending on what your character is doing, it might not be wise to break your action with dialogue if it doesn't fit the scenario. For example, if your character is involved in a fist fight, it'd be hard for him or her to speak.

PURPOSE

As with any other element in a story, dialogue should serve a purpose. Remember, building and developing your character is maybe the most important purpose dialogue serves but there are other things you should consider using dialogue for.

Dialogue can do so many things for your story, but the most important is building your character. You can divulge a lot of information within the words of your character—his or her's interests, intelligence, personality, and life experience, among other things.

Next, use your dialogue as an alternative. What that means is your dialogue can and should be used as another way to present information to your readers. You can only use so much description in the narrative before the average reader gets bored with it. Try writing a fact about something both descriptively and in a character's dialogue and see which way better suits what you're trying to get across. Breaks in your narrative act as a great balance and let you focus on other aspects of your story.

Your dialogue must also further your plot somehow. A lot—not all, as there are exceptions—of what people discuss throughout a story has a direct impact on the story itself. Dialogue can also be a good way to change or alter your plot, should you write a story with plotted twists and turns—it might be the best kind of cliffhanger you could use.

There are exceptions, however, as mentioned, when it comes to furthering the plot with dialogue. Not every exchange of dialogue within a story is going to be directly related the plot. While dialogue is used to advance your story, it's also used to build your characters and a voice that's unique to that character. Listening to what real people talk about when there's nothing of significance to talk about is something that'll help you with that process.

The best example of this is the television show *Seinfeld*. Here's a brief exchange between characters Jerry Seinfeld and George Costanza from an episode titled "The Betrayal":

George: So, how come nothing ever happened between you and Nina? (Getting paranoid) Is there a problem with her? Is she a man?

Jerry: Are you?

George: Well, what's the reason?

Jerry: We were too compatible. Our conversations were so engrossing.

George: How engrossing?

Jerry: If we ever had a problem with Elaine, we could bring in Nina and not lose a step.

George: Wow! Heh. (Half kidding) You don't, huh, have a replacement lined up for me, do ya?

(Jerry snickers, then stares at George, smiling)

Jerry: Anyway, like I was saying, I couldn't make the transition from conversation to sex. There were no awkward pauses.. I need an awkward pause.

George: I'm all for awkward pauses. Fix me up with her.. Wait a minute, Nina just saw me in my Timberlands! Now I have to wear them every time I see her.

Jerry: Why?

George: In any other shoe, I lose two inches. I—I can't have a drop down. We were eye to eye, I can't go eye to chin!

Jerry: So, you're gonna wear 'em no matter what the situation?

George: In every situation. No matter how silly I look.

Notice the everyday subject matter throughout the course of this exchange. It's something that "Seinfeld"—a show considered to be about nothing—made famous and that a lot of people have tried to replicate on the screen and in the page. If you were watching this, you'd notice the dialogue is traded in a sharp, quick, snappy way. If you know the characters, you'd be able to read this without nametags and know who was speaking because each one has their own specific voice.

That voice of a certain character is something which should distinguish him or her from the other characters in the story, whether it's a quirky way of saying something or using certain words only that character would use. Each character's speech should reflect their personality, background and what you've built them up to be in your description. A couple of examples include: if a character is intelligent, then they'll probably have a better vocabulary than most, or if a character didn't go to college or dropped out of high school, they probably will use smaller words and sentences.

Finally, use your dialogue to create conflict and tension in your story. Conflict between characters is a major part of any story, and if they're interacting, arguing through dialogue is the best way to keep that conflict and tension high.

What it really boils down to is this: Dialogue must be in your story for a reason. Never use dialogue as filler to make your story longer or bump your word count. It needs to have purpose, whether it's to build your character, present information in a different way, further your plot or create and build conflict and tension.

GENRE-SPECIFIC DIALOGUE

There are certain stylistic choices to be made when writing dialogue within a specific genre. If you've read stories of any genre—science fiction, fantasy, horror, romance—each one has a specific way of presenting its dialogue.

Science fiction and fantasy will have a bit more formal tone because the subject matter often demands it. Horror and romance tend to skimp a little on the dialogue, as it's not usually an important part of the story. That's not to say it's okay to skimp, however, because your dialogue in genre fiction isn't any less important than the world you're creating.

In the paranormal genre, how does your supernatural creature or person communicate? Do they have a dialect? Are they telepathic? Can they even speak? It's a stylistic choice you have to make as a writer in genre fiction, and it's one which needs to be presented as such. Common forms of paranormal communication include telepathy, non-verbal spirits, non-humans and multiple voices inside one character's mind. Italics work well for things like telepathy and multiple voices, but it's imperative you make it known to the reader and in your manuscript to avoid confusion.

An example from legendary science fiction author Robert A. Heinlein, from his 1956 novel *Time for the Stars*, about a pair of telepathic twins named Tom and Pat. The scene starts with supporting character Mr. Howard speaking and Tom, the narrator, and Pat, telepathically speaking in italics joining in:

> "It has been a century since the inception interplanetary travel; man has spread through the Solar System. One would think that nine planets would be ample for a race too fertile for one. Yet all you know that such has not been the case. Of the daughters of Father Sol only fair Terra is truly suited to Man."

> "I'll be he writers advertising slogans."

> (*"Poor ones,"*) I agreed.

> "Colonize the others we have done, but only at a great cost. The sturdy Dutch in pushing back the sea have not faced such grim and nearly hopeless tasks as the colonists of Mars and Venus and Ganymede. What the human race needs and must have are not these or frozen or burning or airless discards of creation. We need more planets like this gentle one we are standing on. And there are many, many more!" He waved his hands at the ceiling and looked up. "There are dozens, hundreds, thousands, countless hordes of them...out there. Ladies and gentlemen, it is time for the stars!"

> "Here comes the pitch," *Pat said quietly. "A fast curve, breaking inside."*

> (*"Pat, what the deuce is he driving at?"*)

> "He's a real estate agent."

Heinlein makes it clear when one character is speaking and when another telepathically enters into the conversation with the use of parentheses around Tom's dialogue, another way to make the use of telepathy stand out to the reader and in the manuscript.

It's wise to check with your potential publisher and/or editor when considering how to format paranormal communication. Research what's been done in other stories or novels published by whomever you're considering submitting to. Looking at examples from writers within the paranormal genre is helpful as well. Usually there's a precedence that's been set and adhered to and it's not unwise to follow that despite the fact you do need to establish your own writing style.

Whatever you choose to do, however you choose to do it, stick with it. Inconsistency is the biggest threat to your dialogue.

CONCLUSION

Once you've mastered these rules and guidelines through repetition and practice, the next thing you're ready to do is break the walls down and create your own style. That's something that takes a lot of time and effort, even for published authors.

Presenting realistic, interesting and entertaining dialogue is perhaps the most difficult aspect of fiction writing. It's difficult because it gives the character a chance to express thoughts, opinions and ideas to other characters, to the reader and even to you the writer, and if done properly will add great depth to your story. Don't be afraid to edit and rewrite either. If this process doesn't come natural to you as a writer, it will take time to develop.

Dialogue is one of those things which can make or break your story, regardless of how strong the characters are, how compelling the plot is or how cleverly constructed the world is. To keep it simple: Good dialogue is essential.

Dialogue isn't about two people speaking either. It's about building interesting characters, advancing your plot and adding another layer to your story. How do you write that good dialogue that'll catch your reader's attention and establish itself as a strength in your story? Simple: Take a deep breath and relax and let your characters do the same.

REFERENCES

SUGGESTED READING LIST: GHOST CHAPTER

Baldwin, Barbara J., Jerri Garretson, Linda Madl, Sheri L. McGathy. Trespassing Time, *Ghost Stories from the Prairie* (2005) Includes a ghost story for everyone's taste.

Cox, Michael and R. A. Gilbert editors. T*he Oxford Book of Victorian Ghost Stories.* (2003) Includes a chronology of publication of Victorian ghost stories.

Dick, R.A. *The Ghost and Mrs. Muir* (1945) Romantic, sentimental, and amusing. The old movie is good, too.

Dickens, Charles. *A Christmas Carol* (1843) Forget the numerous movies versions and read the real thing. Dickens was a master.

Domingue, Ronlyn. *The Mercy of Thin Air* (2005) The ghost clings to the living in search of answers to a personal mystery she must solve.

Gaiman, Neil. *The Graveyard Book* (2008) Endearing ghosts and chilling villains for YA and adults.

Gran Sara, Come Closer (2003) Not really a ghost story but deliciously supernatural.

Haining, Peter, ed. *The Mammoth Book of Haunted House Stories* (2000) Haining's collections of ghost stories and horror tales are excellent reading.

Harwood, John. *The Ghost Writer* (2005) Good read for Victorian ghost story lovers featuring an interesting structure incorporating short stories in novel. Ghost story telling at its literary best.

____. *The Séance* (2008) More about Spiritualism than ghosts, but a good spooky read of literary quality.

Herbert, James. *Haunted* (1988) A real twist on ghosts and haunting that you will enjoy.

Hill, Susan. *The Woman in Black* (2002) A moody spine-tingling Victorian ghost story.

Jackson, Shirley, *The Haunting of Hill House* (1959) A haunted house classic that none of the movies even come close to doing justice. A truly psychological ghost story. You must read it to get the scariness.

James, Henry. *The Turn of the Screw* (1898) Haunted children play psychological games with their governess. The creepiness is in what isn't said.

Killough, Lee. *Killer Karma* (2005) Meet a ghost detective endeavoring to solve his own murder.

King, Stephen. *The Shining* (1977, re-released 2002) A contemporary classic mixing ghosts and horror. I still prefer the book to the movie.

Michaels, Barbara, Ammie, *Come Home* (1968) Haunting mystery and gothic entertainment.

Moloney, Susie. *The Dwelling: A Novel* (2003) A uniquely creepy haunted house tale.

Sebold, Alice. *The Lovely Bones* (2002) From the little girl ghost's pov as she watches her family fall apart after her disappearance and while her murderer lives on undiscovered.

Stockenberg, Annette. *Emily's Ghost* (1992) Fun, romantic, a bit scary, with a mystery all wrapped in one.

Wagner, Phyllis Cerf and Herbert Wise, editors. *Great Tales of Terror and the Supernatural.* (1994) Good survey of ghost short stories.

Wharton, Edith. *The Ghost Stories of Edith Wharton* (1973) She is the American grand mistress of the ghost story in my book.

FAERIE CHAPTER READING LIST

Silver, Carol G. *Strange and Secret Peoples* (Oxford University, 1999)

Briggs, Katharine. *An Encyclopedia of Fairies* (Pantheon Books, 1976)

Briggs, Katharine. *The Fairies in Tradition and Literature* (Routledge Classics, 2002)

Melville, Francis. *The Book of Faeries—A Guide to the World of Elves, Pixies, Goblins, and Other Magic Spirits* (Barron's, 2002)

Purkiss, Diane. *At the Bottom of the Garden—A Dark History of Fairies, Hobgoblins, and Other Troublesome Things* (NYP, 2000)

Kirk, Robert. *The Secret Commonwealth of Elves, Fauns and Fairies* (Dover, 2008)

Moorey, Teresa. *Faeries and Nature Spirit—A Beginner's Guide* (Hodder & Stoughton, 1999)

Keightley, Thomas. *The World Guide to Gnomes, Fairies, Elves, and Other Little People* (Gramercy, 2000)

Arrowsmith, Nancy with George Moorse. *A Field Guide to the Little People* (Pan, 1978)

Eason, Cassandra. *A Complete Guide to Faeries & Magical Beings* (Weiser, 2002)

Froud, Brian and Lee, Alan. *Twenty-fifth Anniversary Edition Faeries* (Abrams, 2002)

Froud, Brian. *Good Faeries, Bad Faeries* (Simon & Schuster, 1998)

Rose, Carol. *Spirits, Fairies, Leprechauns, and Goblins—An Encyclopedia* (W.W. Norton & Company Ltd., 1996)

Dubois, Pierre. *The Great Encyclopedia of Faeries, Secrets Revealed* (Simon & Schuster, 1999)

GHOSTS

Greer, John Michael, *Monsters.* Woodbury, MN: Llewllyn Publications, 2007.

Guiley, Rosemary Ellen, *The Encyclopedia of Ghosts and Spirits. 3rd ed.* New York: Checkmark Books, 2007.

Haughton Brian, illus. Daniele Serra, *Lore of the Ghost, The Origins of the Most Famous Ghost Stories Throughout the World.* Franklin Lakes, NJ: New Page Books, A Div. of Career Press, Inc. 2009.

Scott, Beth and Michael Norman. *Haunted Heartland.* New York: Warner Books. 1985.

Broughton, Richard S. *Parapsychology: The Controversial Science.* New York: Ballantine, 1992. Hamlin, Garland. *Forty Years of Psychic Research: A Plain Narrative of Fact.* New York: The Macmillan Company, 1936.

Radin, Dean. *The Conscious Universe: The Scientific Truth of Psychic Phenomena.* New York: HarperEdge, 1997.

Rhine, Louisa E. *The Invisible Picture: A Study of Psychic Experiences.* Jefferson, NC: McFarland, 1981.

ONLINE

The Merriam-Webster Online Dictionary
http://www.merriam-webster.com/dictionary/extrasensory
Psychic Information Sites:
http://www.askgrace.com/psychic_powers_intuition.htm
http://www.psychic-experiences.com/psychic-articles/types-psychic-abilities.php
http://www.thelostfound.com/psychic-abilities.html
http://en.wikipedia.org/wiki/Extra-sensory_perception
American Society for Psychical Research http://www.aspr.com/
List of World-Wide Psychical Research Centers
http://www.spr.ac.uk/expcms/index.php?section=49
Psychical Research—Pratum Book Company
http://www.pratum.com/oldpratum/psychic.html

WORLD-BUILDING

Young Adult Paranormals
Blood and Chocolate by Annette Curtis Klause
Evernight series by Claudia Gray
The Silver Kiss by Annette Curtis Klause
Mortals Instruments series by Cassandra Clare
Weather Warden Series by Rachel Caine
The Morganville Vampires series by Rachel Caine
The House of Night Series by P.C. & Kristin Cast
The Twilight Series by Stephenie Meyer
The Vampire Diaries Series by LJ Smith
Blue Bloods by Melissa de la Cruz
Vampire Academy series by Richelle Mead
Wings by Aprilynne Pike
Wicked Lovely books by Melissa Marr
Urban Fantasy Books & Series
Allie Beckstrom series by Devon Monk
Amanda Feral Seattle Zombie series by Mark Henry
Anita Blake Vampire Hunter series by Laurell K. Hamilton
Blood Ties books by Jennifer Armintrout
Cassandra Palmer series by Karen Chance

Corine Solomon series by Ann Aguirre
Crimson Moon series by L.A. Banks
The Dante Valentine series by Lilith Saintcrow
The Dresden Files by Jim Butcher
The Felix Castor novels by Mike Carey
Georgia Kincaid series by Richelle Mead
Guardians of Eternity series by Alexandra Ivy
Jaz Parks series by Jennifer Rardin
Kate Daniels Magic Series by Ilona Andrews
Kitty Norville series by Carrie Vaughn
The Maker's Song series by Adrian Phoenix
The Merrily Watkins books
Moonheart by Charles de Lint
The Morgan Kingsley series by Jenna Black
Mercy Thompson and Alpha & Omega series by Patricia Briggs
The Negotiator Trilogy by C.E. Murphy
The Night Huntress series by Jeaniene Frost
Nightside Series—Simon R. Green
Nocturne City books by Caitlin Kittredge
Poppy Z. Brite's vampire books
The Rachel Morgan series by Kim Harrison
Riley Jenson Guardian series by Keri Arthur
Sabina Kane series by Jaye Wells
The Savannah Vampire books by Raven Hart
Simon Canderous series by Anton Strout
Sisters of the Moon series by Yasmine Galenorn
The Spook Squad Series by Keri Arthur
Sookie Stackhouse Southern Vampire series by Charlaine Harris
Sunshine by Robin McKinley
The Thrall Books by C.T. Adams & Cathy Clamp
The Vampire Chronicles by Anne Rice
The Vampire Files by PN Elrond
Vampire Huntress Legend series by L.A. Banks
Victoria Nelson series by Tanya Huff
Void City series by J.F. Lewis
The Walker Papers by C.E. Murphy

War of the Oaks by Emma Bull
Women of the Otherworld series by Kelley Armstrong
The Zodiac Series—Vicki Petterson

Paranormal Romance Books & Series

Atlantis Series by Gena Showalter
The Black Dagger Brotherhood series by J.R. Ward
The Carpathian Series by Christine Feehan
Casa Dracula Series by Marta Acosta
The Castle of Dark Dreams Trilogy by Nina Bangs
Compact of Sorcerers Series by Eve Silver
The Damask Circle series
The Dark-Hunter Series by Sherrilyn Kenyon
Darkness Chosen series by Christina Dodd
The Darkyn Series by Lynn Viehl
Dragonfire Books by Deborah Cooke
The Dream-Hunter Series by Sherrilyn Kenyon
The Drake Sisters by Christina Feehan
The Fever series by Karen Marie Moning
Immortals After Dark series by Kresley Cole
Lords of the Underworld series by Gena Showalter
The Argeneau Vampires Series by Lynsay Sands
The Mammoth Book of Paranormal Romance (Anthology)
Mackenzie Vampires series by Nina Bangs
Merry Gentry Faerie series by Laurell K. Hamilton
Midnight Breed series by Lara Adrian
Moon Chasers series by Sharie Kohler
The Nikki and Michael Series by Keri Arthur
Nightwalkers Series by Jacquelyn Frank
Prime Series by Susan Sizemore
The Ripple Creek Werewolf Series
The Shadowdwellers by Jacquelyn Frank
The Valorian Chronicles by Vivi Anna
World of the Lupi by Eileen Wilks

Paranormal Chick Lit Books & Series

Aisling Grey series by Katie MacAlister
Broken Heart Vampires series by Michele Bardsley

Jane Madison series by Mindy Klasky
Kismet Knight series by Lynda Hilburn
Succubus in the City by Nina Harper
Undead Series by MaryJanice Davidson

ROMANCE CHAPTER RESOURCE

http://www.erotica-readers.com
A useful site with many e-mail lists, critique opportunities, calls for submissions and stories.
Elements of Arousal: How to Write and Sell Gay Men's Erotica - Lars Eighner ISBN: 1-56333-230-2 Out of print, not easy to find but don't let the title put you off, this book has a wealth of knowledge about writing popular fiction.
Hot and Bothered - Wendy Dennis ISBN 0-586-21440-2 A survey of sexual attitudes, and practices—handy for research
A Natural History of Love - Diane Ackerman ISBN 9780679761839
A Natural History of the Senses-Diane Ackerman ISBN 9780679735663
How to Write a Dirty Story - Susie Bright ISBN: 0-7394-1720-7
Writing Erotic Fiction - Mike Bailey ISBN:0-8442-022-0
Casey Daniels, *Don of the Dead*, Avon, ISBN: 978-0-06-082146-3
Carole Nelson Douglas, *Brimstone Kiss*, Juno, ISBN: 978-0-8095-7304-2
Carline Harris, *Dead Until Dark*, Ace, ISBN: 0-441-00853-4
Lee Killough, *Killer Karma*, Meisha Merlin, ISBN: 189206571-1
Lee Killough, *Wilding Nights*, Meisha Merlin, ISBN: 1-59222-006-1
Lee Killough, *Checking on Culture: an aid to building story backgrounds*, Yard Dog Press, ISBN: 978-1-893687-90-5
*Bram Stoke*r, Dracula
Dwight V. Swain, *Creating Characters: how to build story people*, Writer's Digest Books, ISBN: 0-89879-417-X

PLOTTING CHAPTER RESOURCES

http://www.cannell.com/page.php?id=8&k=ad2e84ef4d5f66e649413 5bff711e66a&t=3
http://www.writing4successclub.com/public/427.cfml
http://oak.cats.ohiou.edu/~hartleyg/250/freytag.html
http://web.cn.edu/kwheeler/freytag.html

http://www.clown-enfant.com/leclown/eng/drama/livre.htm#1STRUC

WINNING AGENTS AND EDITORS

http://www.lynda.com—computer tutorials

LESSER CHARACTERS

Occultopedia: Mermaid. http://www.occultopedia.com

The Aurora Avenue Bridge Troll. http://www.arfarfarf.com/troll/

REFERENCES SHAPESHIFTING

Patricia Briggs and Silver Bullets: http://www.hurog.com/books/silver/silverbullets.shtml

Patricia Briggs, *Cry Wolf*, Ace, ISBN 978-0-441-01615-0

Patricia Briggs, *Moon Called*, Ace, ISBN 978-0-441-01381-4

Charlaine Harris, *From Dead to Worse*, Ace, ISBN 978-0-441-01589-4

Tanya Huff, *Blood Trail, The Blood Books Volume One*, Daw, ISBN 0-7564-0387-1

Lee Killough, *Wilding Nights*, Meisha Merlin, ISBN 189206571-1

Lee Killough, *Checking on Culture: An Aid to Building Story Backgrounds*, Yard Dog Press, ISBN: 978-1-893687-90-5

Carrie Vaughn, *Kitty and the Midnight Hour*, Grand Central, ISBN 0-446-61641-9

WITCHES CITATIONS

Pavlac, Brian A. (June 6, 2006) *Ten Common Errors and Myths about the Witch Hunts, Corrected and Commented,* Prof. Pavlac's Women's History Resource Site. <http://departments.kings.edu/womens_history/witcherrors.html> (April 4th 2009).

Oxford University Press (1945). *Fairy tales from Hans Christian Andersen.* New York, NY: Oxford University Press.

Barnes and Noble Books (1993). *Grimm's Complete Fairy Tales.* New York, NY: Barnes and Noble Books.

Forbes, T. R. (1966). *The Midwife and the Witch.* New Haven, Connecticut: Yale University Press.

Hamilton, C. (2005). *Maiden, Mother, Crone: Voices of the Goddess.* New York, NY: O Books.

Harrison, K. (2004). *Dead Witch Walking*. New York, NY: Harper Collins Publishers.

Jung, C. G. (1964). *Man and His Symbols*. New York, NY: Doubleday.

McCoy, E. (2005). *Celtic Myth and Magick*. St. Paul: MN: Llewellyn Publications.

Rowling, J. K. (2007). *Harry Potter and the Deathly Hallows*. New York, NY: Arthur A. Levine Books.

Bibliography: Lesser Creatures

Fantasy Encyclopedia by Judy Allen—Copyright Kingfisher Publications Plc 2005

Sandburg, Carl. *Abraham Lincoln: The Prairie Years*. Harcourt, Brace and Co., New York, 1926.

Wikipedia: www.wikipedia.org

http://www.fremont.com/fremonttroll.html

http://www.trollshop.net/trolls/history.htm

http://www.nwcreation.net/nephilim.html

http://jewishencyclopedia.com/view.jsp?artid=24&letter=F

http://members.cox.net/mermaid31/merhist.htm

http://www.northstargallery.com/gargoyles/

http://www.halloween-website.com/doppelgangers.htm

http://www.islamawareness.net/Jinn/

http://theoi.com/Georgikos/Kentaurides.html

http://www.eaudrey.com/myth/

YA CHAPTER

Children's Writers and Illustrators Market (annual publishing guide which includes comprehensive information about writing for children and YAs and submission information for books and magazine stories and articles). Published by Writer's Digest Books.

Professional Journals reviewing children's and young adult books in the USA:

Booklist

Bulletin of the Center for Children's Books

Horn Book Magazine

Kirkus Reviews

Publishers Weekly

School Library Journal

Library Journal
VOYA: Voice of Youth Advocates
KLIATT

Online Resources:

Children's Writers and Illustrators Market online (not a complete site yet but worth watching): http://www.cwim.com/

Five Finger Reading Test at The Book Nuts Reading Club
http://www.booknutsreadingclub.com/fivefingertest.html

The Monster Librarian: http://monsterlibrarian.com/

On that website, Horror Fiction List for Young Adults (broadly defined)
http://monsterlibrarian.com/monsterframe.htm

Paranormal: YA Reads Book Reviews (and discussion forums)
http://www.yareads.com/category/book-reviews/paranormal

This site also offers much more, including reviews in other YA categories (look for "Review Categories" down a ways on the far right of the page)

Resources for Children's Writers by Jerri Garretson
http://www.ravenstonepress.com/writeforchildren.html

Society of Children's Book Writers and Illustrators: http://scbwi.org/

Wikipedia Article on the Paranormal: http://en.wikipedia.org/wiki/Paranormal

TIME TRAVEL

MOVIES REFERENCED IN THIS CHAPTER

Back to the Future, Universal Studios (1985) Marty McFly (Michael J. Fox) inadvertently uses a car as a time machine to 1955 where he risks disrupting his own parents' destiny.

Kate & Leopold, Miramax (2001) A romantic comedy about a Duke who time travels from 1876 to the present in New York
and falls in love with a career woman.

The Lake House, Warner Bros. Entertainment (2006) A romance that explores a mysterious mailbox that somehow bridges time. Kate begins writing letters to Alex, who now occupies the lakeside home she had, only to discover that they're living two years apart.

The Love Letters, –Hallmark Hall of Fame (1998) based on a short story by Jack Finney. A letter written by Lizzie in 1863 is discovered in an antique desk by Scotty in 1998 and he responds. A love develops between the two that transcends time.

Somewhere in Time, (1980) The film is adapted from the 1975 novel *Bid Time Return* by Richard Matheson, which was subsequently re-released under the film's title. A playwright becomes so taken by a photograph of a young actress he sees in a hotel that he travels back in time through self hypnosis to the year 1912 to find her.

The Two Worlds of Jennie Logan, American television movie (1979) Directed by Frank deFelitta, who also adapted David L. Williams' novel *Second Sight* into this screenplay. After donning a beautiful antique dress, Jennie is transported back to the turn of the century where she finds intrigue and romance.

BOOKS REFERENCED IN THIS CHAPTER

Beyond the Highland Mist, Karen Marie Moning, 1999, Random House
Carousel, Barbara Baldwin, 2011, BooksWeLovePublishingPartners
Dance Through Time, Lynn Kurland, 1996, Jove
Indigo Bay, Barbara Baldwin, 2001, ImaJinn Books
Knight in Shining Armor, Jude Deveraux, 1989, Pocket Books
Nevada Gold, Barbara Baldwin, 2006, Double Dragon Press
Outlander series, Diana Gabaldon, 1991, Dell Books

OTHER TIME TRAVEL BOOKS (AND BY NO MEANS A COMPLETE LIST)

A Connecticut Yankee in King Arthur's Court, Mark Twain (1889)
Timeless Passion, Constance O'Day Flannery, Zebra Books, 1998 (and other titles by this author)
The Time Machine, H. G. Wells (1895)

SUGGESTED READING FOR YA

ANGELS

Eternal by Cynthia Leitich Smith, 2009
Skellig by David Almond, 1999 (Upper MG, lower YA) (2000 ALA List of Notable Books for Children)
The Palace of Laughter by Jon Berkeley, 2006
Wings by Jason Lethcoe, 2009

DEVILS, SPIRIT POSSESSION

Devilish by Maureen Johnson, 2006 (2007 ALA List of Best Books for YAs)
Repossessed by A. M. Jenkins, 2007 (2008 ALA List of Best Books for YAs)

FAIRIES AND ELVES

Faerie Wars by Herbie Brennan, 2003 (2004 ALA List of Best Books for YAs)
Artemis Fowl series by Eoin Colfer, begins 2001 (also listed as YA)
Impossible: A Novel by Nancy Werlin, 2008
The Moorchild by Eloise McGraw, 1996 (Newbery Honor Book)
(1997 ALA List of Notable Books for Children)
Valiant: A Modern Tale of Faerie by Holly Black, 2005 (ALA List of Best Books for YAs)
Witch Catcher by Mary Downing Hahn, 2006

GHOSTS

Jerri's Ghost Stories Bibliography online (books published 1980-2003, primarily 1990s):
http://www.ravenstonepress.com/ghostbib.html
The Afterlife by Gary Soto, 2003
A Certain Slant of Light by Laura Whitcomb, 2005 (2006 ALA List of Best Books for YAs)
Dead Connection by Charlie Price, 2006 (voices of the spirits of the dead, not exactly ghosts)
(2007 ALA List of Best Books for YAs)
Gilda Joyce, Psychic Investigator and sequels by Jennifer Allison, 2005 (also suitable for MG)
Jade Green: A Ghost Story by Phyllis Reynolds Naylor, 1999
Look for Me By Moonlight by Mary Downing Hahn, 1995
The Secret of Whispering Springs by Jerri Garretson, 2002
The Presence Eve Bunting, *200*
Whispers From the Dead by Joan Lowery Nixon, 1989
All the Lovely Bad Ones: A Ghost Story by Mary Downing Hahn, 2008
Deep and Dark and Dangerous: A Ghost Story by Mary Downing Hahn, 2007
The Ghost of Fossil Glen by Cynthia DeFelice, 1998
The Graveyard Book by Neil Gaiman, winner of the 2009 Newbery Award (also listed as YA)

(2009 ALA List of Best Books for YAs)
The Seer of Shadows by Avi, 2008
The Blue Ghost by Marion Dane Bauer, 2005
The Bake Shop Ghost by Jacqueline K. Ogburn, 2005

LEPRECHAUNS

Artemis Fowl series by Eoin Colfer, begins 2001
Fiona's Luck by Teresa Bateman, 2007
Fluffy's Lucky Day by Kate McMullan, 2002

MONSTERS AND DEMONS

Bonechiller by Graham McNamee, 2008. (ALA List of Best Books for YAs)
Clay by David Almond, 2006 (2007 ALA List of Best Books for YAs)
Doppelganger by David Stahler, Jr., 2006 (2007 ALA List of Best Books for YAs)
Foundling (Monster Blood Tattoo, Book 1) by D. M. Cornish, 2006 (2007 ALA List of Best Books for YAs)
The Haunting of Alaizabel Cray by Chris Wooding, 2004 (2005 ALA List of Best Books for YAs)
Pretty Monsters: Stories by Kelly Link, 2008 (2009 ALA List of Best Books for YAs)

MYSTICISM

Return of the Emerald Skull by Paul Stewart and Chris Riddell, 2009
The Stonekeeper (Amulet, Book 1) by Kazu Kibuishi, 2008, graphic novel. (2009 ALA List of Best Books for YAs)

PARAPSYCHOLOGY AND PSYCHIC PHENOMENA SUCH AS ESP

The Knife of Never Letting Go, Chaos Walking, Book 1 by Patrick Ness, 2008. (2009 ALA List of Best Books for YAs)
Me, the Missing, and the Dead by Jennie Valentine, 2008 (2009 ALA List of Best Books for YAs)
The Road of the Dead by Kevin Brooks, 2006. (2007 ALA List of Best Books for YAs)
Double Life by Justin Richards, 2005
Gilda Joyce, Psychic Investigator and sequels by Jennifer Allison, 2005

(younger YA or older MG)

The Mind Reader by Jan Slepian, 1997. (This book is out of print but a fine, dark example.)

Zap! I'm a Mind Reader by Dan Greenburg, 1996

SHAPESHIFTERS/METAMORPHOSIS (OTHER THAN WEREWOLVES)

Doppelganger by David Stahler, Jr., 2006 (2007 ALA List of Best Books for YAs)

A Fast and Brutal Wing by Kathleen Jeffrie Johnson, 2004 (2005 ALA List of Best Books for YAs)

His Dark Materials series by Philip Pullman, beginning with *The Golden Compass* in 1996 (1997 ALA List of Notable Books for Children)

Under the Cat's Eye: A Tale of Morph and Mystery by Gillian Rubenstein, 1998

TIME TRAVEL

London Calling by Edward Bloor, 2006

Nick of Time by Ted Bell, 2008

Tanglewreck by Jeanette Winterson, 2006

Found by Margaret Peterson Haddix, 2008

Magyk by Annie Sage, 2005 (and sequels; older MG, younger YA)

The Blue Ghost by Marion Dane Bauer

VAMPIRES

Gil's All Fright Diner by A. Lee Martinez, 2005 (2006 ALA List of Best Books for YAs)

Eternal by Cynthia Leitich Smith, 2009

Look For Me By Moonlight by Mary Downing Hahn, 1995

Night Road by A. M. Jenkins, 2008 (2009 ALA List of Best Books for YAs)

Sunshine by Robin McKinley, 2005 (2005 ALA List of Best Books for YAs)

Tantalize by Cynthia Leitich Smith, 2007

Twilight and sequels by Stephanie Meyer, 2005 (2006 ALA List of Best Books for YAs)

There is a plethora of vampire books for teens and a good listing may be found here:

http://www.monsterlibrarian.com/vampiresya.htm

Cirque du Freak (also known as *The Saga of Darren Shan*) series by Darren Shan, 2001 (also listed as YA)

Vampire Island and The Knaveheart's Curse by Adele Griffin, 2007, 2008

The Vampire's Curse (Secrets of the Dripping Fang, Book 3) by Dan Greenburg, 2006

Vunce Upon a Time by J. Otto Seibold and Siobhan Vivian, 2008

WEREWOLVES

Gil's All Fright Diner by A. Lee Martinez, 2005 (2006 ALA List of Best Books for YAs)

Tantalize by Cynthia Leitich Smith, 2007

Blood and Chocolate by Annette Curtis Klause, 1997 (1998 ALA List of Best Books for YAs)

Werewolves are popular, but not as many titles are available as for vampires. This is a helpful listing:

http://www.monsterlibrarian.com/werewolvesya.htm

Werewolf Rising by R. L. LaFevers, 2006. (older MG or younger YA)

WITCHES

Magic or Madness by Justine Larbalestier, 2005 (2006 ALA List of Best Books for YAs)

Raven's Gate by Anthony Horowitz, 2005

Revealers by Amanda Marrone, 2008

Revenge of the Witch by Joseph Delaney, 2005 (2006 ALA List of Best Books for YAs)

Sunshine by Robin McKinley, 2005 (2005 ALA List of Best Books for YAs) Older MG/Younger YA

The Goblin Wood by Hilari Bell, 2003 (2004 ALA List of Best Books for YAs)

His Dark Materials series by Philip Pullman, beginning with *The Golden*

Compass in 1996 (1997 ALA List of Best Books for YAs)
Well Witched by Frances Hardinge, 2008
Wintersmith (and other Tiffany Aching books) by Terry Pratchett, 2006 (2007 ALA List of Best Books for YAs and ALA2007 List of Notable Books for Children)
The Witches Boy by Michael Gruber, 2005 (2006 ALA List of Best Books for YAs and 2006 ALA List of Notable Books for Children)
Witch Catcher by Mary Downing Hahn, 2006
The Witches of Dredmoore Hollow by Riford McKenzie, 2008
A Very Brave Witch by Alison McGhee, 2006

ZOMBIES

Gil's All Fright Diner by A. Lee Martinez, 2005 (2006 ALA List of Best Books for YAs)
You Are So Undead to Me by Stacey Jay, 2009
Zombie Queen of Newbury High by Amanda Ashby, 2009
Double Life by Justin Richards, 2005
Grampa's Zombie BBQ by Kirk Scroggs, 2006
The Vampire's Curse by Dan Greenburg, 2006 (Book Three of Secrets of the Dripping Fang)
The Zombie Nite Cafe by Merrily Kutner, 2007
The Restless Dead: Ten Original Stories of the Supernatural, edited by Deborah Noyes, 2007 (2008 ALA List of Best Books for YAs)

RESOURCES CRITIQUING

Here are a few resources to get you started. My best advice: whichever route you take, if you use an outside critique source (paid or unpaid) do your research and make sure to protect yourself against fraud and other less savory aspects of the business.
http://perfectly-write-words.blogspot.com/search/label/proofreading
http://blog.wylie-merrick.com/2008/07/critique-groups-one.html
http://writing-genre-fiction.suite101.com/article.cfm/online_workshops_for_speculative_fiction_writers
Critters Writer's Workshop—http://www.critters.org/

Writing World—http://www.writing-world.com/links/critique.shtml
Critique Circle—http://www.critiquecircle.com/
Athena Critiques—http://www.athenacrits.com/?page_id=8
Write For Your Field Services—http://writefieldservices.com/
  critiqueservices.html
The Writer's Institute—http://www.dcs.wisc.edu/LSA/writing/awi/critique.htm

CONTRIBUTOR
BIOGRAPHIES

Rosemary Laurey

USA Today Best-selling author Rosemary Laurey is an ex-pat Brit, retired special education teacher and grandmother who now lives in Ohio and has a wonderful time writing and letting her imagination run riot. A split personality author, Rosemary also writes Erotica as Madeleine Oh and Fantasy as Georgia Evans. Please visit her web sites: www.brytewood.co.uk, www.rosemarylaurey.com and www.madeleineoh.com

Rae Lori

Throughout her writing career, Rae has written comic book and film related articles which have appeared in online publications such as Comic Stack, Suite101, CinemaGap and Dark Moon Rising. As a result, her alma mater's English course chose one of her articles as an example for how to write an article. She also served as editor and contributing writer of her school newsletter.

Her manuscript, *Hotel Sunset*, won an Honorable Mention award in the 73rd Annual *Writer's Digest* Writing Competition. Under various pen names, she has written books, novellas and short stories that run the genre gamut of science fiction, fantasy, short roman noir and paranormal romance and many more waiting to drip onto the page.

A fan of David Lynch and Alfred Hitchcock, she also has a love for film, vampires and visual storytelling which she couples with the art of the written word to tell her stories. While penning her works, she loves to create artwork that explores her strong female characters and the men in their lives.

Rae is a member of the Broad Universe and the Paranormal Romance Guild. She also teaches short story and novel writing and currently works as a graphic designer, often creating her own promotional materials and artwork. http://www.raelori.com

Danielle Ackley-McPhail

Award-winning author Danielle Ackley-McPhail has worked both sides of the publishing industry for over fifteen years. Her works include the urban fantasies, *Yesterday's Dreams, Tomorrow's Memories, and The Halfling's Court: A Bad-Ass Faerie Tale*. She has edited the *Bad-Ass Faeries* anthology series, and *No Longer Dreams*, and has contributed to numerous other anthologies and collections, including *Dark Furies, Breach the Hull, So It Begins, Space Pirates, Barbarians at the Jumpgate*, and *New Blood*.

She is a member of The Garden State Horror Writers, the New Jersey Authors Network, and Broad Universe, a writer's organization focusing on promoting the works of women authors in the speculative genres.

Danielle lives somewhere in New Jersey with husband and fellow writer, Mike McPhail, mother-in-law Teresa, and three extremely spoiled cats. She can be found on LiveJournal (damcphail, badassfaeries, darkquestbooks, lit_handyman), Facebook (Danielle Ackley-McPhail), and Twitter (DMcPhail). To learn more about her work, visit www.sidhenadaire.com or www.badassfaeries.com.

Barbara Baldwin

Barbara Baldwin is published in poetry, short stories, essays, magazine articles, teacher resource materials, and full-length fiction. Her fiction ranges from contemporary to historical; ghost stories to time travel; Christmas to romance. She was a 2009 EPPies finalist for her historical titled *Song Of My Heart*. She also wrote and co-produced a documentary on Kansas history which won state and national awards. When not writing, she loves to do crafts like pottery and fused glass, candles, baskets and quilts. Visit her website at http://www.authorsden.com/barbarajbaldwin.

Shannah Biondine

Shannah Biondine is the author of three fantasy novellas and seven novels of historical or paranormal romance, including "Wisful Thinking" and "Magnetism," titles from a guardian angel series published with Double Dragon Publishing. Originally a California native and professional business writer, Shannah now writes fiction exclusively and resides in Colorado with her husband and children.

Shannah won the 2002 Eppie for Best Fantasy/Paranormal Romance, and has seen her works final in the prestigious PRISM, Aspen Gold, and Dream Realm Awards. A complete list of her titles and more information is available at her author site: http://biondine.homestead.com. Readers may contact her at: sbiondine@yahoo.com.

Elizabeth Burton

Elizabeth K. Burton is an author, editor and the executive and acquiring editor for Zumaya Publications LLC and its speculative fiction imprint Zumaya Otherworlds. A native of Pennsylvania, she currently thrives in beautiful Austin, Texas.

An avid reader since she first memorized the words in her Little Golden Books, she has been a finalist in the Writers of the Future for her short story "Simple Sarah and Slippery Sam" and is the author of *The Everdark Wars Trilogy, The Ugly Princess* and a novella set in her alternate world of Karlathia. She has two additional erotic romance titles at eXtasy: *The Sorcerer's Apprentice: Major Arcanum IV, The Emperor* and *Remembered Glory: 6 of Cups.*

Karina L. Fabian

From and order of nuns working in space to a down-and-out faerie dragon working off a geas from Saint George to zombie exterminators, Karina Fabian writes stories that surprise with their twists of clichés and incorporation of modern day foibles in an otherworld setting. Her quirky twists and crazy characters have won awards, including the INDIE book award for best fantasy (*Magic, Mensa and Mayhem*), an EPPIE award for best sci-fi (*Infinite Space, Infinite God*), and top placements in the Preditor and Editor polls. In May 2010, her writing took a right turn with a devotional, *Why God Matters*, which she co-wrote with her father. Mrs. Fabian is former President of the Catholic Writer's Guild and also teaches writing and book marketing seminars online.

Jerri Garretson

Jerri grew up on the plains of Kansas but lived in Europe, Asia, Caribbean and several states as an adult. She currently lives in Florida. She was head of youth services for Manhattan Public Library in Manhattan, Kansas and has done numerous presentations about children's literature at state library conferences and reading association conferences as well as dozens of school visits as an author.

Jerri has been writing for children since 1983, with articles in children's magazines and books for young readers from preschool to young adult. She is also the author of ghost stories for adults and is the owner of Ravenstone Press.

Jerri's books for children include: *Imagicat, Johnny Kaw - The Pioneer Spirit of Kansas, Kansas Katie - A Sunflower Tale, Kansas Tall Tales, The Secret of Whispering Springs, Twister Twyla - The Kansas Cowgirl.*

Jerri's ghost stories for adults are in: *Trespassing Time - Ghost Stories from the Prairie.*

Kelly A. Harmo

Kelly A. Harmon used to write truthful, honest stories about authors and thespians, senators and statesmen, movie stars and murderers. Now she writes lies, which is infinitely more satisfying, but lacks the convenience of doorstep delivery, especially on rainy days.

She has published short fiction in several anthologies including the EPIC Award Winning *Bad Ass Fairies 3: In All Their Glory; Hellebore and Rue, Black Dragon, White Dragon, Triangulation: Dark Glass*, and the forthcoming, *Magicking in Traffic*. Her story "Lies" short-listed for Aeon Award. Her award-winning novella, "Blood Soup," is available from Eternal Press and Amazon.

Ms. Harmon is a former magazine and newspaper reporter and editor. She has published articles at SciFi Weekly, eArticles, and magazines and newspapers up and down the East Coast and abroad.

Read more about Ms. Harmon at her Web site: http://kellyaharmon.com.

Lee Killough

Lee Killough has been storytelling almost as long as she can remember, starting somewhere around the age of four or five with making up her own bedtime stories. Then, in keeping with wisdom that says the golden age of science fiction is about age eleven, that year Lee discovered science fiction and fantasy. From her first SF novel, Leigh Brackett's *The Starmen of Llyrdis,* she was hooked. But along with the pleasure of this marvelous literature came fear. She lived in a small Kansas town with a small library and realized she would soon read the section dry. So to keep from running out of science fiction, she began writing her own. And because the mystery section adjoined the SF/Fantasy section, leading her to discover mysteries about the same time as SF, her stories tended to combine SF with mystery. These have evolved into urban fantasy with supernatural detectives: vampire cop Garreth Mikaelian, werewolf cop Allison Goodnight, and ghost cop Cole Dunavan. Her short story "Symphony for a Lost Traveler" was nominated for a Hugo award. Her books also include a chapbook *Checking on Culture*, a guide for world-building and developing story backgrounds.

Linda Madl

Linda Madl's work includes novels, novellas, short stories, and nonfiction articles. She is an avid reader of ghost tales, fiction and nonfiction. She started collecting ghost story books as a college student in Great Britain. Currently her ghostly library contains over 250 tomes of fiction and nonfiction paranormal stories from North America and Europe. She has served as a Halloween ghost tour guide at haunted Ft. Riley, Kansas, and as a docent for a historical Victorian home in her hometown. She is a contributing author to *Trespassing Time, Ghost Stories from the Prairie*. For a more complete list of her titles go to www.lindamadl.com

Ripley Patton

Ripley Patton is an American writer happily living on the South Island of New Zealand. She has had numerous short stories and flash fiction published both on-line and in print. Her short story, "Corrigan's Exchange" won the Sir Julius Vogel Award for Best Short Story 2009. Her short story, "The Future of the Sky" won the Au Contraire 2010 Short Story Contest. Ripley is also the founder and President of SpecFicNZ, the national association for writers of speculative fiction in New Zealand which launched in August 2010. She is currently working on her first novel, a young adult contemporary fantasy. More information and links to her work can be found on her website: http://www.ripleypatton.com/ and on her blog: http://rippatton.livejournal.com/.

Lee Masterson

Lee Masterson is a full-time fiction and freelance writer from South Australia. She lives in the gorgeous sea-side suburb of Brighton with her extremely spoilt German Shepherd dog (Kaiser).

Lee's freelance work has featured in various print magazines around the world consistently for the past 10 years. Her fiction work has featured in many magazines and ezines, and has also been translated into 5 different languages. While the predominant nature of her freelance work revolves around writing financially related topics, she has also had over 210 writing-related articles published with more than 135 ezines and magazines around the world.

Lee is the founder and editor of Fiction Factor (http://www.fictionfactor.com), an online magazine operating since 1999, which is dedicated to helping fiction writers hone their work and find publication with suitable publishers.

In what little spare time she has, Lee also writes horror, science fiction and dark fantasy in her own name, and has a string of paranormal erotica novels selling very well under a professional pseudonym.

Sheri L. McGathy

"Born in the Buckeye state, I was uprooted in 1971 and replanted amongst sunflowers, tornadoes, and college football. It's a good life."

During the weekdays, Sheri is a Graphic Arts Coordinator/Copy Editor in prepress. In the evenings and weekends, she's a writer...or she tries to be. She is also Managing Editor at The Fractured Publisher online.

Her work includes short stories and/or novellas in various anthologies: *Twice Upon An Eventidem Omnibus – A Collection Of Fantasy Stories, Trespassing Time – Ghost Stories From The Prairie, Twilight Crossings, Twilight Crossings II, From Within The Mist* and *The Stygian Soul*

Her novels include: *Within The Shadow Of Stone, Season Of Gold—Elfen Gold Book One, Season Of Silver—Elfen Gold Book Two*

Kathryn Meyer Griffith

Kathryn Meyer Griffith has had fourteen novels and seven short stories published since 1984 with Zebra Books, Leisure Books, Avalon Books, The Wild Rose Press, and now Damnation Books and Eternal Press. Her novels have been in the genres of paranormal romance, horror, romantic horror, time travel, romance, suspense, and murder mysteries. Her books: *Evil Stalks the Night (1984); The Heart of the Rose (1985); Blood Forge (1989); Vampire Blood (1991); The Last Vampire (1992); Witches (1993);* "The Nameless One" (erotic horror short story 1993); *The Calling (1994); Scraps of Paper (2003); All Things Slip Away (2006); Egyptian Heart (2007); Winter's Journey (2008); The Ice Bridge*

(2008); "Don't Look Back, Agnes" (ghostly short story 2008); "In This House" (ghostly short story 2008); *BEFORE THE END: A Time of Demons (2010); The Woman in Crimson (2010); Always & Forever* (erotic contemporary short story 2011). Many of these older books and short stories will be rewritten and rereleased – in paperback, and in e-books for the first time ever – by July 2012 by Damnation Books and Eternal Press.

Bob Nailor

Bob Nailor is an author who resides on a quaint country acre in NW Ohio with his wife. When not in the RV traveling the country and researching his latest project, he spends his time writing and editing. He is the author of *2012: Timeline Apocalypse* and co-editor of *Nights of Blood 2: More Legends of the Vampire* and a contributing author to *A Firestorm of Dragons, The Fantasy Writer's Companion, The Complete Guide to Writing Science Fiction,* and *Nights of Blood 1* and several other anthologies. He won an Eppie in 2008 for *The Complete Guide to Science Fiction.* Visit him at www.bobnailor.com

Ryan Peverly

Ryan Peverly is a journalist, columnist, short story writer and soon-to-be novelist (pfft, sure). His works haven't appeared anywhere other than lightly-browsed Internet forums and on discolored pieces of printer paper strewn about his cozy, two-bedroom apartment in a rural Ohio town, where he lives comfortably with his girlfriend and two, newly-adopted cats.

Kim Richards

Kim Richards is an author and publisher. She co-owns and works as CEO for Damnation Books LLC, which publishes through Damnation Books (www.damnationbooks.com), Eternal Press (www.eternalpress.biz) and Realms of Fantasy Magazine (www.rofmag.com). Born and raised in New Mexico, she currently lives in Northern California with one extraordinarily supportive husband.

Jane Toombs

Jane Toombs lives on the south shore of Lake Superior with the Viking from her past and their calico grandcat, Kinko. Here they enjoy refreshing springs, lovely summers, gorgeous falls and miserable winters. Jane's edging towards ninety published works in all genres except men's action and erotica, but her favorite genre to read and write has always been paranormal. Her web site is www.JaneToombs.com

CPSIA information can be obtained at www.ICGtesting.com
Printed in the USA
BVOW011337201211

278835BV00001B/214/P